Why We Talk

STUDIES IN THE EVOLUTION OF LANGUAGE

General Editors
Kathleen R. Gibson, *University of Texas at Houston,* and
James R. Hurford, *University of Edinburgh*

PUBLISHED

IN PREPARATION

PUBLISHED IN ASSOCIATION WITH THE SERIES

Why We Talk

The Evolutionary Origins of Language

Jean-Louis Dessalles
translated by James Grieve

OXFORD
UNIVERSITY PRESS

OXFORD
UNIVERSITY PRESS

Great Clarendon Street, Oxford OX2 6DP

Oxford University Press is a department of the University of Oxford.
It furthers the University's objective of excellence in research, scholarship,
and education by publishing worldwide in

Oxford New York

Auckland Cape Town Dar es Salaam Hong Kong Karachi Kuala Lumpur
Madrid Melbourne Mexico City Nairobi New Delhi Shanghai Taipei Toronto

With offices in

Argentina Austria Brazil Chile Czech Republic France Greece
Guatemala Hungary Italy Japan Poland Portugal Singapore
South Korea Switzerland Thailand Turkey Ukraine Vietnam

Oxford is a registered trade mark of Oxford University Press
in the UK and in certain other countries

Published in the United States
by Oxford University Press Inc., New York

Hermes Science Publications and Oxford University Press thank
the French Ministry of Culture for its assistance in the publication of the
French and the English editions of this work.

This book has been published with the assistance of the
French Ministry of Culture (Centre national du livre).

British Library Cataloguing in Publication Data
Data available

Library of Congress Cataloging in Publication Data
Data available

Typeset by SPI Publisher Services, Pondicherry, India
Printed in Great Britain on acid-free paper by
Biddles Ltd., King's Lynn, Norfolk

ISBN: 978–0–19–927623–3

1 3 5 7 9 10 8 6 4 2

Contents

Part II
The functional anatomy of speech

Part III
The ethology of language

Foreword

The question of the origin of the human species is no longer a monopoly of palaeontologists. Those who take an interest in the emergence, over evolutionary time, of a feature of humanity as fundamental as language cannot restrict themselves to the study of fossils. If we are to understand why our ancestors became gifted with the power of speech, it is essential to establish a cognitive model of language behaviour. In the light of such a model, it becomes possible to track backwards from the structure to the biological function, which in turn enables us to define the particular conditions that made the biological function advantageous for the people who possessed it.

There have been remarkable advances of late in the cognitive sciences. Their most marked feature at the present time must be the fact that they now canvass matters which were once tacitly seen as taboo. For instance, emotions and consciousness can now be studied without overstepping the bounds of research on cognition, which was impossible not many years ago. The question of the phylogenetic origin of language is another of these paradoxically novel areas of study.

The scientific study of mental phenomena is usually driven by the desire to understand how human behaviours are produced and eschews any consideration of magical things, whether the soul, psychic energy, or the life force. The basic method is to analyse the structure of such behaviours and to seek their determinants in the biology and learning abilities of individuals. In the case of language, research focuses on analysis of phonological structures, syntactical structures, and semantic structures, as well as on the structures of the neuronal circuits which make language possible. On the other hand, questions of function, in the sense of biological function, are unusual in cognitive science, though they are inseparable from the study of animal behaviour. Why should human beings be seen as an exception? For we too are biological beings, the outcome of an evolution. By and large, our behaviours are not qualitatively different from those of our hunter-gatherer ancestors. They are behaviours which, like those of animals, are possible only because they can fulfil a biological function.

Language lies at the heart of the preoccupations of cognitive scientists. Though the structure of language has been abundantly studied, the same cannot be said of its function. This ignorance of ours in the area of language function is especially regrettable because our way of communicating so as to transmit ideas and judgements seems to be unique in the realm of living creatures. Why do we have this ability and other species do not?

I am convinced that, if we systematically apply evolutionary insights to cognitive science, we can thoroughly transform our understanding of human beings. The evolutionary approach, by linking some structural features of language to the necessity of a biological function, is a way of reducing the apparent complexity of living phenomena and often of bringing coherence to things from which it is absent. One of the questions that this book is going to attempt to address directly is: What biological necessity is there for language?

The scientific community is reintroducing phylogeny into the study of cognition. By way of a contribution to this paradigm shift, I had the opportunity to organize the Third International Conference on the Evolution of Language, held in Paris in the year 2000. I am convinced that the coming together of evolutionary biology and the cognitive sciences, which once seemed so untoward to people working in fields which they had seen for years as totally disparate, will prove to be lasting. The main aim of this book is to contribute to that coming together and to show how fruitful it may be.

A fair number of the ideas developed in this book were shaped during discussions with participants in earlier conferences on the evolution of language. I am very grateful to Chris Knight and Jim Hurford for their belief in me and for having enabled me to have close contact with people working in this area.

For their valuable assistance and support, I give special thanks to Jean-Bernard Auriol, Olivier Hudry, Philippe Monnier, and François Yvon, as well as to Laleh Ghadakpour who helped me develop some of the ideas I present here. I have tried to heed their advice in ways which I hope improve the quality and coherence of my arguments. I am particularly grateful to Eric Bonabeau, one of the first scholars who expressed confidence in my work and who made the initial suggestion that I should write this book. I am glad to take this opportunity of expressing my gratitude for the rigorous accuracy of my translator James Grieve. His shrewd and uncompromising habits of work have enabled me to clarify a fair few obscurities in my original French text. Writing on a subject which has fascinated me for years also gives me the chance to thank my parents, Robert Dessalles, who first explained the principles of evolution to me when I was a child, and Fernande Dessalles who gave me advice and encouragement during my work on the book.

My objective is to give a coherent and reasoned account of the conditions out of which language grew. Readers will encounter a number of original ideas which I hope will stimulate their spirit of enquiry.

Jean-Louis DESSALLES

PART I

The place of language in human evolutionary history

Introduction to Part I

To reconstruct the circumstances which may have led to the emergence of language in the evolution of our ancestors, we can set about it in three stages. First we can put language behaviour into the broader context of the evolution of species. Then we can analyse the structure of language so as to link it to a biological function. Thirdly, we can identify the conditions which may have made such a biological function advantageous. These are the themes of the three parts of the book, each of which contains surprises. Language will come to seem more like a haphazard quirk of our development rather than a necessary outcome. We shall see how its structure suggests the existence of at least two quite separate stages in its evolution. We shall also have to overcome the paradox that language seems prima facie to be disadvantageous for those who use it. The book is designed as a progression: my aim in Part I is to pose the problem; Part II analyses the reasons underlying the functional components of language; and Part III suggests a coherent explanation. A reader who wishes to grasp the logic of this progression should follow the order of the chapters as presented.

A commonly accepted idea is that language is not just natural and self-evident, but necessary. How could there be such a thing as intelligent beings without speech? On this view, language, with all its biological predispositioning, is the inevitable outcome of an evolutionary process which starts with the amoeba and ends with human beings. This implies that language is a behaviour which resembles other systems of communication used by animals but just happens to be more elaborate. The fact that other species of animals do not 'speak' as well as we do means only that their evolution is incomplete, that they have fallen by the wayside in the advance towards the intelligence and culture which enable us humans to share not only our resources but our thoughts. According to this view of things, language is a marvellous asset which has given our species dominion over the natural world. Does anyone need another justification? The usefulness of language can be taken for granted.

The aim of this first part is to show that language cannot in fact be taken for granted.

1 Animal and human communication

Some take the view that language is merely a particular instance of animal communication, whereas others see it as a behaviour which sets us apart from animals. If we are to understand the process which endowed our forebears with the ability to speak, this matter of our separateness or lack of separateness must be faced at the outset. Does the advent of communication through speech constitute an unlikely innovation or should it be seen as only a quantitative improvement on existing systems?

1.1 The biological status of language

The status of human language is a subject of controversy. Advances in ethology have revealed the hitherto unsuspected wealth of animals' modes of communication. Could it be that human communication is only one of these, a more complex extension but basically identical in its principle, after the manner of present-day computers which, despite differences in appearance, still function pretty much as computers did in the 1940s? If we can answer no to that question, if human language is something radically novel, quite unknown in the world of animals, then we must explain how and why it came into being.

There is, of course, something inherently dubious about that second possibility. If ever there was a prejudice that has hindered the advancement of knowledge, it is the idea that the human race is separate from the rest of the natural world, ruled by different laws, and seen as a culmination. Even when nineteenth-century scientists first abandoned the view that humanity was the straightforward outcome of a divine plan, this did not lead them to see our species as a mere haphazard result of evolution. They found it difficult enough to think of human existence as not being necessary, as being nothing more than a contingent product of an accumulation of chance events. Could it not at least be acknowledged that our intelligence and culture set us apart from nature? Even primitive human societies are subject to laws of their own making. If the human can differ to such an extent from the natural, then we surely must occupy a place that is special and unique. According to that way of seeing things, human evolution did follow a different path which distanced us once and for all from the animal realm. The existence of a culture then meant we had to develop new faculties unrelated to our animal substratum, of which language is the archetype.

In scientific circles which are informed about evolution and conversant with examples of elaborate animal behaviours, it has become customary, by way of reaction against such an anthropocentric view, to adopt a radically continuistic position: humans being merely animals like other animals, their characteristics are natural and grounded in their biology, and any differences between their capacities and those of animals can only be quantitative.[1] Saltation is foreign to nature, whether between chimpanzees and humans or the donkey and the horse. This would make human language a system of communication like any other; and any appearance it might have of being much more elaborate than animals' modes of communication can be put down to our ignorance of these.

It is true that advances in ethology have made us rethink many a preconceived notion about the originality of our own species. Since the days when Descartes wondered whether animals were mere mechanical automata, we have learned that they can make tools, learn elaborate strategies, feel emotions that are akin to ours, form alliances, perceive colours beyond our ken, build complex structures, and even construct a culture (Bonner 1980; Wrangham et al. 1994). They can also convey their mental states, tell lies, and communicate about objects that are absent. What else can human beings do? Even laughter or smiling appear to be aptitudes we share with the great apes (Goodall 1971: 243).

In any proper assessment of the originality of humans' mode of communication, it is important not to underestimate the complexity of animal communication. Only a comparison can tell us whether this or that aspect of human language is genuinely original and whether it distinguishes us

---

[1] '[T]he mental faculties of man and the lower animals do not differ in kind, although immensely in degree. A difference in degree, however great, does not justify us in placing man in a distinct kingdom' (Darwin 1871).

from other species in the way that having a trunk distinguishes elephants from the other ungulates.

1.2 Animal communication

All living beings communicate with other individuals of their own species. Communication begins with the search for a mate. Without communication, transmission of genes is impossible; so, by the same token, would be the existence of species. Communication exists also inside the body: our cells have modes of communication which are gradually coming to light. The cells in our immune systems, for instance, recognize each other and can recruit other cells to help defend us against invasion by an antigen. Such phenomena function via a system of transmission of information which in some ways resembles language. For example, our lymphocytes (white corpuscles) recognize the cells of our own body from certain molecules on their surface; when these markers are absent, the lymphocytes produce secretions which alert other cells in the immune system.

All this seems very remote from human language. These signals transmitted between microscopic elements of our physiology are in fact just that, signals. Language enables us to communicate emotions and abstract thought and to convey concrete information about the exact position of things which are absent. It was once believed that the second of these two abilities was restricted to human beings or to a few species among the primates. In the 1940s, everyone was taken by surprise when Karl von Frisch published his observations on the 'language' of bees. It had been known for a long time that honey bees (*Apis mellifera*) had the ability to inform other females in their hive of the location of a source of food. What was unknown, though, was that they used a precise code to convey the information. Von Frisch, by altering the positions of his lures and observing the behaviour of the bees when they returned to the hive, contrived to decipher the famous 'dance' of the bees, which must perforce be considered to be a genuine code (von Frisch 1967).

Another example of animal communication which is also frequently cited and has been closely studied is the alarm calls of vervets (also known as green or grass monkeys). These small monkeys have a varied range of cries which they use for warning of the approach of a predator or the presence of individuals from another troop. The meanings of these alarm calls are very precise, as has been demonstrated in experiments using recordings of them. When individual monkeys hear a recording of the cry indicating the approach of a predator, the reaction they have varies with the warning: if it concerns an eagle, they take cover; if it concerns a snake, they straighten up and scan the grass round about; if it is a leopard warning, they take to the trees. It was thought for a long time that these calls expressed no more than an emotional state, that they were an effect rather than the cause of the animals' taking flight. Experiments with recorded calls show that this is not the case and that the calls are genuine signals (Cheney and Seyfarth 1988). Knowledge of the acoustical structure of the signals is genetically programmed in the monkeys. The approximate meaning of the calls is also genetically programmed, though young monkeys have to learn to get them exactly right; until they are two or three years of age, their alarm cries give warning about species which constitute no danger. For example, the alarm cry that the adult monkeys use mainly for the martial eagle is usually stimulated in the immature monkeys by the arrival of a vulture, which is not a predator (Hauser 1996: 307).

Ethologists have examined the question whether the vervets' vocal signals are in some measure tantamount to words. Any behaviourist psychologist who decided to apply to them the conditioning principle established by Pavlov's well-known experiment would have no difficulty in isolating a simple association of stimuli: once the acoustical stimulus had become systematically associated with the stimulus of the sight of the predator, it would be sufficient to set off the appropriate flight reaction. In such a directly linked association of stimulus and response, there is no role for any mental state representing the meaning of the situation suggested by the alarm call. If this is so, the vocalizations of the monkeys could hardly be seen as embryonic language. As it happens, in this case the behaviourist interpretation is mistaken. Through a series of well-designed experiments, Cheney and Seyfarth have shown that the association between the acoustical forms and the behavioural responses was not direct but that it must be mediated by a form of mental representation. They did this by using a habituation test, designed to diminish the intensity of the behavioural responses by repeated exposure to the stimuli. There comes a time when, having repeatedly heard the same recording of a particular call, the monkeys ignore the message and no longer react to it. In that state, if they hear a quite different signal their reaction is the appropriate one. Habituation is therefore selective. Cheney and Seyfarth's investigation was designed to find out whether habituation could be transferred to neighbouring acoustical forms, or to signals close in meaning. An example from the field of language can be seen in the fact that we can easily associate a word like *fraction* with *numerator* and are not limited to associations based on resemblances of form such as *fraction* and *traction*. The latter pair of words are very close phonetically but they do not usually suggest any closeness of situations, whereas the first pair are often associated in the same context. In such cases, we are sensitive to associations between meanings rather than to phonetic resemblances. So, how do our vervet monkeys perform?

To determine whether the monkeys compare signals in terms of their acoustics, as the conditioning theory would suggest, or in terms of their meaning, Cheney and Seyfarth used recordings of two calls produced during territorial disputes with neighbouring troops: one of these cries was a kind of trill sounding like *wrr* and the other a sharper one that sounded rather like *chutter*. The first one is uttered when individuals notice the presence of another troop; the second one is used when the two troops begin to threaten each other or actually start to fight. The interest of these two sounds is that, though phonetically dissimilar, their meanings are quite close. The experiment shows that monkeys who have been habituated to hearing recordings of *wrr* repeated every twenty minutes barely react when they hear a recording of *chutter* produced by the same individual. However, their reaction is normal if the habituation signal and the test signal have very different meanings, for instance the leopard alarm call and the eagle alarm call. Nor is habituation transferred when the test signal is uttered by another monkey. This leads the authors to the conclusion that signals uttered by the monkeys entail mental representations and that it is these representations which underlie the behaviour. If the link between the signals and the behaviours were direct, acoustical similarity is what would be stressed by the habituation test. In fact, the similarity in question is one requiring a mental construction which takes account of the sender of the message and the situation it suggests. For this reason, communication among vervets has some similarity with communication among human beings. And it is that similarity that we are about to set out in detail.

1.3 From signals to behaviour

One way of marking off human language from animal communication is to present the latter as a reflex behaviour and to maintain that acts of animal communication are directly linked to the behaviour they provoke in the receiver. Before the experimentation by Cheney and Seyfarth, it was possible to see the fleeing of vervet monkeys as an immediate and reflex consequence of the alarm call. If that were the case, one could reduce the effect of the signal to the behaviour that it provokes.

Such a description of animal communication, once favoured by behaviourist psychologists uninformed about the real behaviour of animals in their natural habitat, often turns out to be simplistic. Two successive mechanisms can intervene between a signal and any behavioural response. The first of these is a representational mechanism. The signal is used to construct a mental representation and it is that representation which sets off the behaviour. As we have seen, the experiments by Cheney and Seyfarth argue in favour of seeing this type of representation in vervets, for the animals' associations with the signals relate to the situations to which they belong rather than to their acoustical form. This is why we can posit that the immediate effect of the communication act is the making of a mental representation. If that is the case, then the effect of one of these monkeys giving the call usually associated with the presence of a leopard will be to call to the minds of all its fellows something like the image of a leopard, deriving from the memory of actual situations. Experimental data tend to support this view; but they come nowhere near to proving that the mental representation summoned up by the alarm call is as concrete as that.

What would be the point of a mental representation that intervenes between a signal and a behavioural response? The obvious disadvantage is a slower reaction. Instead of reacting immediately to the signal, in a reflex way, the animal reconstructs a representation of the situation with which the signal is habitually associated. Then it reacts to a comparison between its representation and the present situation. Extrapolating a little from the experimentation by Cheney and Seyfarth, we can say that when the monkey hears the cry indicating the approach of another troop, it makes a representation of them which it projects onto the present situation. This explains why the monkey does not react to hearing another call that belongs to the same situation, even if the other call is acoustically different. What could be the point of going through this sort of complicated mechanism in order to produce an appropriate behavioural response? The advantage of such an intermediate procedure lies in the possibility of taking account of the context. A monkey which hears the cry associated with snakes looks at the ground in its vicinity, so as to localize the danger; it does not dash away as it would if its flight behaviour was a reflex. It imagines a snake and looks for one in the context of its actual situation; and if the context gives no reason for assuming that a snake is nearby, the monkey may not flee needlessly.

The construction of a mental representation of the situation indicated is not the only mechanism that may separate the signal from the behaviour it is supposed to bring about. In many cases, the existence of a mental representation can be useful if it leads to an assessment. If the animal hearing the signal is capable of assessing some aspects of the utterance, then it is not a mere slave of whatever it may have perceived. In particular, thanks to the mechanism of assessment, it can resist being manipulated by the animal uttering the signal. For example, though the precise biological function of territorial birdsong remains in part a mystery, it has been established that females are sensitive to some aspects of the singing of males of their species. The onset of pre-breeding behaviour in female song sparrows, for instance, happens more readily when the songs they can hear are marked by certain characteristics, such as the richness of the repertory (sparrows can produce between five and thirteen types of song) and the contrast between the immediate repetition of a song and its delayed repetition (Hauser 1996: 396). It is clear that the female brings an assessment to bear on what she hears, though the grounds of this assessment and its biological meaning are still partly unknown to us.

Assessment may function on the basis of the signal itself, as one supposes is the case with territorial birds, or else through the representation that the signal gives rise to. A monkey which checks the state of its surroundings before fleeing or not fleeing bases its decision on its representation of the situation. Its behaviour is not an automatic result of the representation it has structured from the alarm call and the context. It appraises the representation; and what determines the choice of proper behaviour is the outcome of this appraisal. Assessment is sensitive to factors such as experience or habituation; and in addition it may integrate contextual factors such as the credibility of the source of the signal. In the

habituation experiments, the monkey went back to paying normal attention when the alarm calls to which it had been habituated started coming
from a different source (Cheney and Seyfarth 1990).

The clearest case of appraisal of a communication situation is where
there exists a threat. It is in the interest of an individual under threat to
gauge as accurately as possible the real intentions of an attacker; and it does
this by attending to the signals uttered by the latter. According to the theory
of John Krebs and Richard Dawkins, this assessment is rendered necessary
and complex because of the risk of manipulation (Krebs and Dawkins
1984). A dog threatens by baring its teeth and crouching in a way that
suggests it is about to leap at its opponent. But is that really its intention?
The objective of such a very visible show may actually be to avoid the act of
aggression with its attendant risks. If the individual under threat is not to
be manipulated, it must make a plausible evaluation of the likelihood of
being attacked. Krebs and Dawkins posit a kind of evolutionary one-
upmanship, since in each of the competing roles opposite interests are at
stake. This leads to signalling which is more and more difficult to gauge and
to evaluative abilities which are more and more sophisticated.

Some behaviours presuppose cognitive abilities intermediate between
reflex and reflexion (Grumbach 1994) and cannot be reduced to a mere
coupling of associations of the stimulus–response variety. This can be seen
in communication within many species. In some of them, the perceiving
of a signal leads to a mental representation which, one may suppose, is an
approximate reproduction of a direct perception of the event indicated.
The ensuing behaviour is thus, in such cases, more closely linked to the
situation indicated by the signal than to the signal itself. The second
mechanism that we have mentioned consists of an assessment of the signal
or of the representation it brings to mind. The existence of such mechanisms gives an inkling of the elaborate mental processes required by animal
communication, which go well beyond mere associations, whether genetically programmed or learned. This is why animal communication without
a doubt resembles human communication. Words spoken by someone
make us summon up mental representations which we evaluate. When we
hear on the weather forecast the words *A southerly depression is on the way*,
we first construct a representation of the situation, then we assess the
unpleasant consequences it will involve for the weekend. Prima facie, this
does not seem all that different from what a vervet monkey does when it

hears an alarm call, then decides to flee in a particular way and with particular urgency.

1.4 Language as code

Discovering a quality which distinguishes language from systems of animal communication seems easy. One of the most striking characteristics of human language is its referential power: words stand for entities. The name *Peter* can stand for a particular person, even in his absence. So language can be seen as a code: we translate a situation into words for an interlocutor, who decodes the message and reconstructs the situation which motivated the act of communication. One of the reasons for the interest aroused by von Frisch's experiments with bees is that they make it impossible to see human language as in any way superior just because it can encode references to absent entities.

Bees' words

Inside the hive, as a bee clambers about the suspended frames in the dark, she does a sort of dance. She advances a short distance in a straight line, waggling her abdomen about fifteen times per second. She then goes back to her starting point, walking normally, but following a semi-circular path. She repeats this cycle, alternating her semi-circles to left and right. The whole dance eventually forms a rough figure of eight, by means of which she manages to convey the position of a source of food.

The most important element in the dance is the central straight line of the figure of eight, where she is walking and waggling her abdomen. The nearest of the bees that follow her about pick up her movements from the faint sounds and the breeze she makes during her dance. The speed and the number of abdomen waggles indicate the distance between the hive and the source of food: the nearer the food, the quicker the dance. A three-second burst, for example, indicates a distance of 500 metres. What is most spectacular is the encoding of direction, as elucidated by von Frisch: the angle between vertical and the direction taken by the bee as she walks her straight line reproduces the angle between the direction of the sun and the direction to follow to locate the food. Bearing in mind that a bee with a message to deliver may dance for about an hour, one realizes that she must incorporate into her dance a gradual correction to allow for the change in the angle of the sun. The existence of the code has been proved by biologists using miniature robots to 'talk' to bees (Kirchner and Towne 1994; Michelsen 1998).

The properties of this bee language are interesting in more ways than one. Despite weighing less than a gram, these creatures can make reference to an entity that is absent (though it should be noted that the bee does pass on to her fellow workers samples of the source of food she is indicating). The reference to the source of food consists of several complementary codes, notably one for the direction to take and one for the distance to cover. These codes are analogue codes, in that the bees can indicate adjacent locations by dances which are very close to one another. They are none the less codes, given that they entail the representation (re-presentation) of a particular field, in this case a pair of spatial coordinates, via a different field. That is, the few centimetres traversed on the frames of wax represents a distance of several tens or even hundreds of metres outside the hive; the vertical direction represents the direction of the sun; the direction of the central straight line represents the direction to follow. What is so striking about such communication is the use of a field, the bee's movements, to represent a different field, spatial locations. All this would be far less interesting if the bee merely guided the others by flying off towards her find.

However, the 'language' of bees does differ in several ways from our idea of our own mode of communication. One of the essential differences lies in the fixed and genetically programmed character of the dance. All the bees of any given species dance and interpret the dance in exactly the same way. There is no need for them to learn anything; the behaviour is coded into their genes. The dancing is rather like filling in a form; it leaves no scope for inventiveness; everything that can be expressed is already laid down, the distance, the direction, and the quality of the food discovered. How different from human communication, in which our freedom seems almost boundless! This freedom may well be, in some measure, illusory (cf. Chapter 14); but it is undeniable if we compare ourselves to bees. Our words and sentences seem infinitely more variable than the patterns outlined by the insect on the frames of the hive. Our freedom comes from the fact that the signs we use are arbitrary conventions.

The arbitrariness of signs

It was a Swiss, Ferdinand de Saussure, who first defined, in the early years of the twentieth century, a fundamental characteristic of language: the fact that the signs we use, words in particular, bear no relationship of likeness to the objects, actions, or phenomena to which they refer. In other words, if we leave aside onomatopoeia, the relation between the signifier (the word) and the signified (the object, the action, etc.) is purely conventional. This can be shown by a simple observation of the variety of words in different languages which all have the same meaning: for example, *enfant, Kind, child, copil, koudak* are different ways of referring to the same thing in French, German, English, Romanian, and Persian. Structural linguists, once they became aware of the relativity of the lexicon, took to seeing each language as a sign system, each with its own laws, regardless of the meaning of the signs. Going even farther in that direction, and often limiting their study to a single language or to filiations among several languages, they came to consider language as a single system, no matter how it might manifest itself in any particular language.

What point could there be in a communication system that uses arbitrary signs? At first sight, it could appear to be a very bad thing. Since each language uses different signs, they must be learned. Children do not speak their language from birth; and the learning of a second language requires years of effort. Also, the conventional character of the sign systems means that two speakers of different languages cannot understand each other. As communication systems go, these are very serious drawbacks. By contrast, systems of animal communication are usually genetically programmed and need little or no learning, though, as we have noted, immature vervet monkeys are aware of only the approximate meaning of alarm calls and it does take them some years to learn the finer points of this skill (Hauser 1996: 306). There are species of birds in which the song of the local population must be learned by the young; and dialectal variations influenced by geography have been observed (Darwin 1871; Hauser 1996: 275). Variability of this sort suggests that the connection between the signals and their function is a relatively loose one.

Because of the arbitrariness of signs, the tragedy of the Tower of Babel for ever repeats itself, in one degree or another, among human populations. Yet it is also this property of language which gives scope for individuals to invent new meanings. Human language works on an open lexicon and anybody can invent new words. Young people's slang, with its constant accretion of neologisms, or the jargons of scientists, are good examples of our creativity. The existence of languages which are foreign to one another is the price we pay for our extraordinary ability to convey new meanings. If we leave aside a few chimpanzees brought up by human beings, no animals seem to have any way of creating new meanings and passing them on to their fellows.

In most cases of animal communication the signals used are in no way arbitrary. The animals' biology constrains them to use those signals and no others. On the other hand, if one reasons from the evolution of species, one can see that there is in fact a fair amount of arbitrariness in the signs used. No honeybee is free to invent a new dance, but the evolution of its species might have led to the invention of a completely different one. Karl von Frisch was concerned to point out how the bees' dancing had evolved out of simulations of flight, performed outside the hive. When the dance is done in the darkness of the hive, the replacement of the angle of the sun by the bee's alignment, vertical rather than horizontal, say, or standing in some relation to the angle of entry to the hive, does entail a certain arbitrariness. Similarly, it seems likely that the alarm calls of many animals bear absolutely no necessary relation to the danger they warn of, other than the relation made between the two in their genetically programmed behavioural equipment. So the arbitrary nature of our language is not a complete innovation. The originality of our communication code may lie in the fact that, as we are about to see, it is essentially digital.

Two types of code

Human communication, like that of honey bees or vervet monkeys, relies on the use of a code. Interpretation of signs produced by the communicating individual is impossible for any other individual who does not know the meaning of them. There is, however, a fundamental difference between the code used by bees and the type of code we use when we speak. In the dancing of bees there is a feature that semioticians describe as 'iconic': just as an image resembles the concrete situation which it represents, so there is a likeness between the pattern of the bee's movements and the behaviour it produces in the hivemates. From a technical point of view, one can say that the iconic aspect of the dance lies in the continuous relationship between the set of patterns and the area containing the locations of the food sources. Systems which maintain such a relation based on likeness are called 'analogue' systems.

There are several analogue aspects in human language. Stress, for instance, is governed in part by strict rules, notably as concerns its position in an utterance; but it can have varying degrees of intensity which mark shades of importance. For example, in recounting some event, to give an indication of how improbable it may be, in English one can vary the stress and the length of the third syllable of the word *unbelievable* in the statement 'It was absolutely unbe*lie*vable'; and in the equivalent French statement one can do something similar with the syllable *in-* in *C'était absolument* in*croyable*. Another analogue aspect of our communication behaviour is seen in the gestures and movements we make: we make systematic use of our hands, sometimes of our whole bodies (though the role of such movements in our communication is not yet clearly understood). When these gestures designate locations or indicate movement away, whether concrete or abstract, they usually do so in an iconic way. The most obvious of these is the demonstrative gesture whereby we indicate a location by pointing towards it. It is interesting to note that chimpanzees are able to interpret such demonstrative gestures, whereas other animals look at the finger rather than at what it is indicating[2] (Premack and Premack 1983: 79; Savage-Rumbaugh and Lewin 1994: 161). A demonstrative gesture is not arbitrary; there is an analogue relation between the gesture and its meaning which can be modelled via a continuous mathematical function.

An iconic link can be established when there is an analogue relation between two domains, the domain of signs and the domain of meanings. This is the case with gestures that describe shapes and spatial relationships, as it is with the resemblances of sounds that underlie onomatopoeia. However, games of mime clearly show how difficult it is to designate entities which cannot have any such analogue relation with a set of signs. Obviously, one can make some attempt at miming notions such as kinship, hope, palaeontology, or transcendency, but it will require much effort and the use of many signs and the chances of success are not great. Human language for the most part relies on a non-analogue code; in the

---

[2] Not that this means the chimpanzee understands the communicative intention of the gesture (Call, Hare, and Tomasello 1998).

main, our linguistic signs bear no resemblance whatever to the things they refer to.

The basic units of language show several properties which are anything but iconic. One of these is their discreteness. A code is said to be discrete when its elements are separable: the distance between any two separate elements of the code cannot be arbitrarily small. Thus the honeybee's dance seems not to be discrete, as it appears that the various angles it can express may be arbitrarily set in relation to one another. In language, phonemes possess the property of separability. This can be easily demonstrated by making gradual alterations of an acoustical signal between two forms, one of which is heard as *pierre*, the other as *bière*. Although the alteration is genuinely gradual, it is not perceived as such: native French speakers taking part in the experiment have the impression of a sharp transition; they hear either one of the words or the other; at no time do they hear anything like a hybrid form intermediate between the two words (Martinet 1967: 22; Mehler and Dupoux 1990: 232).

The value of discrete systems is well known (one need only think of the difference between music as digitally recorded and its analogue counterpart): they transform signal-to-noise ratio into probability of error. Disturbances propagate and accumulate through analogue systems, which are generally linear,[3] and this makes them unusable when high fidelity is required. But discrete systems can tolerate a level of disturbance, as long as the resulting probability of error remains undetectable. These systems are in essence non-linear, which means that any disturbance at input, as long as it is not too strong, will be purely and simply eliminated. This is why an acoustical disturbance, for example a transmission by telephone limiting the frequency bandwidth audible to the human ear to a fifth of its value, will not appreciably affect our perception of the phonemes of language.[4]

So language is essentially non-iconic, but not only because it relies on discrete units. A discrete code may still retain some iconic features.[5]

---

[3] Linear systems function on the principle of superposition. If noise is added at input, it will still be there in some form or other at output.

[4] This ability of ours to reconstitute the correct phonemes despite distortions draws on at least two different levels of codification, those of phonemes and words. It is less effective when it is reduced to unaided phonology, as in the recognition of proper names.

[5] When a signal, for instance a musical signal, is quantified, what one gets is a discrete-value signal. This is a non-linear operation which does not destroy the analogue relation between the signal and the physical phenomenon it represents.

In addresses as codified in Europe, there is a similarity between the order of the house numbers and the relative positions of the houses in the street. In the main, our language relies on the use of a code which is not only discrete but also non-analogue. In many respects, language is a digital system.

The digital aspect of language

As a code, it is a remarkable feature of language that it is digital (from Latin *digitus* = 'digit', 'finger'). A digital code is a discrete and non-analogue code; that is, one in which it is not possible to establish a relation of similarity between the domain of the signs and the domain of the meanings. Though two forms may be acoustically very close to each other, there is no reason to suppose they will have similar meanings, as can be seen in the two words *peer* and *beer*, semantically quite unrelated to one another, and in a pair of very different words, *stone* and *pebble*, which have meanings that are quite close.

This lack of relation between the meanings and the set of signs makes it possible for the set to have its own structure. The way language is organized is nothing like a reproduction of the world as we perceive it. The link between linguistic signs and their meanings is an interface between two systems which are organized independently of each other. It is an interface without straightforward one-to-one correspondences, unlike the ideal relationships of mathematics, in which every expression is univocal. In the early days of analytical philosophy some thinkers fancied they could do away with this difference between everyday language and the language of mathematics by reducing the signifier–signified link to a simple bijection. As we shall see, the interface between the system of signs and their meanings is in fact a complex arrangement in which the part played by ambiguity is essential to its communicative functioning.

The digital character of language is not without its drawbacks, though its discrete aspect means that most distortions have no effect. However, if an error is produced, because of the digital nature of the code it is an arbitrary error. A confusion between *peer* and *beer* may lead to a gross misinterpretation. Bees who misread a dance may set off in a direction which, though it is not quite the one intended, may still be within limits of tolerance. A phonetic mistake may mean that one hears the wrong message, *He's a wanker* instead of *He's a banker*. It is the digital nature of human communication which makes for the possibility of serious misapprehensions. Admittedly, the discrete feature of the code limits the impact of distortions by transforming them into mistakes whose frequency is not unacceptable; but because of the code's non-analogue character, the mistakes have arbitrary consequences. This is the price we pay for having a code that allows for the proliferation of potential meanings.

The range of meanings compatible with a non-analogue code is virtually limitless, given that there is no prerequisite of likeness to constrain the referential potential of the signs used. The lack of correlation between the form of the linguistic signs and what they refer to brings up the novel possibility of putting names to abstractions, for which it would not be easy to invent signs of the iconic variety. However, the code must also be powerful enough to encompass a significant number of the meanings open to expression. Language has acquired this power through its combinatorial aspect.

Human language is an open combinatorial system

Derek Bickerton has pointed out that a fundamental difference between animal communication and language is that 'Language is an open system, while animal communication systems are closed' (Bickerton 1990: 16). We enjoy the possibility of creating new words, of uttering sentences that have never before been spoken. This fine property of language comes from its being a combinatorial system.

Because language is in large measure a digital code, its elements are unconstrained by any relation of likeness to the things they designate. This is why they can possess a structure that is unique to them. It is this feature which enables the elaboration of a combinatorial system in which the signifying units are the result of combinations of other units, after the manner of molecules which are the product of combinations of atoms. Language exploits that possibility, in two particular ways: we combine phonemes to make words; and we combine words to make sentences. It is this property of language which is most commonly held to be what distinguishes it from animal communication. It is what some linguists, in a metaphor which is also something of a pun, have expressed as 'double articulation' (Martinet 1967). This dual combinatorial phenomenon is impressive: when we speak, we choose our words from a vocabulary containing tens of thousands of them; and we 'choose' our sentences from a repertory which is potentially infinite. By contrast, the range of signals used by animals rarely exceeds about fifteen elements.

This variety in language does not result from any gradual modulation of sound forms. We actually use an extremely small number of basic sounds, which linguistics has categorized into a repertoire of phonemes. Languages use no more than a few dozen phonemes, about thirty in the case of French. They correspond roughly to the consonants and vowels (including nasal vowels like *on* and *an*). To go from this handful of sound forms to a lexicon containing tens of thousands of words, we use a combinatorial system of concatenation of phonemes within a certain number of constraints (cf. Chapter 7). In a similar way we are able to turn words into a potentially infinite number of sentences by using the syntactic mechanisms of our language.

This doubly astonishing feature of language has often been celebrated as proof positive of the originality of the system of human communication. But in fact, the digital feature of language is not unique in the world of nature, any more than the fact that it is combinatorial, or even that it entails superimposition of two levels of combination. Male nightingales, for example, have about 200 different types of song which are in part learned. Experiments using selective exposure to segments of song during the birds' first weeks of life have established that their singing is structured into their memory in four hierarchical levels: song-sections, songs, pack-ages, and context. Thus, the bird produces sequences (contexts) during which it will go from one 'package' to another, the packages being memorized combinations of elements sung, which are themselves built out of simpler elements, the sections (Hauser 1996: 286). So, in producing its system of sounds, the bird is using several combinatorial levels, which means that, in that respect, there is nothing new in human language. Besides, combinatorial digital systems are omnipresent in the natural world. They can be seen at work, for instance, in many an expression of genetic information.[6] The elements of DNA are read in threes, which gives

[6] This finding is not accepted by several schools of thought which seek a single organizing principle in living things, one founded for example on self-organization and cybernetic laws of stablization through feedback (Piaget 1967, 1976; Varela 1988). Francisco Varela, a trained biologist, wrote: 'the case of the so-called genetic "code" is paradigmatic . . . For some years, biologists have thought that proteins are coded by the nucleotides in DNA. Yet it is clear that DNA triplets can adequately select an amino-acid in a protein if and only if they are immersed in a cell's metabolism' (Varela 1988: 81). As Varela says, the existence of the 'so-called genetic "code" ' is indeed a great impediment to a unified theory of life grounded in the necessity of stable and self-sustaining forms. The presence of a chemical context in no way alters the arbitrary character of the words making the genetic code; and it is inexplicable within Varela's framework of 'emerging regularities'. The fact that language, in some of its aspects, should also be seen to be an arbitrary code is equally embarrassing for a constructivist theory.

sixty-four combinations, called codons. These are themselves combined and transposed into proteins, the number of which is potentially infinite, there being tens of thousands of different proteins in a cell. The combinatorial feature shows also in the system which controls the expression of genes, due to the combined action of repressors and activators. The immune system too works through several combinatorial systems. The synthesizing of a great variety of antibodies is made possible by a random rearrangement of DNA segments in the lymphocyte, each arrangement of segments being translated into a particular version of the antibodies. Similarly, the recognition of a foreign molecule on the surface of an infected cell functions through the presence of a self marker on the surface. There too the genetic combinatorial system contrives such variability that there is virtually no probability of any pair of individuals who are not twins having the same markers. That cognitive functioning relies in part on digital systems is often disputed; yet the idea underlies many theories, some concerning for example perception (Pylyshyn 1980) and especially language.

So language is a digital code, meaning that it is made of discrete and arbitrary symbols, and it is also doubly combinatorial, none of which makes it unprecedented in nature. The question that must now be raised is whether our way of communicating has any originality at all among living things. My following section may suggest a way towards an answer.

1.5 Communication in human primates

It is commonly assumed that our animal instincts have been replaced by culture, reason, and language. On this view, our descent from animals, obvious ever since Lamarck's formulation of the evolutionary 'transformism' of species in 1800, has become no more than an originary myth, an anecdotal curiosity, a biological etymology quite without relevance to anything touching our true humanity. Yet no great objectivity is required to see animality in human behaviour. When two men come to blows over a disagreement, is this very different from other primates? They clench and bare their teeth; they thrust out their jaws and their chests; they try to give themselves a stronger and more threatening appearance. They probably also feel shivers on their skin which makes their body hair stand up and, if they were as hairy as chimpanzees, would make them look larger and more impressive than they are.[7] Is our animality limited to such situations, in which we may forget that we are civilized beings?

Our way of behaving in society and of communicating is so different from animals' ways that it seems to endow us with some special status, beyond their reach. One of the objectives of this book is to show that this idea is in more than one way plausible. None the less it would be false to think that our way of living in society and our mode of communication have in any way replaced the fundamental social behaviours of the primates that we still are. Our feelings, for instance, and the code whereby we communicate them are not very different from the ways in which monkeys, or even mammals farther removed from us such as dogs, express theirs. This similarity was stressed by Darwin, who took the view that dogs feel and express love, pride, anger, and shame, and that their ways of doing so are perfectly intelligible to us[8] (Darwin 1872). Non-verbal human language resembles that of chimpanzees, with whom we share recognizable facial expressions for anger, threats, curiosity, and laughter. Other human gestures expressing appeasement, protectiveness, and affection are found also among chimpanzees (Eibl-Eibesfeldt 1967); and the care that some people lavish on the skin of their partner or their children is reminiscent of the grooming so prevalent among this same closely related species. Our ways of embracing, which some cultures practise with extreme frequency, are like those of bonobos (Savage-Rumbaugh and Lewin 1994: 109). Like other primates we use the voice, sometimes in non-verbal utterances, to mark our separation from the group, our unhappiness, our grief, our joy, our sexual relations. Our ways of showing submission, even when ritualized, show signs of ancestral movements: a dog will submit by exposing its neck to the fangs of the dominant individual; a gorilla will stoop and look away; a chimpanzee will offer its back. In each of these

[7] 'With mankind some expressions such as the bristling of the hair under the influence of extreme terror, or the uncovering of the teeth under that of furious rage, can hardly be understood, except on the belief that man once existed in a much lower and animal-like condition' (Darwin 1872).

[8] Richard Connor suggests, however, that dogs' expression of emotions similar to ours comes from an unconscious artifical selection in the animals (Connor 1999, personal communication).

cases the individual is trying to adopt a deliberately vulnerable position. It has been argued that our doffing a hat and bowing so as to expose the neck have exactly the same effect (Eibl-Eibesfeldt 1967).

Human communication has often been presented as a phenomenon detached from and largely independent of the immediate contingencies of an individual's environment and present state or situation. Animal communication, on the other hand, is seen as unspontaneous, emotional, and compulsory. What is meant by 'unspontaneous' is that animals allegedly communicate only in response to a stimulus, whether an external one such as the presence of a predator, or an internal one, as when a pang of hunger makes a domesticated animal express a desire for food; and at other times they do not communicate, having, as the saying goes, nothing to say. What is meant by 'emotional' is that their communication seems always to be the outcome of a clearly identifiable feeling, such as fear, envy, anger, etc. And what is meant by 'compulsory' is that acts of communication by animals appear to be reflexes, responses to stimuli, which it is not in the animal's power to resist. These features of animal communication, it is said, are the exact opposite of the salient features of human communication which appears to be spontaneous, non-emotional, and under our intentional control. There is, however, nothing hard and fast in this supposed dichotomy.

A fair amount of animal communication does not fit into the neat threefold classification. A mother crocodile moving about on land will utter periodic sounds to remain in contact with her young. This cannot be seen as a response to a precise stimulus, unless we are to broaden the concept of stimulus in a way that makes it lose all definition. Nor does her behaviour particularly suggest she is in a wrought-up state. Much the same can be said of stereotyped and repetitive acts of communication, which are so frequent in the wild and which seem to have no emotional implications.

Nor is it true that every act of human communication is spontaneous, non-emotional, and intentional. We are often unable to control our laughter; and laughter is a signal, communicating to others the fact that we have noticed a situation in which incongruity arises from mechanical-looking behaviour (Bergson 1940). There are many situations in which this signal is a reflex out of our control. As for emotion, not only are some of our utterances hardly distinguishable from the feelings accompanying them (think of insults), but there are emotions such as indignation which will almost without exception provoke vocalization in those who feel them. However, if we define such cases as marginal and ignore them, it can appear that our everyday use of language does possess the feature of spontaneity so marked by its absence from animal communication. Our speaking seems not to be brought about by any stimulus; instead of being controlled by our environment, it appears to be the outcome of internal cognitive processes. An example may serve, though, to invalidate that way of seeing our language activity. Let us imagine two people in Paris sitting at a table outside a café, and a pedestrian walks by, stark naked. The first of them to notice him will without fail immediately start to talk to the other and a conversation will ensue. An event like that, once noticed, constitutes a stimulus which, even in Paris, has all the properties needed to activate a conversation in a way which is more or less deterministic. Is such a conversation in any way less automatic than the alarm call of a vervet monkey? We shall have occasion to come back to the configurations of stimuli which bring about determined verbal exchanges. For now, let us establish that, if there is a difference of kind between animal communication and human communication, we will not find it in any supposed detachment from our environment, from our emotions, or from our reflexes.

1.6 Use of language by humans

Language, because of its combinatorial features, is an open system. Human beings take every advantage of the combinatorial possibilities that it offers. Very few of the millions of sentences we speak in our lifetime are identical with one another. In that respect, our system of communication really is unique among living things. Animals utter repetitive signals drawn from limited repertories, whereas humans invent new messages every time they say anything. Anyone who sees human language as just a 'souped-up' version of animal communication would have a hard time finding an explanation for such a phenomenon. We may have a notion of the reasons why animals repeat their utterances (Krebs and Dawkins 1984; cf. Chapter 16); but it is harder to explain why humans never (or hardly ever) repeat themselves when using language in ordinary conversation.

Human beings spend a fair amount of their waking hours exchanging constantly varied linguistic messages. It is probably this feature of the newness of each utterance that makes human communication seem so extremely original and without equivalent in the natural world. Quantitative data on spontaneous language use are in short supply. Table 1.1, from Dunbar (1998), suggests that in a range of different cultures the amount of time spent in social and linguistic interaction is of the order of 20 per cent of waking hours. Unfortunately, as the table collates figures from different sources, the category corresponding to free social activity, which largely boils down to engaging in conversation, varies considerably from one author to another.

What human beings are really doing during all these hours they spend talking or listening to others talking must be a question of great interest for anyone who tries to make sense of human nature. Yet comparatively little attention has been paid to this phenomenon, either by ethnologists or sociologists. Apart from generalities like 'exchange of information' or 'social bonding', hardly anything worthy of the name of theory has been said on the exact function of human communication! From a psychological perspective, we speak because it affords us pleasure or because we need to, but that tells us nothing about why, biologically, we have the mode of communication that we have. Though we shall of course return

TABLE 1.1   *Time spent in language use in different cultures (from Dunbar 1998)*

Society	Economy	Activity	% of waking hours
Dundee (UK)	industrial	conversation	20.6
Kapanara (PNG)	horticultural	social interaction	19.4
Maasai (Tanzania)	pastoralist	leisure	17.5
Central African Republic	agricultural	non-work (leisure, dances, visits)	16.8
Nepal	agricultural	leisure/social	32.3
Ivory Coast	agricultural	social	7.2
Upper Volta	agricultural	free time (social, religion, errands)	23.6

to this question, since it is basic to any understanding of the reasons underlying the emergence of language, let us briefly enquire into the very particular language activity of storytelling.

Telling stories is without a doubt a behaviour that marks off our species from others. Our ability to recount past experiences and events, including imaginary events, is unique to us. According to some authors, the emergence of this ability is actually responsible for the emergence of our species (Victorri 1999). Language enables us to share with others references which are remote in both space and time. As the honeybees show, we are not the only ones who can convey spatially remote references; but there are no clear-cut examples of animals using such temporally remote references. An integral element of storytelling is by definition the ability to refer to other places and to step out of the present moment. Every day, we spend a fair amount of time doing this. In any comparison of the totality of human language with any mode of animal communication, such as those we have been making, no equivalent of storytelling will be identified in any of the acoustical, visual, tactile, or chemical signals that fill the lives of animals.

Storytelling is a constrained process. As far as I know, no one has made a systematic study of its structure. Some authors have attempted to describe the linear organization of stories by arguing that it contains constants, rather as books always have introductions and conclusions (Genette 1983). But the constraints on the content of what can be narrated have not been properly explored, which is a pity when one remembers the importance of this activity in human social life.

Not all contents lend themselves to being narrated. What are the properties that a content must have in order to be recounted? Take the following example: 'One day, I got up, I had my breakfast as usual, I sat down with my coffee and switched on the radio, France Info it was. I heard that in exchange [Company A] had bought [Company B]. I wondered what the other item of the exchange was. It was [Company C].' If we suppose that the three companies seem indifferent from the point of view of the two interlocutors, then this narration is not acceptable as it stands. One has the clear feeling that something is missing. The properties of the event recounted are insufficient to appear interesting. We all have intuitions about facts that can arouse interest; and what we expect of stories is that they should involve that sort of facts. What does this concept of narrative interest consist of? What is it that makes the event related in the example insufficiently interesting to be an acceptable narration? We know intuitively either that we are supposed to understand something about A, B, and C or else there is more to come. Anyone listening to such an account is bound to wonder whether it is a send-up or whether the narrator is not quite sane. Certain implicit constraints, which we are often not aware of, apply in human communication. People who are incapable of taking account of these constraints quickly come to be seen as having a mental condition. Any reader can test the validity of this by conducting a small experiment, which would consist of recounting to friends the event figuring in the example above and inserting appropriate names for A, B, and C. The least to be expected is that those hearing the story will say 'So what?', meaning that if they are to make sense of it, they need to be told more.

How can this be explained? On the face of it, the event related is too ordinary; it has nothing original to it. If we try to translate these ideas of ordinariness and originality into more scientific terms, what we come up with is the concept of probability. As we shall see in Chapter 14, probability theory, if properly applied, can help explain some of the interest that we find in narratives. For the moment, let us say we are attentive to events which we perceive as unexpected: coincidences, untoward happenings, exceptions, anything surprising or unlooked for, etc. If we can imagine that the person telling the story in the example works for Company C, and that the listener knows this, then there is a greater likelihood that the narration will be made sense of. The listener will understand immediately the point being made by the narrator: the story turns on a coincidence; it does have a feature of the unexpected, since learning via a radio announcement that one's own company has just been sold off is far from an everyday occurrence.

So we recount odd happenings, coincidental or incredible things that we have experienced. We pay attention to facts which have no direct bearing on our own affairs: the fact that the same man has won the lottery two weeks running is bound to be of interest to many more people than just those who bought a ticket. The things we tell about are that we have run into a childhood friend 5,000 kilometres from home, that there is an airship flying over the house, that we once knew a postman with a Ph.D. The behaviour of telling about unexpected events is a property only of human communication and it makes a genuine qualitative difference between our species and all others.

This does not imply that animals evince no curiosity. It is well known that chimpanzees as individuals are very intrigued by anything new. When one of them stares into the distance, other chimpanzees will look in the same direction. However, they do not make a point of sharing their surprise with others (Call, Hare, and Tomasello 1998). Animals can communicate their emotional and physiological states, their intentions, their presence, their identity, events both concrete (food) and negative (predators), but they have never been described as drawing attention to events whose sole property is that they are unusual or unexpected.[9] Our own way of communicating, which consists of noticing occurrences that run counter to our expectations and telling about them, draws on subtle mechanisms. For instance, in order to appreciate the importance of the event recounted, one must have some idea of the frequency of occurrence of analogous events. On being told that a neighbour owns an XBS45, for example, if you have no idea how many people own such cars, you have no way of gauging whether there is anything noteworthy in what you have just learned, and if you catch sight of one of these cars in your neighbourhood, you will probably not see it as something worth telling to other people. A notion of rarity can be deduced from frequency; but it can also come from one's knowledge of the world. We know, for instance, that it must be unusual for a sports car to be equipped with a tow bar, as we have reason to suspect that the two do not go together.

The fact that storytelling focuses on rare or unexpected occurrences can be verified by observing good narrators. There is an art to the recounting of happenings in a way that captures the interest of one's audience, which entails both laying stress on some details and overemphasizing some others so as to enhance the unlikely character of what is being retailed.

Our narrative method in communication can be defined as Shannon's method. Claude Elwood Shannon revolutionized communication theory with his definition of the idea of information (Shannon 1948). According to this concept, the more unlikely an occurrence seems, the more information it affords. This conception of information has led to a redesign of the functioning of telecommunication systems in ways which increased

---

[9] It should be noted that theories based on conditioning see any such behaviour as impossible, since only situations that recur with some regularity can lead to learning and hence to behaviours.

their efficiency.[10] If we transpose Shannon's idea to the storytelling situation, it gives a neat definition of part of what it is that makes an occurrence interesting. From a narrative point of view, an occurrence may be considered to be interesting to the extent that listeners can find enough information in it.[11] Use of language for the conveying of such information appears to be without equivalent in the world of wildlife.

1.7 The originality of language

We have been discussing whether, among the properties of human language, there might be one which is qualitatively unique. Neither the arbitrariness of signs nor the digital and combinatorial features of language can be seen as being without equivalent in the world of animals. Though it is undeniable that these properties are abundantly exploited in spoken communication, they do not represent anything genuinely unprecedented. Is it true, as Darwin says more than once in *The Descent of Man*, that the mental faculties of humans differ only in degree, but not in kind, from those of the higher animals? It is an idea that is taken up by some primatologists: 'Language, in its basic dimensions, may no longer rationally be held as the characteristic that separates humans from animals' (Savage-Rumbaugh et al. 1994: 332). Our brief examination of human communication behaviour reveals that it is really mankind's non-verbal communication which is qualitatively comparable with similar behaviour in the anthropoid apes. Language appears to be an extra ability proper to our species.

One of language's most genuinely innovative features lies in the narrating activity which makes us pass on to someone else any occurrence that can be seen as unexpected. Of itself, the existence of this narrative behaviour makes human language a unique mode of communication, rather than a mere extension of animal communication. Our spontaneous language behaviour, in this narrative dimension, accords with Shannon's rule on information, which is why we can define it as different. For an

---

[10] Shannon's main contribution, which ran counter to ideas accepted at the time, was to show that up to a particular level, noise does not interfere with communication, as long as the transmission rate remains limited.

[11] This finding will be further refined in Chapter 14.

ethologist, this behaviour ought to appear as not just a curiosity, an idiosyncrasy of the human species, but as something quite incomprehensible. Why should human beings spend so much of their time using an elaborate combinatorial code to tell each other about situations that are often quite trivial? It is this feature of human communication behaviour, utterly unprecedented and at first sight paradoxical, which will be the key to our understanding of the reasons why language developed.

2 Culture, languages, and language

Language study immediately confronts us with the diversity of languages. Is it conceivable that there could be a single faculty for language with a possibly biological origin when it is clear that human beings use radically different communication systems? Languages are systems which possess their own internal logic. Though it is no doubt absurd to think that a few individuals might have invented them by design, it can at least be argued that they are the emergent results of a need to communicate. The members of a community contrive to understand each other by using words to refer to objects; then they put words together so as to express thoughts; gradually agreement is reached on the meanings and a new language appears. This way of seeing things would mean that human communication systems are more or less independent of one another; and that the only necessary feature common to languages would be the straightforward urge to communicate and be understood. On the other hand, if there really is a genuine faculty for language which lays down the specifications for a human code of communication, then an examination of languages in all their diversity and their resemblances is a very good way of outlining the limits of such a predisposition.

2.1 Why are there many languages?

On a radio broadcast one day a child asked why all human beings do not speak the same language. The answer given mentioned the arbitrariness of signs and the variability it leads to. However, no language is reducible to its lexicon; and across the whole range of languages, there is also a great diversity of phonological and syntactical structures, as there is of the complex rules which govern their use. How can human beings have created communication systems that are at once so different from each other and so sophisticated? If we take the view that there is some definite faculty for language inherent in us, then there is something mysterious in this. But there is something equally mysterious if we take the view that languages are simply social constructs. If we adhere to the first view, there should indeed be only one language, with possible variations in vocabulary. If we adhere to the second, the incomprehensible thing is the sheer complexity of the structures. Why is there no such thing as a simple language?

The idea of language as a universal system is an abstraction with little bearing on the immediate evidence afforded by observing human beings communicating with each other. What is immediately apparent is that people speak a particular language and that languages differ from one another depending on geographical location. Some 5,000 different languages are spoken in the world, though this total is approximate, given the difficulty of distinguishing between languages and dialects. One of the greatest problems in linguistics is to resolve the apparent contradiction between the extraordinary diversity of the linguistic structures and lexicons used throughout the world and the proposition that there might be a single language faculty common to all human beings.

One of the aims of this book is to explore the factors which may have enabled the emergence of a faculty of language. It takes for granted that in essentials human communication derives from an aptitude shared by all people in good health who are integrated into a society, and that this aptitude, which animals do not have, makes us spend a fair amount of our time in verbal exchanges. However, before considering this faculty of language and its possible origin, we must make a fuller assessment of the diversity of languages. Each of the elements making up this diversity must be inspected separately from the shared aptitude. The purpose will be to establish how much of the presupposed universal language aptitude remains after the examination of the great range of linguistic diversity to be found on the face of the planet.

There are very obvious contrasts among languages. Some languages are flectional, that is to say changes are added to the root of a word when it is used in syntactical combinations. Typical of this are the Indo-European languages. In French, for instance, conjugation of verbs requires inflections: in different tenses, *faire* becomes *fis* and *ferai*. Other languages are described as agglutinating, for example Turkish, in which all variations to words are done by means of suffixes appended to the root which is always at the beginning. Turkish verbs can have suffixes which express a great variety of different meanings, such as necessity, possibility, condition, negation, reflexivity, passivity, etc. The word *almamalısınız*, for example, meaning 'you must not take', is made from *alm-*, the root of the verb *almak* ('to take'), the negative suffix *ma*, the suffix of necessity *malı*, and the suffix *sınız*, indicating the second person plural (Malherbe 1983).

Turkish is also the most commonly cited example of a language with vowel harmony, which means that matching vowels are used in morphological constructions. For example, a word will contain either vowels of the type *a*, *ı*, *o*, and *u* or the type *e*, *i*, *ö*, and *ü*, without the slightest possibility of a mixture of types (except for words of foreign origin). In semitic languages, such as Arabic or Hebrew, the basic meaning of a word depends on its root consonants; often any vowels in the word will have the function of forming derivatives of it. Thus the consonants *k.t.b.*, forming the root of the Arabic verb meaning 'to write', turn up in *aktubu* ('I write'), *taktabu* ('you write', masculine, second person singular), and *katabtu* ('I have written'). In Arabic dictionaries, words are listed in the alphabetical order of their root words, which is why a word like *istiqlal* ('independence'), derived from the root *q.l.l.*, expressing the idea of rarity, will be found under the letter *q* (Malherbe 1983).

The diversity of languages is also seen in the use of class morphemes. These are elements obligatorily affixed to the noun group (Chinese, Vietnamese, Bantu languages) or the verb group (languages of northwestern America, New Guinea, and Australia), indicating physical attributes of objects, spatial situations, or modes of apprehension of the world (Hagège 1985). For example, the word-for-word meaning of the Chinese word *yī-zhī-qiānbǐ* is 'an-object (in the form of a stick)-for lead writing'. Its translation as 'pencil' does not capture the meaning given by the presence of the class morpheme *zhī*. Speakers of European languages can be greatly flummoxed by many other features of Chinese, for instance the existence of the vocalic modulations known as tones. The Chinese spoken in Beijing has four tones, whose modulations are represented by the marks ˉ, ˊ, ˇ and ˋ. In Cantonese and Vietnamese, there are six of them. The presence of a tone is often decisive in the recognition of a word, *běi* meaning 'north' and *bèi* 'the back'.

A not unusual reaction among scholars faced with this diversity is to attempt to identify features which recur in different languages and which may even be universals. In his book *L'homme de paroles*, Claude Hagège takes pleasure in showing that this search for universals 'of substance' has produced in fact little of substance. It might be thought, for example, that in every language under the sun there is bound to be a word expressing a concept as basic as 'to possess'. But this is not the case. Instead, people say things like 'X is Y-possessor' (Quechua, spoken in Peru and Bolivia), 'X is Y-ified' (Australian languages), 'Y of X exists' (Jacaltec, spoken in Guatemala), 'Y is to (for, at, in, with) X' (Russian and East African languages), 'X is with Y' (Central African languages), 'X has, holds, Y' (Romance and Germanic languages, and Slavic except Russian). Similarly, one might expect there to be a simple noun for 'man' and a straightforward verb for 'to see'. Yet in Diegueño (Mexico) 'man' is ʹiskʷ-ič ('he who is tall'); and in Kalam (New Guinea), 'to see' is expressed by a compound meaning '(with the) eyes-to perceive'. The Kalam language is also remarkable for the small number of basic verbs it uses: twenty-five everyday ones and a grand total of just ninety-six (Hagège 1985: 51).

This variability among languages shows also in syntax. Languages such as Arabic or Tahitian put the verb first in the sentence, before the subject. There are many languages in which the verb comes last in the sentence: Armenian, Persian, the Indo-European languages of India, the Turkic languages, Mongol, Japanese, Korean, Tibetan, Quechua (belonging to the Amerind family), Nubian, and even German, in subordinate clauses (Malherbe 1983). As far as syntactical categories are concerned, it can be said that many languages do not have adjectives. A language such as Turkish makes no distinction between adjectives and adverbs (yavaş means both 'slowly' and 'slow'). In Japanese and Korean, the concepts of adjectives and verbs are not separate and some adjectives can appear to be conjugated: the adjective 'big' exists not in such a straightforward form but only in the form 'to-be-big' which can bear inflections for the past and the future (Malherbe 1983). In Basque, little distinction is made between nouns and adjectives.

This linguistic variability is bound to make one wonder what a faculty for language might be. If such a thing does exist, it would appear to be reducible to a few very general principles such as the need to communicate or the fact that the code we use is a combinatorial one. We shall revert to this question when the time comes to notice that the unity of human language goes much farther than is suggested by appearances. For the moment, what is undeniable is that languages are extremely diverse and that such superficial similarities as there are must be explained as mere incidental features of their historical derivation.

2.2 The myth of the mother language

Backwards in linguistic time

Although languages more often than not differ greatly from one another in their vocabularies and grammatical organization, they can still at times show unexpected similarities. Such similarities between Latin and Greek were traditionally interpreted as meaning that Latin had grown out of Greek. However, the evidence for these links was anecdotal; and there was no serious attempt to ground them in a coherent body of knowledge. In the nineteenth century, it was by this method, more ideological than scholarly, that Hebrew was deemed to have given birth to all other languages. In 1786, in colonial India, Sir William Jones, a lawyer who made a hobby of studying languages, drew attention to disconcerting similarities between certain Greek, Latin, Celtic, Gothic, and Sanskrit words. From his analysis of these languages and a few others that he was familiar with, such as Arabic, which did not show the same similarities, he formed the hypothesis that the first group of languages derived from a single language, now extinct. The English word 'star', for instance, corresponds to words like *setareh* (Persian), *tara* (Bengali), *asdgh* (Armenian, $gh = r$), *stella* (Latin, Italian), *Stern* (German), *stered* (Breton), *estrella* (Spanish), and *étoile* (French). The equivalent Arabic word *nejma* is obviously unrelated to this group, an illustration of the relative disparity between Arabic and the languages of the Indo-European group. Similarly, there are affinities between English *day* and *dina* (Sinhalese), *din* (Bengali, Hindi), *dien* (Russian), *deiz* (Breton), *día* (Spanish), *Tag* (German), and *giorno* (Italian), which clearly mark them off from the Arabic words *yaoum* (day of the month) and *nahar* (the opposite of 'night'). Many other examples could be cited to show that there is nothing fortuitous in these similarities between the Indo-European languages.

Jones's hypothesis was the first to be founded on properly analysed evidence. It caused something of a sensation and was to be followed by numerous other comparative studies which led to the fuller definition of the family of Indo-European languages. Many other families of languages have been proposed since, for instance the Altaic group, comprising languages spoken from Turkey to Mongolia. The more extensive such groupings become, the less do linguists agree on where to draw boundaries between them. Attempts to blend these families into super-families, including the hypothesis, formulated in recent years by Merritt Ruhlen, that there is an overall unity among these families and that they all derive from a single one (Ruhlen 1994), are controversial. Ruhlen broadens the methodology to identify common source words from different semantic domains, for example by arguing that a similarity can be detected in words like *aqua* ('water' in Iquito), *yaku* and *hoq'o* ('water' and 'to get wet' in Quechua), *oqo* ('to swallow' in Aymara), *ko* ('water' in Mapudungun), *iagup* ('water' in Genneken), and *aka*, ('lake' in Yamana), and that this supports the hypothesis of a close family relationship among these native-American languages. Ruhlen selects his groups of meaning from a basic vocabulary covering senses like 'I/me', 'you', 'two', 'who?', 'tooth', 'heart', 'tongue', 'no', 'water', 'death'. Words in this vocabulary are rarely borrowed from any other language, unlike words for foods or manufactured objects, such as 'coffee', 'tobacco', or 'television'. Just as linguists have managed to reconstruct a fair number of words that must have been part of proto-Indo-European, a language spoken 5,000 years ago to the north of the Black Sea and the Caspian, Ruhlen claims to have uncovered a number of roots common to all languages, corresponding to the words of a language spoken perhaps in Africa tens of thousands of years ago. These roots include *tik* ('finger'), *pal* ('two'), *par* ('to fly'), *mena* ('to think of'), *mana* ('to stay'), *meno* ('man'), *aq'wa* ('water'), etc. There may be something mind-boggling in this way of going backwards through linguistic time; but there are non-linguistic arguments that can back up Ruhlen's theory.

The evolution of languages

Similarities between languages do not invalidate Saussure's principle of the arbitrariness of signs. Indeed, all the similarities noted appear to indicate a close historical relationship, the links between signs and their meanings having been handed down from generation to generation. Languages appear to behave like living species, evolving, being born, dying out, diversifying over time. Darwin stressed the parallel between language and species, drawing on many arguments to show that it implies a similarity between the two evolutionary mechanisms. For one thing, Darwin says, both processes are gradual. The traces left by evolution, whether of languages or species, are revealed by the fact that each of these can be classified into groups with intricate internal relationships. Some languages, like some living species, have gone extinct. Once a language has died out, it can never come back to life. Nor, conversely, can any language ever have two separate geographical origins. Variation in individuals, which Darwin saw as the essential feature enabling biological evolution, may also be seen in language, with the non-stop appearance of new words. Just as, analogously, certain physiological characteristics can only be explained by the history of species (for instance, the goose-flesh effect that cold weather has on our skin, the function of which was to make fur stand up), so languages contain vestiges of their own past, like the *m* of *I am*, quoted by Darwin as a sound which was once the marker of the first person in the parent language but which English no longer needs, as can be seen from its absence from most verbs. In addition, for Darwin the mechanism of linguistic evolution is a mode of struggle for survival, as some words prevail and prosper by satisfying criteria such as concision, ease of pronunciation, or even novelty and fashion (Darwin 1871).

There are many aspects to this explanation of the fact that the lexicon evolves over generations. One of these is the creation of words such as, say, the French *redingote*, a product of a borrowing from the English compound 'riding coat'. To a native speaker of French, it is a straightforward word, quite unrelated to the making of its morphology. Other aspects of lexical evolution are less obvious, such as the systematic sound changes that have been observed in the evolution of languages, and can reveal lexical similarities which the layman may never notice. An example of this is the fact that, in particular contexts, the consonants *p*, *t*, and *k*, which are unvoiced, tend to be replaced by their voiced counterparts (*b*, *d*, and *g*), as for instance in the French word *second*, where *c* is sounded like *g*. In the same way, Latin *aqua* has turned into Spanish *agua*. In the early 1800s Jacob Grimm made the discovery that some consonants in the Germanic languages such as *f*, *th*, and *ch* came from the consonants *p*, *t*, and *k* of proto-Indo-European, that *b*, *d*, and *g* came from the fricatives *bh*, *dh*, and *gh*, and that *p*, *t*, and *k* came from *b*, *d*, and *g*. Such systematic sound changes demonstrated that there were concealed relationships, like the one between Latin *piscis* ('fish') and German *Fisch* or between Greek *genos*,

Latin *genus*, and English *kin*. These phonetic shifts which happen among related languages remain in large part mysterious.

Language and genes

It might be thought that the life of any given language is in part independent of its speakers. Languages interbreed; they change through phonetic alteration and word creation; they are transmitted from one generation to the next, from an invader to a subjugated population, from a ruling class to the rest of society. However, linguistic changes of this sort occur much more rapidly than the biological changes which underlie ethnic diversities, some of them being noticeable within the space of a generation. This will strike anyone who listens to the soundtracks of newsreels from before the Second World War, spoken in an accent that has very likely died out, or who hears the sounds of what is now known as 'Estuary English'. Such changes and their modes of transmission are cultural in essence and have nothing to do with the biological changes which affect our species through adaptation to environment or the mixing of different populations. And of course there are examples of people of very different ethnic backgrounds who speak the same language. This can be seen especially in countries with large immigrant intakes: in California, for example, the native language of children of European, African, and Asian descent is English. There is a clear theoretical grounding for the lack of interdependence between linguistic things and biological things. However, it is flatly contradicted by the facts.

Studies in population genetics, facilitated nowadays by the existence of databases deriving from genetic analyses of blood samples, reveal extraordinarily close correlations between genetics and linguistics. Populations are marked by different genetic frequencies. Variants of a particular gene, for instance one of those contributing to the marker of the well-known rhesus factor, are common in some human groups but uncommon in others. Measurements of these genetic frequencies can help to reconstitute the history of migrations of populations, making it plain, for example, that native Americans actually derive from peoples who crossed from northern Asia, that southern Chinese are genetically relatively remote from the Koreans, and that Koreans are close to the Japanese. It is remarkable how closely this genetic evidence correlates with data drawn from comparative linguistics (Ruhlen 1994; Langaney 1999). The families of languages uncovered by Joseph Greenberg, whose work has been taken farther by Ruhlen with the aim of discovering the original mother language, correspond pretty exactly with the categories arrived at through completely independent work in population genetics, notably that of Luigi Luca Cavalli-Sforza (Cavalli-Sforza 1999). This striking confirmation strengthened the position of Greenberg, who had been severely criticized, in particular for having postulated the existence of a super-family of languages, the Nostratic family, which brought together Indo-European and the families of Altaic, Uralian, Dravidian (southern India), and Afro-Asiatic (Berber and Ethiopian languages). The idea of associating Indo-European languages with these other groupings was seen as untenable. But genetic analysis of individuals who speak languages from those other families has given strong support to the argument that there is a common origin.

This very close correlation between linguistics and genetics is of course fortuitous. It derives from the fact that both divergence among languages and genetic variation have a common historical cause: population migration. People who migrate take with them not only their genes but also their language. Linguistic transfers between two separate populations, particularly in matters of basic vocabulary, seem to be an exception. By and large, people speak the language of their biological parents. This is why there is such a close correspondence between biological filiation, measured across populations, and linguistic kinship, as shown by comparative methods.

The limits of the concept of a mother language

The myth of the mother language, with all its mystery and glamour, may well derive from a historical reality. In linguistics, no one disputes that the languages spoken today are related in a manner reminiscent of the genealogical tree of common descent posited by Darwin for species. The coincidental relation with the findings from population genetics can only reinforce the likelihood of linguistic filiations. Where opinions differ is on the reliability of the tools available to comparative linguists for linking the different families of languages into super-families and thus tracing their development from the mother language. What this means is, if we see the genealogical tree of similarities in its historical dimension, that there is disagreement over whether comparative methods are valid for data stretching back seven to ten thousand years into the past. What is at issue is whether the common roots that Ruhlen sees as evidence for the existence of a mother language are in any way likely to correspond to words actually spoken by people who lived on the Earth thirty to fifty thousand years ago.

If all languages spoken nowadays, with the possible exception of creole languages, do derive from a single original language, that would appear to strengthen the hypothesis of the cultural creation of language. It would mean that in the beginning a code of communication was invented by a population somewhere in Africa and that it was later handed down from generation to generation, changing as it went. But such a historical scenario can be doubted, for two reasons.

The first reason is related to the demographic past of our species. By analysing genetic dissimilarities between individuals, it is possible to estimate the length of time separating them and their common ancestor. The fact is that most of the changes wrought in DNA through filiation are products of pure chance and accumulate over time. The number of them is therefore proportional to the time elapsed since the lifetime of the common ancestor.[1] In this way it is estimated that the human populations of the various continents experienced great demographic growth about 60,000 years ago and that human beings of today are the descendants of a population which at that time did not greatly exceed 10,000 individuals (Lewin 1999: 180). This demographic bottleneck could not have allowed dozens of families of languages to be passed down to the following generations. So it is not surprising that all the languages spoken today can appear to derive from a single language, or from a few, spoken at that time. Consequently, it is to be expected that there should be close relationships among the languages spoken nowadays, whether language is a cultural invention or not.

The second reason for not extrapolating a cultural origin for language from the genealogy of languages lies in the mechanism of linguistic propagation. If a language dies out through lack of speakers, the genealogical branch (a fictitious one, of course) containing all the languages it could have given rise to 'disappears' with it. The place of this branch is

---

[1] These analyses are preferably done on mitochondrial DNA, which has the peculiarity of being transmitted through mothers to daughters and of being unaffected by the genetic mixing that the genes of the cell nucleus are prone to. So any changes in it can give a precise calculation of the time elapsed since the divergence of any two lines.

taken by other branches. If one starts from a pool of 100 languages, the genealogical trees which ramify from them are in fact in competition with each other. Even with a constant stock of 100 languages, it is extremely unlikely that all of the original hundred will continue for all time to have descendants. Given a long enough time, the random outcomes of successful filiations will mean that all languages eventually have the same ancestor (see Figure 2.1). If we invert the reasoning, the fact that it might be possible to rediscover a mother language, in the sense of an ancestor of

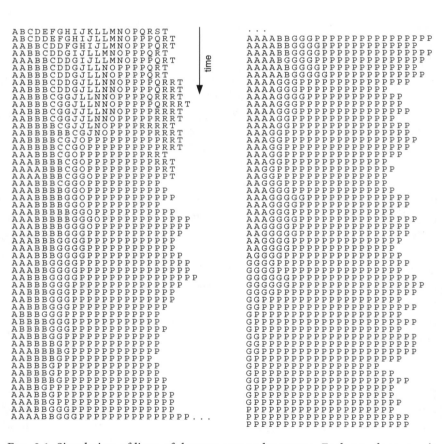

FIG. 2.1 Simulation of lines of descent among languages. Each new language is represented by the letter standing for its mother language. Random disappearances eventually produce a situation where all the languages descend from the same original language.

all the languages spoken nowadays, would not prove that such a language was the only one spoken in its day. In other words, the hypothesis of the mother language is perfectly compatible with the fact that there may always have been a considerable number of different languages spoken simultaneously on the Earth. If this is so, the argument for a mother language loses all validity and cannot lead to any conclusion about the cultural invention of language.

What can be learned about the origin of language from the study of the evolution of languages? For proponents of the idea that language behaviour began as an invention, on the model of the invention of writing, say, it is of primary importance to study the origin of languages. By grasping the genealogical relations among languages and prospecting as far into the past as possible, they hope to be able to define where and when the invention originated. However, proponents of the idea that we have a biological predisposition to language may tend to believe that the origin of languages is of merely anecdotal interest. It must be said that such a view would be excessive. It is true that historical accidents which favoured some languages against others are irrelevant to the matter of understanding how and why an aptitude for language made its appearance among our forebears. Even so, the study of filiations among languages is valuable if we are to avoid assuming that some of their aspects indicate a predisposition of human beings, when they may represent nothing more than a shared cultural heritage.

The observation, for example, that many languages use adjectives may lead one to the conclusion that the faculty for language makes humans use adjectives. But if one then notices that these languages are historically related, the conclusion appears less obvious. It comes to seem more plausible that reliance on adjectives is a culturally inherited property, of the kind that can be seen, for example, in the verb ending -*t* which marks the third person in Indo-European languages. So an awareness of relations of filiation among languages is important if we are to avoid spending time on false universals. Another consideration to be borne in mind is the dynamics of these changes, the fact, for instance, that the order of syntagmas in the sentence has shown rapid changes over the history of languages. The reasons therefore why the verb–subject–object order is relatively rare must first be clarified, with a focus preferably on cognition.

A link between observable everyday language behaviour and a faculty for language as a component of human nature built into our biological make-up would be more evident if all peoples on the Earth spoke the same language. However, knowledge of the languages of the world shows not only their extraordinary diversity but also a mode of relationship that does not arise from historical origins. The challenge facing linguistics is to understand what a faculty for language capable of producing such remarkable variety might consist of and to distinguish between whatever might be the result of historical accident handed on orally and what might be seen as deriving more directly from a predisposition to language.

2.3 Language and the palaeolithic revolution

There is such a great contrast between what we might expect of a faculty common to all human beings and the bewildering multiplicity of languages spoken in the world that one may well wonder whether the notion of a universal oneness of language shared by us all is not a mere functional abstraction. Our faculty for language might be limited to a communicative function, without reference to the particular means by which we put it into practice, which might be produced by different cultures:

While the human brain obviously has a capacity for language in a general sense, it might take the form of a broad potential for communication and representation, rather than a preset language system with precise specifications. (Donald 1998: 50)

This would mean that our faculty for language was limited to a rather general need to communicate, everything else being supplied by the collective ingenuity of society and tradition. As we shall see, this view is reinforced by evidence from palaeontology.

A cultural revolution

There is broad agreement on the idea that the emergence of language not only corresponds to the emergence of culture but is actually the motive force for it:

All we know is that every people that has ever lived on the Earth, humankind in its oldest and humblest manifestations, has been acquainted with articulated language, and that the emergence of language coincides exactly with the emergence of culture. (C. Lévi-Strauss, in Charbonnier 1961: 188)

If we take that for granted, it becomes possible to date the appearance of language to a particular moment in the past of our species, by linking it to the appearance of culture. Some authors, stressing the importance of a very significant historical phenomenon which occurred some tens of thousands of years ago, take language as we know it to be a cultural invention. For instance, the psychologist William Noble and the archaeologist Iain Davidson see it as having arisen several thousand years before the so-called 'palaeolithic revolution', well aware that our species, *Homo sapiens*, is actually twice as old as that. They reason in part from a genuine paradox which concerns our 'recent' past. A few hundred centuries ago, throughout all parts of the planet where human beings were present, something like a veritable cultural revolution did take place. Humans started to produce complex artefacts such as finely worked spearheads, jewels, flutes, statuettes; they made paintings and engravings of quite extraordinary realism. We have evidence of religious practices, in particular burial sites and the systematic use of ochre, which in hunter-gatherer societies is universally associated with magic (Knight, Power, and Watts 1995). Most of these changes appeared between 40,000 BC and 30,000 BC. This was also the period of the conquest of the Australian continent, which implies the intentional crossing of open sea on craft designed for navigation. According to Noble and Davidson, this palaeolithic revolution is the visible consequence of the invention of language:

[Language] was a product of behavioural discoveries rather than biological events. The evolutionary changes in biology had set up the circumstances in which the behaviour of language would have the form it does: use of the vocal-auditory channel with prolonged learning during infancy in a social context. The nature of language as a symbolic communication system 'created' the human mind, capable of logistics and planning apt for all environments, of reifying concepts, of distinguishing 'us' from 'them', of the invention of the supernatural, of investigating its own workings and the past. (Noble and Davidson 1996: 214)

The strength of this cultural argument as an explanation of the emergence of language is that it solves the mystery of a species which, without undergoing any biological changes, suddenly acquires great mastery over its environment, discovers art, and makes its first acquaintance with spirituality. If we can see the invention of language as the spring of this progress we can explain why such a stupendous cultural revolution had not taken place before and why it appears to have affected the whole planet. It is easy to imagine how the invention of spoken communication could increase the knowledge of individuals and their awareness of one another, enabling them to talk together about not only material concerns but also matters relating to aesthetic things or to death. However, if we closely inspect this cultural scenario for the emergence of language, it raises many more problems than it solves.

Human beings were biologically identical before and after the palaeolithic revolution, neither more nor less intelligent than we are today. Were they brutish and devoid of culture for half of their existence as a species? Can the invention of a code of communication have been enough to give them a sense of art, a grasp of technology, and inklings of the sacred? That is what Noble and Davidson ask us to believe.

The palaeolithic revolution, which brought about a sudden change in the behaviour of our species, is not the only one requiring explanation. About 10,000 years ago another cultural revolution took place in different parts of the globe. It was the agricultural revolution; and just like the one before it, it cannot be explained by any biological developments. Another perplexing example of an important discovery, from an even more remote period, is the domestication of fire, which was to result in so many alterations in eating habits, the structure of the habitat, and mastery of the environment. There is no reason to suppose that this achievement was the doing of some species other than *Homo erectus*, which had been in existence for more than a million years and would last for another half million. The acutely bothersome thing about such revolutions is that one tends to assume they must have been produced by biological changes. When one species replaces another, what is usual is that there are observable changes in behaviour; and conversely it is difficult to imagine a species that makes huge alterations in its patterns of behaviour without going through any notable biological change. There would be something very mysterious in such a set of events. What remains to be explained is, first, whether one or other of these revolutions, the palaeolithic for example, can be explained by the hypothesis that language had just been invented, and, second, why it should explain that revolution rather than any of the others.

The nature of cultural progress

One likes to imagine that important cultural changes arising at a particular time in the life of a species must have causes that are equally important;

and it seems hard to believe that changes as far-reaching as those experienced by *Homo sapiens* during the palaeolithic might just be spontaneous. The technological advances of the last two centuries present a picture of regular, almost foreseeable progress.[2] Each generation comes along with its share of innovations, thus adding to what was created by the generation before. However, to see such a conception of progress as representing human experience in the past would be a great mistake. In modern western culture, innovation is valued for its own sake. Economic competition among nations lives off innovation and hence gives it an organized form. In such a context, we expect to see not developments as epoch-making as those of the palaeolithic but rather an accumulation of discoveries all contributing to make what we call progress.

In hunter-gatherer societies, cultural innovation, instead of being fuelled by economic competition among groups, is mainly the outcome of chance. There is no evidence that people living in such societies ever make a conscious attempt at innovation. Their minds are turned towards different aspects of material and social life which do not include any concern for inventing tools or thinking up new techniques. Even in industrialized societies, technological innovation is the domain of a minority of specialized individuals; in artistic things, those who attempt to innovate are not always influential and they are rarely among the most highly regarded. So we may assume that our ancestors had no special interest in being inventive and that any innovations were arrived at quite fortuitously.[3] However, as with other natural processes, this type of cultural progress does have self-catalyzing aspects, in the sense that an innovation may foster its own development. For instance, the very first bow ever made was presumably very unlike the bows we see being used nowadays in international archery competitions. It was probably not even bent. It may have been the outcome of a game thought up by an imaginative child. Whatever the exact conditions were that gave rise to a concept

---

[2] One thinks of developments in the technology of electronic circuits, whose capacity has doubled regularly every eighteen months over a period of thirty years, though such progress requires continuous innovations in chemistry, physics of materials, and electronics.

[3] The role of chance in scientific discoveries has been played down and Newton's apple has come to be seen as a mere anecdote for people who have a taste for stories rather than for equations. However, though scientific research may seem to be an inexorable progression when seen in the long term, it should not be forgotten that chance can often be instrumental in putting research on the right track (Lot 1956).

like the bow, we may be sure that they led its inventor to the making of a very imperfect object. What is important, however, is what came next: the existence of the first bow led people to reproduce it, and to improve it, two processes which, unlike innovation, are characteristic human behaviours. If one's neighbour has a bow, it is important to have a bow oneself and if possible a better one than his. The self-catalyzing phenomenon is promoted by such competitive emulation. Any innovation is repeated and elaborated until the objects concerned have reached local perfection, that is to say they cannot be improved without further innovation.

A concomitant of this phenomenon of self-catalyzing elaboration is that cultural progress, in its spontaneous form, progresses by fits and starts. Sudden changes may well appear, but they are separated by longer or shorter periods of stagnation.[4] The usual thing is that changes of this sort will vary in their importance and effect, ranging from the creation of a new object to profound cultural upheavals. This intermittency of cultural evolution lets us see the palaeolithic revolution as a less dramatic occurrence. There may well be something satisfying to the mind in seeing a single event as being responsible for significant changes such as the coming of art, the birth of religion, the making of ornaments, the infancy of navigation, etc. Yet these things came to pass over a considerable length of time, covering about a tenth of the lifespan of the species *Homo sapiens*. In such circumstances to speak of a 'revolution' is somewhat misleading; and there is a sort of reductive overstatement in an idea like the 'invention' of art or religion. All we have to go on, after all, is an assortment of manifestations of art or religion; and artistic activity may well not have been restricted to cave paintings or engravings, just as sacred ideas may have found expression in things other than the design of burial sites. The paintings or the burial places which we can see appearing about the mid-point of the existence of our species are mere cultural innovations, not to be confused with the behaviours, the quest for the beautiful and the pursuit of the sacred, that gave rise to them.

In such a context, the importance of the palaeolithic revolution can be seen differently. For one thing, it consists of a set of events which are not necessarily interrelated. For another, *pace* Noble and Davidson, these events do not represent changes as radical as the advent of religion, art,

---

[4] This phenomenon is the cultural analogue of the punctuated equilibria which are features of the evolution of species (cf. Chapter 5).

or the ability to design and plan, but merely new manifestations of such behaviours. Just as music existed before jazz or the art of fugue, and language existed before writing, so art, religion, and technology were in existence before the palaeolithic 'revolution'.

Even so, we may still wonder about the role of language in the origin of the palaeolithic innovations. According to Noble and Davidson, not only is language the cause of them, but the absence of language also explains why they did not happen earlier. It should be noted, though, that there is nothing inevitably causal about any link between language and art, technology, or spirituality. First, it is quite possible to imagine a form of communication which, though very unelaborate, would still be very useful, while being too restricted to lend itself to any representation of the sublime or the sacred. Nor is there anything unimaginable in a mode of art or magic that could function without the combinatorial verbal communication of articulated language. And of course one can also imagine a mode of purely social communication, focused solely on relations among individuals and making no difference to the organizing or concrete planning skills of those who speak it. The fact that we can imagine all these possibilities shows there is something lacking in the idea that the recent success of our species is a consequence of language. Language is often deemed to have many and varied virtues, such as being the source of numerous abilities which we have come to think of as being well nigh impossible without it. But that is an assumption that cannot be taken for granted; and what still needs to be demonstrated is that language is both necessary and sufficient to the emergence of those abilities. In other words, the supposed correlation between the emergence of language and the revolution that happened in the life of *Homo sapiens* about 40,000 years ago has no sound theoretical basis and derives from a mere desire to correlate mysteries in the hope of reducing them in number.

2.4 The equal complexity of languages

The idea that language is a pure cultural construct presupposes that there is no biological grounding for a specific universal capacity for it. One very bothersome circumstance for those who entertain this cultural hypothesis is the fact that the complexity of languages bears no relation to the

complexity of the cultures which speak them. Here is what Darwin had to
say on the matter:

The perfectly regular and wonderfully complex construction of the languages of
many barbarous nations has often been advanced as proof, either of the divine
origin of languages, or of the high art and civilisation of their founders. Thus
F. von Schlegel writes: 'In those languages which appear to be at the lowest grade
of intellectual culture, we frequently observe a very high and elaborate degree of
art in their grammatical structure...' But it is assuredly an error to speak of any
language as an art, in the sense of its having been elaborately and methodically
formed.[5] (Darwin 1871)

Cultural evolution has produced impressive changes: the palaeolithic
revolution, the domestication of animals, the invention of agriculture,
writing, and everything that has flowed from them. Not that this cultural
evolution has affected the richness of any language (leaving aside the
prodigious filling-out of the lexicon that derives from writing and formal
education); and the languages spoken by the hunter-gatherers who still
inhabit certain parts of the Earth are every bit as sophisticated as our own.

   There is a correlation between the richness of a lexicon and the degree of
sophistication of the culture that uses it, as is especially obvious when one
compares societies which rely on oral tradition and societies which have a
written culture. On the other hand, it would be well nigh impossible to
establish any such correlation through a comparison of their syntactical
structures. Grammatical complexity is, of course, a difficult factor to
measure. How more or less complex than one another are the use of
inflections, the reliance on cases and declensions, the use of class morphemes or affixation, conjugations, the number of verb tenses, types of
agreement, etc.? English is an example of a language that is generally
supposed to be syntactically simple, in that its morphology is minimal,
it makes hardly any use of case, mood, or verb tenses and it has little in the
way of constraints of agreement. And yet to some it can be a very
confusing language because of the inflexibility of word order in its sentences. Such constraints on the placement of words must also be taken
into account in any measure of syntactical complexity. The same goes for
irregularity and the presence of exceptions which, because each one must be

---

[5] Here Darwin is arguing that languages are the product of evolution by cultural
selection, against the idea that language was a consciously designed and thought-out
system.

learned by heart, may significantly affect the degree of complexity. The upshot of all this is that, whatever definition is used for the measuring, it is highly unlikely to find one that correlates with any degree of cultural sophistication.

As far as syntax is concerned, this lack of correlation between language and culture is utterly incomprehensible if one takes language to be an expression of a culture. If language really is nothing but a convenient construct invented by a community to meet its needs in communication, how are we to explain that high-tech cultures which juggle a multiplicity of abstruse concepts have never elaborated codes any more complex than those in use among tribes of hunter-gatherers? On the other hand, if the grammar of languages comes at least in part from a particular faculty for language, then not only is it not surprising to find that complex languages are used in cultures that we think of as uncomplicated, it is actually what we should expect. If human beings are gifted with abstract cognitive structures which influence the possible design of any sentences they may form, then we must be able to find constructions of equivalent complexity in any language spoken anywhere in the world.

The great diversity of languages might lead one to the conclusion that speaking, using syntax, and abiding by rules of phonetics and conversation are the outcome of a straightforward cultural construction which, generation by generation, has gradually devised an intricately designed and finely wrought instrument to meet a need to communicate. An analogy can be seen in the art of the baroque fugue: as practised in the first half of the eighteenth century, it was the product of a cumulative cultural evolution made possible by the contributions of many musicians, some not very talented, some geniuses, each of whom copied and improved the handiwork of their predecessors. Perhaps it is possible to see language as not very different: every generation makes its own use of the preceding generation's code of communication, improving it as it goes. This process may result in a highly elaborated system: just as fugue has its rules about recapitulation of the principal subject and the counter-subject, its principles governing harmonic transitions, its combinations of notes, and its vocabulary of chords, so language has its rules on phonetics and syntax, its conventions of usage, and its lexicon. This way of conceiving of language does appear to be in accordance with the history of language, insofar as we can reconstruct it, and to give some prima facie consistent explanation of language as having sprung from an invention and then having undergone a process of gradual cultural refinement. However, a closer inspection of the reality of human linguistic practice shows that the theory of the cultural creation of language is at variance with a number of facts.

Some of these facts will be presented in the next chapter as part of an argument for the existence of a specific biological basis for language. This argument in no way rules out the importance of culture in the functioning of that faculty. We have just seen that language makes itself manifest through different languages, that they are the emergent result of inter- actions between people, that they are transformed over time, and that their use is inseparable from immersion in a culture. What must be established now is that there are some aspects of our language behaviour which cannot be mere products of a culture.

3   The biological roots of language

If language is not an invention, then we must have a natural predisposition to speech. It is the aim of this book to explain the emergence of that predisposition. What does it consist of? In the preceding chapter we took some account of how diversely it manifests itself in different languages. What we must do now is assess how much of human language behaviour depends on biological faculties and which of these faculties are particular to language. One way of doing this is to analyse certain evidence which reveals the biological roots of our capacity for language. In addition to anatomical and behavioural data, we shall inspect attempts to teach language to chimpanzees.

3.1 The organs of language

It is impossible to make chimpanzees speak, in the sense of uttering words. Though we share 98 per cent of our genome with chimpanzees, there are still certain morphological differences between them and us, one of which lies in the structure of the larynx. The human larynx is highly original, with an unusual structure that marks us off from the other primates; and there can be no doubt that this morphological peculiarity is related to the use of language.

Our phonation apparatus is amazingly well adapted to language. Was this anatomical arrangement selected to comply with the need to speak? Or was it the other way round, language taking the articulated form that is familiar to us because of an already existing speech apparatus that had been selected for another function? Human beings have no difficulty in sounding up to fifteen phonemes per second, an achievement made possible by an extremely accurate control over the vocal cords, the larynx, the tongue, the lips, and the palate. Chimpanzees do not have this accuracy of control (Deacon 1997: 248). In addition, there are considerable differences between the anatomy of our voice apparatus and those of other great apes. The main difference concerns the size of the human pharynx, which extends as far as the sixth cervical vertebra (Figure 3.1), whereas in other mammals such as the cat or the pig it reaches only the third, in dogs the second, and in equidæ the first (Barone 1976). The larynx, corresponding to the part of the trachea leading to the pharynx, is voluminous in humans (being even larger in men than in women). Our voice is a product of the many and varied ways in which laryngeal sound can be modified as it passes through the different parts of the vocal tract. Our overlarge pharynx and larynx mean we can make vowel sounds which are powerful and delicately controlled, for which the pharynx functions as a resonance chamber. Together, they are extremely mobile, facilitating in particular swallowing, despite being situated so low in the throat. Philip Lieberman stresses the importance of this anatomical difference, which though it plays this essential role in language, entails disadvantages,

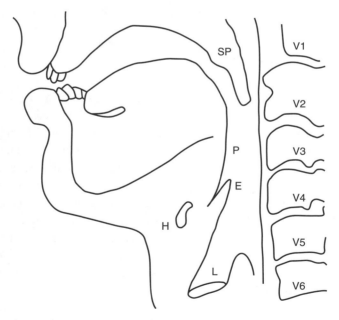

FIG. 3.1 Concise anatomy of the pharynx (P), showing its extension from behind the soft palate (SP) down to the larynx (L) situated at the level of the sixth cervical vertebra (V_6). The diagram also shows the epiglottis (E) and the hyoid bone (H).

especially the danger of food being accidentally taken into the trachea (Lieberman 1992).

The idea of the cultural origin of language, to be consistent, ought to be able to give a convincing explanation of the anatomy of our phonation apparatus without reference to any linguistic function. The properties of living beings, apart from certain very particular cases, correspond to precise functions.[1] The anomaly is here all the more blatant, given that it is a feature which in other respects is something of a handicap. If the low position of the larynx is genuinely unrelated to the biological evolution of language, then it must be explained as serving some other function. However, the fact is that nothing plausible has ever been suggested. What type of vocalization or respiratory function could ever require such a morphology? Some have argued that the anatomy of our pharynx may have been a consequence of bipedalism (Aiello 1996). Others point out that in the species of hominids that preceded us, though they too walked on their hind legs, the anatomy of these organs was more or less that of other primates and not so abnormally low as it is in us (Lieberman 1984). Nor is it clear how bipedalism might have had the inevitable effect of pushing our pharyngeal apparatus to such a deep position, given the difficulties this can cause with swallowing. And of course it would also be necessary to explain how a biomechanical constraint such as bipedalism could have wrought the miracle of a vocal organ capable of making and controlling such a range of varied sounds. Among the primates, *Homo sapiens* is the only one able to produce non-nasal vowels like those heard in words such as 'see' and 'put'. According to Lieberman, it is easier to distinguish such sounds than those that other primates can utter. The only plausible explanation is that the larynx and pharynx of human beings have been modified by natural selection in ways that allow the production of articulated language. If one takes this view, language cannot have been a mere product of culture.

---

[1] These very particular cases are those organs which continue to be present even after their function has disappeared, such as the eyes of blind cave-dwelling fish or what Gould and Lewontin call 'spandrels': fortuitous features associated with features selected (Gould and Lewontin 1979), for example the green colour of bile.

3.2 Neuronal circuitry dedicated to language

The shape of the larynx is not the only anatomical peculiarity of human beings to have a direct bearing on speech. The biological roots of language are clearly seen in forms of aphasia caused by particular cerebral lesions. In the middle of the nineteenth century, the French physician Paul Broca was the first to prove beyond doubt that there was a correlation between brain damage and a mental disorder, in this instance a mode of aphasia which prevented the patient from speaking the words and sentences of his native language. The lesion in question was situated on the cortex, in the left prefrontal lobe, a zone known ever since as 'Broca's area' (Figure 3.2). Broca was convinced that this finding proved conclusively that language is a specific function, governed by a particular zone in the left hemisphere of the brain. Later research showed this conclusion to be too radical; and there are several areas which are necessary to language. One of them does happen to be Broca's area in the left prefrontal lobe, though this is a part of the brain that in fact includes several different areas with separate functions (Deacon 1992). Another cortical area essential to language is Wernicke's area, located in the left temporal lobe. Carl Wernicke was a German neurologist who demonstrated the role of this second area in language comprehension little more than a decade after Broca's discovery. The case for seeing language as the expression of a specific biological predisposition is strengthened by the existence of regions of the brain which appear to be dedicated to language.

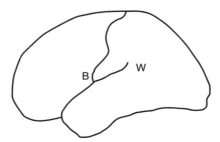

FIG. 3.2 Simplified diagram of the brain's left hemisphere showing the main cortical areas involved in language, Broca's area (B) and Wernicke's area (W).

This is a view which can be qualified in several ways. First, there is the discovery that many other parts of the brain, including the right hemisphere, seem also to play a role in the treatment of language. Such discoveries result not only from study of pathologies caused by various spontaneous lesions of the brain but from studies of direct brain stimulation done by neurosurgeons during operations, as well as from modern studies in cerebral functional imagery. The last of these are made possible by various techniques, such as positron emission tomography (PET scans), Nuclear Magnetic Resonance Spectroscopy (NMR), and encephalography. These techniques are gettting better all the time, though caution may be required in interpreting some of their findings. They certainly represent major advances in study of the brain. What is striking is to see that images of the brain's functioning, particularly when it is engaged in linguistic tasks, quite closely corroborate facts established by the study of pathologies. It is quite clear that, in normal people, Broca's area and Wernicke's area do play a part in language tasks. They are, however, not the only areas that do this. Many other cortical regions are involved in the processes linked to language, though the disorders caused by their accidental destruction are less easy to detect and characterize than with damage to Broca's and Wernicke's areas and some others.[2] So the neuronal correlates of language should not be seen as a localized module, a sort of optional plug-in added to the prelinguistic brain of a primate (Deacon 1997: 293). What we have is rather a set of circuits, some of which are also used for other functions.

Brain plasticity, though it is rather limited, especially in adults, does not enable us to demonstrate conclusively that the cortical zones associated with language are the result of a specific biological predisposition. For instance, though part of the temporo-occipital area happens to be involved in learning to read, no one would claim that reading, a recent historical invention, is a biologically determined behaviour. Moreover, Wernicke's area is close to auditory areas, just as Broca's area is close to motor areas in charge of the organs of phonation (Deacon 1992), which seems to suggest that these two areas may be recruited during the learning of language, as happens with reading. However, such a hypothesis is at variance with evidence which supports the idea of a specific

[2] For example, the supplementary motor area, which is essential to the initiation of speech, or the counterparts of Broca's and Wernicke's areas in the right hemisphere, damage to which causes prosody deficits (Deacon 1997: 313).

neuronal predisposition. This includes the fact that language is almost entirely confined to one hemisphere, the left for 97 per cent of subjects, which means there is at the very least a bias in favour of it for the processing of symbolic information. Also, disorders arising from damage to the corresponding areas have practically no direct bearing on the type of language spoken by patients or their culture,[3] whereas the existence of a cortical zone involved in reading obviously depends on whether a person has learned to read.

Mention must also be made of some rather striking evidence, which might seem anomalous if the specialization of the areas in question were a simple result of learning language. It concerns aphasias observed in deaf patients whose first language is sign language. It turns out that their disorders, whether lexical (inability to make the correct sign), syntactic (mistakes in linking of signs), or semantic (using one sign for another), correlate just as closely as do those of patients who are not deaf with damage to Broca's area and Wernicke's area (Hickok, Bellugi, and Klima 1998). This implies very strongly that these areas really are specific to language, given that their functioning is indifferent to whether language is spoken or signed. Consequently, it is difficult to maintain that their involvement depends on their position or on the auditory character of normal communication. In the light of this, one may wonder why these areas are located in the very places where one would expect them to be if cortical specialization were completely a product of ontogenesis. No doubt their position in the geography of the cortex is not fortuitous, though the reasons for this circumstance should more properly be sought in phylogenesis, that is in the evolutionary origin of the cortical specialization for language. In the past of our species, earlier forms of Broca's and Wernicke's areas, which once processed phonation and acoustical signals, evolved into specialized processors of linguistic information. The rather strategic position of these areas could therefore be explained not as ontogenetic specialization but as a result of our species' acquisition of a biological predisposition to language.

---

[3] The effects of damage to Broca's area on disorders of grammar vary considerably, depending on whether the patient speaks a highly inflected language such as Italian or a largely uninflected language like English (Deacon 1997: 307).

3.3 Language learning in animals

Language cannot be reduced to phonation. We do, of course, possess organs of phonation quite unlike anything to be found among our close relatives the primates; and it is these that give us the power of speech. Against that, sign language as used by the deaf shows that phonation is not an essential ingredient of language. Any attempt to assess the biological roots of language must canvass the question whether chimpanzees, despite their inability to utter the same sounds as we do, possess the ability to communicate by signs.

Sarah

Since the 1960s, several research teams have been trying, not without some success, to teach language to animals, chimpanzees in particular. In previous tests dating from the 1930s and 1940s, chimpanzees had been brought up like human children and their adoptive parents had tried to have them learn a few words. Unfortunately, this had ended in total failure, as the animals had never managed to speak even a word or two correctly. In Nevada, in 1966, Allen and Beatrice Gardner tried a different approach, which consisted of teaching a female chimpanzee by the name of Washoe the rudiments of the sign language used by deaf mutes (Gardner and Gardner 1992). After four years, Washoe was capable of making appropriate use of about 150 signs. In California, about the same period, another famous project of similar type was initiated by David Premack. In this one, a young female chimpanzee called Sarah was being taught to express herself with plastic symbols. Premack's main aim was to test Sarah's ability to manipulate 'words' to answer questions, put them together in sentences, understand and express negation, grasp abstract concepts, etc. The results, as described by Premack and shown in audio-visual documentaries, were very impressive. For instance, Sarah could write sentences like *Randy cut fig* or *Mary give apple Gussie* and could understand sentences entailing reasoning, such as *No Sarah honey cracker take* or *red on yellow—if-then—Sarah take chocolate*. She could respond to tests on *same* and *different*, pointing when asked at an object identical to the one in question. Similarly, to describe the relation between a plastic symbol and an object, she could indicate it by the use of *name of* or *not-name of,* as in *apple name-of (real apple).* She could also tell the proper relation between two objects, as in *red not colour-of banana* (Premack and Premack 1983).

These achievements were greeted with admiration and disbelief. Could the chimpanzee really understand what she expressed? When she made a sentence, did she understand the sense of it from the meaning she gave to each of its component words? The most immediate objection was raised by critics who compared Sarah's achievements to those of a circus animal. There are some animals that can be trained to do very impressive tricks; and Sarah had been literally trained. By Premack's own admission, for her to learn a single word it sometimes took several hundred attempts. Each time she got it right, she was given a reward. Unsurprisingly, her first successes with symbols involved food. The animal's linguistic behaviour was therefore the outcome of conditioning or training. Can it be said of a dog which gives its paw when asked to that it has any subtle understanding of the sentence *Give your paw*? In defence of the linguistic genuineness of Sarah's behaviour, Premack could cite the creative aspect of her spontaneous productions. At times, when they asked her *Is yellow on blue?*, referring to cards of those colours, her reaction was unexpected. Instead of just answering *No* (since blue was actually on yellow), she would first place the yellow card on the blue, then give the answer *Yes.*

The most serious criticism levelled against these experiments on the language-learning abilities of animals came from one of the researchers, Herbert Terrace. His chimpanzee, Nim, had acquired more than 100 signs and could produce many spontaneous two-word combinations like *more banana* or *give apple.* Nor was the order of these combinations a matter of chance. For example, transitive verbs like *give, tickle,* or *hug* were usually placed in front of the object. Did this represent the emergence of spontaneous syntax in the chimpanzee? The team studied video recordings of some 20,000 of Nim's productions and gradually came to the conclusion that Nim was not really able to produce language, in the human sense, but that he was just imitating whatever his teachers put to him. In other words, according to Herbert Terrace, the notion that chimpanzees were capable of making sentences on a definite pattern, however simple, was a mere illusion.

People wondered whether it could at least be maintained that these talking chimpanzees had a vocabulary and that they had an understanding of its words; but even that appeared to be doubtful. According to Sue

Savage-Rumbaugh, known especially for her work on the bonobo Kanzi, the first chimpanzees that were trained to speak, albeit with signs and plastic symbols, had no real grasp of the referential meaning of the 'words' they were using. In a situation whose context was designed, they could make use of a symbol to have access to an object or an activity. But they were unable to decode these very same symbols when used by humans to make simple requests (Savage-Rumbaugh and Lewin 1994). With the aim of showing that chimpanzees could use symbols whose referential meaning they fully understood, Sue Savage-Rumbaugh devised a new type of experiment designed to have two of them communicate with each other.

Austin and Sherman

The experiment consisted of bringing two chimpanzees, Austin and Sherman, to communicate with each other through symbols. For the apes, as had always been the case in the previous experiments, this communication was a way of earning a reward. In this case, however, the reward was not in itself the object of the communication; and Savage-Rumbaugh had designed a situation in which it would be possible to know with certainty that chimpanzees do use symbols whose meanings they understand. With that in mind, she gave them a task that they could only solve by cooperating. The experimenter hid a sweet inside a container in the presence of one of the two apes, without the other one knowing about it. The one who had the knowledge, Austin, say, also knew that opening the container (there were six different ones) would require a particular tool, a key, for example. Since Austin lacked the tool, he had to ask Sherman for it, which he did by going to the keyboard and pushing the lexigram corresponding to the required key. Sherman, who was in the other part of the room behind a pane of glass, could read the symbol. He went to fetch the key and passed it to Austin through a little trap-door; and Austin used the key to get the sweet which he then shared with Sherman.

This basic situation could entail many variants: the sweet could be changed, the container could be changed, the tool required could be changed, and the roles of the two animals could be exchanged. Whatever the combination, the chimpanzees had no problems in accomplishing their task. In accordance with Savage-Rumbaugh's design, communication was not focused on the ostensible aim of the exercise, the sweet, but on a fortuitous intermediary thing, the tool required. The animals had to focus their attention on the act of communication so as to select and interpret the appropriate lexigram. Savage-Rumbaugh, in the knowledge that the symbol was associated with a neutral object, the tool, deemed that the experiment could not succeed unless each of the apes were able to establish a two-directional association between the symbol and the object it referred to. In the case of Sarah, the plastic word she used to denote a banana may not have been a word meaning 'banana', but only an action that got human beings to give her a banana. Speaking personally, I have never imagined that the code on my bank card might mean the money I withdraw from an ATM: pushing the buttons to enter the code is just a motion to be gone through enabling me to withdraw the cash. At that moment, my code has no existence as a signifier; it is at most an act associated with getting at money. However, with Austin and Sherman, the most straightforward explanation is to accept that they associate the lexigram of a key with the real key. To show just how unambiguous this interpretation is, Savage-Rumbaugh tells of how Sherman sometimes mixed up the lexigram for the key and the lexigram for the wrench. During one experiment, he asked for a key, though it was a wrench that was required:

[Sherman] watched as Austin began to look over the toolkit in response to the request. Austin picked up the key, and Sherman looked surprised, turned to look at the keyboard, which still showed the *key* request he'd made, and realized his mistake. He rushed to the keyboard and corrected himself by tapping on the wrench symbol to draw Austin's attention to the changed request. Austin looked up, saw what Sherman was doing, dropped the key, and took the wrench to the window to give to Sherman. (Savage-Rumbaugh and Lewin 1994: 82)

The success of this experiment was made possible by previous work. The two apes had already learned to share food, to name the tools and the sweets through the use of symbols, and to understand how the containers worked. They had also learned a simpler task than the one in the eventual experiment, in that the chimpanzee that was aware of where the sweet was had to put a name to it. The sweet would not become accessible unless the other chimpanzee could also name it correctly. The object of the exercise was to find out whether, having learned all these things and without further training, the apes could then accomplish the task of communication related to the tools. The experiment showed that they could: when Sherman and Austin were put for the first time into a situation where active cooperation was required, they contrived to produce and interpret symbols of tools so as to solve together the problem that they were faced with.

Thus a system of communication based on the use of symbols denoting objects had been learned and used by animals. Unlike the parodies of communication made of linked pairs of stimulus and response (Epstein, Lanza, and Skinner 1980), communication between Sherman and Austin appeared to have been mediated by mental representations. This was the only way to explain not just the spontaneous success of the two apes but also their ability, equally spontaneous, to notice and correct their mistakes. Savage-Rumbaugh's work argues very strongly for the ability of chimpanzees to construct mental representations. Compared to the behaviour of Sarah or Washoe, which could be seen as the outcome of a conditioning that made direct associations between signals and actions, the behaviour of Sherman and Austin seems to require the mediation of a mental representation. When Sherman asked Austin for the tool that he needed, it seems proper to assume that the animal imagined the tool and was not just obeying a reflex set off by the recognition of the type of container with the sweet inside, as can be seen in particular when Austin offered the wrong tool.

Kanzi

The most remarkable case of an animal learning a system of communication similar to human language is without a doubt that of Kanzi, the bonobo (also known as pygmy chimpanzee) brought up by Sue Savage-Rumbaugh. It was not until relatively recently that the bonobo (*Pan paniscus*) was recognized as a different species from the common chimpanzee (*Pan troglodytes*). Although genetically closer to other chimpanzees than to humans and thus equally distant from us, bonobos were seen as more human-like in appearance and in their social and sexual behaviours. Savage-Rumbaugh, who worked at the Language Research Center in Georgia, wanted to explore the linguistic abilities of this human cousin, something she was able to do at the Yerkes Regional Primate Research Center in Atlanta, where she was entrusted with the task of teaching to Matata, the adoptive mother of Kanzi, the language used by Sherman and Austin. All attempts at making Matata use the symbols on the keyboard failed. After two years and nearly 30,000 tests, the animal had mastered no more than six of the symbols, and that only in a limited way. Kanzi, at a few months old, had always been a nuisance; and much of the research team's time went into distracting him so that Matata could concentrate on her exercises. Savage-Rumbaugh recounts an episode which, as she says, was to revolutionize the study of language learning in animals.

When Matata weaned Kanzi and had to be separated from him for a time so as to breed again, he was left alone. The research team thought they might be able to try teaching him what they had failed to teach Matata, though he had never shown any interest in her keyboard, except to push keys at random. But his behaviour, once he was separated from his mother, upset this plan: as soon as he was left to himself, he spontaneously started to touch keys on the keyboard, not at random or in response to a prompt, but in a way that announced his own actions. For example, he would touch the lexigram for apple, then go and fetch an apple. This proved that not only did he know the meaning of the symbols on the keyboard, unlike Matata, but that he had learned them quite spontaneously. This observation was, to say the least, unexpected. Teaching the lexigrams to the chimpanzees had been a laborious business; their attention had first to be drawn to the activity and they then had to be induced to choose a proper symbol for the effect they desired, and all this occupied sessions that were repetitive and tedious. So the fact that Kanzi had learned the meaning of several lexigrams quite unprompted and apparently without effort was a great surprise. Reasons canvassed to explain this achievement included his early age, the circumstances in which he had become acquainted with language, and the fact that he belonged to a different species (it was later established that this was not a determining factor). Savage-Rumbaugh decided to explore farther the circumstances of his acquaintance with language, eschewing directive methods and using the symbols only when a situation might make them relevant from the animal's point of view. That is, in organizing acts of communication, her idea was to take her cue from the animal's own focus of interest, from sweets, from play or going for walks, social activities and the like. This approach turned out to be very apt, and Kanzi quickly learned several dozen extra symbols. He is at present credited with knowing about a thousand different symbols.

The second thing in Kanzi's behaviour that caused great surprise among the research team at the Language Research Center was that they came to realize he could understand a number of English words. For example, if they happened to say the word *light* when talking among themselves, he would look at the switch or even went over and turned it on. No other chimpanzee, not even Austin or Sherman, had ever been able to understand spoken words. Through systematic testing of Kanzi's oral comprehension skills, it was discovered that he knew quite a few words associated with the symbols he used. The researchers resolved to talk to him in all their everyday doings and in this way Kanzi came to have a rather extensive passive vocabulary, a fact that makes his achievements even more spectacular.

Kanzi's originality lies mainly in the spontaneity both of his learning and his use of language. Savage-Rumbaugh stresses the fact that he properly understands the symbols making up his vocabulary. Washoe had the ability to produce signs as required but she did not always recognize the same signs when they were used by one of the experimenters. Kanzi, however, has no difficulty of that sort, which appears to prove that he makes a proper connection between the symbol and the thing. That is why Savage-Rumbaugh's findings are so authoritative and why Kanzi is genuinely impressive.

3.4 Does animal communication entail syntax?

It may appear paradoxical that the achievements of Austin and Sherman, then those of Kanzi, were given a cool reception by Savage-Rumbaugh's scientific peers. The crucial point at issue was whether animals could use a language entailing syntax; and the very unfavourable conclusions of Herbert Terrace seemed to have closed off further investigation.

Spontaneous animal communication in the wild had provided no unambiguous evidence implying the use of syntax. The example of the vervet monkeys shows that their acts of communication are made of a single 'word' apparently devoid of inner structure. The various signals used by mammals express a whole range of different information, such as location (territorial signalling, calls), emotional states (pleasure, anger, etc.), intents (threats, signs of sexual advances), alarm, and so on. Most of these signals entail a gradation. For instance, a dog's joyful or threatening behaviour may be more or less marked by the varied intensity of the signals that manifest it. The vocal system of chimpanzees enables them to play on the pitch of the sounds they make, the intensity and length of them, in ways that add affective information to their acoustical signals, as when the calls they utter about the presence of food show the degree of pleasure associated with whatever type of food it may be (Savage-Rumbaugh and Lewin 1994: 228).

Against that, the signals that animals use are always qualitatively the same for a given meaning. It is true that in the dance of honeybees, there can be gradual variation in some of the parameters, such as the inclination of the dancing insect's circuit or the speed at which she does the dance, and this can alter the meaning of the message. However, qualitatively speaking, it is always the same circuit.[4] The only variations in the message are in its quantitative parameters; but it has a fixed qualitative structure. The presence of syntax can be seen in messages with qualitative variations in structure. A human being can of course graduate the expression of anger by speaking the same sentence in voices of different strengths. But we have the additional possibility of varying our vocabulary and using words which are more or less provocative. Qualitative variations in the elements of our sentences can change their emotive effect from teasing to insulting. That is, the meaning of a sentence depends systematically on the ways in which we combine its component signs. As far as is known, no similar case of the use of syntax has ever been demonstrated in animal communication.

There remained, however, the question whether the anthropoid apes who were the subjects of experiments in teaching symbolic language might be capable of combining symbols in structured messages. As we have seen, Sarah was able to produce proper sentences, though Premack prefers to speak of 'constructions'. It is a fact that the internal organization of a real sentence is in part independent of its meaning. For instance, the position of the object in relation to the verb, a thing that varies from language to language, is unaffected by whatever state of reality any sentence may be describing. And that, of course, cannot be said of Sarah's linguistic constructions (Premack and Premack 1983). In Premack's view, a construction like *Mary give Sarah ice cream* borrows its organization from the situation it describes. Though Sarah may learn to distinguish between *Mary give Sarah ice cream* and *Sarah give Mary ice cream*, this distinction

---

[4] It is noteworthy that when the source of food is less than fifty metres away from the hive, the bee does a different type of dance, which is circular in shape rather than a figure of eight.

only holds for the parts played by the entities to which these words refer, in this instance the giver, the action, the object, the receiver. When Sarah states *Blue on red*, all she is doing is naming first the colour that can be seen because it is on top of the other one. In other words, Sarah has no grasp of the grammatical functioning of the words as subject, verb, complement. Premack contrasts Sarah's behaviour with the way a child will sometimes say things like, 'Daddy come home' or 'Where did Mommy go', and at other times just, 'Come home?' and 'Where go?' The reason why the child appears to make these omissions is not that they denote any definite entity, but rather that they are always the subject of the sentence (Premack and Premack 1983: 114). But nothing of the kind can be observed in Sarah's behaviour.

As we have seen, there was doubt about how well Sarah actually understood the words she used and even more about her 'sentences'. As for Kanzi, however, he seems to have much greater comprehension not just of the elements of his vocabulary but of the combinations of words that he uses. So if it turned out that Kanzi also observed constraints in the order of the symbols that he expressed, the phenomenon would be difficult to ignore. Over a period of five months when he was five-and-a-half years of age, his 13,691 utterances were recorded, about 10 per cent of which contained two or more elements. Half of these 'sentences' were spontaneous, in the sense that they were unprompted by any member of the research team and so could not be explained as an imitation of their acts of communication. Kanzi came to follow a rather strict order, putting the action first and the object second, as in *Hide peanut, Bite tomato*, etc. It seems reasonable to suppose that he had learned this rule of English word order from the systematic structuring of the sentences to which he was exposed by the human experimenters. Not only could he learn such rules, he could also invent them. Many of his combinations were made of touching a lexigram on the keyboard followed by a pointing gesture, as in *Tickle* + a gesture towards the person designated to be the tickler. This gesture was always made after the touch on the lexigram, even when the person pointed at was right next to him and the keyboard was on the other side of the room, which meant he had to go over to it first. Savage-Rumbaugh sees this as a genuine rule of syntax, invented by Kanzi himself (Savage-Rumbaugh and Lewin 1994: 161), whereas according to Premack's criteria it is a mere rule of construction, having a bearing not on grammatical categories but on the roles of action and agent making up the situation. The fact remains that the rule exists, it sets the order of the signs in an arbitrary way, and the animal appears to have adopted it spontaneously.

3.5 Language learning and universals

The achievements of Kanzi led Savage-Rumbaugh to draw the conclusion that there is a natural likeness between these animals and human beings in their communication abilities:

[T]he fact that Kanzi is able to invent such rules is strong evidence for the continuity theory—that is, the idea that the mind of man differs in degree from that of the ape, but not in kind. (Savage-Rumbaugh and Lewin 1994: 163)

The continuity theory, with its basis in the linguistic accomplishments of trained chimpanzees, is vehemently opposed by Noam Chomsky, who makes the analogy that if human language is like a bird flying, then the communication that laboratory chimpanzees are capable of is an attempt to jump a little higher. The flight of a bird is not just a better jump; it is a mode of locomotion of a different kind. To get chimpanzees to use the communication code that experimenters thrust upon them, much effort must be expended, whereas children spontaneously pick up the language they hear being spoken, without any need to be taught.

Language is not learned the way mathematics is. Some people see language as something that just happens to children and compare it to other events like puberty or learning to walk, rather than as a thing acquired that needs to be actively learned, like how to read or play bridge. This was the focus of the famous debate organized between Jean Piaget and Noam Chomsky in 1975 at the Abbey of Royaumont (Piattelli-Palmarini 1979). The question at issue was whether children's learning of their native language was the outcome of general abilities or rather due to particular and specialized predispositions which enable them rapidly to acquire the language spoken all about them. One of Chomsky's main arguments in favour of this latter hypothesis concerns the spontaneous and extraordinarily effective way in which children pick up their native language, despite the fact that their exposure to the range of its possible syntactic variants is in fact only partial. In particular, children appear to acquire very early in life certain constraints related to language; and for

Chomsky that would only be possible if their learning is guided by a specific predisposition, which might consist of an innate awareness of certain structures of language. A corollary of this theory is therefore that all human languages must share some structural properties, since the predisposition cannot be one related to any particular language. By way of example, here are two sentences. First: *He says that John is ill*, in which *He* and *John* cannot indicate the same person.[5] And second: *John says that he is ill*, in which *John* and *he* may indicate the same person, though not necessarily. Such a constraint can apply in sentences which are much more complicated: *The fact that he says the cousin of the person to whom John sold his car was a crook doesn't cast any aspersions on James*. There again, coreference between *he* and *John* is impossible, though *he* and *James* may well be coreferential. As will be seen in Chapter 9, the linguistic explanation of these examples bears on the position of the pronoun in relation to the proper names in the syntactic tree. This is a phenomenon that exists not only in languages like English or French but in all languages. Chomsky sees this as a universal property of the faculty of language (Chomsky 1975). Consequently, an awareness of this constraint is innately available to children and they do not have to deduce it from the sentences spoken in their hearing.

Some psycholinguists have tried to confirm this conjecture about the innate awareness of certain linguistic phenomena. For instance, Stephen Crain studied preschool children aged between two and five, using sentences like this: *When he ate the hamburger, the Smurf was in the box*. The sentence is ambiguous, for it is not actually clear whether it was the Smurf who ate the hamburger, or possibly Gargamel, another character in the scene. So both possibilities were put to the children, who were then asked, via a little game, whether the sentence was true or not (the aim being to give a reward to a frog when anything it said was true). Seventy-five per cent of the children accepted the sentence as true, no matter which character was eating the hamburger. Crain then tested sentences like this one: *He ate the hamburger when the Smurf was in the box*. This sentence is unambiguous, since the syntax forbids *he* to refer to *the Smurf*. To test

---

[5] It is rather remarkable to observe that any attempt to get round this impossibility ends up entertaining the idea of a splitting of personality, after the manner of Caesar in the *Gallic Wars*, where he divides himself into the Caesar who narrates and the Caesar who acts.

whether the children knew this, Crain presented them with a scene in which the Smurf ate the hamburger in the presence of Gargamel, who was portrayed as disliking such food. Though the appearances were designed to mislead, the children were not in fact misled and 87 per cent of them, including some as young as two or three, said the sentence was untrue (Crain 1991).

According to Chomsky, this type of innate awareness of certain obligatory aspects of language enables children's learning to be so spectacular, giving them the ability to make complex sentences by the age of three or four. This theory holds that children begin life with such a rich awareness of what the syntax of a language might be that all they have to do is recognize some parameters in what they hear so as to determine what type of grammar they are dealing with. This means that certain grammatical concepts, such as subject, complement, cases, or pronouns, are intuitively available to any human being. Once a child has recognized the grammatical category of words overheard, little time is required to determine for example whether the language is of the subject-verb-object variety or of the subject-object-verb variety. Learning of this sort would require a considerable time if it proceeded only from general inductive principles giving no indication of what is to be learned. In Chapter 9, we shall revert to the question of innate awareness of syntactical relations.

3.6 Linguistic abilities in neonates

If linguistic predisposition is as precise as some linguists suspect, it must surely appear in very young children. To enquire of newly born infants what they know about language may appear to be utopian. Yet psycholinguists have contrived to do that, by means of a pretty simple device: they measure the eagerness with which babies suck on a dummy. The design of the experiments never varies: by repeated exposure to a stimulus, the baby is habituated to it; if the baby's sucking rhythm changes when the stimulus is changed, then it can be assumed that the child has perceived the variation. In this way it is also possible to test the responsiveness of very young infants to subtle phonetic variations, a procedure which has given astonishing results. For instance, an infant habituated to hearing the sound *pa* will not notice slight alterations to the sound which are still recognizable as *pa* to adult ears; but if the sound becomes *ba*, the child will react. Animals, notably birds, are capable of extremely fine acoustical discrimination, and yet Japanese quails require between 4,000 and 12,000 attempts before they can learn to touch a key each time they hear a syllable starting with the phoneme *d* (Mehler and Dupoux 1990: 234). So from their very first days of extra-uterine life, babies are capable of brilliant and quite untutored linguistic achievements. Thanks to their predisposition to processing the sounds of language, they learn very quickly: by the time they are four days old they can distinguish the language they have been hearing from a different language, apparently relying on prosodic features (Mehler and Dupoux 1990: 216).

These findings give a picture of the abilities of neonates which is at variance with the long-held view that the new-born child was a mere blank consciousness ready to receive everything from its contact with the world. Such empiricism is simplistic, for it masks the complexity of the learning process that would be required for the child to be capable of such language acquisition. Neonates appear to come into the world already equipped with predispositions which enable them to analyse quite rapidly the phonemes of the surrounding language. Some may even go so far as to fancy that the child's learning started back in its intra-uterine life and imagine that it acquired an acquaintance with phonology while still afloat in its amniotic fluid; but that would be ruled out by many things, such as the acoustical distortions of the liquid medium, the body sounds which surround the child inside the mother's womb, the fact that after its birth the neonate has a special phonetic ability but no specialization in the phonemes of the surrounding language, etc. A foal, at birth, has hooves and knows how to walk; and similarly, a new-born human child comes into the world already equipped with a number of functional behaviours such as sucking, seeking the mother's breast, and even walking.[6] Evidence of this sort suggests that infants also have a specific capacity for learning the sounds of the surrounding language.

But the abilities of very young children are not limited to their phonetic skills. Analogous tests have shown that by their third or fourth day of life, they can discriminate between groups of two objects and groups of three (Dehaene 1997: 55). By measuring how children focus their attention, psychologists have demonstrated that babies of five months actually have

---

[6] A new-born baby who is held up shows all the reflexes of walking. This is one of the tests commonly applied to be sure of a child's health at birth.

arithmetical knowledge: they show surprise, which translates as a slowing of the sucking rhythm, if someone tries to make them believe that 1 + 1 does not equal 2. This can be done by hiding an object with a screen and very obviously adding a second object; if one of the objects is surreptitiously removed before the screen is lifted away, the child will be surprised to see only one object where there should be two, a reaction which is repeated if the child discovers three objects (Dehaene 1997: 62). In ways like this, it can be shown that a child is far from the *tabula rasa* dear to the empirical tradition. Children are born with numerous aptitudes, in particular a predisposition to acquire their language. As we shall see, they already have the ability to create a language.

3.7 The deaf children of Nicaragua

The historian Herodotus learned of an amazing experiment which had apparently been conducted by an Egyptian sovereign by the name of Psammetichus (seventh century BC). He had two new-born babies brought up by goats, in the hope that they would spontaneously start to speak in a language which it was believed would have to be the original tongue, the one from which all others derive. According to Herodotus, the first word uttered by the children was *bekos*, a Phrygian word meaning 'bread'. This single royal experiment was enough to establish both the indisputable superiority of the Phrygian language and the fact that human beings were born with the gift of language (Hewes 1992).

Nowadays, cases of children being brought up in total linguistic isolation would appear to be unthinkable or at least extremely rare. Yet that is exactly the situation of deaf children. If they happen to live without the benefit of being integrated into a community that can provide them with a sign language, then they live in an extremity of linguistic aloneness, able to express by signs only their most immediate needs. In western countries it was over two centuries ago that the deaf were first cared for. In France in the late eighteenth century, the Abbé Charles Michel de l'Épée undertook a programme of teaching of a code based on signs, the success of which is well known. Young deaf people adopted the code and perfected it, managing to transform it into a language with syntax that is in many ways similar to the syntax of spoken languages. These young people invented a language out of the code thought up by the Abbé de l'Épée, following a procedure which unfortunately has left no trace. However, as luck would have it, the same phenomenon has not only repeated itself, quite spontaneously this time, but in a way that could be observed scientifically.

The revolution that happened in Nicaragua in 1979 put that country's deaf children into an unprecedented situation. The previous regime had provided no semblance of care for children suffering from serious hearing disorders. Left to themselves, these children contrived to communicate with the members of their families by using an extremely limited vocabulary of no more than about twenty signs. Because of these limitations they were looked on as mentally deficient and lived under a great social stigma (Kegl, Senghas, and Coppola 1999: 199). Under the new national education scheme, the children were sent to school and put in the charge of primary-level teachers who, however, having received no special training for dealing with the education of deaf children, tried to teach them to read. This turned out to be a waste of time and effort—how could children understand the meaning of an alphabetical system full of letters and syllables based on sounds they could never hear? It became clear that these first children, already adolescent, had a greater desire to communicate with each other than to attend to what the teachers wanted to give them. Within a few months, without the active participation of any adult, hearing-impaired or not, they had made up their own extended vocabulary of signs. Quite by chance, an American linguist, Judith Kegl, was able to observe and study this process almost from the beginning; and she eventually gave a circumstantial account of the development of these children and those who came after them (Kegl, Senghas, and Coppola 1999).

Judith Kegl's interest was aroused initially once she realized what the teenagers she was observing at the Learning Centre in Managua had invented. They spontaneously strung signs together to express thoughts and kept inventing new ones. In studying the structure of their sign sentences, Kegl and her colleagues noticed that these were quite unlike the sentences in any known sign language. Grammar was all but absent from their exchanges and all interlocutors had to make sense as best they could from any message. When contexts or constraints are familiar enough, deducing from a clue or two what someone is saying is not difficult, as anyone can appreciate by remembering conversations with, say, a foreigner who though he possesses only a very few words none the less contrives to make himself understood. In this way, one can cope with concrete subjects and express straightforward emotions, but it becomes much more difficult to convey any complexity in situations or ideas. For instance, without syntax, it can be a tricky business even to explain a situation concerning three characters. Syntax is of considerable assistance in our understanding of the meaning of statements, since the word order is full of helpful information. An unsyntactical statement like *Cat neighbour dog chase* could mean either that the cat chased the neighbour's dog or the exact opposite, whereas statements like *The dog will chase the neighbour's cat* or *The cat will chase the dog as far as the neighbour's place* are much more meaningful and less ambiguous. Having no syntax, the deaf adolescents studied by Kegl were doomed to engage in communication that was limited only to simple situations. This was, of course, a considerable advance on their previous experience, when they had lived at home, isolated among people who could hear; but the restrictions built in to their code of communication also meant that what they had invented was not a real language. The arrival of younger children was to radically alter this situation.

Kegl went to observe children in a primary school in Managua. They were younger, six years of age or less, and they had been quick to take up the signs invented by the older ones. But they had also stylized them and had created other signs of a different kind. The most salient feature of the signs made by the teenagers was their iconic quality, that is, the clear relationship between the sign and the signified. For example, the gesture meaning 'fall' was a vertical hand movement. In some ways, their system was a form of miming, whereas for the younger children the gesture meaning 'fall' was stylized, the vertical hand movement was barely noticeable, and the relationship between the sign and the signified was purely etymological.

What Kegl realized was that, as she watched, the younger children were actually inventing a real language with its range of grammatical constraints. For example, a speaker could point at an arbitrary point in space and make the sign for a particular entity; then the making of a sign for a verb in the same direction meant that the entity mentioned was an argument of the verb, either its subject or its complement. Thanks to such grammatical links, the deaf children of Nicaragua possessed a medium of expression of impressive fluency and precision. There is a striking contrast between a story told by a deaf person whose schooling did not begin until adolescence, before the development of a genuine sign language, and the same story told by a young child skilled and steeped in such a language. The basic story in the first version is easy enough to grasp, given the iconic nature of the signs, the logic of their sequences, and the relative slowness of their delivery, whereas, told by a younger child, with signs that are much less iconic, often reduced to fleeting gestures, and linked together, the story is much richer in details and can only be understood by people who have a close familiarity with the code.

The deaf children of Nicaragua are remarkable in two ways. One of these is the spontaneous character of their code of signs, which was all their own invention, since their well-meaning teachers not only had no hand in it but gave them no encouragement to communicate in this way. The other remarkable thing is the rapidity of the whole process: they invented a language from scratch not over several generations but in the time it took them to reach adolescence. Is this not a signal invalidation of the idea that language is a cultural invention? It would be impossible to find anywhere in the range of spontaneous gestures used by Nicaraguans with normal hearing any precedents for those used by the deaf children, the bulk of whose words, and the totality of whose syntactical code, were the outcome of spontaneous but shared creativity. As far as syntax is concerned, their invention was made possible by an ability that is latent in children up to about seven years of age but which disappears by adolescence. The deaf children of Nicaragua provided science with the experiment dreamed up by Psammetichus. The result of it is quite unambiguous: though human beings have probably nothing resembling an innate awareness of a primitive language, we do have an *a priori* ability to make up a language from scratch, should the conditions be right. And the prime condition is that, by the age of six or seven, children should be put in the situation of communicating with enough other children of their own age.

3.8 Language is a compulsory activity

There is a fundamental property of language that helps to make it different from cultural constructs and that philosophers, anthropologists, and linguists do not appear to have detected: the compulsory character of language activity. Healthy individuals, almost without exception, cannot prevent themselves from engaging in conversational activity. In their social relations they cannot help using language. Though this may appear to be a truism, it is anything but. We have at our disposal enough non-linguistic signals to enable us to socialize perfectly well at a particular level. If language were a cultural invention like jazz, writing, or pottery, it ought to be possible to opt for total silence, just as one can opt out of playing jazz, writing, and shaping vases from clay. But in language that is not in fact an option. Language learning is something that just 'happens' to us in our earliest years; and all human beings who are in good health and thoroughly socialized seek the conversation of some of their fellows.

Language activity is a response to a genuine urge; it is a need we feel in certain circumstances, as when a silence goes on too long. This need to speak words can also be motivated by quite precise stimuli. The episode of the naked man in Chapter 1 is a case in point: an event of such unexpectedness sets off in anyone witnessing it the automatic reaction of talking about it to someone else. There, speaking is a reflex action. Another example can be seen in the correcting reaction: when someone says something that we know to be untrue and that we can show to be untrue, it can be very difficult to abstain from doing so; if for example someone claims in conversation that the population of Tunisia is as great as that of Algeria and you know this is wrong, you feel the need to state what is right, especially when several other people are present. This need to communicate, like the previous one, appears to be a reflex. These two modes turn up also whenever you start to comment to someone else on something you are reading: a particular passage makes you interrupt your reading so as to disturb the person beside you with an account of it. Whenever you come upon unexpected revelations or glaring absurdities in a text, you take the opportunity to respond to this reflex of communication.

Thus there is something compulsory in speaking. The fact that there are definite situations which produce the reflex of communication fits well with the view that language is a natural behaviour provided for by our biological constitution. If language were a pure construct, this reflex aspect of it would be inexplicable. Konrad Lorenz, one of the founders of ethology, showed that in natural behaviour there are several characteristics that distinguish it from behaviour learned through training. In particular, natural behaviours are provoked by configurations of stimuli which are precise, universal, and generally simple. Lorenz speaks of an innate release mechanism (*angeborener Auslösemechanismus*). For example, breeding is possible in rock pigeons only when the female is in the appropriate state of readiness and her partner is showing the proper colours and goes through the right motions. The female demands that the male feed her, then they preen each other's feathers, exercising great care behind the wings, before she accepts him (Lorenz 1965: 140). When a natural behaviour has not been able to express itself for a longish period, what Lorenz calls '*in vacuo* activity' may be observed: there is a lowering of the stimulus threshold and the animal will go through its behaviour in response to weaker and weaker stimuli or even in the absence of the stimulus. A dog will worry a shoe as though it is prey; a cat starts hunting imaginary mice; a caged bird sets about building a nest though it has no nesting materials (Lorenz 1978: 102). In other words, a natural behaviour whose expression has been prevented will at length be executed, even though it may be irrelevant. Apart from Lorenz and Eibl-Eibesfeldt, few have ever looked for traces of such natural behaviours in human actions.

Admittedly, most human actions do appear to manifest an intentional will, which makes them radically different from the sort of instinctive behaviour studied by Lorenz. Our speech behaviours appear to be among our most deliberate actions: we choose our interlocutors, we are aware of what we say, we try to exercise conscious control over both the form and the content of what we say. The words we speak feel much more like the outcome of a conscious choice than of an instinctive reaction. And yet observation of the conditions in which we engage in speech brings to light phenomena reminiscent of the mechanisms identified by ethologists. Our language acts can be stimulated in an almost systematic way, showing the compulsory aspect of language that we have just discussed. A highly unexpected situation or an absurdity acts on us like a release mechanism, setting off almost invariably a speech reaction. The speech behaviour of people who engage in conversation with pet animals, with their car, or with themselves can be seen as analogues of Lorenz's *in vacuo* activity. Such phenomena of stimulation and lowering of the stimulus threshold make us see language from a different point of view, a more biological one, which posits language as a natural behaviour and not a completely invented social construct. Language activity, to which we devote about a fifth of our waking hours, instead of being the outcome of a habit inculcated in us as infants, comes to be seen as responding to a need that is well-nigh physiological. This in no way diminishes the intentionality of our control over our utterances. This control, however, should not be seen as the only source of all our language activity, but rather as a modulation of a natural behaviour whose roots lie deep in our biology.

3.9 The faculty of language

The evidence that we have just reviewed—the absence of any simple language; the universal and spontaneous nature of language; the way it is learned; the fact that we have areas of the brain and organs of phonation dedicated to language; the existence of complex linguistic universals; the experience of the deaf-mutes of Nicaragua—serves to show that human beings are naturally predisposed to the use of speech. These facts, along with many others, make the hypothesis of a cultural invention of language untenable.

One reason for the continuing belief among the scientific community in a historical origin of language lies in the contiguity between two concepts, expressed in French by two separate words *langue* and *langage* but conflated in English into the single word 'language'. In one of its senses, language (French *langage*) is a universal and exclusively human capacity, independent of whether this or that language (French *langue*) is spoken in this or that place. The most fundamental question that can be asked about language is whether our aptitude for it is specific or whether it is rather the application of a general form of intelligence to communication. In this chapter my aim has been to show that in fact language relies on a specific aptitude. The hominid lineage evolved to speak, which means that our forebears who lived 100,000 years ago had exactly the same linguistic abilities as we do.

Why is our species endowed with a specific biological faculty which enables us to communicate via a combinatorial code using the vocal tract? Why do other primates not communicate in this way? Answers to these questions can only come from the study of the past of our species and a consideration of the rules of biological evolution. As will be seen, discussion of this matter of the phylogenetic origin of our faculty for language has often been inapt, which was an effect of the uninformed prejudices and out-of-date conceptions on the evolution of species brought to the subject by authors interested in language.

4 Misapprehensions about the origins of language

The whole matter of the evolutionary origin of our capacity for language has been bedevilled by misconceptions. Whether one takes the view that language is merely an outcome of the general intelligence of us human beings, or whether one believes, as many authors do, that language gives a decisive selective advantage to those who use it, the appearance of language comes to seem self-evident and there is nothing that needs to be explained. Language is seen then to be the expected result of the process of hominization. The trouble with that sort of explanation, though, is that it creates a mystery which is just as impenetrable as the one it claims to solve. If language is really so advantageous, then why do apes not speak? This is a bothersome question. For the sake of consistency, those who believe in the evolutionary necessity of language are obliged to imagine that non-human lines of descent such as the other primates, cetaceans, and others either did not manage to evolve towards language or have not had enough time to do so. This chapter aims to show that such ideas are fallacies.

4.1 That language was a necessary outcome of evolution

A man who has never left home may think there is only one road, the one leading to his own village. The road has clearly been made for the purpose of coming from far away to his native place, a fact that gives the village great importance. Also, it would be absurd for there to be roads leading somewhere else, since everything happens in the village, with its market place, the church, the local pub. Human beings tend to think like that about evolution too: the road that leads to them had to exist, since their species exists. What they overlook is that their village was built on the road and that there are many roads, with other villages which have exactly the same importance or insignificance as theirs. The human village is, of course, different; it does have several local specialities, such as articulated language, technology, art, and religion, among others. Human beings imagine that life without these things would be impossible, a mere mode of survival, rather as people brought up in France see life as impossible without cheese and wine. If there are other villages along the road leading to articulated language, their denizens must be benighted incomplete beings who had neither the time nor the intelligence to develop spoken communication.

The process of hominization, when seen through the anthropocentric lens generally favoured by various authors, is a deterministic one, leading us from a monkey-like condition to our present status as intelligent, self-aware beings, endowed with language. It seems self-evident that the present state of our species, with its easy dominance over nature, is the inevitable outcome of a selective process tending for ever, or so the story goes, towards the production of species which keep on becoming more and more efficacious. If other species did exist between us and the common ancestors we share with the anthropoid apes, they are bound to have been, according to this version, mere staging-posts along the road to intelligence, consciousness, and language. And of course language does have excellent virtues: it enables us to share our experiences, our knowledge of the world, our technological expertise; it means we can undertake coordinated and collective endeavours and settle disagreements; all of which facilitates extensive social life for individuals unrelated by family. This way of seeing the obvious usefulness of language is well illustrated by the two following comments:

Vocal language represents the continuation of the evolutionary trend towards freeing the hands for carrying and tool use that started with upright bipedal hominid locomotion. The contribution to biological fitness is obvious. The close relatives of the hominids who could rapidly communicate *Look out, there are two lions behind the rock!* were more likely to survive, as were hominids who could convey the principles of the core and flake toolmaking technique in comprehensible sentences. (Lieberman 1992: 23)

The immediate, practical benefits that hominids would have gained from communicating with one another in even the simplest form of protolanguage are obvious enough. (Bickerton 1990: 156)

Other species did not manage to 'discover' language, despite the accepted wisdom that it would have enabled them to be much more effective in their struggle for survival. They adopted other strategies, behavioural specializations and modes of communication which are deemed to be 'embryonic' when compared to language. According to this view, our own species was the only one to cross the Rubicon of intelligence and accede, through language, to the dominance of nature. As for other species, either they have not had time to do this or else the possibility never presented itself. The broad highway leading to human-kind was therefore fully visible, though its starting point remained hidden from all species but ours. Once this process had been set in motion, it was bound to lead to a species endowed with language. If some other species, dolphins for instance, had managed to find the turn-off leading to the same level of intelligence as humans, it too would have been bound to acquire a language which, apart from its phonatory aspect, would have been akin to our own. This deterministic feature of the emergence of language is stated by Steven Pinker:

It is possible to imagine a superintelligent species whose isolated members cleverly negotiated their environment without communicating with one another, but what a waste! There is a fantastic payoff in trading hard-won knowledge with kin and friends, and language is obviously a major means of doing so. (Pinker 1994: 367)

Once again language is presented as a characteristic with extraordinary virtues, allowing those endowed with it to greatly increase their life expectancy. It is amusing to note that all three authors quoted use 'obvious' to describe the advantage conferred by language. It is a word which generally conceals ignorance. I once had a maths teacher who used to forbid us to use it; and things we describe as 'obvious' are often things we find it very difficult to demonstrate. The usefulness of language for survival, which is too often taken for granted, can be shown to be extremely problematical. From the point of view of those who see lan-guage as some kind of miracle solution to every problem of life in the wild, it is hard to find fault with the idea that our species is the expected fulfilment of some inevitable evolutionary process which began with the first Australopithecines, or even with the very first primates. As is well known, evolution favours solutions which are advantageous for survival. If language is one such solution, the fact that it happened once shows that discovery of it was possible, which could appear to imply that it was inevitable. Not only is this line of thought mistaken, it leads its proponents into serious difficulty, as we shall see.

4.2 That evolution towards language was slow and gradual

There is something of a consensus that, from an evolutionary point of view, language is a good thing, a faculty which favours the success of the species endowed with it. This makes language a sort of attraction force: anything that bears the slightest resemblance to it has to be favoured by natural selection. Speaking technically, there must have been selection pressure towards any change in the communication system used by hominids that could bring it closer to language as we know it. If there really was selection pressure, what must be explained is why hominids did not immediately develop a language that was every bit as elaborate as ours. To which must be added the problem of why animals do not speak. What is not clear is how selection pressure could have been resisted so as to prevent other species from developing language comparable to human language in structure and expressive power. One has only to posit that language of the human type, a digital, combinatorial communication code (cf. Chapter 1), is advantageous for any and every species, or at least for some species of higher mammals, and the uniqueness of it in the whole living world becomes a problem.

One possible solution to this difficulty, implicitly adopted by many authors, is to argue that evolution is a slow process. Evolution, as is well known, functions over lengths of time which dwarf the scope of human memory; typically, periods of hundreds of thousands of years must pass for any notable changes to appear. Our common ancestor with chimpanzees lived at least five million years ago, the first primate about eighty million years ago, the first mammals more than 200 million. Seeing such large-scale transitions as a determined but imperceptibly slow progression fits with the idea that they are stages in a process leading from the simple to the complex, from the amoeba to creatures that are more and more sophisticated, more and more 'highly evolved' as the saying goes, and ending with human intelligence at the top of the pyramid. From the point of view of the human village, the evolution process took so long to produce us that it must have been extremely slow. And it is this argument from the slowness of evolutionary change that apparently accounts for why human beings are the only ones to possess language. Other species have not had time to manage it yet. The role of random factors in evolution being well known, our species was just luckier than others and happened to be the first to find the way towards intelligence and its correlative, language.

Such a conception of the evolution of human faculties is flawed in several ways, in particular the way it leaves many other species wandering in the wilderness that surrounds the promised land of language. Chimpanzees, gorillas, possibly even dolphins and dogs have almost reached it; and if they were given another four or five million years to work on improving their system of communication, they might just get there. The problem is, though, that none of these species shows the slightest evidence of being on any road that might lead to language.

In the natural world, there are many instances of species which possess an original characteristic that no other species has acquired or even 'tried' to acquire, such as, for example, the elephant's trunk or the beaver's expertise in constructing dams. These are outstanding achievements: with one and the same instrument, its trunk, which is the equivalent of the nose in other species, a huge animal can accomplish some feats requiring immense strength and others of the utmost delicacy; while the beaver knows how to bring about a rise in the water level that will make the entrance to its lodge inaccessible to predators. There is nothing mysterious about the usefulness of such systems to the species endowed with them: among other things, an elephant is able to feed on leaves that it can reach at the tops of trees; and a beaver can protect its young which otherwise would make easy prey. Yet the uniqueness of such adaptations is not a matter of astonishment; it is clear that they represent local biological strategies and that there is no universal usefulness in having a trunk or being able to make dams. Most species would have no use for either feature, since they do not eat leaves or make lodges.

If the usefulness of a system of communication as efficacious as human language really was universal, we ought to be astonished by the uniqueness of it, since isolated morphological or behavioural adaptations generally respond to very particular needs. When a need is universal, what is usually observed is cases of convergence. We speak of convergence when the same two organs or behaviours appear independently of each other in two species and are not derived from a common ancestor. Among many possible examples, one can cite the shape of martins' and swallows' wings, which are so similar that it was wrongly believed for a long time that the two species were closely related; the fact that cetaceans have a shape which is not very different from the shapes of large fish; and that the sonar used by dolphins functions through a system not unlike the echolocation of bats. The idea is, roughly, that the function creates the organ: if a sufficiently generalized need exists, it is often observed that several different species have responded to this need by developing more or less analogous organs. For instance, needs such as those of a bird of small dimensions that never stops flying, the need for hydrodynamic efficiency, for the sighting of prey and avoidance of obstacles and predators in dark or opaque conditions, are relatively general and can easily arise in several different species. Some species have independently developed similar adaptations. If, as we are often told, there is a widespread need to communicate information, then we should expect to find cases of convergence. Despite which, there is no evidence to assume that the members of any species other than ourselves spend a sizeable part of their time in exchanging all sorts of information on a variety of subjects.

Various arguments canvassed in Chapter 1 led us to see language as unique to human beings. Communication as used by other species neither relies on open digital systems nor functions in narrative mode. Nor is there anything to suggest that such systems of communication might one day evolve into one comparable with ours. Language is *sui generis*, very likely an innovation. Arguing from the slowness of the evolutionary process is no way to explain why other species lack a language equivalent to ours. This uniqueness of human language inclines one to the belief that it was a local adaptation and its emergence an isolated process whose genesis it would be futile to seek somewhere outside the line of descent of our own species.

4.3 That language was an outcome of intelligence

One way of resolving the paradox between the uniqueness of language and the necessary discontinuity of the evolutionary process leading to human beings is to say that language was not possible, or that it had no usefulness for creatures capable of it, until such time as they had something to say. In other words, evolution would not have created any system of communication akin to language in other species for the simple reason that no other species had been able to reach the degree of intelligence achieved by our hominid ancestors. Like a runner passing on a baton in a relay race, the prior development of intelligence must have favoured the later selection of language.

The idea that the development of intelligence preceded and enabled the development of language can be found as far back as Darwin himself:

The fact of the higher apes not using their vocal organs for speech, no doubt depends on their intelligence not having been sufficiently advanced. ... The lower animals differ from man solely in his almost infinitely larger power of associating together the most diversified sounds and ideas; and this obviously depends on the high development of his mental powers. (Darwin 1871: 89, 85)

Not only do the mental powers mentioned by Darwin make language possible, they very likely make it necessary. What would intelligence be for, and how could it benefit from knowledge, if it was unaccompanied by the faculty of speech? Even if it was theoretically conceivable, we find it hard to imagine intelligence without language. In the work of some science fiction writers, imaginary species endowed with intelligence are common: though such creatures are clearly the products of fertile if anthropomorphizing imaginations, always possessing exotic features (animal-like shapes, out-size brains, supersensory powers), they are never presented as lacking an aptitude for language. The intelligence of any species would seem singularly limited if its members only ever behaved as individuals and were incapable of coordinating their actions. Also, intelligence seems as though it ought to come with the need to communicate; it is assumed that individuals who have reached a particular degree of understanding will realize how useful it would be to pool their knowledge. Thinking of this kind makes it unsurprising that a code of communication grew up among intelligent beings. Once one assumes that hominids managed to develop a particular degree of understanding, the emergence of language seems to stop being a problem. However, it merely turns into another problem: the emergence of intelligence.

Intelligence seems prima facie to be a good thing for survival. A being capable of detecting causal relations, of foresight, planning, the discovery of analogies, analysis of its own mistakes, etc., is bound to be better than its less skilled competitors at practising the arts required to reach the age of procreation. Given all this, can anyone doubt the existence of selection pressure towards ever greater intelligence? After all, this must surely be how hominids became more clever, before going on to acquire the ability to exchange their knowledge via language. The problem of the appearance of language turns out to be a rather incidental one: when it happened becomes the only question, since why and how are now explained. The uniqueness of human language comes from the fact that our ancestors were the only species of animal 'highly evolved' enough in intellectual things to 'feel' the need to speak. Unfortunately, this argument entails several questionable assumptions.

The first difficulty raised by this scenario of hominization is the necessary link it makes between intelligence and language. Do intelligent beings require a complex language? And is it necessary to be intelligent to speak? Ontogenetically, it is doubtful. Acquisition of language does not wait for the development of intelligence: children of four or five speak perfectly, though they have yet to acquire mastery over some basic conceptual relations like the laws of conservation of quantities, changes of points of view in space, the idea of chance, or the idea of justice (Piaget 1932; Piaget and Inhelder 1947, 1951). There are pathologies such as Down's syndrome which entail a significant cognitive handicap, yet affected individuals still manage to cope quite well with their native language. Ethnographically, one might expect that the level of language activity would depend on the complexity of the ideas being conveyed; but there is no quantitative correlation between daily use of language and a particular type of culture or the level of the knowledge exchanged. None of this seems compatible with the idea that language is the means through which intelligence expresses itself. So observation of contemporary humanity gives no evidence that the evolution of language depends on the evolution of intelligence.

The second flaw in the argument that language is an outcome of intelligence is the idea that symbolic communication requires a certain level of intelligence. Even if that were the case, it would still be necessary to define the quantitative or qualitative threshold that enables language to happen. Sue Savage-Rumbaugh, who devotes her life to the study of the linguistic and cognitive capacities of chimpanzees, makes no bones about stating that the intellectual aptitudes of these animals are quite adequate for communication. Whatever phenomenon it was that made for the development of articulated language needs to be sought elsewhere:

The ability to produce spoken, symbolic language depended, therefore, on the appropriate development of the vocal tract in early human ancestors, not on the evolution of the requisite cognitive capacity. Even in primitive form, such a system of communication would have had considerable survival advantages ... (Savage-Rumbaugh and Lewin 1994: 249)

Savage-Rumbaugh is among those who see language as a decisive bonus in a competitive Darwinian system. But her view that it was the fortuitous alteration of the vocal tract which created the conditions required for the emergence of language runs counter to the position of Darwin himself, quoted above. The fact is, she declines to explain that emergence by any growth in the intelligence of our forebears.

The real difficulty inherent in the evolutionary scenario of language deriving from mind capacity lies in the fact that the mystery of emergence is merely transferred from the former to the latter. Human intelligence possesses the very properties which made language an enigma of evolution: (1) it appears to be very advantageous for survival; (2) it is qualitatively unique in some respects; (3) the level attained by humans is in fact quite disproportionate compared with anything in the animal kingdom. At first sight, the second of these points may seem debatable. For the moment—we shall return to this in Chapter 15—it can be said that a basic component of human intelligence, the ability to draw up a plan, is different in kind from anything that animals are capable of. However, points 1 and 3 are quite sufficient to posit the problem. Intelligence, from an evolutionary point of view, is not of itself a positive value. As the old Greek poet says, 'The fox knows many things, but the hedgehog knows one big thing.' By what miracle did our ancestors become beings endowed with intelligence, while no other species evolved so clearly in that direction? Since the miracle did not happen for other species, no doubt we must once again attribute this to the slowness of evolution and the theory that they have not had time to acquire enough intelligence to achieve language. In Chapter 6 we shall have occasion to show that this argument is untenable.

As a way of conceiving of the link between mind and language, the idea that there might be a threshold of intelligence necessary to symbolic communication, that intelligence did not make an early enough appearance, that there were proto-humans who were intelligent enough to speak and too intelligent to keep quiet, has no serious basis. If there is an order of precedence in the link between our faculty of language and our mental faculties, it is no doubt not the one implicit in the idea that language is an outcome of the power of thought.

4.4 That in the beginning was the word

Jacques Monod has a very original point of view, one which inverts the order of things in the interpretation just criticized. He points out that there must have been a very close relation of interdependency between the phylogenetic development of the brain and the development of language:

> One cannot but assume that there was a very close linkage between the special evolution of the central nervous system in humans and the evolution of the unique achievements which are its hallmark, making language not just the product but one of the initial conditions of such evolution. (Monod 1970: 145)

Monod goes on to conjecture a causal link which is the opposite of the one commonly supposed and posits that language was instrumental in the development of the brain:

> In my view, the most plausible hypothesis is that, given the very early appearance of the most rudimentary symbolic communication in our line of descent, because of the radically new possibilities this offered, it was one of the initial 'choices' which determine the whole future of the species by creating a new selection pressure. This selection could only have favoured the development of our linguistic ability itself and consequently the performance of the organ making for that ability, the brain. (Monod 1970: 145)

The same idea is propounded by Bickerton, who sees language as the prime mover of a process which turned our species from an animal into a human:

> While it would be absurd to suppose that language in and of itself provided everything that differentiates us from the apes, language was not only the force that launched us beyond the limits of other species but the necessary (and perhaps even sufficient) prerequisite of both our consciousness and our unique capacities. (Bickerton 1990: 4)

This is an attractive idea, one which is also put forward by Terrence Deacon (Deacon 1997). It lets us see symbolic communication as a kind of new ecological niche which our ancestors, perhaps as far back as the Australopithecines, were the first to discover. Once a species of ape had discovered how to communicate meanings, however rudimentary, via an open combinatorial system, it is conceivable that there was every scope for such a system to grow in complexity and that the wealth of meanings to be communicated, which is linked to intelligence and the size of the brain, grew correlatively.

However, let us not jump to conclusions. Such a scenario takes for granted several hypotheses which are invalid. The very first of these is the idea that a symbolic combinatorial system is exclusive to human language, which as we saw in Chapter 1 is not the case. Nature seems to have little difficulty in evolving combinatorial systems, as can be seen with the functioning of the immune system or the structure of birdsong. So it is certainly inordinate to see symbolic communication as some kind of all but inaccessible Eldorado. The next stage in this reasoning is the inevitable idea that communication is advantageous for the individuals who go in for it, whether speakers or hearers, this being the only way to explain the setting in motion of a process of selection favourable to communication and, through communication, favourable to the advancement of mental capacities. But the existence of such a mutual benefit, as will be seen in Chapter 16, is anything but self-evident. Thirdly, if such a selection pressure did exist, one may well wonder why it did not result more quickly in the linguistic and intellectual powers of modern human beings, rather than marking time for millions of years at the relatively unimpressive levels of the Australopithecines and *Homo erectus*. So if the Monod scenario were to be convincing, it would need to be considerably reinforced.

Nevertheless, there is still something very attractive in the idea that language lies at the origin of intelligence. If there really was a selection pressure favourable to the communicating by individuals of complex meanings—and that is something that remains to be clarified—, then we could readily accept that it might have indirectly created conditions favourable to a significant increase in intellectual abilities. This would mean human intelligence was mainly oriented towards the invention and understanding of meanings, that the uses it was put to in practical things such as controlling behaviour or planning actions were of secondary importance, and that our disproportionate mental capacities were a by-product so to speak of our aptitude for language. We shall come back to a reconsideration of this view of the primacy of language. Summing up for the moment, we can say that Monod's idea that the increase in intelligence in our species was really a consequence and not the cause of our linguistic practice is an appealing one, for the reason that it lets us see language as the single qualitatively differentiating thing marking us off from all other species. On the other hand, what it does not do is explain why such a differentiation happened, short of leading us back to anthropocentrism and a faculty that was universally advantageous but difficult to discover. Symbolic communication is not a gold mine with its entrance hidden from the eyes of all species but our own. Or rather, if we can adapt the metaphor a little, it is a gold mine open to all species, but its gold only had a value for the single species that began using it as currency.

4.5 That language is a vestige of past evolution

It is tempting to search for what might have been the spark that set our ancestors to using and valuing symbolic communication. Many authors take the view that evolution towards a language of human type was necessary and just waiting to happen, but that, before the numerous benefits inherent in such language could begin to be exploited, what was required was a felicitous coming together of factors. What could have provided that initial spark? Whatever the answer is, it may well also provide us with a problem, for language can be used in many ways; and if we isolate any one of these as our explanation for the emergence of language, we may find we have to bypass the others.

Some explanations of the origin of language refer to the need to coordinate hunting, to negotiate between partners, to detect social cheats (Dunbar 1996), to avoid dangers, and the like. This would mean that language emerged for a precise purpose, even though we use it now in a variety of different ways. In particular, we may feel that culture has taken over language and profoundly transformed it, as it created mathematics by transforming the universal human ability to count small quantities (Dehaene 1997). If that is so, then any study of language as exploited by human beings in modern societies would be of very little help to us in understanding the phylogeny of language:

Among the systems that humans have developed in the course of evolution are the science-forming capacity and the capacity to deal intuitively with rather deep properties of the number system. As far as we know, these capacities have no selectional value, though it is quite possible that they developed as part of other systems that did have such value. (Chomsky 1975: 58–9)

Here, it is rather astonishing to see Chomsky supporting his hypothesis about the non-adaptive character of language by means of an analogy with scientific and mathematical abilities. Throughout his work, he maintains the specific and innate character of language, which distinguishes it from intellectual activities with a much more marked cultural content (Piattelli-Palmarini 1979). If one looks on language and mathematics as cultural products derived from a very narrow biological base, it makes sense to imagine scenarios in which language might have emerged for a very particular purpose which is no longer extant. This would mean that the biological aspect of language could be seen as a kind of vestige of a primitive mode of communication, a fossil, and that culture has built it into the system that has come down to us. This would make language the outcome of a cultural diverting of a primitive and innate communication behaviour. For instance, we might be biologically equipped to exchange simple orders, so as to coordinate cooperative actions like hunting, and from that biological basis culture has elaborated the multifunctional language that we use, much as it has elaborated mathematics or baroque art.

The same argument applies, whichever use of language we choose to see as the reason for its emergence. We may well define five, ten, or thirty uses of it in contemporary society; but we cannot argue that, in the past of our species, language was selected for five, ten, or thirty reasons at once. If we did so argue, then we would have to explain why not a single one of these reasons ever applied in the evolution of other species, whether chimpanzees, dolphins, or whatever. So one of these uses must be chosen as the 'true' reason for the emergence of language, whether it be the detection of cheating (see below, Chapters 16 and 17, especially sections 16.4, 16.5, and 16.6) or the art of chatting up young females. But in that case, what becomes of the four, nine, or twenty-nine other uses of language? To which the answer will be no doubt that they are mere cultural inventions diverting language from its primitive biological objective.

There are several arguments against this way of reasoning. The first of these is that, if there had really been a primitive use of language which was solely responsible for its emergence, one should expect that it would still constitute the bulk of linguistic interactions. But the disagreements among authors trying to identify which use of language it was that created an evolutionary advantage show this not to be the case. If the hypothesis of a primitive use is right, it would mean that culture has contrived to confuse the issue by inventing other uses for language which nowadays play roles that are of equal importance. It is difficult to accept that, in the lives of human beings today, almost everything that is of importance in language was not of importance over the whole history of the species.

The second argument against the idea that there was a particular primitive use of language derives from the systematically spontaneous character of the whole range of ways in which we use it. Of those that come readily to mind, whether giving orders, courting, speaking ill of cheats, complaining, and so on, many are systematically used by all healthy people. But the same cannot be said of cultural creations like mathematics, baroque music, golf, or baking cakes: many people who are quite normal in all respects engage in none of these activities. Most uses of language are universal; they are practised everywhere on the planet, in all cultures, which is manifestly not the case with cultural things such as engaging in mathematics.

An extra argument comes from the way the different uses of language are learned. In addition to the fact that no particular one of them appears first in the development of human children, all the universal ones found among adult speakers crop up spontaneously in children. Unlike mathematics, chess, or golf, none of these uses of language requires instruction; they just happen spontaneously in the behaviour of children.

Lastly, the main argument against the idea of a particular primitive use of language comes from the fact that not one of the plausible candidates suggested can serve as a determinant to explain the emergence of spoken communication. If any system of communication is to become established, each of the participants must derive some benefit from it. Anyone who tries to reduce language to any of its particular uses should surely be required to demonstrate how that use is in the interest of both speaker and hearer. In Chapter 16 we shall find that this requirement is particularly difficult to satisfy.

It is unlikely, for all the reasons just examined, that the emergence of language in the descent of human beings was due simply to any one of its particular uses rather than to the others. Language was not selected for any direct usefulness it might have in this or that situation. This does not mean language has no biological function, but rather that the function for which it was selected should not be sought among the immediate effects of a single mode of speech.

None of these various scenarios of hominization offers a clear reason why a single species took advantage of the communication of symbolic information. All the fallacies refuted in this chapter derive from a conception of language as a universal benefit and from the theory that there was an inexorable if difficult evolution towards the promised land of language. The next chapter will inspect a scenario which is the exact opposite of that, in which language will be seen as a feature just as fortuitous as the elephant's appendage or the building behaviour of the beaver.

5 Language as an evolutionary curiosity

One conception of evolution sees species as evolving in definite directions. It sees hominids as species which evolved towards ever greater complexity and intelligence, until they turned into human beings with their necessary accompaniment of language. It is a mistaken conception. At most, we might be able to see our own species as rather original, but that is a value judgement. As Stephen Jay Gould has shown, the appearance of new species follows no pre-established tendency, a fact that is as true for our species as it is for those which preceded it.

5.1 Evolution's directionless advance

By way of explanation of the fact that language and intelligence, though apparently extremely advantageous for the survival of individuals, did not appear earlier in the evolution of species, one may be tempted to believe that it was all a matter of time. The evolution, through natural selection, of complex characteristics requires an accumulation of many advantageous elementary variations which all contribute to the forming of those characteristics. By definition, such variations are rare; and many of them get lost among the random hazards of selection. A view quite commonly expressed by some people who are impressed by their status as human beings is that the human mind is the most complex thing in the universe.[1] That being the case, it should not be at all surprising that evolution took

---

[1] Such a statement is based no doubt on a belief rather than on any calculation. It is easy to calculate an upper bound of the algorithmic complexity of the brain, or at least of its innate genetic base: about 100 megabytes, a figure based on the useful genetic information contained in our cells. This amount of information corresponds to the complexity of a random sequence of that size, of which many can be found in nature. As genetic information is highly redundant, the actual complexity of the brain must be much lesser.

some time to produce such a wonder. In its advance towards the production of ever more complex forms, it must have brought several species to the brink of intelligence, awareness, and language, until quite by chance one of them, which happened to be us, took the lead in the race towards the mind. This sort of scenario helps explain the uniqueness of human characteristics like language, intelligence, and some of their consequences such as culture. We are unique because we outdistanced our competitors. There are, however, two conditions which should be fulfilled if such a scenario is to make sense: there would have had to be selection pressure towards ever greater intelligence and capacity for communication; and the evolutionary process would have had to be slow enough for the five million years between us and our ape-like condition to correspond to a lead taken by us in the race for intelligence. But on both counts, it can be seriously doubted whether anything like that really happened.

Proper understanding of the phenomena of evolution is often counter-intuitive, which is why its mechanisms, in their relative simplicity, can be misinterpreted. In the idea that our line of descent underwent a slow and gradual transformation, leading from the first primates to ourselves, during which process intelligence, social organization, and communication became ever more complex and eventually led to mankind, there are mistakes of perspective. The main one of these is the 'human village' fallacy (cf. Chapter 4). A focus on our line of descent, tracing it in isolation from its origins up to its preordained point of arrival, gives us the false impression that we are the goal of evolution. Take the genealogical tree of the legitimate descendants of Louis XV: a man who is proud of his descent from this monarch places himself on it and shows how a succession of marriages over many generations have eventually led to him. Reciting these unions, like reciting the generations linking Abraham to Jesus as told in the first chapter of St Matthew, gives an impression of determinism, as though the eventual birth of the descendant had been implicitly programmed from the start. The only thing that gets omitted, of course, is the fact that Louis XV and Abraham had many other descendants.

Stephen Jay Gould has pointed out the errors that such a deformed way of looking at things can lead to (Gould 1996). He uses the example of the evolution of the Equidae from *Hyracotherium* which lived fifty-five million years ago to the genus *Equus* which includes our horse, three species of zebras, and four species of donkeys. This example is an interesting one, having often been used to demonstrate the idea of evolutionary tendency.

Starting with an ancestor smaller than a small gazelle, which had three toes on its hind legs and four on its forelegs, we eventually come to the modern horse, with its imposing height and its single toe, after an apparently regular progression: *Hyracotherium (eohippus), Orohippus, Epihippus, Mesohippus, Miohippus, Parahippus, Merychippus, Pliohippus, Dinohippus,* and *Equus.* The height of the animals increases regularly, the lateral toes decrease in size, stop touching the ground, and eventually regress more or less completely. All this gives the impression of a knowingly directed evolution, tending towards the provisional perfection of the horse, that fine, familiar, noble animal, designed for racing. This line of descent of horses often figures in manuals as an example of the slowness and the directed nature of evolution. But the trouble with that way of seeing the evolution of horses is that it gives a woefully distorted picture of the reality. The first error consists of seeing the branch but not the tree. As it happens, the genealogical tree of the descendants of *Hyracotherium* is particularly well known. It is actually so dense and thick that it is more like a bush than a tree; and this is why any telling of its full evolutionary history as though it had eventually to produce *Equus* is singularly mis-leading. In the genealogical bush there are numerous genera of all sizes; some species are not much larger than the common ancestor; and many of them kept three toes. Nor should it be thought that the flourishing of the genealogical bush happened only recently: if we restrict ourselves only to the descendants of *Parahippus,* between eleven and eighteen million years ago there figure no fewer than thirty different genera. Farther back into the past, despite the lesser frequency of fossils, it can be seen that *Miohippus* separated from the *Mesohippus* line, then coexisted with it for at least four million years. Furthermore, each of these genera consisted of several species which coexisted with one another. At the same period, a site in Wyoming (all of these species lived in the New World) has given evidence of three species of *Mesohippus* and two of *Miohippus.*

Gould enjoys imagining the reaction of those who see the horse as the endpoint of such a rich genealogy if the only survivor of the family had been *Nannippus* rather than *Equus,* a far from fanciful scenario: *Nannip-pus,* a descendant of *Merychippus,* went extinct two million years ago after its four identified species had lived for eight million years, which was much longer than the four million years of *Equus.* In fact, all the genera deriving from the ancestor *Hyracotherium* died out in the New World, including *Equus* which only survived because it belatedly colonized the old world. It could very easily have been *Nannippus* that migrated in that way; and if it had survived, no one would speak of the regular tendency of evolution allegedly working for fifty-five million years towards ever larger dimensions and fewer toes, for *Nannippus* (the term means 'little horse') was about the size of a small gazelle and had three toes. The horse that we know is just an insignificant representative of a group of species which once dominated the New World and it owes its survival to a fortuitous migration. This, by the way, is also the case with many other links in its lineage, including the ancestral *Hyracotherium* which was a mere shadow of the former glory of the odd-toed Perissodactyla, an order that lives on nowadays only in horses, rhinoceroses, and tapirs, but which once included all the giants among the mammals. There was a time when the most varied and abundant group of all mammalian animals was the rhinocerotoids, which included dwarf species as well as *Paraceratherium*, the tallest mammal there has ever been, standing more than five metres high at the shoulder (Gould 1996: 72). This clearly demonstrates the pointlessness of seeking definite trends in such a large-scale evolutionary tree.

This is a fact that runs counter to intuition. When one looks at the evolution of primates, one cannot help thinking in terms of progress and perceptible long-term tendencies, for instance in connection with the hemispheric specialization of the brain:

Everything points towards a biological evolution leading to the specialized and progressive competence of the cerebral hemispheres, a movement which had probably been under way for a long time and which can be seen in the family Pongidae, in non-human primates, and actually in most mammals. (Brenot 1984)

The history of the primates seems to show that anthropoid apes and humans are a considerable improvement on the first primates, which were more like varieties of lemurs. It is often said that they are manifestly more 'highly evolved' than these smaller ancestors, which are considered to be more primitive. This idea is not without foundation, as long as one leaves aside the implicit value judgement that the lemurs and present-day tarsiers are living fossils less well adapted than ourselves, for the truth is that their species have survived perfectly well until now, no differently from other living primates. The value judgement arises from the feeling that the great apes, especially humans, are more sophisticated, both in their neuronal anatomy and in their individual and social behaviour. If we take this reasoning a step further, we are also more complex than the fish and unicellular organisms which were our ancestors. It is a mode of reasoning informed by a notion of irreversible progress; it sees the evolution of living creatures as proceeding from the simple to the complex so as to culminate at the pinnacle of humanity. Stephen Jay Gould insists that this way of seeing things is once again wrong. Short-sighted reasoning of this kind mistakenly makes us believe that evolution follows a design or at the very least a direction. In reality, the increased complexity is due, as will be seen, to an increase in variance and not to a definite trend.

Therein lies an important difference, illustrated by Figure 5.1, which shows three alternative conceptions of evolution. Let us suppose we are interested in a single parameter, concerning for example a measure of the complexity of living beings. The different species are initially grouped about a mean value, shown by the black distribution curve.

In the first scenario (a), it is supposed that evolution has no inherent tendency to either increase or decrease the parameter. What is observed is, given the increase in variance due to diversification, a spread in the distribution of the group which remains symmetrical. However, if evolution obeys a tendency, as at (b), we find not only a spread due to diversification but also a shift in the direction of the trend. The mean value of the parameter increases, which was not the case at (a). A study of the size of species of plankton supports scenario (a): conducted by a colleague of Gould's on 342 species of plankton, it shows that the variation in size between a species and its parent species follows a symmetrical Gaussian distribution (Gould 1996: 161). In this case, evolution shows no bias towards increases or decreases in size.

There are, however, many evolutionary situations where a disturbance occurs through what Gould calls the 'wall' effect. In Figure 5.1, (c) shows

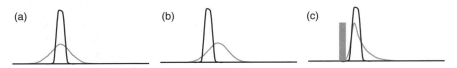

FIG. 5.1 Schematic evolution of the distribution of a group of species in relation to a single parameter, showing three competing hypotheses: (a) simple diversification; (b) tendency; and (c) diversification in the presence of a wall.

that when one of the two directions of variation of the parameter is blocked by a 'wall', to the left in this diagram, the spread of the distribution comes to have an asymmetrical shape. If we take the example of the height of trees, biomechanical constraints make it impossible for them to grow taller than about 100 metres. Distribution of species of trees is thus limited in the parameter of height. In the matter of complexity, however, the opposite happens. Under a certain level of complexity, organisms become unviable. That is the situation illustrated by (c) in Figure 5.1: complexity is free to increase, which results in skewed distribution once diversification has played its part. From the finding that the average complexity of living beings increases over geological time it is but a short, and mistaken, step to conclude that evolution has an inherent bias towards complexity, whereas the truth is that there is a disymmetry created by the presence of a built-in lower limit. Besides, if such a tendency towards increased complexity did exist, the simplest species ought to be less and less represented, which is not the case. For instance, 80 per cent of multicellular animals are arthropods (insects, crustaceans, myriapods, arachnids). The different species of plankton are a good example. Although it is a fact that when speciation (the appearance of a new species) occurs there is no bias towards an increase in size relative to that of the parent species, nevertheless the absolute average size has increased over geological time. This movement is not due to the disappearance of the smallest species, which continue to flourish, but to the existence of a lower limit on size below which the organization of this type of creature is not viable.

Gould draws the lesson that evolution always was and still is blind. Apparent trends are the 'result' of mere wall effects. When diversification encounters a limit, it spreads out in other directions, which gives the false impression that evolutionary change is a march towards progress. In particular, any increase that may be observed in the complexity of living beings results from mere diversification. The idea that there might be some directed evolutionary tendency leading from amoebas to humans, from vertebrates to humans, or even from apes to humans, is nothing but an illusion. All we are is a fortuitous result of wholesale diversification. The same must be said of the alleged tendency towards increased mental capacity or aptitudes for communication in vertebrates or mammals, with humans as the point of arrival: what is illusory is the tendency; what is true is the diversification. In Chapter 6 this lack of tendency in evolution will be distinguished from evolution falling to mere chance; and it will be seen that the principle of the blind character of selection must not be applied blindly.

5.2 Nature appears to jump

As an experienced palaeontologist, skilled in the inspection of fossils, Gould not only denies that evolution is directed; he also appears to doubt one of the founding dogmas of Darwinism: the hypothesis that the transformation of species was a gradual process. This could have a profound bearing on our thinking about the origin of language. Did language arise as a gradual transformation of an animal system of communication or did it appear suddenly?

Darwin took great care in enunciating his principle of continuity, restating Leibnitz's famous dictum that Nature does not jump (*Natura non facit saltum*):

Mr Mivart is further inclined to believe, and some naturalists agree with him, that new species manifest themselves 'with suddenness and by modifications appearing at once'. For instance, he supposes that the differences between the extinct three-toed Hipparion and the horse arose suddenly. He thinks it difficult to believe that the wing of a bird 'was developed in any other way than by a comparatively sudden modification of a marked and important kind'; and apparently he would extend the same view to the wings of bats and pterodactyles. This conclusion, which implies great breaks or discontinuity in the series, appears to me improbable in the highest degree. (Darwin 1859)

Darwin's principle is that it is extremely unlikely that functional organs, those which appear made for a purpose, should appear as though by magic:

It certainly is true, that new organs appearing as if created for some special purpose, rarely or never appear in any being;—as indeed is shown by that old, but somewhat exaggerated, canon in natural history of *Natura non facit saltum*. (Darwin 1859)

Gould and Niles Eldredge take an opposing view with their theory of punctuated equilibria (Eldredge and Gould 1972). While remaining basically faithful to Darwinian thinking, they question the principle of continuity in the transformation of species. That is, they take seriously the appearances of the fossil record and assume that discontinuities from one set of fossils to another, such as those observed among the different ancestors of the horse, are real and not just to be explained by a dearth of samples, unlike what Darwin believed:

[T]he sudden appearance of new and distinct forms of life in our geological formations, supports at first sight the belief in abrupt development. But the value of this evidence depends entirely on the perfection of the geological record, in relation to periods remote in the history of the world. If the record is as fragmentary as many geologists strenuously assert, there is nothing strange in new forms appearing as if suddenly developed. (Darwin 1859)

According to Gould's idea that evolution proceeds by steps, which is the exact opposite of Darwin's gradual evolution, species live out their existence without transforming. In this stable state, natural selection works solely to maintain stability. Changes by steps are abrupt and lead to new species, which makes it unsurprising that there should be discontinuities in the fossil record, since fossils can bear witness only to the periods of stability. This theory of punctuated equilibria would appear to reduce considerably the importance of natural selection, which becomes a way of maintaining what exists rather than a factor of evolution. So it is not surprising to see that Gould argues against the idea of directionality in evolution. In his view, transitions from one species to another are sporadic events on the scale of geological time and are largely the outcome of chance. The direction they take and the time of their occurrence are utterly unforeseeable:

[C]an a reasonable story of continuous change be constructed for all macroevolutionary events? (my answer shall be no) ... (Gould 1980: 156)

Gould's advocacy of a discontinuous view of evolution brings him to share the idea of 'hopeful monsters' developed by Goldschmidt in a book published in 1940:

Macroevolution proceeds by the rare success of these hopeful monsters, not by an accumulation of small changes within populations ... As a Darwinian, I wish to defend Goldschmidt's postulate that macroevolution is not simply microevolution extrapolated, and that major structural transitions can occur rapidly, without a smooth series of intermediate stages. (Gould 1980: 156–7)

If we apply this theory to the appearance of our own species and the emergence of language, it brings us back to the positions of Chomsky and Piattelli-Palmarini who see language as one of these 'hopeful monsters', a product of a macromutation.

5.3 The role of macromutation in the emergence of language

Seeing evolutionary change in species, as Gould does, as an aimless process gives strong support to the argument that speciation is a purely random phenomenon. When a species happens to split into two different species incapable of interfecundity, it is not because it is responding to any need to adapt to the environment but rather the result of a chance accident. The prime mover of speciation becomes separation, whether this is geographical, genetic, or behavioural.[2] What occurs is completely fortuitous: a group of individuals happens to have become isolated from the main population, taking with them only a part of the shared gene pool, and they are then subject to a process of spontaneous diversification which has no reason to run parallel to the diversification affecting the main population; they are also subject to possibly different environmental conditions that induce divergent adaptations through natural selection. This would lead eventually to a divergence so great that loss of interfecundity between the two populations would be inevitable.

Such a way of seeing the evolution of species rules out any possibility of determinism. Important changes affecting living creatures in ways that result in the appearance of a new species come from accidents as gratuitous as geographical or genetic separations. This could account for the chance origins of Australopithecus in east Africa five million years ago because a population of anthropoid apes had become isolated from its kin (Coppens 1983). A similar geographical accident could explain the appearance of *Homo sapiens* about 200,000 years ago; and the capacity for language of that species might be no more than a fortuitous consequence of that isolation. This is certainly Chomsky's way of seeing things:

Evolutionary theory appears to have very little to say about speciation, or about any kind of innovation. It can explain how you get a different distribution of qualities that are already present, but it does not say much about how new qualities can emerge. (Chomsky 1981: 23, quoted in Pinker and Bloom 1990)

In reaction against the view of language as a complex construct which appeared as a response to an adaptive need, other writers follow the lead of

---

[2] Genetic separation can arise for example from a rearrangement of chromosomes. Small alterations in nuptial displays or breeding rituals can also lead to the genetic isolation of individuals.

Gould and Chomsky in order to argue against the adaptive nature of language.

The specificity and the gratuity of linguistic principles make perfect sense under the hypothesis of an exaptive (i.e., non-adaptive) and discontinuous origin of language. (Piattelli-Palmarini 1989: 22)

This idea that language is fortuitous and gratuitous, that the form it takes owes nothing to any adaptive need, especially to any communicational need, is one which recommends itself to Chomsky, who has always disputed the force of functional ideas as applying to language. In his view, the fact that language may serve to communicate may have nothing to say about its structure:

Searle argues that 'it is quite reasonable to suppose that the needs of communication influenced the structure' of language, as it evolved in human prehistory. I agree. The question is: What can we conclude from this fact? The answer is: Very little. The needs of locomotion influenced the fact that humans developed legs and birds wings. The observation is not very helpful to the physiologist concerned with the nature of the human body. Like physical structures, cognitive systems have undoubtedly evolved in certain ways, though in neither case can we seriously claim to understand the factors that entered into a particular course of evolution and determined or even significantly influenced its outcome...We know very little about what happens when 10^{10} neurons are crammed into something the size of a basketball, with further conditions imposed by the specific manner in which this system developed over time. It would be a serious error to suppose that all properties, or the interesting properties of the structures that have evolved, can be 'explained' in terms of natural selection. Surely there is no warrant for such an assumption in the case of physical structures. (Chomsky 1975: 58–9)

The theory of evolution, if applied to language as Gould applies it to the evolution of the ancestors of the horse, would appear to require us to agree that language arose by pure chance. The existence of its phonetic or syntactic structure, the complexities of which Chomsky was among the first to demonstrate, is not a response to any need. In other words, it was not the function that created the organ. Yet it was also Chomsky who was the first to come up with the following comparison:

Why, then, should we not study the acquisition of a cognitive structure such as language more or less as we study some complex bodily organ?...The idea of regarding the growth of language as analogous to the development of a bodily organ is thus quite natural and plausible. (Chomsky 1975: 10–11)

If the organ of language did not come into being during evolution in response to selection pressure, how are we to explain its appearance? If we follow Gould to the letter, then we must abandon entirely the notion of selection pressure with its assumption that language is an adaptive response to a need. For those who subscribe to this way of thinking, the only solution is to see language as having appeared suddenly:

In evolution, novelty can also come by jumps. In a nutshell, what the new evolutionary theory is saying is that full-blown evolutionary novelty can also suddenly arise, so to speak, *for no reason*, because novelty caused by sheer proximity between genes is not governed by function and it, therefore, eludes strict adaptationism. (Piattelli-Palmarini 1989: 8)

Gould does note that speciation phenomena, which correspond in fact to real evolutionary change, occur with great rapidity on a geological scale. On that scale, the genetic alteration of an isolated population or a chromosome change happens instantaneously. According to this view, language as a feature of our species must have been a fortuitous aptitude which made a sudden appearance. What must be accepted, against the theory that it was an adaptive property requiring hundreds of thousands of years of directed selection, is that the appearance of language was abrupt, an outcome of a macromutation:

The evidence surveyed above indicates that language could not have developed gradually out of protolanguage, and it suggests that no intermediate form exists. If this is so, then syntax must have emerged in one piece, at one time—the most likely cause being some kind of mutation that affected the organization of the brain. Since mutations are due to chance, and beneficial ones are rare, it is implausible to hypothesize more than one such mutation. (Bickerton 1990: 190)

Chomsky's idea that human language is for many reasons different in kind from forms of animal communication fits well with the theory of a sudden appearance at some point in the evolutionary history of our lineage:

Popper argues that the evolution of language passed through several stages, in particular a 'lower stage' in which vocal gestures are used for expression of emotional state, for example, and a 'higher stage' in which articulated sound is used for expression of thought... His discussion of stages of evolution of language suggests a kind of continuity, but in fact he establishes no relation between the lower and the higher stages and does not suggest a mechanism whereby transition can take place from one stage to the next. In short, he gives no argument to show that the stages belong to a single evolutionary process. In fact, it is difficult to see what links these stages at all (except for the metaphorical use of the term 'language'). There is no reason to suppose that the 'gaps' are bridgeable. There is no more of a basis for assuming an evolutionary development of 'higher' from 'lower' stages, in this case, than there is for assuming an evolutionary development from breathing to walking; the stages have no significant analogy, it appears, and seem to involve entirely different processes and principles. (Chomsky 1968: 60)

Chapter 1 made the argument that the aptitude underlying language is not a mere extension of animal communication. Language really is a genuine biological innovation; and if we accept Gould's view of it, we are bound to see its emergence as being typical of any changes which accompany the appearance of a new species, that is, abrupt, gratuitous, purposeless.

It would appear that Chomsky, in arguing that language was an accidental mutation without any particular function, was partly responsible for the fact that, for more than two decades, the question of the emergence of language was not adequately dealt with. To Chomsky's great credit, it must be said that he fought hard to put language on the scientific agenda. In the climate of the 1950s and 1960s, language was seen as a mere conventional system of signs. It took all of Chomsky's energy to gradually establish the idea that humans have an underlying aptitude, a linguistic competence, which was as deserving of study as any individual language. From the initial assumption that certain linguistic features were universal, he argued that our capacity for language had its roots in biology and compared it to an organ with a structure that should be studied. The object of linguistics was utterly transformed: instead of just studying a conventional system analogous to the highway code or the provisions governing election to the upper houses of parliamentary systems, the purpose now became the attempt to understand the structure of a natural system. This was all well and good. But in his next step, which was quite naturally to raise two questions (What is the biological function of this system? How had it emerged during evolution?), Chomsky took the astonishing view that both questions were pointless, thereby completely obscuring the necessity to discover an origin for the capacity for language. In so doing, he closed the door he had just opened, the one leading to a naturalistic conception of language and through it to the search for an evolutionary origin for this most characteristic human behaviour.

Steven Pinker and Paul Bloom must be credited with having relegitimized that search, with their article published in 1990 in *Behavioral and*

Brain Sciences, in which they made a spirited attack on the lack of foundation in the anti-adaptive position on language. They remind us that language is an astounding contrivance and that for it to have appeared spontaneously via a macromutation would be too close to a miracle. The structure of language, like the structure of eyes, can only be the outcome of the unremitting workings of natural selection. But, if that is the case, where is the mistake made by those who believe in the possibility of a macromutation? Is Gould's whole view of evolution just wrong? The next chapter will show that the problem arises from mixing up two different time scales. Gould is certainly right to maintain that evolution displays no tendency over the periods of tens of millions of years that it takes for genera and orders to diversify. However, it may be directional in the short term, the reason for which we shall have occasion to examine.

The position of writers like Chomsky, Bickerton, and others who take the anti-adaptive catastrophist view of the emergence of language leads ultimately to absurd consequences. It has even been suggested that language, with its double combinatorial open system, its strict and universal constraints governing syntactic arrangements, its open system of meanings, its narrative and argumentative mechanisms, just appeared accidentally out of a single mutation and that it had little or no purpose. Such a conjectural mutation would be tantamount to letting an ape type at random on a keyboard in the expectation that it would write the Universal Declaration of Human Rights. There would be something risible in such a conjecture, were it not for the fact that it comes supported by such authorities.

Let us clear some ground. Unless we are to believe in miracles, there had to be some chance that the grand mutation which took the ancestor we had in common with chimpanzees from non-language to the language characteristic of our species would be discovered. About 10^5 generations separate us from that common ancestor, let's say 10^6 to be on the safe side. In each generation, the whole population of the world amounted to fewer than a million individuals, an estimate derived from demographic extrapolations from populations of hunter-gatherers and comparisons with populations of great apes. The whole of the past of the *Homo* lineage gives therefore fewer than 10^{12} viable births. If we suppose that 'luck' was on our side and that, if there was a rerun of the film of evolution, we missed the appearance of language 999 times out of a thousand, that still leaves a probability of an individual being born with the right mutation of the order of 10^{-15}. And how much information does that represent? About fifty bits.[3] This means that if we could code the difference between apes and humans which enables the latter to have language as using fifty bits, then a million individuals over a million generations would have about one chance in a thousand of bridging this gap through unaided chance. And if we were actually dealing with sixty bits, evolution would have about one chance in a million of producing language. But can anyone really believe that apes need only fifty or sixty bits of information to accede to language? Obviously, it cannot be ruled out, given that we are hampered by great ignorance of the genetic mechanisms underlying behaviours. However, in the present state of knowledge, such a hypothesis is improbable. One can easily imagine how little information amounts to fifty bits. It needs more than fifty to represent the information contained in this sentence. Some writers, faced with such an insurmountable difficulty, try to get round it by seeing language as a capacity derived from some other aptitude that was already there.

5.4 Could language be the outcome of a quite different ability?

The only reasonable way to argue for the abrupt and non-adaptive appearance of language would be to identify a characteristic of chimpanzees or hominids out of which it might have grown. This is not to fall back on the continuistic argument that language is merely an extension of the vocalizations produced by the other primates. Continuism is in fact a mode of gradualism, requiring natural selection to have acted without let-up so as to bring such vocalizations to the degree of sophistication we see in language. On the other hand, the idea that language might be a by-product of some other behaviour is compatible with the Gouldian catastrophist view argued by Chomsky and Piattelli-Palmarini.

This interpretation would make language a kind of parasitical ability, something like a side effect. Not only does it make language a gratuitous behaviour, devoid of any special function for which it might have been

---

[3] Tossing a coin fifty times would give one chance out of 10^{15} of hitting on the right combination.

selected, but it could also explain how, with very little information, non-language can turn into language. If the buildings of a former military barracks are transformed into a complex of student residences, a whole new campus can be set up at no great cost. The complex as such can appear quite suddenly and may require little in the way of conversion, compared with the time and labour that would be needed to build it from scratch. If language did arise by transposition from an existing system, it could have appeared suddenly and without the need for great transformations.

So which systems might have been available to serve as the scaffolding, so to speak, of language? There is no self-evident answer to that question; and though there are several potential answers, none of them appears clearly to supply the substratum that language would have required. Chomsky makes mention of an idea of Richard Gregory's about grammar having 'its roots in the brain's rules for ordering retinal patterns in terms of objects' (Chomsky 1975: 228 n.7); but he does not accept the idea. André Leroy-Gourhan takes the view that language is a transposing to the articulatory domain of the ability to make and manipulate tools (Leroy-Gourhan 1965). Robert Worden argues that social intelligence is the basis for language (Worden 1998). He sees chimpanzees as being able to have a representation of a situation such as: 'If X cries and Y is X's mother, then Y reacts'. Worden models this representation with what he calls a 'script', that is to say a graph representing the individuals and their actions; and he observes an analogy of shape between the scripts and the syntactic and semantic structures of language.

The trouble with scenarios of this kind, which present language as a by-product of some other more fundamental ability, lies in the unconvincingness of the structural analogies proposed between language and the domains which are supposed to have served as its precursors. The structural richness of language seems to be vastly greater than anything that can be imagined in these different domains. The following chapters will examine some complexities of phonetics, syntax, semantics, and argumentative mechanisms. Each of these four functional levels of language has its own structure; and no clear parallel has ever been suggested between this range of structures and any particular domain, whether vision, the design of the movements required by tool-making, or the managing of social relations. If one is really determined to seek an analogy of form between this or that aspect of language and some property of a non-linguistic cognitive domain, then no doubt one will end up finding one. For instance, the syntactic structure of a sentence is naturally represented by a tree diagram and it is also possible of course to represent some aspects of cognitive processing, such as planning, by a tree diagram. But the analogies are superficial. A phrase structure tree contains built-in constraints, certain asymmetries for example between what is placed in the upper or lower parts of the tree (we saw something similar in Chapter 3 with the sentence *He says that John is ill*, p. 67). And in planning there is nothing remotely equivalent.

Palaeontologists who have contrived to reconstruct the technique required for the making of stone tools have realized that knapping off flakes was a far from haphazard business. Every stroke with the knapping stone must hit precisely the right spot, at the right angle, with the right force. In addition, all these parameters must be aptly varied according to the context, the shape of the stone, its type, the quality and weight of the knapping stone. Achieving a satisfactory result requires not only a degree of manual dexterity beyond the abilities of any beginner, but also quite unambiguous knowledge of which materials to use and which actions to make, as well as experience in planning that includes the ability to evaluate the intermediate stages (Pelegrin 1990). A formal description of these activities of stone technology would probably lend itself to a tree-like diagram or graphs showing the sequences of actions and decisions; and any such abstraction may present some resemblance to structures found in language. But it is the superficiality of the analogy that will strike the linguist. Is there anything in the knapping of a stone tool that could correspond to the plural, to case marking, to morphological inflecting, the passive voice, or impersonal subjects? In tool-making activity not only is there nothing that exactly matches those particular features of syntactic structuring, but there appears to be nothing that could have been a precursor of them, even at a simplified level.

As for Robert Worden's alleged analogy between language and the representation of social relations in chimpanzees, it should be noted that the representation may really be Worden's rather than the chimpanzees'. Not that chimpanzees do not have representations of the world they live in, including their social world, but we shall have occasion to doubt that the form of their representations has the form that Worden sees in them. Furthermore, the analogy he describes could at most explain the origin of certain semantic representations, since any resemblance between his 'scripts' and syntax trees remains extremely superficial.

It is perfectly legitimate to seek precursors of language in the cognitive abilities of chimpanzees. As often happens in the evolution of species, natural selection 'turns the old into the new' (Jacob 1970). But what seems less well founded is the hope of finding any precursor that is more or less formally identical with language. Clinging to such a groundless hope is a form of wishful thinking, showing only the strength of some people's desire to reduce the gulf separating non-linguistic animals from us human beings and some of our ancestors. Those who believe in the sudden and non-adaptive appearance of language are reduced to a pointless search for a closely matching analogue of it in the behavioural repertoires of apes.

5.5 Dr Pangloss's explanation of language

The idea of a macromutation is an extreme version of Gould's theory which it is impossible, in all reason, to accept. In the next chapter we shall see not only that it is possible to sidestep the view of speciation as instantaneous, with macromutations and monsters, but that it actually runs counter to a proper conception of the phenomenon of punctuated equilibria. For the present, let us focus on the basic argument, which in essence is Gould's: that speciation phenomena are infrequent; that they occur rapidly on the scale of geological time; and that their direction is unforeseeable. If we apply these principles to language, the crowning achievement of *Homo sapiens* can no longer be seen as the pinnacle towards which all other species have, with varying degrees of success, been trying to evolve, and turns out to be only a chance behavioural peculiarity that just happened to appear in one strain of primate, much as the elephant's trunk appeared in the family of the proboscidians. This rather negative way of seeing human language will be seen later in a different light. In the mean time, let us not deprive ourselves of the pleasure and the intellectual profit to be derived from Gould's criticism of what he calls 'the Panglossian paradigm' of some thinking on evolution, as it applies to the sorts of overhasty explanations of the emergence of language that one can read in some authors.

The argument that language evolved out of gradual improvements in a system of communication, for the simple reason that it is a useful system, is of itself more than dubious. It is the argument that says 'X is used by Y, therefore Y is the evolutionary cause of X'. Authors like Gould and Richard Lewontin take the view that, more often than not, such reasoning is greatly mistaken. Noses may be used to rest glasses on, but this does not mean of course that the existence of glasses explains why human noses exist. Language vastly increases the ability of humans acting as a group to dominate nature, because of the pooling of their knowledge. Was that why language was favoured by natural selection? This may appear obvious; but it is mistaken.

According to Gould and Lewontin, this mistake is typical of out-and-out adaptationism (Gould and Lewontin 1979; Lewontin 1987). They see a real danger in seeking—and finding—adaptations where there are none. The mode of adaptationism criticized by Gould and Lewontin interprets all characteristics of living things as the result of a conception, the originator of the conception being no longer God as was once the case but natural selection. Not only is it believed that each and every characteristic is functional in life, but it is the best possible for its function. This way of seeing the world is a clear reminder of the teachings of Master Pangloss in Voltaire's *Candide*:

Pangloss taught metaphysico-theologico-cosmomoronology. He proved to perfection that there is no effect without a cause, that, in this best of all possible worlds, the castle of His Highness von Thundertentronckh was the finest of all possible castles, and that Her Highness was the best of all possible baronesses. 'It is conclusively demonstrated,' he would say, 'that things cannot be otherwise. For, since everything was created for a purpose, everything is of necessity for the best of all possible purposes. *Nota bene,* noses were created for the express purpose of wearing spectacles. And so we wear spectacles. Legs were visibly created so that breeches could be invented. Therefore we wear breeches! Stone was created for the especial purpose of being sawn into blocks, so that castles might be built. Therefore His Highness has a most beautiful castle. The greatest baron in the province must be the best housed. And, since pigs were created for the express purpose of being made into pork chops, it follows that we must eat pork all year round. Therefore, those who maintain that all is well have in fact uttered a nonsense. They *should* maintain that all is for the best in the best of all possible worlds.' (Voltaire, *Candide*, 1759)

Gould and Lewontin ridicule what they call the 'Panglossian' interpretation of the theory of evolution which sees all characteristics of living things as perfect. In demonstrating the inappropriateness of this reasoning to such situations, they introduce the idea of a 'spandrel', a technical term in architecture which, though its proper meaning is the roughly triangular wall space included between the shoulders of two contiguous arches, has now become part of the basic vocabulary of evolutionary science. Gould and Lewontin take pleasure in pointing out how well the spandrels of the cathedral of San Marco in Venice appear to have been designed for the decoration on them, which is so well adapted to the triangular surfaces on which it has been done. Even non-architects can grasp, *pace* Dr Pangloss, that the spandrels are there for a completely different reason, being mere fortuitous by-products of the fact that a dome has been built on top of arches. A more biological example of the figurative 'spandrel' would be the colours of blood and bile, in the sense that very likely these colours, by being hidden away from sight, played no part *per se* in the evolution of vertebrates.

Gould and Lewontin inspect a range of factors which could replace natural selection as an explanation of this or that property of a living creature. For instance, genetic drift randomly affects the gene frequency in a population; and the smaller the group is, the greater the effect. This drift promotes the evolution of the average of the individuals, though this is an evolution that owes nothing to natural selection. Another factor that might explain how forms appear without natural selection or despite it relates to relative growth constraints and more generally to constraints of patterns of organization. In insects, as in vertebrates, the organization plan makes for symmetry and segmentation. The loss of one segment might create insects with only four legs; but it is extremely difficult to conceive of a major exception to this design, such as five-legged insects. Relative growth can also explain many an evolutionary mystery, such as the front legs of Tyrannosaurus rex. The life-size Tyrannosaurus in fibre glass in the Boston Museum of Science intrigues visitors not just because of its huge jaws but also by its absurdly short forelegs, which do not even reach to its mouth. What were they for? Did they help the animal to get up from a lying position? Gould and Lewontin remind us that before we set about seeking a particular adaptiveness in them, without reference to the rest of the beast, the question to be asked is whether their smallness is not relative to the size of the hind legs and whether the latter are not simply an outcome of an embryogenetic growth differential between the front and rear parts. So the size of Tyrannosaurus's forelegs may be a mere 'spandrel' and any hardline adaptationist who tries to find a special evolutionary meaning in it is mistaken.

When applied to language, 'the Panglossian paradigm' leads some people to jump to conclusions, in ways reminiscent of those misapprehensions discussed at the beginning of Chapter 4. An example is Lieberman's claim that it is clearly in the interests of humans to communicate to their fellows the theory and practice of stone knapping, and that this is the reason why they use language to do so. The most immediate and unfortunately the most often used Panglossian explanation consists of saying that human beings are obviously made to communicate, and so they communicate. Voltaire's Pangloss, in his eagerness to see the world he lives in as the best of all possible worlds, manages to justify the existence of all things in it. In the same way, we, it is said, use language to warn our fellows of a danger and to teach them techniques; and, given that nothing in the best of all possible worlds comes from chance, just as stones exist for the especial purpose of being sawn into blocks and building the Baron's castle, language must have been created for this very purpose of utilitarian communication.

One of the main butts of Gould's and Lewontin's satirical sallies is 'just-so stories'. Tyrannosaurus's forelegs were short so that the animal could stand up; members of the human race have two breasts because of the possibility of twin births. Any story will do, if what we are trying to do is account for existence by function. As explanations for things, the relative growth of segments of the body or the existence of a symmetry plan which makes some bodily organs exist in even numbers may well be less stimulating for the imagination, because they are not functional explanations.

As far as language is concerned, it must be admitted that there is no shortage of nice stories purporting to explain the appearance of spoken communication in the human line of descent. The explanatory strategies are nearly always the same. The first of them, language being an unprecedented characteristic, is to see it as a consequence of some other original property of our lineage, such as bipedalism (Aiello 1996), social intelligence (Worden 1998), the level of general intelligence (Darwin 1871), or the morphology of the larynx (Savage-Rumbaugh and Lewin 1994), to quote only a few examples. In each case, what we have is a semblance of explanation: the emergence of language in a single species, ours, ceases to be astonishing because it results from a property that only hominids possessed. There is a ready acceptance of the idea that exceptional causes, such as bipedalism or an abnormally low larynx, can produce an effect as exceptional as language. Causality, unfortunately, does not come unscathed out of such explanations. How could bipedalism or the anatomy of the larynx be the cause of language? Why did language not appear without them? As we shall see, these questions reveal that explanatory hypotheses such as those we have just mentioned are at best very incomplete and at worst groundless.

A second explanatory strategy consists of singling out one of the effects of language so as to make it the reason for the evolution of language. For example, the following beneficial effects of language, and others, have all been seen as the reason why it became part of our evolutionary heritage: the possibility of uttering precise alarm calls or pooling knowledge (Lieberman 1992); the strengthening of social bonds or the detection of uncooperative individuals (Dunbar 1996); negotiation (Pinker and Bloom 1990); or even the possibility of clarifying one's own thoughts and thinking 'off-line' (Bickerton 1995). Gould's and Lewontin's criticism of these explanations of the existence of language would consist not of a demonstration of their falseness but merely of the fact that they are stories, something shown by the multiplicity of them. How could anyone choose one of them rather than another? For Gould and Lewontin, telling such stories should have no place in a scientific approach to evolution. It is always possible to spin a yarn to shore up the adaptive origin of this or that feature:

Often, evolutionists use *consistency* with natural selection as the sole criterion and consider their work done when they concoct a plausible story. But plausible stories can always be told. (Gould and Lewontin 1979)

Understanding of evolutionary phenomena requires reasoning of an unusual order. Evolutionist reasoning is fraught with peril, for more often than not it amounts to an inverting of the temporal relation between cause and effect. The theory of natural selection, as formulated by Wallace and Darwin, stipulates that some of the spontaneous variations which affect the offspring of living things will be favoured because of their advantageous effects for the individuals affected. So the phenotypic effects of the variations are the causes of their success or elimination. There is therefore a strong temptation to account for the existence of a particular organ by saying its appearance during the course of evolution was due to one of the effects it produces in observable individuals. Unfortunately, one cannot just take at random any effect and conclude that it was responsible for setting in motion the evolutionary process that led to it.

In language, effects are numerous. As the authors quoted above point out, language enables us to utter precise and effective alarm calls, to pool our skills, to strengthen social bonds or denounce cheats, to negotiate with our fellows, or clarify our own thoughts. But it also enables us to do many other things: with it we can squabble or sing, we can greet other people, court somebody, make up poems or puns, give orders, political speeches, or sermons, tell lies or tales of fantasy, affirm our authority, complain, insult people, display our abilities, become a scientist, etc., etc. We could choose any one of these different uses of language and deem it to be the 'true' reason for its emergence. Whichever one we might choose would stand every chance of being added to the anthology of Panglossian theories of language.

However, it is quite easy, such is the persuasiveness of Gould, to go from one extreme to the other, not only to shun strict adaptationism but to entertain the thought that there is no such thing as adaptation, that all characteristics of living beings are fortuitous, which is equally absurd. Not that this is the position of Gould, who sees himself as deriving directly from Darwin. The problem, though, if one accepts that natural selection does have a role to play in at least some cases of the development of organs and their proper functioning, is where does one draw the line?

The criticisms made by Gould and Lewontin should be seen in their proper perspective, which is that they are a warning not against acceptance of Darwin's theory but against excesses deriving from misuse of the theory of evolution by natural selection. Two fundamental points should not be lost sight of, for without them no progress can be made in our understanding of the genesis both of the living world and of language.

The first is that, ever since scientists stopped believing that God's will explained the origin of all things, including the shape of the nervures on the wings of each of the 20,000 species of bees so far identified, *the only known source of design for functional organs is natural selection*. No one has ever suggested any other credible mechanism to explain in particular the adaptation of forms to their functions. Chance, for instance, is unable to bring about the appearance of complex forms with structures corresponding to the demands of a precise function. Why do the bodies of dolphins have their elongated shape? Why is the woodpecker's beak pointed? Why do ducks have webbed feet? An orchid *Ophrys apifera* imitates the olfactive, visual, and tactile signals made by small female solitary bees, a mechanism that induces copulative behaviour in the males, thus enabling the orchid to transfer pollen to the insect, which will then carry it to other flowers of the same species. Such fine adaptations did not just appear out of thin air, completely formed; their design was the outcome neither of the mind of an engineer nor of the will or the habits of the animals themselves. They come from the fact that all beings living nowadays descend from individuals which, in each generation, were often slightly better equipped than their fellows. This does not mean that all characteristics of living beings were independently determined by the action of natural selection, but only the functional characteristics. Gould's and Lewontin's comments apply almost exclusively to non-functional things or to mistakes made by naturalists in determining functions. In the case of language, the determination of function will be a necessary step in our search for an evolutionary explanation.

The second point not to be forgotten is the extent of the workings of natural selection. Natural selection acts on phenotypic differences which affect the relative reproduction of individuals.[4] If a particular property enables individuals endowed with it to have on average more progeny than their fellows, the principle of natural selection stipulates that this property will spread through the population. Two significant consequences flow from this principle. First, it is expected that there will be a whole range of evolutionary phenomena unaffected by natural selection. This is the case with phenotypically neutral genetic modifications, phenotypic modifications that do not affect reproduction, or even ecological variables such as the size of a population or the success of a species, parameters whose variations make no change in the *relative* reproduction capacity of individuals (Williams 1966). Secondly, however, the same principle stipulates that if a property creates a phenotypic difference that might affect relative reproduction, then it will be subject to the working of natural selection. The property will have to either disappear or take over the whole population. Or else, in certain quite precise cases, it will achieve an equilibrium in which only a definite proportion of the population will possess it. In other words, natural selection does not permit the random evolution of what it acts on.

The relevance of this for language can be seen in a straightforward step of reasoning. (1) Language, insofar as it is universal, shows a quite marked feature of design, which means of necessity that it is a product of natural selection. (2) It would be difficult to argue that, other things being equal,

---

[4] My form of words is an approximation, since in some cases the appropriate unit of selection is not the individual (Dawkins 1976; Dessalles 1996a).

capacity for language has no bearing on the relative reproduction of individuals. Even in modern societies, a proficiency in language has an important effect on the social contacts that people make and can ultimately impinge on how they contribute to future generations. So that gives two reasons why, *pace* the believers in macromutation, language is not a haphazard development and is of necessity subject to the workings of natural selection. Consequently, like any characteristic shaped by natural selection, human language has to be explained in terms of function, even if one eschews hardline adaptationism. That said, we must also eschew any Panglossian explanation. Most mistaken or unfounded explanations of the emergence of language arise from ignorance of the constraints of evolution. As will be seen, it is not always as easy as Gould and Lewontin would have us believe to think up plausible scenarios that account for the evolutionary emergence of natural characteristics. And language is one of these.

6 The local optimality of language

The aim of this chapter is, so to speak, to reconcile Gould and Darwin on the dual question of the gradualness and the directional quality of evolution. I wish to show that the two positions, Gould's saltationism (evolution by jumps) and Darwin's gradualism, are both valid, albeit on different timescales. The point is that macroevolution should not be confused with microevolution. By and large, differences of opinion on the emergence of language arise from mixing up two timescales. Once that is accepted, two further points, which prima facie seem to contradict each other, can be made: (1) that language really is an accident in the evolution of primates; like most of the innovations which characterize entire genera, its occurrence was fortuitous and was in no way a normal outcome of any evolutionary tendency; (2) that language is not due to a macromutation; it serves an adaptive function for which it is locally optimal.

6.1 Between chance and necessity

Chapter 5 left us with a problem. If we accept Gould's and Eldredge's theory of punctuated equilibria, then the direction taken by speciations is indeterminate. So the appearance of *Homo sapiens*, fully equipped with language, was an abrupt event and was in no way a response to an adaptive need. Such a way of seeing language is diametrically opposed to the view, contested in Chapter 4, that evolution towards language was gradual and slow, though inexorable. How can an exclusive choice be made between these two interpretations of Darwinian theory? To decide between them is to decide whether language, as the prerogative of our species, was fortuitous or necessary.

Gould's thinking is at odds with the idea that evolution goes in a determinate direction, whether it is a matter of increases in size, specialization, intelligence, or complexity. If evolution is aimless, how are we to explain the apparently constant increase over time in the volume of the cranium in hominids? The increase in their technical control of their environment through the making of more and more elaborate tools and the discovery of fire similarly reinforce the idea that there really was something like a process of hominization. Gould's idea seems to mean that evolution functions like a haphazard exploration of the broad range of possibilities. But that seems incompatible with the very idea of selection. By definition, evolutionary change through natural selection, the heart of Darwin's theory, makes for dissymmetry among the spontaneous variations by which individuals in a generation are differentiated, by singling out the favourable variations. In other words, we should not expect evolution to be isotropic, occurring in all directions, despite what Gould has shown in the evolution of genera and orders.

The phenomenon known as selection pressure is one which does result in an evolutionary tendency. For example, in an ecological context like the Amazon forest, trees are not tall by chance. In the struggle to absorb sunlight, being tall has its rewards. This makes for competition of a kind that Richard Dawkins compares to an arms race favouring increases in size until the maximum possible is reached (Dawkins 1976). Such increase in average sizes is not fortuitous; it is a response to selection pressure. Can the principle of selection pressure be reconciled with Gould's principle which, strictly interpreted, rules out the existence of trends?

The dichotomy confronting us here is the one that Jacques Monod once famously used as the title of a book: chance and necessity. In making us pass from one species or genus to another, evolution with its unforeseeable directions seems to be left to chance. Yet, when we inspect species themselves, their physical make-up or behavioural abilities, we are bound to be struck by the necessity for them as products of evolution. It is no fluke that cat's teeth are sharp; nor is it by chance that the dolphin has a body like a shark or a tunny fish. In the same way, our language abilities seem to be well adapted to the function for which we use them. Forms like these can be seen as expressing a certain necessity. In the light of such things, is it conceivable that the workings of evolution are blind? The answer to that question lies in an understanding of the dynamic aspects of evolution.

6.2 The slow and the fast in evolutionary change

Evolution is generally seen as a process of inordinate slowness. A period of a million years is something we can find it extremely difficult to have a notion of; yet that is the timescale on which we need to think if we are to have any hope of observing notable change in the history of a species. We acquire the habit of thinking that evolution is intrinsically slow and that it can never entail rapid change, a perception that derives from a mistaken assumption about evolution's constant speed. According to Gould's and Eldredge's theory of punctuated equilibria, periods of evolutionary change are very brief, the rest of the time being stagnation. This is a new perspective, giving an inverted image of the workings of evolution, making them seem extremely rapid when measured on a geological timescale. Gould proposes an extreme version of this contrast. On the one hand, there is macroevolution, a very slow process working itself out over millions of years and producing, for example, the line of descent of *Hyracotherium*, which over fifty-five million years evolved several hundred species, including those of the genus *Equus*. Macroevolution is completely blind, though it manages to produce diversification of species. On the other hand, there is microevolution, the poor relation in Gould's theory. He sees microevolution as being largely due to chance macromutations or genetic changes which, though possibly slight, have major phenotypic consequences. That is to say, for Gould, such events are not just rapid but well-nigh instantaneous. Evolution via 'hopeful monsters' is an extreme version of this process; and microevolution may amount to no more than the birth of a single individual.

Going from one of these extremes to the other may well leave one with an uneasy feeling. All of Darwin's cautious attempts in *The Origin of Species* to give a colouring of plausibility to the appearance of complex functioning organs become just irrelevant. The elimination of gradualness would also eliminate the only plausible explanation of forms which give evidence of design, such as eyes, wings, or language. The mistake lies in a mixing-up of the mechanisms of macroevolution and microevolution; and this affects not only gradualists, who apply to macroevolution what they have understood through microevolution, but also standard saltationists, who feel their position obliges them to deny the existence of a mechanism belonging to microevolution. An example will show that macroevolution really is, as Gould maintains, a slow, discontinuous, and non-directed process, but that microevolution, though rapid, is not instantaneous, and in particular that it is gradual and directed.

An artificial example of evolution

In a book called *L'ordinateur génétique*[1] (Dessalles 1996a) I analysed in detail several situations of artificial evolution. By the use of genetic algorithms, one can create in the memory of a computer a situation resembling the evolution of species and thereby observe in real time phenomena which we have reason to suspect existed in the history of life. Punctuated equilibria, dear to the heart of Gould, are a case in point, turning up in all spontaneity in the evolution of a genetic algorithm. With artificial evolution speeded up and happening as we watch, we can observe the functioning of the mechanisms of macroevolution and microevolution and see what differences there are between them.

Figure 6.1 (a) shows three successive levels in the evolution of a genetic algorithm. The programme in use here is set the problem of getting out of a maze. A standard programme would first choose a random path, then try to improve it step by step, avoiding backtracking, until it found the shortest way to an exit. A genetic algorithm proceeds a little differently. In the memory of the computer it sets in motion not a path but a population of 100 paths. Each of these paths (called 'individuals') is characterized by a binary sequence called 'genome'; and it is this genome which encodes the behaviour of the individual inside the maze. The individuals making up this virtual population are subjected to severe selection. To begin with, they are random, which leads of course to erratic behaviours in the maze. The ones which prove to be best at avoiding backtracking through the maze are then selected and 'reproduce' until they have begotten a new population. As a result of this artificial selection, behaviours quickly become less random and lead to a locally optimal path. The situation is illustrated by the curves of Figure 6.1 (a): the black one shows the performance of the best individual in each generation; the grey one shows the average of the population. The performance, shown on the vertical axis, is calculated from the number of backtrackings, with a bonus mark awarded when an individual manages to get out.

---

[1] The title means 'The genetic computer' [JG].

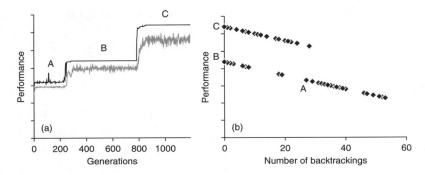

FIG. 6.1 The genetic algorithm as illustrated here tries to get out of a maze. It selects individuals which best avoid backtracking. On the left, the curves show the evolution of performances from one generation to the next. On the right are shown the best individuals in each generation.

The levels in the left-hand diagram, marked A, B, and C, correspond to three different strategies. At A, the best individuals follow a direct path, but it comes to a dead end. At B, the best individuals in the population are those that take a cyclic trajectory, which means they never backtrack. At C, the algorithm has found a way out. Individuals that manage to get out receive the bonus mark, which explains the difference in performance between levels B and C.

It is striking to observe the similarity between this type of evolution and the one that predicts the theory of punctuated equilibria. The algorithm stagnates for long periods, which are interrupted by sharp jumps leading to notable differences in performance. If one accepts this experiment as an indication of what natural evolution might be like, it would appear that we must also accept Gould's saltationism with its idea that nature does make jumps, despite its contradiction of Darwin and his dictum borrowed from Leibnitz. However, such a conclusion would be premature. The curve implies that the population exists in three successive forms, which we are tempted to see as three species. The performances of these species get better, in accordance with the marks given by the algorithm in recognition of the number of backtrackings avoided in the allotted time. The presence of abrupt jumps in performance suggests that evolution does proceed by 'hopeful monsters' as in the theory that Gould wishes to rehabilitate. In the context of the maze, a hopeful monster would be an individual so radically different from its fellows as to find straightaway a new and significantly better solution. Such an artificial Adam could be seen as the founder of a new species which in its turn would enter a long period of stagnation, awaiting the next Adam who would bring it to an end. This description, however, in the case of the genetic algorithm, is a distortion of reality.

The discontinuities in the curve are misleading. Figure 6.1 (b) reveals gradualness in the performances, which means in a way that Darwin is just as right as Gould. It shows the distribution of the best performers as recorded by the computer's memory over successive generations in terms of two parameters: the number of their backtrackings on the horizontal axis and their performances on the vertical axis. Each backtrack makes for a lower performance, which explains why individuals are distributed along two straight lines, one made of those who are still inside the maze at the expiry of the allotted time and one made of those who managed to get out and thereby won a bonus mark. The points shown as A, B, and C in Figure 6.1 (b) represent the three stages of the curve. If evolution proceeded solely by jumps, we ought to see only these three points, which is obviously not the case. The diagram shows that there were many other individuals with a claim to be the best in their generation. They lived during the brief transitions between one stage and the next. What can be observed is that there were many intermediate performances, meaning that the algorithm did not proceed solely by jumps.

If we extrapolate the results of this experiment to the real situation that obtains in life, we must conclude that Gould is right to contradict the idea of regular, steady-paced evolution, and that Darwin is also right to contradict the idea of radical discontinuities. The apparent existence of discontinuities like those in the black curve in Figure 6.1 (a) is an illusion created by the timescale of observation. On the scale familiar to a palae-ontologist like Gould, working mainly with fossils, discontinuities in the evolution of genera and orders become blatant. They mainly disappear, however, if one can see the real sequence of lines of descent. They become transitions which, though not instantaneous, are just very rapid relative to the long stagnations. They are an effect of the speed of microevolution, which most palaeontologists are unaware of. Table 6.1 summarizes differ-ences between macroevolution, Gould's main focus, and microevolution, which is where the Darwinian principles of natural selection apply. In discussing the various elements of this contrast, we shall draw on the evidence provided by the maze experiment.

TABLE **6.1** *Summary of contrasting features of macroevolution and microevolution*

Macroevolution	Microevolution
Discontinuities; equilibria punctuated by abrupt transitions	Gradualness; phenotypic continuity
Slow evolution	Rapid evolution
Absence of selection pressure; isotropic progression	Selection pressure; directed progression
Chance	Necessity
No apparent optimization	Local optimization; attractors
Proliferation of species	Little proliferation
Very infrequent innovations	Frequent innovations

Discontinuities or gradualness

The maze experiment sheds light on the periods of stagnation that Gould and Eldredge showed to be inherent in macroevolution. The genesis of the three equilibria revealed in Figure 6.1 (a) is easy to understand. The population is in a constant state of equilibrium; at any given moment, most of the individuals in the genetic algorithm are following more or less the same path inside the maze. There are of course mutants which try other paths; but since their genome offers them no useful instructions on how to find their way through areas into which their ancestors have never ventured, their performances are very poor and they are almost certain to be eliminated by the selection working through the algorithm. The population remains trapped inside the solution it has discovered, though it will later turn out to be not as good a solution as others. This is a state known as a local optimum, that is, a position that cannot be bettered by a slight change. The population can spend whole generations exploring a dead end (as at A) or in a cyclic trajectory (as at B), without ever discovering how to get out of them, for the simple reason that the variants that try exploring the rest of the maze are not as good as their conservative fellows. A day may come, though it is unlikely, when a particularly lucky mutant performs quite well, at least as well as the current standard. This gives it some possibility of leaving descendants or even of founding a new species which will follow the path that it contrived to find. The new species will be in a new state of equilibrium at a different local optimum which will be better than the previous one.

It should be noted that the transition from one local optimum to another, though rapid, is not instantaneous. In Figure 6.1, no offspring of individuals at A are to be found at B. Similarly, several generations must pass before any mutants that escape from B have offspring of type C. Evolution works in a way that affords transitions from one local optimum to another, but it never does this instantaneously.

As for the idea of the 'hopeful monster', that role could well be filled by the particularly lucky mutant who discovers a radically new path through the maze. In Figure 6.1, the mutant that appears at generation 784 is lucky enough to find a way out, which earns it the bonus and the possibility to leave abundant progeny in its own image. Its performance jump is mitigated, however, by the fact that it backtracks about thirty times along its new path. Not only that, but if its genome is analysed it shows very little difference from that of its contemporaries. The fact that it has taken an unexplored path through the maze may of course be seen as monstrous, but it is the outcome of a genetic configuration that hardly differs from the average genetic configuration of the population. Some estimate of the genetic innovation of this Adam is provided by how long the equilibrium preceding his appearance lasted. In the maze experiment, the coming of the Adam who begat the C population was awaited for about 500 generations in a population of 100 individuals. With hindsight, it can be estimated that his genetic configuration had about one chance in 50,000 of being produced and passed on. This means that for the population's state of equilibrium to be disturbed, it took a genetic change bearing on about sixteen bits of the genome. Yet the mutation of this Adam was nowhere near that: in relation to his parents, he may have differed by as little as a single bit, the one that altered the direction to follow on one crucial location of the maze and made him turn into the new path. The other fifteen properly positioned bits of his genome were there by chance, both in him and in his parents. That being the case, it would be an exaggeration to call this founding Adam a monster, though he was certainly 'hopeful'.

If the equilibria correspond to local optima, the punctuations correspond to transitions from one local optimum to another. It is in the transitions that microevolution happens. Adam, by virtue of his better performances, has offspring with 'normal' individuals; and there is a good probability that he will hand down to them what made him different. So in the maze almost half of them join him on the new path that he opened. The individuals making up this sub-population go on to have offspring with the offspring of the broader population. A new phase of competition rapidly begins, however, in which the individuals on the old path will eventually drop out of the race. And not many generations later this competition leads to a new local optimum, that is, a path through the maze which it is difficult to improve by slight alterations.

Speed of evolution

This interpretation of the phenomenon of punctuated equilibria in terms of a change of local optimum leads to a comment on the other lines in Table 6.1. Microevolution is rapid because there is open competition among individuals. In equilibrium, this competition is no longer open, as all the best available solutions have been found. A sudden transition happens with the appearance of an improbable Adam who opens a new area of possible improvement. There then follows an extremely rapid phase in which competition leads, in a relatively small number of generations, to a new equilibrium.[2]

Selection pressure and the directional working of evolution

Microevolutionary competition enables selection to do its work and to create a pressure which pushes evolution in a given direction, that of the next local optimum. In the maze, competition pushes the population towards improvement in the trajectory followed until it has eliminated all backtrackings that penalize individuals. This improvement is gradual and directed, just as Darwin predicted. It leaves little scope for variants, since competition eliminates all but the best solutions. Macroevolution, by contrast, is much more unpredictable, as Gould likes to stress. It is hard

---

[2] The rapidity of microevolution is due not only to the existence of open competition but also to the phenomenon known as implicit parallelism. This is linked to genome crossover, which makes the genes independent of each other. When an individual is confronted with natural selection, all his or her genes are implicitly evaluated. The genes are thus selected by chunks, the remaining chunks being redistributed at each generation. So genes which are the best locally emerge rapidly. This rapidity gives genetic algorithms a technological interest as a method of optimization (Goldberg 1989; Dessalles 1996a). The same mechanism explains the rapidity of microevolution.

to foresee the direction in which any punctuation of equilibrium will happen, and the longer an equilibrium lasts, the harder this becomes. So while microevolution can be seen to be a directional phenomenon, macroevolution is marked by isotropy.

Nevertheless, the example of the maze seems to suggest that changes of local optimum always happen in the direction of progress, which appears to contradict Gould's idea of change happening in unforeseeable directions. Do we not observe slow but inexorable progression towards ever better performances? If this is so, then macroevolution too shows a trend. However, this objection can be answered. The natural context is much more varied than that of our genetic algorithm. In the context of the maze, all paths can be compared to one another and only the best on that single scale survive. Living beings live in different ecological niches. If through speciation a species manages to change niches, its performances cannot be compared with those of its parent species, so the very concept of progress becomes inapplicable. In such cases, Gould is right to deny any concept of progress in evolution. What is true, however, is that if speciation occurs in the same niche, the new species will have every chance to replace the parent species; and that could properly be seen as progress. Even so, it is not appropriate to speak of directional evolution. Though it may be possible at times to foresee progress in cases where speciation is unaccompanied by a change of niche, morphological changes related to speciation still remain completely unpredictable. Gould is once again right to say that the phenotypes of species do not succeed each other in a definite direction.

It might be possible to maintain that *Homo sapiens* represents progress with regard to *Homo erectus* and that *erectus* may have represented progress with regard to its predecessors, as long as it could be shown that these different species occupied the same ecological niche. However, *erectus* was not carrying the seed either of *sapiens* or of any of the other species which it might have led to and which would have replaced it if chance had brought them into being. There is no direction in macroevolution.

Chance and necessity

Why does an Adam appear at one moment rather than at some other? Why should it be this Adam rather than that? When an equilibrium is well established, the discovery of a new evolutionary path is an unlikely phenomenon which leads to a major change. Generalizing metaphorically from the maze experiment, we can say that the punctuation of an equilibrium implies a 'bifurcation' in the phenotypic expression of individuals. The more stable the equilibrium of a species, the greater the bifurcation that releases it, since all the small potential bifurcations have already been explored. And the greater the bifurcation, the more unlikely it is. The moment at which the salutary bifurcation may occur, and its direction in relation to other bifurcations which, though equally unlikely, would have been equally advantageous, are subject to no necessity. In the interplay of chance and necessity which is a feature of the evolution of life (Monod 1970), it would appear that chance dominates the domain of macroevolution.

But it is in the domain of microevolution that necessity, in Jacques Monod's sense, takes on its full significance. Microevolution brings about local optimization for a species which is out of equilibrium. The fact is that in general there are not many local optima available at any given position in the phenotypic space. This suggests that purely locally the conformation of a species has a 'necessary' character. A biomechanician might undertake to demonstrate that, as far as deformations of a hand are concerned, the foot is the best possible one for bipedalism. The fact that other configurations were not only possible but potentially better, for instance walking on fingers as birds do, is irrelevant, given that the optimality under consideration here is purely local. Since anthropoid apes walk on the hands of the hind limbs laid flat, it is not difficult to agree that, once the principle of bipedalism was established, there was an inevitability in the evolution of the foot.

Evolution and optimization: local attractors

It might be thought that the concept of necessity, in Jacques Monod's sense, would lead to another Panglossian error of the sort criticized by Gould and Lewontin. Transposed into evolutionary science, this error consists of seeing perfection in all living things and believing that nothing could ever be other than it is, the perfection manifest in every species deriving not from divine action, but from the workings of natural selection. With Voltaire's help, Gould and Lewontin ridicule such a way of conceiving of life, pointing out that the changes which lead to the appearance of new species are the work of chance and not of any force making for progress. The maze experiment does show, however, that chance is not the sole agent of speciation. Given the rapidity of microevolution, every species occupies a local optimum; and that fact has very significant consequences for our concept of species. In particular, it will require us to look again at the Australopithecenes and *Homo erectus*, both of which are often mistakenly seen as very imperfect early versions of *Homo sapiens*. Another idea that will be of great importance when we come to try to understand the functional character of language is that of the local optimality of species. Against those who present language as having been produced solely by a fortuitous macromutation with an arbitrary result, I shall argue its locally optimal character, which can be established in accordance with criteria that are quite separate from evolutionary considerations.

A good way not only of clarifying the difference between macroevolution and microevolution but also of avoiding Master Pangloss's ways of thinking is to apply the metaphor of the attractor. Let us imagine a space containing all possible phenotypes, that is to say the space of all the forms that living beings can have. Individuals are points inside that space; species are haloes, more or less concentrated. As they evolve, species are going to move from their places. In this metaphor, the action of natural selection works through local attractors: whenever a species comes close to an attractor, it is affected by its attraction and evolves in a determined direction. This is how microevolution works. When the species is under the influence of the attractor, it is in a state of equilibrium and there is little possibility that it will move from its place. However, when the halo representing the species is affected by the zone of attraction of a neighbouring attractor, the species may move in this direction if the attractor is more powerful. The species may also split apart. That is how macroevolution works. What is unforeseeable in this case is the direction in which the move will take place: among all the neighbouring attractors, which of them will be the one to affect the destiny of the species in question cannot be predicted.

The image of the attractor is helpful because it puts the potential advantageousness of language into perspective. Everything suggests that chimpanzees are remote from the attractor of language and that there is no reason why their species would begin to adopt a form of communication akin to ours. And this reasoning applies to all the species which preceded us. In relation to *Homo erectus*, we stumbled upon an attractor that may have been more powerful, though the phenotype space is so rich in attractors that many others would have been available. There was no necessity in the evolution of *erectus* towards *sapiens*. In any possible rerunning of the film of evolution, it is highly improbable that it would follow the same course.

Proliferation or transformation of species

With reference to Table 6.1, we may wonder why macroevolution, which affects the punctuations of stable equilibria, promotes great proliferations of species, an example of which was presented in the previous chapter with the ancestors of the horse, and why microevolution does not promote speciation. The main reason is related to the size of the major changes which bring on the end of a stable equilibrium. When these changes are large enough, divergent individuals may move to a new niche and no longer be in competition with their conservative parents. This is a situation which favours speciation. Conversely, the rapid improvements selected in the transitional phases of microevolution are unlikely to promote proliferations. In a state of disequilibrium there is little probability that two incompatible innovations of equal value will happen at the same time and give rise to two independent lineages, without one of the latter dominating the other. In a situation of open competition, there is room only for the best.

In nature, changes of species rarely happen on the spot. When the end of a stable equilibrium comes about through the isolation of a small sub-population and genetic drift ensues, speciation is likely. Gould sees this mechanism as the most likely explanation for macroevolutionary change (Gould 1980). The new population, now isolated in a different ecological context, evolves in a direction that moves it away from the parent population until the two sub-species come to occupy separate niches and become genuine species. It is always possible, if this sort of splitting of a population occurs during a rapid phase of open competition, that speciation might come about; but the probability is very low.

The foregoing considerations make it possible to define the conditions for the emergence of language. In discussing the evolution of the human line of descent and more particularly the genesis of our linguistic capacity, what needs to be clarified now is the role of macroevolutionary phenomena and what could perhaps be explained as microevolutionary optimization.

6.3 Macroevolution and microevolution in the emergence of language

A metaphor from economics

Interpreting evolutionary phenomena would be easy if one could always clearly distinguish between macroevolution and microevolution. Any idea about the direction of evolution is profoundly affected by that distinction. In a microevolutionary situation where a particular selection pressure defines an evolutionary direction, there are always changes happening which go in the right direction; and the species evolves rapidly till it reaches a local optimum. At the other extreme of straightforward macroevolution, the species is in a state of lasting equilibrium. There is no selection pressure, hence no prescribed evolutionary direction. The only effect of natural selection is then to keep the species in its state of equilibrium. This state is a stable local optimum, a sort of regional optimum in fact, which could only be disrupted by a significant bifurcation leading in an unforeseeable direction. It is not difficult to imagine an intermediate situation, somewhere between the two extremes, with the presence of selection pressure, but the absence of innovation going in the right direction. The species would then be in an unstable equilibrium.

A metaphor borrowed from economics can help clarify the different situations in which a species may be. Macroevolution resembles a stable economic situation, with demand satisfied and competition keeping companies in a state of equilibrium. If a new demand appears, new companies are created to satisfy it, which is the microevolution situation. The third situation would represent a lasting state of unstable disequilibrium: demand left unsatisfied by inadequate supply. This is a metaphor that will prove valuable in our attempt to define and possibly invalidate quite a few explanations of the emergence of language.

Three lessons from the rapidity of evolution

Several lessons can be learned from the fact that the evolution of a species happens in fits and starts, with phases of rapid evolution separated by long periods when, in the terms of the economic metaphor, supply and demand are in a state of equilibrium.

The first lesson, coinciding with Gould's energetic demonstrations, is that on the macroevolutionary scale there is never any demand left unsatisfied. To be precise, on the scale which takes in the evolution of the whole group of primates, *there is nothing remotely resembling a need to communicate either more or with greater efficacy*. On that scale, genera are in equilibrium, adapted to their ecological niche, and no simple change will help any individuals to have more descendants. We must set aside all the 'stories' which purport to see the genus *Homo* as the arrival point of some trend or other deriving from other families of primates, whether the Pongidae or the Lemurians. With them we must also discard any idea of a regular increase in intelligence or a gradual improvement in the efficiency of intraspecific communication. As Gould has shown (cf. Chapter 5), the illusion of there being a progression comes from a biased description of the evolutionary tree of species.

The second lesson has to do with the rapidity of microevolution. Here what must be discarded are ideas about the great length of time required for the development of bipedalism, mastery of tools, or of phonatory articulation. The evolution of such achievements, insofar as they were subject to selection pressures, must of necessity have been extremely rapid on the geological timescale. Microevolution can do its work in a limited number of generations. Consequently, if changes do not appear where an evolutionist expects to see them, *the reason must be that there was no relevant selection pressure*. This means that the individuals would stand to gain nothing, in terms of reproduction, if they underwent change in the direction supposed by the evolutionist. In particular, anyone who thinks the Neanderthals were unable to articulate the vocalic sounds we can make (Lieberman 1984) must accept the fact that, locally, it was not in the evolutionary interest of individuals of that species to acquire such a capacity.

The third lesson concerns the supposed obstacles to the evolution of advantageous forms. Many explanations of the emergence of language amount to a demonstration of how the coming of a new characteristic 'unlocked' the process leading to the appearance of spoken communication. Any such explanation could only make sense within the intermediate situation somewhere between macroevolution and microevolution: the presence of a selection pressure, but a lasting absence of any 'supply' that might respond to it. However, the four conditions in which such a situation might come about are very restrictive. The event responsible for restarting the evolutionary process must appear unlikely; it must have a causal effect on the restarting of the process; there must be no more likely option that might have played the same role; and the evolution following from it must be rapid. As far as language is concerned, *none of the explanations of this kind that have been put forward passes all four of these tests.* Let us inspect some examples.

Evolution is never 'restrained'

Is there any force in the argument that language is a case of 'locked' microevolution, a situation of unsatisfied demand being 'unlocked' by some more or less fortuitous evolutionary event such as the lowering of the larynx, bipedalism, or the advent of this or that intellectual capacity? Constraints of embryogenesis rule out some of the conceivable variations, for example that there could be insects with five or seven legs. This fact is sometimes used to argue for evolution that is directed but restrained by a lack of supply going in the right direction. Though this is an argument that has been abundantly exploited in consideration of language, closer inspection of this kind of hypothesis shows that the scenarios described lose much of their persuasive force.

Some authors take the view that the lowering of the larynx was a mechanism enabling the production of the sounds of language and thereby the emergence of language itself (Savage-Rumbaugh and Lewin 1994). It is hard to see, though, what might be said to have been unlikely in this transformation, that is to say what might have made it an evolutionarily improbable achievement. The changes leading to an increase in the size of the larynx are gradual; and if there had been the slightest selection pressure in that direction, why was there no earlier evolution towards an increase in size of the larynx among our predecessors the hominids or even among apes? Conversely, the fact that such an increase in size did not happen casts serious doubt on whether there was selection pressure in the direction of the production of vocalic sounds. So the argument that we have language because of an increase in the size of the larynx turns out to be a specious one. The true state of affairs is quite clearly the opposite: one can see how the emergence of language could have created selection pressure for the production of vocalic sounds, but what is not clear is both why the ability to produce them would have spontaneously appeared and how that ability might have 'unlocked' a process of emergence of language just waiting to happen. Nor is there anything to be gained by supporting this argument with another based on the alleged slowness of evolution:

It seems quite reasonable to suppose, as we have seen, that the transformation which was crucial for the acquisition of speech—the lowering of the larynx—may date back to ancestors of ours who lived at least 200,000 years ago. This does not mean of course that Eve's descendants became Enrico Carusos and Maria Callases overnight. It must have needed at least a good 160,000 years for the voice apparatus to attain its present conformation and in particular for the brain centres in charge of speech to become properly organized. It was not until then that true language could have developed, giving human beings the means whereby they might create a culture and build a civilization. (de Duve 1995: 403)

That is not evolution's way. When selection pressure exists, a quantitative alteration such as the lowering of the larynx would take nothing like 160,000 years, which would make about 8,000 generations. The process of optimization via selection happens much more quickly. So it is hard to make the argument that the lowering of the larynx is a causal factor in the appearance of language. Once again, if language was as advantageous for individuals as we are led to believe, why should its appearance have had to await such a development? A lowered larynx could facilitate the utterance and control of powerful vocalic sounds, but such abilities are neither necessary nor sufficient for the development of language. If selection pressure towards a digital communication system was already present, it could have been satisfied in many ways, through gestures or sounds, even without vocalic sounds of a musical type.[3]

For reasons that are similar, many of the factors mentioned by various authors as explanations of the onset of an evolutionary process leading to language are unacceptable at face value. These include the influence of bipedalism (Aiello 1996: 279), appropriate development of the vocal tract (Savage-Rumbaugh and Lewin 1994: 249), the emergence of the ability to handle tools (Leroy-Gourhan 1965), increasing immaturity in human neonates (Aiello 1996: 280), the appearance of a mimetic capacity (Donald 1998: 64), increase in intelligence (Darwin 1871), increase in social intelligence (Worden 1998), or a growth in the size of groups (Dunbar 1996).

---

[3] Vocalic sounds, like musical sounds, are periodic.

Bipedalism, for instance, is argued to be the cause of the lowering of the larynx, which then caused the appearance of language (Aiello 1996). But can it be believed that selection pressure towards more effective communication could remain unsatisfied for a long time, waiting until a fortuitous growth in the size of the larynx made for a functional vocal tract? Bipedalism is also purported to have freed the hands, thus giving hominids the opportunity to start using tools, then to form concepts, and eventually to communicate them (Leroy-Gourhan 1965; Aiello 1996). If each of the links in this chain was of the slightest advantage, why would it have had to wait for the preceding one to happen? The evidence seems to lead to very different conclusions. One need only look at the delicate manual achievements of the great apes (Matsuzawa 1994) to realize that bipedalism has nothing to do with it. In transforming two of our hands into feet, it certainly neither created nor facilitated the skills required to use tools, let alone the ability to exchange small talk with our fellows. Equally mistaken is the idea that the great apes have not had time to develop sufficient ability to form concepts and find a way to communicate them, given that when there is selection pressure the process of evolution is a rapid one.

Another argument used by Leslie Aiello is the immaturity of new-born humans, a consequence, she says, of the narrowing of the pelvis, itself a result of bipedalism: the brain of a child forced by mechanical reasons to be born when less mature was exposed to a rich environment while it was still rapidly growing and developing, which would have created very great selection pressure for its evolution (Aiello 1996: 280). Here, though, the problem lies in imagining any evolutionary mechanism capable of bringing to bear the sort of selection pressure alleged by Aiello. She argues that, given a context in which hominids' brains had to cope very early with a wealth of information, greater brain size would result in the birth of more children. Unfortunately, Aiello provides no evidence that would enable us to grasp this link between cause and effect. The argument can be turned back to front to support the opposite impression, namely that new-born babies with a large brain might actually be a handicap for a bipedal species. If there really was selection pressure for increased brain size, it must have had little to do with bipedalism.

The same flaw can be seen in the explanation of language by mimesis (Donald 1998), that remarkable ability we have of being able to imitate the actions of our fellows. If this skill of reproducing someone else's behaviour had really been of advantage, why did it not develop sooner? Why should communication, also presented as advantageous, have had to wait for the development of an imitative ability? Any hypothesis suggesting that the earliest language acts were done by parroting apes is bound to shed little light on the real reasons for the emergence of language.

In the previous chapter we dealt with the idea, dating from Darwin himself, that language was an automatic consequence of intelligence. Apart from the fact that it merely replaces the mystery of the emergence of language with the mystery of the emergence of intelligence, it too raises several difficulties. The main one of these is that the intelligence of individuals has no bearing upon whether or not it is in their interest to exchange information. No aptitude for language will ever develop in a system of agents, even very intelligent agents, if the ones supplying the useful information end up less advantaged than the ones who simply take advantage of the information supplied. It stands to reason that general intelligence, to which Darwin was referring, cannot be the sole factor in any explanation of the emergence of language. So, what about social intelligence?

According to Robert Worden, social intelligence was one of the preadaptations which led at little cost to the beginnings of language. Social intelligence is what enables any person engaging in group interactions to understand the intentions or even the ulterior motives of others. As we know, higher primates are all quite gifted in the arts of foreseeing the acts of their fellows and planning their own interactions (de Waal 1982). Worden's view is that relations between social roles show all the richness of relations between the linguistic components of sentences in language (Worden 1998), a position that we have already had occasion to question (see Chapter 5.4). At best, such a preadaptation might give greater plausibility to the appearance of language as we know it rather than the appearance of some other mode of communication, but it cannot explain why people communicate. To have an accurate perception of social relations is one thing; to communicate information, whether of a social nature or not, is quite another.

The main purpose of this search for preadaptations as a way of explaining language, whether concerning the lowering of the larynx, imitative abilities, skill with making tools, general intelligence, or social intelligence, is to identify whatever mechanisms may have facilitated the beginnings of language. But none of these alleged preadaptations has a clear causal effect on the promotion of a selective process in favour of language. Simply stated, no perfected larynx is going to induce speech in someone who has nothing to say or in whose interest it is to remain silent. Conversely, once it was in the evolutionary interest of hominids to communicate with each other, for reasons that we have not yet discussed, the only function of any possible preadaptations was to switch evolution in some definite direction.

Those who stress the importance of such preadaptations always base their arguments on the same premise: they see communication of the human type as being something useful by definition but hard to achieve. That is to say, they try to adopt a position somewhere between macroevolution and microevolution, where there could be a selection pressure in favour of language that remains unfulfilled because of the limited range of morphological changes available. However, this type of hypothesis is extremely improbable. There is no reason why the advent of an open digital communication code should present a major difficulty if one presupposes some selection pressure such as the need to communicate precise and factual information. After all, nature has already produced several systems of this type, such as the singing of certain birds, the immune system, or the transmission of heredity through genes. The real question is how selection pressure to communicate a variety of facts about the world could arise. In other words, what must be determined is the reasons why language became advantageous for individuals when it had not been advantageous before.

6.4 What's the point of communicating?

Most attempts to explain the emergence of language address the wrong question. What is required is not to find out how protohumans contrived to communicate with each other, but to understand why our ancestors contrived to leave more children through communicating with each other. It is, of course, possible to see a link between humans' new acquisitions and language: bipedalism, which may have favoured a lowering of the larynx; the low larynx, which may have altered our abilities in phonation; intelligence, which may be linked to a capacity for semantic representation, etc. But what is not apparent is a link between these evolutionary events and any unlocking of the microevolutionary process that might have led to language. What is not self-evident, if the appearance of language was advantageous, is the reason why, in order for it to become a possibility, it should have had to wait for these other events. This is not to say that any and every potential selection pressure is automatically satisfied in nature, but merely that, in the case of language, any scenario premissed on the appearance of bipedalism, the use of tools, or the lowering of the larynx as ways of accounting for the appearance of a capacity for communicating which was already all but present misses the point, which is to explain why that capacity for communicating did not manage to come to pass in some other way.

The most fundamental question, which is not addressed in such scenarios, still remains to be answered: what type of selection pressure can explain why human beings communicate with such intensity? Any search for conditions which might have first delayed, then unlocked the corresponding evolutionary process is secondary, not to say absurd, if uninformed by a knowledge of why it is advantageous for individuals to communicate information to their fellows. The real question has therefore a macroevolutionary focus. In our economic metaphor, what must be understood is how a new demand could have appeared and what it consisted of, rather than which historical accidents might have delayed the supply which eventually satisfied it. The reasons for the emergence of language are mysterious enough to invalidate sketchy hypotheses such as analogies between language and the use of tools or between language and social intelligence. Even if such analogies can appear relevant with hindsight, they cannot possibly suffice to solve the enigma of the appearance in our lineage of the elaborate communication behaviour that we indulge in for hours every day.

If we are to determine the new role that language played for the ancestors of humans, that it could not play for other primates, we would do well to begin with its structure. Language, like most characteristics of life, is the outcome of microevolution. So it contains locally optimal aspects. Its optimality corresponds to a biological function; and studying its structure can inform us about that function. In Part II we shall inspect various aspects of the structure of language, with a view to determining in each case whether they are fitted to the performing of a precise biological function.

PART II

The functional anatomy of speech

Introduction to Part II

In an area of study like medecine, functional questions have always accompanied, and at times taken precedence over, structural questions. In the early nineteenth century, Franz Josef Gall found it easy to allot a function to each zone of the cortex. The same holds good for the philosophical tradition. Descartes had an idea about the function of the conarium (pineal gland). It is astonishing that language should be the exception. Despite the fact that, over the last century, language as a system has been the subject of thorough structural studies, the question of the functional role of the entities defined and described by linguists has often been skimped. Examples are the stressing of syllables or case marking which, though described in depth, have rarely been inspected by anyone interested in the way they function within language considered as a vehicle of communication.

If we wish to comprehend the reason why language evolved, we need to be able to understand its biological function. With that in mind, it is surely best to try to link in detail structural elements of language with their functions. It is not always easy to define a function and can often be a risky exercise. This is why we shall sometimes do no more than raise the question, while requiring that there should be a necessary fit between structure and function. In this Part II, we shall consider successively some aspects of phonology, syntax, and semantics, and the finding will be that many features of language do not owe their existence to chance. During this consideration, we shall be more and more rudely reminded of the flimsiness of the traditional idea of language as a simple means of exchange of information among human beings.

7 Putting sounds together

Each of us has some degree of awareness of the sounds we use in speaking our own language; and this awareness is heightened in certain societies by the use they make of alphabetical script. When a child or a foreigner makes a mistake of pronunciation, we not only notice it in a reflex way but are able to analyse and correct it. For instance, if a German friend pronounces *petit enfant* without making the liaison by sounding the final *t* of *petit*, or pronounces *batch* instead of *badge*, we are aware of the mistake and can conceptualize it as a lack of liaison or a difficulty with pronouncing the sound 'ge' [ʒ] in the context of the word *badge*. We are also capable of identifying regional accents, recognizing them from clues which are at times minute. Every language and every accent has its own sound system governed by strict laws. The slightest departure from these rules reveals a speaker to be an outsider, somebody who was not immersed in the local linguistic environment as a child. What is the nature of these phonetic laws? Are they really laws, and if so, do they have a biological function?

7.1 The articulatory gestures of language

In Molière's *Le Bourgeois Gentilhomme* (1670), there is a celebrated lesson in phonology:

PHILOSOPHY MASTER: Let me tell you that letters are divided into vowels, called vowels because they express what we call the voices, and consonants, called consonants because they sound with the vowels and serve solely to mark the divers articulations of the voices. There are five vowels or voices: A, E, I, O, and U.
M. JOURDAIN: I grasp all that.
PHILOSOPHY MASTER: The vowel A is formed by opening wide one's mouth: A. M. JOURDAIN: A. A. Yes.

PHILOSOPHY MASTER: The vowel E is formed by bringing one's lower jaw close to one's upper jaw: A, E.

M. JOURDAIN: A, E, A, E. Upon my soul, yes, indeed! My, what a fine thing!

PHILOSOPHY MASTER: And the vowel I is formed by bringing one's jaws even closer to each other and sending the corners of one's mouth towards one's ears: A, E, I.

M. JOURDAIN: A, E, I, I, I, I. Why, 'tis true! Isn't knowledge a wonderful thing?

PHILOSOPHY MASTER: The vowel O is formed by parting one's jaws and bringing the corners of one's two lips together, the upper and the lower: O.

M. JOURDAIN: O, O. Never was a truer word spoken! A, E, I, O, I, O. How marvellous! I, O, I, O.

PHILOSOPHY MASTER: The opening of one's mouth forms a little circle which has the shape of an O.

M. JOURDAIN: O, O, O. You're right! O. My, what a fine thing it is to know things!

PHILOSOPHY MASTER: The vowel U is formed by almost closing one's teeth but not quite, while pushing out both one's lips and bringing them also quite close together but without letting them touch: U.

M. JOURDAIN: U, U. Exactly as you said! U.

PHILOSOPHY MASTER: Your two lips protrude as though you were making a face. And it is a fact that, should you ever wish to make a face at somebody and insult him, all you have to do is say U at him.

M. JOURDAIN: U, U. That is true. Oh dear, had I studied when I was younger, I too could have known all that.

Monsieur Jourdain's phonetics lesson raises the question of the basic constituants of language. Should we analyse language in terms of vowels and consonants or should we begin with more fundamental elements such as articulatory gestures? If vowels and consonants, the elementary sounds of language, are defined by articulatory gestures, then they cannot be considered as the primary building blocks of language. This is an important question. One of the most basic properties of language is that it is a productive digital system that relies on a combinatorial mechanism (cf. Chapter 1). If we are to understand this mechanism and see clearly what may have motivated its appearance in the history of our species, then the most essential knowledge we can have is knowledge of the type of entity on which it functions. And combining articulatory gestures is not the same thing as combining sounds.

In reaction against the traditional view that phonemes are the atomic particles of language, some linguists argue from evidence that appears to mean that articulatory gestures came first. Human vocal organs have evolved into a sort of polyphonic instrument that we can play by availing ourselves of its different possible channels (Lindblom 1998). Evolution has transformed the straight and inflexible vocal tract of primates into a curved conduit containing several parts which can work independently of each other. In particular, the tongue muscle has become very versatile, offering us three degrees of freedom, with the relatively independent movements of the rear part, situated in the throat, the tongue body with its relation to the palate, and the tip or blade which can make contact with the teeth. It is the independent and parallel control over the various elements of our vocal apparatus that enables us to converse at a rate of ten to fifteen phonemes a second, which makes about 150 words a minute. Some authors argue that description in terms of articulatory gestures is more economical than description in terms of phonemic components. For instance, the babbling of infants is rather confusing if seen from a strictly phonetic standpoint, whereas it takes on new significance if analysed in terms of articulatory gestures. A child of fifteen months who tries to repeat the word *pen* may produce a range of words as phonetically diverse as *mant-e, mbo, bah,* and *buan,* which sound as though they have no relation to each other or to the target word *pen.* However, analysis of the child's articulatory gestures shows that they are close to those required by the pronunciation of *pen*: closing the lips, opening the glottis, raising the tip of the tongue, alveolar closure, and lowering the soft palate (Studdert-Kennedy 1998). The main difference is that infants may get the sequence of articulatory gestures in the wrong order: if they try, for instance, to say the initial [pʰ] of *pen* by closing the lips, opening the glottis, and raising the soft palate, they produce the voiced *mb* to be heard in *mbu.*

According to Michael Studdert-Kennedy, phonetic descriptions can help to define but not to explain mistakes of pronunciation. What the child is trying to reproduce is not a sound but a correct combination of elementary articulatory gestures. By way of justification of this change of perspective from the traditional concept of a phonetic performance, various writers suggest that our representation of the sounds of our language is not a phonological one, but is made up from the range of different motor components required for the production of the sounds. Just as we can apprehend the bodily postures of people and are able to imitate them immediately by controlling our muscles, we appear to be able to conceive of others' articulatory gestures. The truest atoms of language might therefore be elementary articulatory gestures such as closing the lips or touching the palate with the tip of the tongue. Our ancestors might have evolved in a way that enabled them to have representations of articulatory configurations and to reproduce them, but not to have representations of phonemes and the corresponding ability to reproduce them. This, however, is an idea that we cannot accept holus bolus.

7.2 Was language gestural before it became oral?

In the evolutionary analysis of some authors who conceive of language as a combination of articulatory gestures, what is stressed is the skills of the vocal apparatus and the human aptitude for motor imitation. This can lead to an explanation of the emergence of language which draws an analogy between the ability to combine articulatory gestures and the ability to combine the movements used, for example, in the making of tools. In Chapter 6 we saw Leroy-Gourhan make some such link between words and tools. Or we might try to see articulated language as a by-product of some pre-existing sign language: if language is an outcome of an ability to combine elementary motor skills, then it may matter little whether it makes use of movements of the hands or of the vocal apparatus. There is certainly no shortage of evidence apparently supporting this idea of gestural origins, at first manual, then articulatory: the proximity between cortical areas controlling the right hand and Broca's area; the spontaneous movements which are a systematic accompaniment to speech; the ability of the deaf to express themselves by sign language; the spontaneous ability of us all to communicate through signs at times when verbal communication is not possible; the way we use mime, etc. If the roots of language lie in the ability to combine elementary motor components, there would be nothing surprising or fortuitous in the prevalence and range of these abilities.

An apparently decisive argument in favour of seeing gestural communication as a precursor of oral communication can be drawn from the naturally iconic and figurative quality of manual signals. There is a prima facie difficulty in accepting that signs as abstract as sounds could have been straightforwardly associated with concrete concepts. So there is something attractive in the hypothesis of there having been a primitive stage of language as gesture and movement, because it seems to facilitate the step from the signified to the signifier (Corballis 1991: 229). Gestures, signing, or mime might have naturally described concrete realities; and words could gradually have supplemented them when it came to the expression of more abstract meanings. After all, work done on language disorders in the deaf seems to support the idea that our faculty of language is independent of the vehicle used, whether it be oral or gestural (Hickok, Bellugi, and Klima 1998). This could lead to the conclusion that, if there was a transfer from gesture to word, this step could have been taken without loss of the benefit of the initial phase, the ability to combine gestures or movements. Upon closer inspection, though, it is clear that this hypothesis raises several problems and that the analogies it posits are superficial.

First of all, we must make a distinction between the spontaneous movements which accompany speech and sign language as used by the deaf. They are, in fact, two completely different behaviours: movements accompanying speech are unconscious, obligatory, and non-arbitrary, used solely in conjunction with spoken language; whereas the signs used by the deaf are intentional, conscious, and mostly arbitrary. If we want to find a precursor of verbal language, the only suitable candidate becomes this coded and self-sufficient mode of sign language used among the deaf. But there are plenty of arguments against this derivation of language, some of which are set forth by Peter MacNeilage (MacNeilage 1998). For one thing, if sign language represents a kind of behavioural fossil, our present behaviour should have retained some traces of it; yet this is not the case. Coded sign language arises only in very particular conditions, when deaf children are being brought up together; deaf children being brought up separately do not develop it spontaneously to make themselves understood by people. Normal individuals do not spontaneously use it to communicate among themselves[1] or with deaf children. The fact that the use of sign language is possible, but that it never arises spontaneously in the course of normal everyday life, does cast doubt on the notion that at some time in the more or less distant past our ancestors relied on a code of communication exclusively made of signs. If they had, the complete

---

[1] Reference is sometimes made to sign language as used for example in bargaining or sending messages among stockbrokers, but these codes are of very limited semantic scope, quite unlike anything one expects from a vehicle of linguistic expression. The meagreness of them (e.g. the underwater code used by divers) is actually an argument against the existence of any gestural competence peculiar to communication.

disappearance of such a code would be a mystery. A second problem raised by MacNeilage concerns the possibility that a signing ability was transferred to an articulatory one:

It is difficult to imagine the nature of the selection pressures that could transfer some *abstract* capability of one motor system, such as the sequencing capability independent of what is being sequenced, from one set of brain loci to another. (MacNeilage 1998: 232)

MacNeilage goes on to point out the impossibility of any direct gesture-to-gesture translation between the manual modality and the oral modality, the shape, orientation, and movement of the hand bearing no plausible relation to any of the motor controls for voicing consonants or the articulatory gestures required for positioning the tongue or the lips. Iconic gestures in the two modalities refer to different entities in the world, sign language describing mainly forms and voice imitating sounds. A transfer from one modality to the other would therefore have been accompanied by a radical shift in the range of meanings conveyed iconically. MacNeilage then argues that deaf infants exposed to sign language show no greater propensity to sign manually than do normal infants, though they do show a 'tendency to make longer series of rhythmic repetitive movements' (MacNeilage 1998: 236). One might be tempted to see this as an analogue of the babbling of normal infants, which could support the idea of a development of language capacity regardless of the modality through which it is expressed. However, although repetition is basic to articulatory modulation of the voice, with its alternation between opening and closing of the oral cavity, these very periodic features are absent from any system of signing. Hence, if babbling does have a role to play in the acquisition of language, it is restricted to the oral mode. Once again, true equivalence between the two modes is lacking. All this is evidence against the argument that there is something primal in the manual-visual channel. Human language probably developed from the outset through a principal focus on the vocal-auditory channel, with complementary support from the manual modality. Not that this in any way lessens the importance of gesture and movement in communication; their spontaneous use as an accompaniment to language is an integral part of our ways of communicating (McNeill 1992: 19), not a behavioural fossil, a vestige of an ancient and obsolete system of communication.

7.3 The atoms of language: gestures or phonemes?

The German linguist Wilhelm von Humboldt is generally credited with having been the first to identify and describe the combinatorial mechanisms whereby language makes infinite use of finite resources. This is the general principle, also applicable to chemistry or biology, of digital combination, which involves the existence of invariable particles which, like atoms in matter, are in a state of ceaseless rearrangement and give the infinite variety of the world about us. If language really does have this combinatorial character, we should expect to be able to identify quite unambiguously the atoms of linguistic chemistry, which must have a universal existence. What then are the atoms of language? We have just raised the possibility that they might be articulatory gestures, though there is a standard and rather intuitive interpretation according to which it is phonemes that fulfil this role. Actually, there is something problematical in referring to either of them as atoms, since neither articulatory gestures nor the sounds of language are invariable. It is extremely difficult for any speaker to say a single sentence twice in exactly the same way; and of course different speakers make for further differences. There is a continuum of variability in articulation and the sounds it produces. The idea of isolating invariable elements, whether they be the most basic articulatory gestures or phonemes, may seem more like an idealized approximation made up to suit the purposes of linguists. Here I shall attempt to show that this is not the case and that language is a genuine Humboldtian system, a kind of phonetic chemistry combining true atoms.

Traditional analysis of language takes as its starting point the hearer's perspective, by seeking distinctive features in words, the minimal clues which make a native speaker either identify this word rather than that or even hear a non-word. The definition of phonemes in particular derives from this way of thinking. The discrete and non-gradual nature of the components of language inheres in language itself. The lack of phonetic gradation between pairs like *peer* and *beer* or French *pierre* and *bière* is not something ordained by linguists (Martinet 1967: 22; Mehler and Dupoux 1990: 232). Native speakers will hear one or other of these words, but never a mixture of both or anything like an intermediary word. This is what obliges us to recognize the discrete and combinatorial character of language. Speakers act essentially not by shaping a malleable substance of sound but by assembling things. They are builders rather than sculptors.[2] The fact that they build with bricks that are variable is no drawback, as long as the variability of them is properly recognized. If language were not combinatorial, any variation in pronunciation would entail a change of meaning; but the fact that it *is* combinatorial accommodates a measure of variability in its basic elements, and this both helps it to resist deformations and offers the possibility of modulation. If one experiments with saying *beer* ten times in a row, giving the phonemes ten different lengths or intensities or changing the mode of articulation in ways that stress shades of insistence, despair, or exclamation, the word remains exactly the same word. But if we introduce the slightest alteration, turning the initial *b* into a *p*, say, then we have a different word. This behaviour is typical of digital combinatorial systems with contained variability and abrupt transitions (cf. Chapter 1).

What needs to be determined is whether the combinatorial system manipulates phonemes, standard articulatory gestures, or some other elementary feature. The functioning of articulatory gestures is more detailed than that of phonemes. Each vowel or consonant may be analysed into a set of these gestures. Pronunciation of the phoneme *p*, for instance, requires momentary closing of the lips and, to prevent the vocal cords from vibrating, also of the glottis. However, articulatory analysis is often too detailed, as anybody can see by trying to pronounce a vowel such as *a*, for example, while holding a pencil crosswise in the mouth: the sound is perfectly identifiable as a vowel, even though the articulatory gestures are unusual. This little experiment would appear to show that articulatory gestures represent a means to an end; and it is an end that is different in nature from them. Björn Lindblom (Lindblom 1998) makes a comparison between our vocal apparatus and a polyphonic instrument, a simile we may extrapolate a little. Musical instruments like the guitar, lute, or banjo offer the possibility of using different fingering to produce the same note. There are pieces of music which are set out on the conventional pattern, with the notes on a score; but there are others which are printed in the form of a fingering chart or tablature. In terms of the musical analogy, we need to know whether our idea of language is more like a score or a tablature. On the latter it is very difficult to establish relations between the

---

[2] There are of course aspects of phonology for which this does not hold true, for instance intonation, in which there can be gradual variation.

sounds: it is not easy to see when a passage for guitar and banjo is exactly the same, and it is difficult to transpose a piece by shifting it up a tone,[3] things that are much more straightforward when the music is noted on a conventional stave. If our capacity for language, as regards pronunciation, is to be understood in exclusively articulatory terms, which corresponds to the tablature in the analogy, then certain relations between sounds become implicitly complex.

At first sight, the question whether the system of language should be defined in terms of articulations or of sounds appears to be a difficult one. Something of this may be seen from a few examples. In the two words *rain* and *train*, the *r* does not stand for the same sound; nor is it made by the same articulatory gesture. However, we are dealing not with two different phonemes, but with what are called allophones of the same phoneme. By definition, two phonemes are enough to distinguish two words from one another. That, though, is not the case with *rain* and *train*, since no two English words are distinguished only by the difference in pronunciation of the phoneme *r*. This shows the limitations of any description in terms of phonemes that takes no account of allophones. Similarly, in French, the historical replacement of the rolled *r* by the uvular variety cannot be defined in purely phonemic terms. Another example is the 'rule' that constrains successions of certain phonemes, such as French *b* followed by *s*, *t* followed by *z*, *g* followed by *s*, or *z* followed by p. It seems to oblige French-speakers to opt either for *ob̲zerver* or *op̲server*, *t̲sar* or *d̲zar*, *Straz̲bourg* or *Strasp̲ourg*. If expressed in phonetic terms, there is nothing simple about the rule, as all possible sequences of incompatible consonants must be enumerated: *pz*, *ds*, *kz*, *vt*, etc. But if defined in terms closer to the articulatory reality, it can be expressed more concisely as a constraint on any sequence of two consonants, one of which is voiced (e.g. *b*, *d*, *z*, *g*, *v*) and the other unvoiced (e.g. *p*, *t*, *s*, *k*, *f*).[4] This constraint is very marked in a language like French; and as it appears to result from a mechanical impediment (the slow opening of the glottis), perhaps it is an effect inherent in the functioning of the vocal organs rather than a rule of phonology as such. Whatever the case may be, it is a constraint that is

---

[3] Transposition requires changes of fingering because of the notes played on open strings, and the tablature must be completely recast.

[4] This constraint thus stated facilitates definition of formation of plural endings in English: *cat/cat[s]*, *judge/judg[iz]*, *slave/slave[z]*.

defined clearly by the voiced/unvoiced contrast, which is a feature belonging to articulation. The same goes for many phonological phenomena. In fact, most phonological rules are defined with a focus on articulatory movements. For example, Noam Chomsky and Morris Halle use strictly articulatory terms to define the thirty-odd distinctive features of their phonological theory:

Vocalic sounds are produced with an *oral* cavity configuration in which the most radical constriction does not exceed that found in the high vowels [i] and [u] and with vocal cords that are positioned so as to allow spontaneous voicing. ... Coronal sounds are produced with the blade of the tongue raised from its neutral position. (Chomsky and Halle 1968: 302)

It might appear therefore that the only useful terms for describing phonological phenomena are those related to articulation. That, however, is not quite the case. It should be noted first of all that some of the features focused on by linguists are not elementary from an articulatory point of view. The description of vocalic sounds just quoted, for instance, mentions both the vocal cords and the configuration of the oral cavity. Secondly, a more fundamental point is that some distinctions more clearly appertain to the ear than to the mouth, as in the case of vowels. Table 7.1 shows that the number of vowels used in different languages is quite variable, ranging from three to fifteen (the figures relate to vowel qualities and ignore phonemic variations such as nasalization or length). The study by Crothers focused on 209 languages, Maddieson's on 317. A good number of languages have five basic vowels, though a not negligible number have only three, for example Kabardian, spoken near the Black Sea, Múra, an Amazonian language, and Alabama, a northern Amerindian language. The vowels used in these minimal vocalic systems are [a], [i], and [u]. These three vowels are found respectively in 88 per cent, 92 per cent, and 84 per cent of the languages in Maddieson's study. Languages containing four to six vowels use also [ɛ], [ɔ], and a central *i* [ɨ], intermediate between [u] and [i]. The vowels [e] and [o] are used only in systems which have at least seven. This relative universality of vocalic systems cannot be entirely explained in strictly articulatory terms. It can, however, be very neatly explained by recourse to acoustical evidence.

Figure 7.1 shows the distribution of the vowels just mentioned in relation to their first two formants. Vowels being vibratory sounds, the formants are the resonant peaks in the frequency spectrum, which enable

TABLE 7.1 *Distribution of languages according to number of vowels*

Number of vowels	% of languages studied (Crothers 1978)	% of languages studied (Maddieson 1984)
3	11%	5%
4	11%	9%
5	29%	31%
6	17%	19%
7	12%	15%
8		5%
9	3%	8%
10		5%
11 or more		3%

the ear to distinguish them. As the figure shows, the vowels [a], [i], and [u] are the farthest apart. It has been demonstrated that these vowels are the most distinct that the phonatory apparatus can utter simply. It is also clear that vowels such as [ɛ], [ɔ], and [ø] are very well placed to be distinguished from the others. Once it has been pointed out, this preference of languages for distinct vowels seems obvious. There would, however, be nothing obvious about it if the comparison were made on purely articulatory evidence. For instance, the parting of the jaws in the pronunciation of [i] (or [o]) makes for a very slight acoustical contrast. Linguistic systems have become stabilized about sets of clearly distinct vowels. The articulatory system, through being learned, has had to adapt to these constraints. In short, the vowels of any particular language exist in their own right, which cannot be deduced merely from articulatory constraints. In terms of the musical analogy, vocalic contrast translates more naturally as a score than as a tablature.

The example of vowels brings to light something bothersome at first sight. If the basis of language is a combinatorial system of sounds or of elementary articulatory gestures, one might expect that there would be a measure of universality in such a system. Yet some vowels are completely unknown to speakers of different languages, as can be seen for instance in the difficulty some English-speakers have in pronouncing a French *u* ([y]). It would appear therefore that the basic atoms of different phonetic

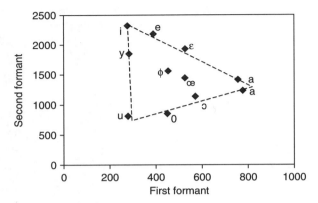

Fɪɢ. 7.1 Distribution of the main French vowels, spoken by a male voice, according to their first two formants.

systems are in part the outcome of a learning process. This would mean that not only the combinatorial system of language itself is learned, but also the elements combined, whether they are phonemes or articulatory gestures. Does it follow from this that the only biological basis for the phonology of language consists of undefined articulatory constraints which set a limit to the range of sounds we are able to utter? If so, it would be futile to speculate about how natural selection might have affected the genesis of the phonological combinatorial system. In fact, how important biology was can become clearer only when we have a definition of the respective contributions of cultural emergence and the predispositions of individuals.

7.4 Phonological structuring of languages

The variability of phonological systems must make us wonder how important biology was in the shaping of them. It is not just that phonemes and the rules constraining their sequences vary widely from one language to another; there is also the fact that phonological aspects which are widespread, such as the prevalence of the vowel system [a], [i], and [u], seem to be explainable by the general constraints on our powers of auditory discrimination and speech organs. Some authors have shown how a consideration of constraints on acoustical discrimination and constraints on ease of articulation can produce a vowel system close to the one shown in Figure 7.1 (Carré 1996; Lindblom 1998). Their findings include the fact that languages which use few vowels tend to use those which are easiest to make. By simulating the idea of articulatory cost with a simple model of the vocal apparatus, they explain why vowels that are articulatorily more complex, such as the breathy *a* [a̤] or the creaky *o* [o̰], which give excellent acoustical contrast, are not used in languages with few vowels. Lindblom's basic working hypothesis is that the phonology of a language is a system in which everything is connected. In particular, some of the articulatory mechanisms used for making a phoneme may be reused for making a different phoneme, as happens for example in French with the four nasal vowels ([œ̃], [ɔ̃], [ɛ̃], [ã]), as heard in *un bon vin blanc*,[5] which are produced by the same articulatory gestures as the respective unnasalized vowels ([œ], [ɔ], [ɛ], [a]). Lindblom takes account of these articulatory relationships in estimating not the cost of the phonemes taken singly, but the cost of the phonemic system as a whole. Carré also shows the necessary nature of the simplest vowel systems, going solely on the notional ease of production of the sounds (modelling the larynx with a simple adaptable tube) and on the physical contrast between the signals, ignoring the real physiology of the organs of production and perception of sound. From such studies we may conclude that by and large the vowel systems of human languages are locally optimal as compromises between economy of articulation and ease of discrimination. The mechanism that allows this optimization remains to be seen.[6]

At first sight it might be thought that optimization is entirely the outcome of cultural evolution. The effects of random historical change involving word borrowing, phonetic drift, and even trendyism, tend to make languages diverge in their phonologies. However, along with these centrifugal forces, other forces (the need for people to understand each other; the requirement for easy learning by children of the phonetic system of their language) work towards a locally optimal system. Articulations

---

[5] The phoneme pronounced in *un* is non-existent in certain accents spoken notably in the Paris region.

[6] The meaning of the concept of local optimality is identical here to the meaning it had in the chapters dealing with the evolution of species. In this context, it is largely unrelated to Paul Smolensky's and Alan Prince's theory of optimality, according to which a sequence of phonemes must be optimal with respect to a set of constraints (Prince and Smolensky 1993).

that are too complex are gradually simplified or distinctions that make for insufficient discrimination are clarified, unless that would result in lexical confusion. For instance, in standard French pronunciation, the difference between [a] as in *patte* and [ɑ] as in *pâte* is lessening. Conversely, some sound shading may be introduced to stress a contrast. This may be the case in French with the [ŋ] of *camping* or the [dʒ] of *gin*, both sounds once borrowed from English and still surviving. By means of such changes, languages may be achieving a constantly renewed compromise, a type of dynamic equilibrium, between their centrifugal forces and systemically cohesive forces. This could mean that each of them has reached a local optimum, the emerging consequence of the need for intercomprehensibility among speakers and the constraints of production. Such adaptability of languages would leave no apparent role for biology to play.

There is something tempting in the idea that language is merely a closed system entirely ruled by its own internal laws. An approach like this has proved to be fruitful in the context of structuralism as applied to linguistics. It is also possible to interpret the way languages evolve and adapt their phonetic arrangements into locally optimal systems as another effect of internal adjustment rules. But if one considers such a system from the outside, the question that must be answered is what enables it to exist. Languages stand on a biological substratum; and any attempt to understand the reasons why they emerged during the prehistory of humanity should also attempt to identify that substratum. The ability of human beings to produce sounds that make effective communication possible depends on three different adaptive mechanisms: biological evolution by natural selection; cultural evolution; individual learning. A systemic approach often leads to the conclusion that these mechanisms are independent of one another, which is not the case. The effects of natural selection are both direct and indirect. People have the ability to utter sounds that are clear and distinct because the voice apparatus of their ancestors, differing in this from other primates, was directly selected for that ability. But natural selection has also endowed us with the ability to learn linguistic sounds and to assemble them in certain ways; and it is this ability which, indirectly, frames and directs diachronic change in languages. It is obvious that no language can ever include elements that could not be pronounced or that children could never learn. Slightly less obvious, though of equal importance, is the fact that the organization of a language cannot be based on any randomly arrived at phonological structure. In what follows I suggest that what we have is a predisposition to use phonological structures such as syllables. If one accepts this line of argument, the biology of our species does not determine the language we speak; but it does determine in large measure what a language can be.

7.5 Mental structures underlying the assemblies of sounds

All speakers are more or less aware of the existence of regularities in their native language. Any English-speaker, for instance, will recognize the following corresponding features (Durand 1990: 114): *divine/divinity*; *crucify/crucifixion*; *satire/satiric*; *sane/sanity*; *abstain/abstention*; *volcano/ volcanic*. In each of these pairs, the vowel underlined in the first word is a diphthong, that is, it is pronounced as two vocalic phonemes, [aj] in the first three, [ej] in the second three. When a suffix is added, the diphthong disappears automatically. The same shift occurs with other vowels, as in *cone/conic*, where the vowel [ow] turns into [ɔ]; *profound/profundity*, where [aw] becomes [ʌ]; or *assume/assumption*, where [ju] becomes [ʌ]. There is thus a systematic aspect to the contrast between the diphthong and the basic vowel. This phenomenon, which under some circumstances can change a long stressed vowel into a diphthong, and vice versa, is one of the phonological regularities encountered in language which are some-thing of a conundrum for linguists. The most favoured hypothesis is that such regularities are not merely statistical curiosities and that speakers are doing more than just reproducing forms learned by heart. Anybody who speaks applies unconscious mechanisms, and it is these that many lin-guists are trying to discover and set out in the form of rules. Here is another example, concerning speakers brought up in southern parts of France. They apply a systematic rule to the phonology of words containing the middle vowels [e], [ø], and [o], which they replace in certain condi-tions by [ɛ], [œ], and [ɔ] respectively. This can be seen in their ways of pronouncing these vowels in pairs of words like *fait/faites*, *heureux/heur-euse*, *faux/fausse*, in which the underlined vowel of the first word is closed and the second open. Although in standard French there are pairs of similar type (*sot/sotte*; *différé/diffère*; *entier/entière*; *bêtise/bête*) and though the phenomenon is sometimes orthographically marked as in *poétesse/poète*, it is far from generally observed. In southern speech, how-ever, it is systematic, as can be seen even in the pronunciation of words that are unfamiliar to the speakers. How can such regularity be explained? One feature to be noted is the presence of a [ə], called a schwa, in the syllable following the open vowel. So the *o* in *sotte* should be open because of the [ə] that follows in the southern accent: [sɔtə]. The vowel is closed when the following syllable contains a normal vowel or if there is no following syllable. So in southern speech both *sot* and *sottise* should be pronounced with a closed *o*. Unfortunately, the rule just stated does not cover all situations: the vowels underlined in *resté/reste* and *posté/poste* are all open, although the rule requires that the ones followed by the syllable *té* should be closed. It can be seen that discovering the logic behind a regularity is not always easy. Sometimes it can lead to the devising of complex rules, which have to accommodate so many exceptions that it seems clear the phenomenon has not been properly understood. In this case, however, it is possible to arrive at a satisfactory rule (Durand 1990: 223). It entails a consideration of the syllable containing the vowel to be opened. If this vowel is not terminal in the syllable, the vowel is pronounced open; and if not, it stays closed. So the vowel in *faux*, terminal in its syllable [fo], is closed, whereas the vowel in *fausse* ([fos] or [fosə]) considered as monosyllabic,[7] is not terminal and must be open. In that position, southern speakers of French will see a closed *o* as improper. The rule explains well the systematic regularity of the phenomenon, including some facts which would otherwise be bothersome, such as the opening of the vowel in *prestidigitateur* despite its closing in *préstimulation*, since the division between syllables is considered to come after *pres* in the first word but after the prefix *pré-* in the other.

The fact that speakers abide by systematic practices like the one just described in detail shows two basic properties of the mental mechanisms which we activate when we speak. The first is that there is every reason to believe that such mechanisms exist; the second is that they rely on structures. In the example concerning the opening of French middle vowels, the simplest hypothesis is that syllables exist and that there is a mechanism sensitive to the structure of syllables. A syllable is generally considered to be organized about one or two vowels which constitute its nucleus. The nucleus is preceded by the onset and followed by the coda.

---

[7] Some phoneticians prefer to see this as two syllables which they define as forming a foot, as in poetic meter. A middle vowel will be closed if and only if it ends a foot.

Taken together, the nucleus and the coda form the rhyme, as in the following diagram:

The rule on the opening of French middle vowels serves as a good illustration of the role of the coda:

When the coda is not empty, as in *fausse*, the middle vowel of the nucleus, as pronounced by a southern French speaker, must be open. Representing syllables in the form of tree diagrams seems a good way of explaining quite a few phenomena in different languages. In French, for example, it clarifies liaison in some respects. Although *oie* and *watt* are very close phonetically [wa; wat], liaison of the plural article *les* is made only with the first of these words: *les-z-oies* [lezwa]; and one pronounces *les watts* [le wat], and *les westerns* for that matter, without liaison. This difference is explained by the structure of the syllables:

The word *oie*, with its empty onset, supports liaison, which is not the case with *watt* (Kaye and Lowenstamm 1984: 139). Similar sense can be made of the exceptions to the rule of syllabic contraction (syneresis) in French. Words like *louer, rieur,* and *ruelle,* which derive from the roots *loue, rie,* and *rue* with the addition of a suffix, can be pronounced in a single syllable. For instance, *louer* can be pronounced [lwe] by replacing [u] by the semivowel [w], thus avoiding a hiatus. This is a fairly general principle. If syllables contain two vowels, one of them will often be turned into a semivowel, as is the case in *pierre* [pjɛ:r], *lueur* [lɥœ:r], *mouette* [mwɛt], *fier* [fjɛ:r]. However, there are systematic exceptions to this rule of syllabic contraction: while *louer* [lwe], *tuer* [tɥe], and *lier* [lje] can be pronounced as a single syllable,[8] words like *trouer, (in)-fluer*, and *plier* are always pronounced as two syllables, with two full vowels. One possible explanation of this might be that syllabic contraction is blocked by the presence of a consonant plus a liquid at the beginning.[9] This seems to be confirmed by *prouesse, prière, brouette*, and *bleuet*, all pronounced as two syllables. But in that case why can one make a single syllable of *croire, trois, pluie*, and *groin*, which all start with a consonant plus a liquid? The answer is that in these words there is no syllabic contraction, as it is already present in the root word: the root of *croire*, for instance, already contains two vowels, while *prouesse, prière*, etc., are derived from words which at least etymologically do not allow syllabic contraction.[10] Jonathan Kaye and Jean Lowenstamm analyse this lack of contraction via a comparison of syllable trees (Kaye and Lowenstamm 1984: 146):

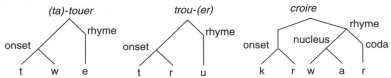

Syllabic contraction brings the vowel into the onset as a semivowel; but when the onset contains a consonant plus a liquid, this is not possible. So, unlike *-touer*, a word like *trouer*, made from a morphological apposition of two syllables (*trou-er*), cannot reduce to a single one, in accordance with the constraint just mentioned. Nor can it acquire a structure like that of *croire*, which does not result from syllabic contraction.

How do speakers apply such mechanisms? The examples just discussed show that we are dealing here not with mere regularities, but with rules, and that these rules apply to structures. If these rules are more than constraints inherent in articulatory functioning, then they are mental objects and we must try to understand their function.

---

[8]   This is not the case in the speech of some regions of Quebec, where the phenomenon happens only when the root contains more than one syllable. So, there, *lier* is always pronounced [lije] and *confier* [kõfje] (Kaye and Lowenstamm 1984: 139).

[9]   Liquid consonants in French are *l* and *r*. They are in the same phonemic category as semivowels.

[10]   *Prouesse* comes from *preux*; *brouette* is a diminutive of *beroue* (*bi-roue*).

7.6 The nature of the rules of language

An apparently general rule such as the constraint on pairs of consonants, one voiced, the other not, may perhaps be seen as a straightforward consequence of our phonatory anatomy. The fact is that it is physiologically difficult to pronounce in sequence [p] plus [z], or [b] plus [s]. An abstract rule made out of something that looks more like a bodily impediment may be a faulty one, if its real basis is the tongue muscles rather than mental function. Nevertheless, though the important role of articulatory constraints has been stressed in this chapter, they cannot be seen as the only phenomena governing the phonological structure of languages. For example, it is not any muscular impediment that makes the verb form *troua* be pronounced in two syllables, since *trois* can be pronounced in one without difficulty. Nor can this difference be explained as a result of the morphology of the words, for though *troua* derives from the root of a verb, that is also the case with *roua*, which can be contracted into one syllable. According to Kaye and Lowenstamm, speakers of French are sensitive to constraints associated with a structure, the syllable. It was this structure that helped us understand the phenomenon of the opening of middle vowels in southern speech. As we have seen, it also clarifies the behaviour of liaison with initial [w] in French; and it can similarly shed light on the absence of liaison before words such as *hibou* or *onze* (Encrevé 1988: 197). There are some phonological phenomena that operate on structures larger than the syllable. The functioning of liaison itself is the outcome of an exact calculation based on the syntactic components of a sentence. There are some liaisons, as in *les amis* [lezami], that are universally observed, some that are optional, and some that are never made, according to the grammatical relationships between any words thus linked: there is, for example, no liaison between a subject and its verb; but there may be one between a verb and its complement. Such phenomena are far removed from articulatory considerations and deserve to be seen as genuine mental procedures.

Linguists may debate the theoretical validity of rules they draw up, but it is difficult to question the assertion that there are complex aspects to the operations accomplished by speakers. These operations resemble the workings of a programme rather than the reproduction of particular forms that have been learned by heart. French speakers never learn as children all the pairs of words between which liaison is acceptable. What they do is discover some systematic principles which help them to link words appropriately, including words they may rarely use. In the sentence *Les idiolectes ataxiques outrent tout académicien acrimonieux*, which contains several out-of-the-way words, French speakers will make at least two liaisons (with the *s* of *Les* and the final *t* of *tout*) and at most three (with the *s* of *idiolectes*). The complexity of the processes of pronunciation may, of course, only be apparent; and speakers may be using simpler ones, though applying them to forms that are more abstract than the individual words or sounds that they encounter. The rule of opening of middle vowels would be complex if one needed to memorize separately the behaviour of every single word affected by it; but, once one has grasped that it concerns solely the form of the rhyme in a syllable, it turns out to be a thing of transparent simplicity. However, this simplicity is misleading. For southern speakers to apply the rule, they have to be able to divide syllables and analyse the inner structure of them, an operation which is not entirely straightforward, as can be seen in the example *pres-tidigitateur/ pré-stimulation*. In short, complexity may lie more in the task of identifying the structures to be processed than in the processes themselves.

The requirement for a speaker to undertake elaborate operations does not necessarily mean they are the outcome of procedures specific to language. They might be much more general mechanisms, such as analogy. For instance, a speaker who has made up a feminine form of the name *Quentin* [kɑ̃tɛ̃] and who is unsure how to pronounce it might, by analogy with the pair *marin/marine*, deduce *Quentine* [kɑ̃tin], in which the second [n] is pronounced and the second vowel is denasalized. However, the simplicity and generality of a mechanism like analogy masks the complexity of its application. Analogy can only function if it brings together two matching structures, which presupposes that the speaker must be aware of them. That is to say, the complexity of the analogy lies not in the duplication mechanism but in the matching of structures. Trying to match structures can be a tricky business, as is shown by attempts to do it by computer (Yvon 1996; Pirelli and Yvon 1999). In the example of *Quentin*, even leaving aside the spelling, it feels right in French to match the final *-in* with the ending of *marin*, rather than with other final syllables which, though they sound exactly the same, *-eint*, for example, as in *atteint*, or *-ain* as in *hautain*, form their feminines in different ways (*-einte, -aine*). So it is clear that the mechanism of analogy, which is not peculiar to language, plays a role in our cognitive processing of pronunciation. But it can only do that because it is working on structures like syllables or morphological components which we can recognize thanks to a capacity that *is* specifically linguistic. It should also be noted that the functioning of analogy is not systematic: one can never be sure that an analogy will be applied or, if it is, whether it will be properly applied. Left to its own devices, analogy would be incapable of producing behaviours like those we have inspected, liaisons between determinant and noun, the opening of middle vowels, or the constraints of syllabic contraction.

Underlying the often systematic behaviour of people speaking sentences in their native language, there cannot be just simple and general mechanisms. In particular, such behaviour does not arise from mere memorization. It is produced, at the very least, either by complex procedures or by simple procedures applied to structures that are not elementary. What needs to be determined is the relation linking these procedures and structures with the biological determining of human beings. To the extent that such procedures vary from language to language, they cannot be predetermined in their actual form. The procedure that makes for systematic opening of middle vowels is not imprinted as such in the DNA of people living in the south of France. None the less, it would be difficult to maintain that our human genetic inheritance does not constrain the types of linguistic treatment we are capable of or the type of linguistic structures we can process. The evidence considered in Chapter 3 very strongly inclines us to the view that there is a biological basis specific to language, which we have and animals do not; and such a biological predisposition is bound to be apparent in one way or another. The least we may assume is that we have a competence for applying some classes of treatments to some classes of linguistic structures. We might, for example, have a biological predisposition to processing syllables. In any given language, cultural evolution and learning might lead us to consider only syllables of a certain type, for instance, syllables with simple onsets and codas, such as those used in Yawelmani, a native American language from central California (Kaye and Lowenstamm 1984: 128). It might also be that a cultural environment selects a number of constraints on these syllables, such as the one discussed under syllabic contraction in French which has the effect of prohibiting onsets made of consonant-liquid-semivowel (see p. 156). If we are able to learn such structures, it is because we have cerebral equipment that makes it possible. It would still be necessary to explain in some way the existence of such equipment, by showing that it fulfils a biological function.

7.7 The biological function of phonological ability

One of the main aims of research in linguistics is to draw up concise descriptions of languages with the aim of delimiting which sequences can be spoken and which cannot. In the process, a model of speakers' linguistic ability is also drawn up. Although this work is far from complete, it has already provided us with hypotheses that give some idea about the phonological ability of human beings. This raises the question why such an ability exists and why it has the form we see in it. Among the aims of Chapter 6 was to show that species are locally optimal. If our species has a predisposition to use a phonological system, then the predisposition must be locally optimal for a biologically adaptive function. What function, though?

A first reply to that question could be that phonetic processing is a coding process that contrives a compromise between the speed of transmission of information and the accuracy of the transmission. And it must be said that this idea is attractive. From an engineering point of view, the possibility of offering maximum contrasts, like those just examined in vowel systems, is one that makes perfect sense within a system of digital transmission of information. The fact that, acoustically, vowels like [a], [i], and [u] are maximally distinct makes it easy for hearers not to mistake one for the other if the signal encounters interference or is distorted. This also provides speakers with a safety margin, in that they can use a higher rate of delivery of speech than if the vowels were acoustically close to each other.

This type of reasoning, however, which favours seeing the phonetic level of language as an optimal transmission code, cannot be accepted at face value. A typical speaker produces ten to fifteen phonemes per second. Why not more than that? Any suggestion that this rate represents an articulatory limit or the limit of hearers' decoding abilities misses the point. What we are talking about is equipment fashioned by natural selection. Is it conceivable that, if it had been useful to transmit more information, natural selection could not have done better than to evolve a system transmitting the equivalent of about fifty bits per second? Why are we not endowed with a system capable of transmitting the equivalent of, say, a kilobyte per second? Once we accept the principle of local optimality, there is no avoiding the answer: our phonetic apparatus was selected so as to function at about fifty bits per second, and it is this rate which is a locally optimal compromise. Consequently, our phonatory apparatus and our procedures of phonetic decoding have evolved to use a particular range of contrasts which are sufficient to achieve that rate. We are not dealing with a conventional engineering situation in which the aim would be to maximize the transmission rate without exceeding an acceptable limit of errors. Our phonetic system is regulated for a particular transmission rate; and if it is optimized in relation to something, it must be in relation to factors like the expenditure of muscular energy or the cost of processing. This answer, however, merely postpones the question of the function of language. Why should a rate of about fifty bits per second be locally optimal?

Our phonetic system, with its optimal acoustic contrasts, is not there just by chance. We may conclude from the foregoing that the phonetic rate of speech is regulated to ensure the transmission of an amount of useful information. Is there any way to measure that information rate? This is a question that takes us to the heart of our enquiry into the role of language. To measure the information exchanged between interlocutors, should we focus on phonemes, on words, on sentences, or on the thoughts expressed by the sentences? In the following chapters, we shall consider these different points of view. For the moment, let us establish that the effective rate of phonetic communication, in terms of the amount of information transmitted, is actually less than the rate of fifty bits per second that we have stated. This is a consequence of the redundancy implicit in any sequence of phonemes.[11] Some phonemes, such as [s] in French, are more frequent than others, such as [g], and long sequences of consonants are unlikely.[12] So, as some phonemes perceived are more or less expected, they carry less information than they would if completely unpredictable. Redundancy in the sequences of phonemes used in any particular language derives from the anatomical limitations imposed by our articulatory apparatus and by phonetic rules. Is there any usefulness in such

---

[11] In technical terminology, speech at the phonetic level has no maximum entropy.
[12] Alex Taylor cites the German word *Impfpflicht* (compulsory vaccination), containing a sequence of six consonants, all pronounced.

redundancy? Once again, engineering offers a partial answer. Remembering that speech is basically a mode of digital communication, we can say that redundancy in digital transmissions is a way of guarding against mistakes. In the transmission of data, binary symbols are grouped into 'words'. The receiver tests the validity of words received and can thus correct most transmission errors. This is exactly the system used in speech. Children hearing a new word for the first time can recognize that it is a word belonging to their language; they can analyse its composition, for example its syllabic components, and in this way are not likely to memorize a faulty version of it. To do this, they rely on the phonological rules of their language. Mistakes made by children are revealing in that respect: *frotsy* for *frosty*, *perkle* instead of *purple*; *thilthy* for *filthy*, *mashrooms* for *mushrooms*, *hostipal* for *hospital*, *Harold be thy name* for *hallowed be thy name*, *hair conditioning* for *air conditioning*, etc. It is obvious that such mistakes are infrequent, if we take into account that children acquire up to ten new words every day.[13] Furthermore, phonologically, they are mistakes of some subtlety, which supports the idea that our system of phonological decoding is one of remarkable efficiency. Because phonological rules put constraints upon possible sequences of phonemes, a process that produces redundancy of information, they are the main source of that efficiency. Children recognize the syllables of a new word because the syllables of their language are not random assemblages of sounds.

Phonological rules also have a role to play in the understanding of familiar words. For adults as for children, the bulk of phonological decoding consists of recognizing words. A French-speaker hearing the sequence [tɥaãʒemənã], has no trouble in recognizing the question *Tu vas manger maintenant?* (= 'Are you going to eat now?'), despite the dropping of several consonants. An achievement like this is possible not only because we are familiar with the words making up the question, but also because the words making up the language differ phonologically from one another. Just as our phonetic system, together with the possibilities of articulation, makes for the production of acoustical contrasts, so phonological rules make for contrasts among syllables and contrasts among words. So a rule such as the opening of middle vowels has the effect of facilitating the segmentation of syllables. For example, in the

---

[13] By early adolescence, they can understand some tens of thousands of words though they have lived for no more than a few thousand days.

south of France, the two statements *Elle saute à la corde* ('She's skipping') and *Elle sauta la corde* ('She jumped over the rope') do not have the same pronunciation. The two ways of pronouncing ([sɔt-a] and [so-ta]) produce a different division of the syllables and hence of the words. The use or non-use of liaison can produce something similar: in the sentence *Le petit arbitre la rencontre*, the two words *arbitre* and *rencontre* can be either nouns or verbs, depending on context, and the statement can mean either 'The little referee meets her' or 'The youngster is refereeing the contest', depending on whether the liaison of the final *t* of *petit* with the following vowel is made or not made.

My purpose here is not to show that all phonological rules have a functional role to play in disambiguation, but rather to assess what importance we may see in the human capacity to detect phonological structures and to apply systematic procedures to them. Without some such capacity, we would have no way of making words discernible. The words making up the lexicon of a language are not haphazard sequences of phonemes; they possess an internal structure, and in particular they are composed of syllables which possess an internal structure of their own. These structures, and the rules that apply to them in each language, have the effect of separating out the words that are phonologically possible in any language from the indiscriminate sequences of phonemes, thereby greatly facilitating recognition of them.

Given these facts, there is a clear usefulness in any biological programme that enables detection of phonological structures and the application to them of systematic constraints. In any context where the ability to exploit very extensive vocabularies is an advantage, some such faculty is indispensable. The fact that natural selection has endowed us with this ability can therefore be explained by independent considerations drawn from the engineering of digital transmission. Engineers structure binary data circulating on networks into words, packets, messages, or sessions. Each structure contains instructions that are superfluous to the useful information but which guard against errors of transmission or routing. The same principle can be seen at work in language: hearers expect that acoustical signals will be recognizable phonemes belonging to their language, properly formed syllables, words familiar to them, and sequences of appropriate words. However, once again, what must be stressed is an important difference between the methodology of network engineering and the capacity for language. Engineers are interested in achieving ever greater transmission rates but human language is regulated for a given rate of information which we must suppose is locally optimal. Natural selection has endowed us with a phonological mechanism enabling us to exchange inside a minute some 150 words selected from a vocabulary of several tens of thousands of lexical components. Why do we not exchange 1,000 words a minute? Why do the rules of phonology not allow us to discriminate among a million or even ten million words short enough to be transmitted at that speed? Without the slightest doubt, the answer to these questions is not that natural selection has been unable, or has not had the time, to endow us with a super-phonology of that order. The answer can only be that it is not in human beings' biological interest to exchange words at such a rate. That, however, is an answer that merely raises further questions. A satisfactory answer will depend on a more thoroughgoing understanding of the function of language.

8 Protolanguage

Protolanguage is an idea coined by the American linguist Derek Bickerton. His study of pidgin and creole languages and of the differences between the two has led him to posit the hypothesis that in the past the progenitors of our species spoke a less elaborate form of language, which he calls protolanguage. A vestige of this form of communication survives in our modes of behaviour. What type of communication was possible through protolanguage? And what can we know about the intelligence of those who spoke it?

8.1 Communicating just with words

The phonological system affords us the possibility of making a great number of quite distinct words. What else might be required for speaking? As things stand, the universe of meanings that we can communicate is substantial; and the ability to speak just with words and without syntax is considerable. Obviously, speaking is more difficult if one must do without the wealth of grammatical structures that enable the expression of complex relations. This difficulty translates as slowness of communication and problems with defining abstract ideas or describing situations completely unfamiliar to interlocutors. But just putting one word after another does enable human communication to happen. In introducing the concept of protolanguage, Bickerton has done more than just give a name to the possibility of communicating without syntax. He notes that this mode of communication constitutes a functional system, on a par with language, and points out that there are communication situations in which even we contemporary human beings resort to protolanguage. He goes on to argue that protolanguage was the vehicle of communication of the species that preceded us on the earth, *Homo erectus* (Bickerton 1990).

Bickerton came to the idea of protolanguage through the study of Hawaiian pidgins, which he compared with other pidgins and with the creole languages that often grow out of them. A pidgin is a simplified mode of verbal expression, typically spoken by adults who speak also a native language which is different. People may find themselves constrained by a variety of circumstances to communicate without using an established language. The best known of these circumstances is slavery, which brought people from very disparate linguistic backgrounds into contact with each other. In the Caribbean, for example, thousands of Africans transplanted from different ethnic groups found themselves suddenly thrown together; and in conditions of forced labour, they were cut off from all contact with other speakers of their own language. More recently in Hawaii, economic and commercial reasons brought together people from various parts of the Pacific, such as Japan, Korea, the Philippines, etc. Finding that they have to communicate with one another, or just responding to the normal human instinct which makes the normal person speak to other people, such adults very quickly devise a code of communication by adapting the only linguistic resource they happen to have in common, which in Hawaii happened to be either English or Hawaiian. Under normal circumstances, foreign immigrants soon pick up a modicum of competence in the local language. But when the number of simultaneous immigrants exceeds a certain level, the standard form of the language becomes less accessible to them and ceases to function as a model, and a form of pidgin soon emerges. Pidgin is a language apparently without syntax, reminiscent of the speech of the character of Tarzan. Here are a few sentences, unconnected with each other, from Taï Boï, a French-Vietnamese pidgin (Bickerton 1995: 163):

Moi faim. Moi tasse. Lui aver permission repos. Demain moi retour campagne. Vous pas argent moi stop travail. Monsieur content aller danser. Lui la frapper. Bon pas aller. Pas travail. Assez, pas connaître. Moi compris tu parler.[1]

The next extract is from Hawaiian pidgin (Bickerton 1990: 120), followed by English equivalents, the first of them word-for-word:

---

[1] Approximate equivalents in English-based pidgin: *Me hungry. Me cup. Him have permission rest. Tomorrow me return country. You no money me stop work. Sir happy go dance. Him hit her. Good not go. Not work. Enough not know. Me understand you speak.*

Aena tu macha churen, samawl churen, haus mani pei
And too much children, small children, house money pay.
And I had too many children, very young ones, and I had to pay the rent.

This type of rudimentary speech is not confined to colonial situations. Bickerton quotes an exchange from Russonorsk, a commercial language used for almost exclusively mercantile purposes among Russian and Scandinavian sailors (Bickerton 1990: 121):

R: What say? Me no understand.
N: Expensive, Russian—goodbye.
R: Nothing. Four half.
N: Give four, nothing good.
R: No brother. How me sell cheap? Big expensive flour on Russia this year.
N: You no true say.
R: Yes. Big true, me no lie, expensive flour.
N: If you buy—please four *pud* [measure of 36 lb]. If you no buy—then goodbye.
R: No, nothing brother, please throw on deck.

The subject under discussion is bartering flour for fish. The structuring of the sentences, in its almost total lack of grammar, is very close to that of the two extracts from pidgins. What is remarkable is that the people who are speaking like this are all perfectly capable of expressing themselves properly in their native languages. Bickerton compares this way of speaking to the speech of Genie, the Californian child who was kept locked up by her father from the age of eighteen months and discovered in 1970 when she was thirteen years old. Her inability to speak was reminiscent of Victor, the wolf-boy discovered in 1798 in the Aveyron district of France whose story was made into a film by François Truffaut. Despite all the efforts of her tutors, Genie could never learn to express herself normally and what she did say was very close to pidgin: *Father take piece wood hit. Cry.* (Bickerton 1990: 116). Bickerton also draws a parallel between this form of speech and the speech of children of about two years of age. There is a clearly observable moment when children begin to make statements of several words, such as *Danny wait*, meaning 'We are waiting for Danny'. Bickerton even compares such modes of expression to what trained chimpanzees are capable of (cf. Chapter 3).

Bickerton's structuring idea is that protolanguage, related in his view to pidgins, the speech of very young children, or the language used by Genie, is not a debased form of normal language, but is a functional system of communication in its own right:

Genie knows what past tense means, knows when it is appropriate to use it, and even knows at least one of the ways of marking it in English. But she cannot incorporate this knowledge into her normal ongoing speech. ... This suggests not that she has merely *failed to acquire* a full version of human language, but that she *has* acquired *something other than full human language*—an alternative means of communication that incorporates some features of language but rigorously excludes others. (Bickerton 1990: 117)

Bickerton sees protolanguage as a fossil, a behavourial vestige with which each of us is endowed. We are able, effortlessly and instantaneously, to adopt a pidgin form of speech, using words from our native language. Without the slightest reflexion, words come to us naturally, in an approximate order; we just spontaneously omit grammatical words, articles, prepositions, relative pronouns, markers of tense or aspect. In Bickerton's view, this reveals the presence of a fossilized competence, an innate expertise which was once the normal form of communication among members of *Homo erectus*, the species from which our own derived. It is a vestige of their speech that survives in us and which we can fall back on at times when expression through normal speech is impossible.

8.2 A language that is not learned

The example of the deaf children of Nicaragua (cf. Chapter 3) fits very neatly with Bickerton's hypothesis on the existence of a protolinguistic competence. The level of communication achieved by the deaf adolescents who have been to school is a form of pidgin. The signs they put together are more or less separate from each other and the sequences are brief, rather like statements in pidgin which are usually restricted to four or five words. Two other features of their communication that are reminiscent of pidgins are the fact that the protolanguage of signs was developed rapidly and spontaneously by the youngsters themselves, and of course the fact that they seem to have been already too old to learn how to make their protolanguage evolve towards a language with syntax.

Like Genie, the deaf children had lived in isolation from a normal linguistic environment ever since infancy. Their linguistic difficulties show that acquisition of language must happen during a very limited period of a person's life, before the age of eight or nine. If exposure to language does not occur during that period, it appears that a person, though still capable of picking up some form of communication, will never fully master the syntax that is characteristic of human languages. In Bickerton's view, what such individuals do spontaneously learn is a protolanguage, a phenomenon made possible by the fact that, unlike normal first-language learning, there appears to be no crucial limiting period. This could mean that a competence in protolanguage is not only a capacity with deep roots in us but that it just lies there ready for use and never needs to be toned up through a lasting exposure to a linguistic environment. There is still, of course, the problem of acquisition of vocabulary. But the capacity to link words into a protosentence, then to link protosentences into a discursive sequence appears to be a faculty that we all possess and have no need to learn.

The idea that protolanguage of the sort seen in pidgin languages is a faithful reflection of the type of language used by *Homo erectus* is obviously a conjecture. The only speakers we can observe nowadays are *Homo sapiens*, who are undoutedly far superior to *H. erectus* in the linguistic competence and intelligence which enable them to reconstitute meanings. Modern human beings, who have the ability to spontaneously develop a language in the full sense of the term, do not develop a protolanguage except in the very particular conditions just discussed. If a sufficient number of children under six years of age are put into a situation where they can interact spontaneously, they develop a language equipped with a syntax that resembles the syntax of any other language spoken anywhere in the world. In this way, if the children of pidgin-speakers are brought up together, it takes them a single generation to develop a new language, a creole language, which they make up from the lexicon of their parents' pidgin. It was in just this way that, when the younger deaf Nicaraguan children were brought together, they spontaneously developed a sign language with real syntax, which is often considered a creole language. Creole languages are not just an amplification of the pidgins that preceded them. They are fully fledged languages, with all the syntactic attributes of any other language in the world, notably grammatical words and embedded phrases, which are absent from protolanguages like pidgins.[2] So it is

---

[2] Bickerton restricts the definition of pidgin to pseudo-languages spoken by adults. There are, however, circumstances, for instance when a pidgin is used as a second language, as in Papua New Guinea, or when the social structure does not accept the existence of communities of children of the same age, in which a pidgin may evolve into a slightly more sophisticated form, though it still does not lead to a genuine creole.

no easy matter to make comparisons between human beings who are forced to use a protolanguage and *Homo erectus* who, as Bickerton suggests, had neither the ability to manipulate syntactic structures nor understand the meaning of them.

Nevertheless, Bickerton's hypothesis is undeniably attractive. By positing a protolinguistic competence for *Homo erectus*, it reduces the width of the gap separating us from species without language. Mind you, if this transition did take place in two stages, first from non-language to protolanguage, then from protolanguage to language, then we need to explain two steps instead of just one, though this would also make each of them slightly less of a miracle. Furthermore, if there really is some vestige of an ancestral mode of communication subsisting in us, that would afford a neat explanation of Bickerton's observation of an autonomous protolinguistic competence in contemporary human beings. That this competence coexists with our capacity for language would appear to make it largely superfluous; and on the face of it, that might seem something of a mystery. However, if it is a fossil, a survival of the normal mode of communication of the species that engendered our own, then its presence in us becomes understandable.

So the Bickerton hypothesis has a convincing ring to it, though it must be said that it stands or falls on the single assumption that protolanguage is a genuine competence. What would happen, though, if what Bickerton calls protolanguage turned out to be merely a debased form of normal language, just a way of speaking in which syntax is largely dispensed with? That would mean protolanguage would have no existence separate from language itself and could not be seen as any sort of competence handed down by our ancestors. If we are to accept the protolanguage hypothesis, it is important not to restrict our consideration of it to an enumeration of its negative features, that is, to what it lacks in comparison with normal language. The form of language found in pidgins has two essential properties: it is functional and it is spontaneous. These two properties are lacking in any debased forms of language that we might observe or imagine. Protolanguage does enable hearers to construct meanings which roughly fit the meanings that speakers have had in their thoughts, though this requires that the contexts be sufficiently restricted. For instance, the protosentence *And too much children, small children, house money pay* says enough for us to be able to grasp at least the gist of the speaker's lament. That is a very positive quality, which might well be absent from other conceivable simplifications of normal syntax, such as omitting all nouns or every second word. If all the semantically weak parts of a statement are omitted, like the grammatical words or the inflections of nouns and verbs, this can often prevent the meaning from being plain. Such omissions from the sentence *The girl whose money was stolen has gone* would result in *Girl money steal go*, which might make it appear that it was the girl who stole the money. In protolanguage, the words *money* and *girl* would be juxtaposed and the statement would probably be made in two sentences: *Steal money girl. Girl go.* There is still an ambiguity; but the wrong meaning is not so unavoidable. Protolanguage is not the result of a rough simplification of language; it is a tool for communicating meanings that has its own organization.

The second of the essential properties of protolanguage, its spontaneity, has a way of being produced systematically by certain conditions, as we have seen, in the form of pidgin languages. If the conditions are slightly less unusual, for example if people are learning a second language while immersed in the foreign linguistic environment and without the benefit of formal instruction, then they go through a phase in which they express themselves through pidgin: *Quentin me jouing* is a sentence spoken by a French-speaking child of six to let an English-speaking adult know he was playing with his brother. Conversely, in cases of poor intercomprehensibility, we may help a foreigner by simplifying our own language in a particular way, which turns it into a protolanguage: *You cold, I get blanket.* However, no one has ever adopted a type of language completely without verbs, though it is quite possible, at least in theory, to speak like this: 'However, the adoption by no one of a verbless type of language, despite the perfect theoretical possibility of such speech' (Carstairs-McCarthy 1998). Protolanguage is a kind of second nature. Although speaking without verbs requires a certain concentration on the words we use, we have no need to take account of details of form if we use Tarzan-speak. We could, of course, with much training and practice, achieve mastery of a verbless way of speaking, just as we can learn to express ourselves in back slang. But protolanguage needs no learning. Because it is functional and spontaneous, it can properly be considered as a true competence. Bickerton's argument follows more or less automatically: the continuing existence of such a competence, parallel with language, can only be understood as a fossil, which means protolanguage was the form of expression of one or other of the species from which we trace our descent, most likely *Homo erectus.*

If we accept that conclusion, and if protolanguage was one of the characteristic behaviours of a species of hominids, it must be possible to show it was locally optimal (cf. Chapter 6), that is to say that no minor variation in the competence could have made it any better at fulfilling its biological function. The difficulty that arises when we propose to evaluate its local optimality is that we have still not defined what the function of protolanguage was. A glance at its structure tells us that the main feature of it is that it includes all the semantic elements essential to comprehension and only them. The result is an economical system which, though not nearly as accurate as language, none the less does provide a measure of efficacy. A closer glance, in particular at word order, shows that the absence of definite syntax does not make for a total lack of order. We saw an example of that with *Girl money steal* and *Steal money girl.* A conclusion that appears natural is that protolanguage is locally optimal for communicating meanings of a particular sort and that word order is chosen so as to facilitate the hearer's construction of meaning. So if the intended meaning is that somebody stole the girl's money, the preferred order will be *Steal money girl,* since *money* and *girl* belong to the same semantic component and must be juxtaposed.

The principle of protolanguage could be stated as follows: in its utterances, it groups words into semantic components. Seen from this perspective, it is uncluttered by the grammatical elements (relative pronouns, conjunctions, inflections) which recur in normal language but which, because they have no separate semantic function, could not contribute anything. In pidgin languages, demonstrative adjectives, interrogatives, or certain prepositions may be used, but only infrequently, which is consistent with the limited contribution they make to immediate comprehensibility (Bickerton 1990: 126). So it is possible to accept the idea that as a linguistic system protolanguage is optimized to facilitate access to meanings. The corollary of this, however, is that it also entails a markedly greater degree of ambiguity than obtains in the language we speak. Does this mean that *Homo erectus* was not 'lucky' enough to achieve language and that protolanguage was optimal only in the sense that it lacked the innovation of syntax? If we remember to adopt the proper macroevolutionary point of view and bear in mind that *Homo erectus,* as the species is currently defined, lasted for nearly two million years, it is unwise to see the ability to use syntax as some sort of miracle that hominids eventually stumbled upon after much trial and error. The evidence reviewed in Chapter 6 should foster scepticism towards any explanations that confuse microevolutionary optimization with the haphazardness of speciation. Consequently, it is wiser to see protolanguage as a system which, well adapted as it was to its function, had no need for syntax as we know it.

8.3 Protosemantics

This hypothesis will achieve greater coherence if we try to understand what sort of meanings protolanguage can express and how it is adapted to convey them. In what follows, we shall argue that protolanguage is adapted to the expression of protosemantics, that is to say a field of meanings accessible to *Homo erectus*. What might such protosemantics consist of? In accordance with the principles established in Chapter 6, protosemantics cannot amount merely to a weaker version of *Homo sapiens*'s abilities in semantic representation. It has to be a mode of cognitive organization that is functional and locally optimal. So any arbitrary division, such as restricting its scope to concrete entities or to immediately visible objects, would be inappropriate. If protolanguage ever existed as a means of communication proper to a species, then we must assume that its existence necessarily involved a form of protosemantics. Members of that species communicated about something, and it is that something that we must try to reconstruct. This is an endeavour fraught with potential dangers, as what we are about to embark on is an attempt to reinvent if not the mind of *Homo erectus*, at least some aspects of the cognitive functioning of that mind. The main danger is that, in the absence of subjects on whom to test any hypotheses, we might get carried away and end up piling conjecture upon gratuitous conjecture in a world where the only limit to such things is imposed by authors' lack of imagination. I suggest a more prudent course. The problem facing us (how are we to define protosemantics in relation to protolanguage?) is relatively constrained in four parameters, as follows: (1) protosemantics must be a functional field of meanings; (2) it must be locally optimal for a given biological function; (3) it must subsist in modern humans, either as a fossilized competence or as a functional subset of our semantic competence; (4) protolanguage, as we understand it from the study of pidgin, must be locally optimal for the expression of this protosemantics. It is clear that if we accept these constraints, the danger of fanciful conjecture will be greatly reduced. Added to that there is the fact that our objective is the relatively modest one of positing, if possible, a few minimal hypotheses aimed at making more sense of the existence of protolanguage, in the full knowledge that they may well be criticized and require revision.

The basic idea is that the words put together in protolanguage are a way of bringing to mind concrete scenes, either experienced or imagined. On hearing a word like *cat* we may picture either a prototypical cat or else a particular one that is familiar to us. Similarly, *door-mat* readily brings to mind the image of an object. In a particular context familiar to two speakers, both words would very likely convey the image of a particular animal, the household cat, and the image of a particular object, the mat at the front door. Combining the two words into the statement *cat mat* requires us to join the two images together. We possess the ability to combine images in a way that is not arbitrary. Clearly, there was a strong chance that the cat in the example might be on the mat, if they both belong to the same house. But there are an infinite number of other possibilities: the cat might have been lying under the mat or to one side of it; the mat might well be under the cat but in the bedroom; both the cat and the mat might be floating about inside the kitchen; the cat might be either walking towards the mat or away from it; or the cat might even have changed colour or shape to look like the mat; and so on. Most people, however, if the circumstances are right, will spontaneously picture the first image of the cat dozing on the mat by the front door. This human ability to combine images in a particular way that will be foreseeable by another person is largely a mystery. It must rely on the use of actual situations seen as more or less prototypical, such as a cat that is in the habit of dozing on the mat by the front door. However, we also readily create scenes that we have never experienced by combining images that are purely imaginary, such as the cat lying under the mat or balancing the mat on its nose. This astonishing competence no doubt uses our ability to associate in order to recall memorized visual elements and appraises the scene envisaged with reference to constraints inherent in each entity (the respective sizes and weights of the objects, their power of autonomous movement, etc.) and to their expected behaviour (typically, a motionless cat is lying down and is asleep). Nevertheless, it must be acknowledged that this process of synthesis of mental images remains largely obscure. No doubt future advances in psychology and the technologies of virtual reality systems will shed light on this.

If we assume that this ability to construct scenes out of our combining of mental images is real and that *Homo erectus* also possessed it, we can understand how the link between protolanguage and the making of images can happen. In a given context, words bring to mind either images or, more generally, memorized perceptual prototypes; the combination of words makes the hearer construct a scene; this combination grows gradually as semantic components are worked into it. The statement *Girl money steal go* is semantically analysed by its components, probably from left to right, as $(((((Girl)\ money)\ steal)\ go)$ or perhaps by grouping *money* with *steal*, $(((Girl)\ ((money)\ steal))\ go)$. (*Girl*) will refer, say, to the daughter of the speaker, who is well known to the hearer. $((Girl)\ steal)$ gives a typical image of somebody stealing, and here it is clearly a girl who is doing the stealing. Obviously, as human beings we are able to process such a sentence without going through all these images, but what is under discussion here is a form of protosemantics totally based on combination of images. The other possible way of looking at it would be that the hearer would make an image corresponding to $((money)\ steal))$ before linking this image to the one of the girl. Then the hearer would encounter the problem of the word *go*. It is difficult to make a static image of someone stealing money, typically from a cupboard, say, and leaving at the same time. The solution might be the construction of a dynamic scene, a sort of mini-film, in which the character first steals then goes. We are all capable of visualizing such a scene.

It is clear that combination of images is an unreliable process; and for this there are two reasons. The hearer risks combining images in a completely unexpected way or failing to combine any at all. It is therefore the responsibility of the speaker to describe the scene in a way that facilitates the hearer's task. Without the active cooperation of the speaker, this mode of communication cannot work. In the example, if the meaning was that somebody stole money belonging to the girl, the speaker will prefer to say *Steal money girl. Girl go.* By putting *money* beside *girl*, the speaker biases the hearer towards making an image in which the money belongs to the girl; by separating *steal* from *girl*, the speaker biases the hearer away from imagining a scene in which the girl does the stealing; and by repeating *girl* in front of *go*, the speaker helps the hearer to make a scene in which it is the girl who leaves.

Can we say that protosemantics, as discussed above, meets our four constraints? The answer is certainly positive for constraints numbers 1 and 3: if we accept that our ancestors possessed the mechanism of combination of images and scenes, then it is obviously a functional system still extant in modern human beings. Constraint number 4 requires that protolanguage must be locally optimal for conveying representations of protosemantics. This is not an easy point to verify, though we do possess two pieces of evidence pointing in the right direction. One is, as Bickerton observes, that the words of protolanguage as suggested by pidgin are all words with semantic content. Even modern human beings, who are able to use words that are more or less empty of separate meaning, such as prepositions, conjunctions, or relative pronouns, omit them when expressing themselves in protolanguage. The second comes from word order. Although protolanguage is supposedly devoid of syntax, its word order is not entirely arbitrary. The grouping of words into semantic components is crucial for the drawing of any proper interpretation. It should be noted that this constraint is greatly relaxed in normal speech. In the sentence *I sent, on the day before she came, John's book which was on the table to Mary,* the words *sent* and *Mary* are separated by five words with semantic content, a thing which would be quite impossible in protolanguage. The structure of protolanguage looks as though it is determined by the requirements of protosemantics, which strongly suggests that it is a linguistic system well adapted to its function, in accordance with constraint number 4.

Constraint number 2, relating to the adapted character of protosemantics and its local optimality for a given biological function, is much more difficult to verify. The fact is we have not yet broached the function of protosemantics. Can we define what usefulness individuals might see in using the words of protolanguage to communicate an image or a concrete scene to their fellows? In Bickerton's view, the use of protolanguage obviously serves the survival of individuals; but the evidence inspected in Chapter 4 shows that this conclusion is illusory rather than obvious. If we are to gauge the optimal character of protosemantics, we must establish a relation between the properties of the scenes conveyed by protolanguage and the use that a hearer will make of the scenes. The first thing to be established is that the scenes brought to mind by words are very imprecise. We 'see' the cat on the mat, but is it a striped cat or a Siamese cat? Can we see the colour of the mat? Is the floor wet? Is it summer or winter? What can be seen behind the cat? All these questions, as well as many others, are likely to remain unanswered. The images we combine on hearing concrete words are extremely sketchy compared with perception. However, they are still images; and we can say for sure that the cat is on the mat, outside the house, say, sitting there and facing us. But can we say that this sketchiness, which is what releases the evocative power of protolanguage, is enough to ensure that the scenes will have their proper effect? Without pronouncing definitively on what the function of these scenes may be, we can say they are at least good enough to allow a comparison with scenes memorized. If we limit the function of communication among hominids to that partial description, then we can say that protosemantics and the protolanguage which serves protosemantics appear to be adapted to that function.

One undeniable objection that can be raised here is the fact that this system is inherently limited by the concrete aspect of the visual or more generally perceptual images conveyed. It is this concreteness, taken with the extreme sketchiness of the images, that makes Bickerton reluctant to see anything semantic in them:

Let's say that you are one of those who think they think in images. You have an image of a cat on a mat, and indeed you can immediately dress it out as 'The cat sat on the mat'. If words failed you, you could draw it; if drawing failed, you might be able to point to actual cats and mats in the room. But such a test is too easy. Take something more like 'My trust in you has been shattered for ever by your unfaithfulness'. Now have the mental image to which this sentence corresponds. (Bickerton 1995: 22)

The argument is certainly convincing. Though there may be some people for whom fidelity and trust summon up an image, there is no image that any of us would recognize as even a remote equivalent of the complete sentence quoted by Bickerton. His conclusion is that we think exclusively in words. If this idea is tenable, then any notion that human beings have retained a functional protosemantics of images must be abandoned. However, the argument can be refuted, oddly enough, by Bickerton's own method. To counter the view that there is no language without syntax, he points to pidgins; to counter his view that thinking does not take place without words, we can point to the ability shared by all humans to combine images conveyed by concrete words. Granted, some abstract ideas cannot be represented in any perceptual way. But that proves only that protosemantics and semantics are not the same thing. Bickerton tries to deny that the combination of images plays a part in our comprehension of spoken statements. And yet, without that ability, many statements would be incomprehensible. Take this fine sentence of Hortense Vlou's: *He felt so lonely in this desert that sometimes he would walk backwards just to see tracks in front of him.*[3] Any understanding we have of this character's seeing his own tracks really derives from our ability to see statements as images. Bickerton should accept the existence of this ability to elaborate scenes as a component of our representational abilities in the same way that he argues for the existence of protolanguage as an integral part of our linguistic abilities.

Does the fact that image-forming is limited to concrete entities rule out protosemantics, as Bickerton seems to suggest? An answer to that question should not be based on the abilities of present-day humans. Concrete protosemantics might have been quite adequate to the needs of hominids who had no access to abstractions. Abstractions like the fidelity or trust cited in Bickerton's example are qualitatively different from the images that concrete words can bring to mind in a reliably systematic way. If I say *cat*, I can make a pretty sure guess at the type of mental image you will form, especially if the context is clear, for instance if we have both just seen a cat walk past. If I say *fidelity*, I have no way of knowing what image you will form, if you do in fact form one. In the first case, communication is possible, because the speaker can foresee the signified as constructed by the hearer; in the second, Bickerton is right to hold that communication cannot take place if it has to rely solely on the construction of an image. Hominids must have been able to function in the first of these two modes, communicating through the exclusive use of concrete words which were adequate to conveying scenes in a way that was more or less deterministic. If one accepts this description of communication among hominids, it is reasonable to conclude that they had no abstract representational abilities and that this constitutes a fundamental difference between protosemantics as used by them and semantics as used by us.

8.4 Prelanguage, a language without sentences

In elaborating the concept of protolanguage, Bickerton saw it as an attribute of *Homo erectus*, the corollary of which is that, in his view, this

---

[3] Winner of the RATP-Télérama poetry competition.

species was devoid of language as we know it. This reasoning seems impeccable. *Homo erectus* do not appear to have come anywhere near our level of intelligence; their tools were stereotyped; and as far as we know, they left no evidence of symbolic culture. We would find it difficult to accept that such a creature, one that we usually picture as a sort of brute beast, could have possessed as versatile an instrument of expression as our own. On the other hand, we are dealing with a humanoid being which serves as a rampart between us and animality. As *H. erectus*'s children, it is not for us to hold them in too much disdain. For after all they were able to control fire and conquer the whole of the ancient world, adapting to a wide variety of conditions of life. It is tempting to think that their means of communication might have resembled ours, while remaining qualitatively different from it. Protolanguage closely fits this description. In the absence of evidence to the contrary, we can only share Bickerton's view. A question arises, however, about the species which preceded *Homo erectus*: what type of communication should we posit for *Homo habilis* or even *Australopithecus*? If we accept Jacques Monod's argument (cf. Chapter 4), language, or at any rate a form of communication akin to human language, was an initial 'choice' which determined the whole further development of our line of descent. Did *Australopithecus* possess protolanguage? That way lies the primrose path of pointless speculation. It must be said, nevertheless, that there is a relatively sensible way to posit the problem of attributing levels of linguistic competence to our ancestors.

As we saw in Chapter 6, the macroevolutionary transitions that give rise to new species correspond to qualitative changes. Conversely, speciation events are the only known causes of qualitative changes in the evolution of species. Broadly speaking, palaeontologists choose to distinguish four main transitions in human lineage, corresponding to the emergence of the four genera or species *Australopithecus, habilis, erectus*, and *sapiens*. There is some complexity in the case of *erectus*, in that the term groups into a single species some older individuals with a cranial capacity of 700 cc and other more recent individuals with a cranial capacity exceeding 1,200 cc. It is not at all certain that they belong to a homogeneous species; and it is perfectly possible that in our line of descent there were several qualitative transitions involving speciation in addition to those recognized as such and that the fossil record of skulls is too discontinuous to enable us to distinguish these transitions from a regular quantitative increase in brain size. To match these possible morphological transitions we could hypothesize a number of qualitative changes in the language competence of our ancestors. If we observe the principles of macroevolution set forth in Chapter 6, any transitions in language should correspond to transitions of species. Conversely, if we take Monod's point about the central importance of language in the evolution of our lineage, we would expect that the succession of speciation events that have punctuated our descent should correspond to qualitative leaps in our language competence. If we accept this correspondence, we should endow each of the species that have preceded us with an original linguistic capacity. Even if we apply this principle less strictly, it remains a valuable guide for reconstructing the communication abilities of our ancestors. The obvious risk is that we may mix up species and endow one of them with a competence that should belong to another. However, if we bear in mind that any reconstruction of competences associated with fossil species is bound to be a step-by-step process, entailing its share of hypotheses advanced then refuted, it is an acceptable risk.

So it is legitimate to wonder, given that *Homo erectus* may have expressed themselves via protolanguage, what form communication among *Homo habilis* might have taken. Let us review which possibilities of transition in language capacity there might have been. Ray Jackendoff suggests that the single-word stage represents a functional state of communication among our ancestors (Jackendoff 1999). He points out that a fundamental property of human words is that they are not attached to a particular situation, unlike the call of an animal which is. For instance, the cry that a chimpanzee utters to announce the presence of food will not be the one uttered to urge its fellows to go and fetch the food, whereas an infant will indiscriminately use the word *cat* or an equivalent of it to mark the presence of a cat, to enquire where the cat is, to call it, to indicate that something looks like a cat, and so on (Jackendoff 1999). The reason why some authors like Jackendoff or Deacon see the relaxing of the signified–signifier link as a decisive moment in the evolutionary history of language is no doubt that at one and the same time it originates ambiguity and semantics. Meaning ceases to be a simple reflex association and requires some cognitive processing. A system of communication in which every speech consists of one word and in which every word is essentially ambiguous becomes the simplest system using semantics. We could call this system 'prelanguage'. For it to be a biologically valid competence attributable to a species of hominids, the principles set out in Chapter 6 would require prelanguage to be not only functional but also locally optimal for its function.

When a word is uttered in isolation, of what use can it be? As we saw in the case of protolanguage, it can serve to convey a scene. If it is to do this, the hearer must be aware of the link between the word and the scene. Such a system, if it involves rigid associations between words and situations, may appear to be totally lacking in flexibility. However, the context can play a vital role, since the same word in different contexts will not bring to mind the same scene. A child who says the word 'Cat' when a cat has just arrived may mean no more than that; but if the same word is spoken about a half-eaten roast, it may summon up the image of the family cat on the table eating the meat. If this function is the same as that of protolanguage, it is difficult to see how prelanguage could be locally optimal, for it is undeniable that scenes will be conveyed much more efficiently and reliably through the combinations of words in protolanguage. An utterance like 'Cat eat roast' leaves a hearer much less scope for ambiguity than the single word 'Cat', which transfers most of the effort of interpretation to analysis of the context of the situation. In these circumstances, one may well wonder how prelanguage could have existed as a faculty peculiar to a species. If a group of words function more effectively than a single word, it is difficult to see what would keep a species in a state where the only possible acts of communication were isolated words.

The answer may lie in how competent a hearer is at semantic decoding. If hearers are unable to combine the images presented by a group of juxtaposed words into a single scene, then protolanguage becomes un-usable. Prelanguage would have its own presemantics, with something of the evocative power of words found in protosemantics, though without its potentiality for combining images into scenes. The conclusion we arrived at after discussing the mechanism governing the combination of images was that, in the present state of knowledge about this type of mental process, it was largely mysterious. We may assume that animals are without this mechanism, which presumably appeared in one of the species of our lineage. This is an essential assumption if we are to believe that prelanguage could have been a functional form of communication.

Experiments with chimpanzees like Kanzi suggest that some animals possess presemantics. Kanzi is able to interpret a word like *ball* with regard to its context, for example by going to look for the ball. What is more bothersome is that Kanzi is able to understand, and can even produce, combinations of words like *open orange*. This would appear to mean that the chimpanzee analyses the expression as two separate words, each with its own semantics, the *orange* calling to mind the image of an orange and *open* referring to an action unlinked to any context of oranges. There is a documentary in which one can see Kanzi obeying Sue Savage-Rumbaugh when she tells the animal to put the keys in the refrigerator. This behaviour is very impressive, given that it amounts to an original act, so bizarre that it seems to require some preliminary interpretation, a combination of images, typical of protosemantics. It looks as though Kanzi contrived to combine the image of the keys with the image of the refrigerator, which enabled him to carry out what was expected of him. If that was what happened, the whole idea of prelanguage with its associated presemantics would be untenable. However, it is possible that Kanzi's 'reasoning' was different. Because he has been through numerous experimental sessions, he expects that he will be expected to accomplish some act. On hearing *keys*, he goes through the action of taking the keys, as this is what he has always done when keys are mentioned. Then he hears *refrigerator* and puts what he is holding into the refrigerator, as that is one of several actions he can accomplish when the refrigerator is part of the act. In short, the animal is going through a sequence of motions and is not combining images, a difference that is far from insignificant. A combination of actions requires two things: that each operation be given its operands; and that the operations can be sequenced in time, the result of the preceding one linking with the prerequisites for the one following. This is nothing like a combination of images. When one hears *cat mat*, a decision in favour of the cat's being on the mat requires a different mechanism from the one that makes for temporal sequencing of actions. So it is possible that Kanzi is using merely presemantic abilities to interpret the instructions of the experimenter. Not that this finding in any way detracts from his achievements. The hypothesis positing that prelanguage was succeeded by protolanguage merely suggests that communication among our ancestors exploited a capacity that was different from the one that the chimpanzee demonstrated with the keys and the refrigerator.

The achievements of Kanzi illustrate the contrast between the representational abilities of animals and protosemantics. One important characteristic of prelanguage and protolanguage is that they are both referential. Words refer to objects in the perceptual world. In general, what animals communicate is their emotional states, though the vervet monkeys discussed in Chapter 1 show that the use of referential signals by some animals cannot be ruled out. However, the semantics of those used by vervets is in large measure innate, whereas human and very likely prehuman communication is referential and its semantics must be learned. Needless to say, prehumans must have been able to use words as simple signals to reveal their emotional states, but their great originality was that they must have spontaneously used words to refer to concrete objects and events, something that Savage-Rumbaugh did manage to reproduce with Austin and Sherman, but only through a course of intensive training (cf. Chapter 3). No doubt animals like chimpanzees possess a quite developed capacity for representation of images, though it is unlikely to be anything like the capacity we have, which *Homo erectus* probably had too, of combining images to make up imaginary scenes. That capacity, defined here as protosemantics, appeared at some stage during our descent. Referential communication must have preceded it, building on the simple ability to summon up a memorized scene, corresponding to the ability we have called presemantic.

If *Australopithecus* or *Homo habilis* could speak, though without having access to protosemantics, then prelanguage could have been a locally optimal means of communication. Uttering isolated words, individuals contrived to bring to their hearers' minds the scenes they wished to communicate, when the context lent itself to this. Jackendoff suggests that some of our behaviours are fossils of this mode of communication. Certainly, interjections such as *ouch!*, *dammit!*, *shh*, *wow*, *pst*, etc., and the various oaths that people use, function like sentences without being structured like sentences. It is doubtful, however, whether such exclamations, intentional or not, are used for any evocative purpose. They are probably just non-linguistic signals. Jackendoff also mentions isolated words like *hello*, the *yes* of encouragement, and the dissuasive *no*:

I would like to think of such words as these as 'fossils' of the one-word stage of language evolution—single-word utterances that for some reason are not integrated into the larger combinatorial system. (Jackendoff 1999)

The idea of seeking a fossil of prelanguage in present-day human language is a commendable one, but it is unclear whether any such fossil could ever be unearthed. We sometimes express ourselves with isolated words: *Out, Done, Hit, Missed, Sunk, Land*. There may be some evocative power in these words which thus lend themselves to interpretation when they are used. In other respects, however, it is impossible to distinguish prelanguage from the subset of protolanguage comprising one-word sentences. So for the moment we shall consider prelanguage to be an interesting hypothesis, logically consistent for now, about a possible stage in the evolution of language.

8.5 The lexicon of protolanguage

Phonology

Human beings have a phonological combinatorial system that enables them to form mental lexicons composed of large numbers of words of manageable proportions and easily distinguishable from one another. The constraints that we spontaneously impose on phonological sequences have the effect of clearly separating linguistic forms within the set of possible phonetic forms. Such a system would only ever have evolved in response to a demand for a voluminous vocabulary. The words of prelanguage or of protolanguage make a link between phonological form and meaning. The demand that had to be met by the phonological system was for a very large number of meanings. Since prelanguage has no mechanism for combining words, the need to align signifiers with signifieds no doubt required a considerable lexicon, so that ambiguity should not exceed the constraint of construability in context. If that is the case, it is reasonable to assume that phonology is coeval with prelanguage. This argument stands, however, on a dubious premise, for we have no idea of how many different meanings the earliest hominids might have wished to communicate. If they needed a mere dozen or so, then any phonological system would have been superfluous.

Our hypothesis on presemantics assumes that these species communicated about concrete situations, though no doubt not just for the purpose of describing them. Bearing in mind some aspects of communication among contemporary humans, to be analysed in Part III, we may suppose that the earliest hominids were trying to indicate events or situations that were 'salient'. By and large, no one speaks for the purpose of pointing out that the neighbour's house is still there or to draw attention to the continuing presence of the forest. By their very nature, there is something unexpected in salient situations: the unannounced return of a friend who has been gone for a year, the approach of a cloud of locusts, the presence of an albino animal. It is not possible to indicate such situations if the vocabulary is too restricted, unless of course one deals with an extremely small number of potentially salient situations and only speaks of them about once a year. It is more likely that the earliest hominids, in their inability to combine words and the representations associated with them, could draw upon a lexicon of appreciable size enabling them to indicate concrete situations with enough precision for the hearer to grasp their salience. The words of this lexicon could not have been mere unstructured grunts barely distinguishable from each other. It therefore seems quite consistent to accept that the origins of phonology are to be found at the beginnings of prelanguage.

Grammatical categories

Were all the words of protolanguage of the same order, or did our ancestors make grammatical distinctions such as verbs, adjectives, and nouns? As we know, some of these distinctions are only relative. Until the end of the Middle Ages, for example, grammarians did not see adjectives as belonging to a different category from nouns, though they made a clear distinction between finite verbs and their past participles (Matthews 1974: 44). In Lakota, a Sioux language, there appears to be no separate category for adjectives; and words like *big* or *red* behave like verbs or else they are composites of the nouns they qualify, which can also happen with verbs (Van Valin and LaPolla 1997: 28). It would appear, however, that every language in the world makes a distinction between verbs and nouns. Could such distinctions have played a role in prelanguage and protolanguage?

The hypothesis we applied to understanding the function of protolanguage assumed that it served to indicate concrete situations. The hearer either constructs mental images or reconstructs and combines earlier perceptions. The efficacy of protolanguage can be gauged from the fact that the mental constructs match what the speaker had in mind, the most important thing being that the hearer should have a proper grasp of the salience of the situation communicated. In such a system, is there any need to make distinctions between nouns, verbs, adverbs, and adjectives? From the fact that such distinctions are made in pidgins spoken nowadays it cannot be concluded that prehumans were able to make them. The use of nouns, however, would appear to be self-evident: since protocommunication is supposed to be concrete and referential, the use of nouns to indicate entities in the perceived world may seem inevitable. Could our ancestors do without verbs? How could the fact that 'John is coming' be spoken of without the verb 'to come' or an equivalent? The use of adjectives and adverbs seems equally indispensable if one wishes to indicate for instance the presence of 'a very tall man running quickly'. The problem with this type of reasoning is that it derives from a human conception of language; and as far as prelanguage is concerned, if we can assume it existed, nothing leads one to suppose that the use of verbs, adverbs, and adjectives might have been of advantage to its speakers. If, as we assume, hearers were unable to combine several images to construct a scene, speakers would have been restricted to a single word for indicating a salient situation; and in my view, such a word could only have been a noun. However, though nouns represent the only possible form of pre-lexicon, it is not really possible to talk of a lexical category. In a language where everything is a noun, there are no nouns. On the other hand, it is likely that speakers of protolanguage had a more differentiated lexicon, since they had, one supposes, the ability to combine the meanings of their words. However, this point cannot be taken as proven. An equivalent of *man height* could be used to express the fact that somebody is tall, or something like *John food* to mean that he is eating. Distinctions between nouns, verbs, and adjectives are both semantic and grammatical. Are they indispensable in a concrete language without grammar?

In many languages, distinctions between grammatical categories, seen from a semantic perspective, are blurred by the fact that there are some words which can serve indiscriminately as verbs, nouns, or adjectives. Take the English noun 'verb', which can function as an adjective in 'a verb phrase'; and as is well known, in English 'you can verb any noun'—*water* and *house* can mean things or actions. The word *orange* can be either an adjective of colour, a noun of colour, or a noun meaning a fruit, the first two being close semantically, which suggests that the grammatical category is not decisive in determining meaning. There is no special reason for systematically augmenting semantic distinctions (colours, animate beings, sexes, vegetables, round objects, or foods) with abstract distinctions (quality, entity, action, manner) which equate to our notions of adjective, noun, verb, and adverb. The distinctions we make between adjectives, nouns, verbs, and adverbs are first and foremost grammatical;

but if we consider them from a purely semantic point of view, they have no more and no less reason to figure in the broad range of lexical categories of protolanguage than many another category that our ancestors might or might not have been interested in.

Morphology

If we accept that our ancestors needed a considerable number of words, we may wonder how they made them up. There is no difficulty about inventing new forms well within phonological constraints, but there is a great risk, when they are first used, that they will not be understood. A way of forming new words that is common to many of the languages spoken in the world is to make them up from already existing words. A glance at the vocabularies of present-day languages shows that words are not always the atoms of meaning. The word *reasonable* has a morphological structure, in that it contains a simpler signifier, the noun *reason*. This type of morphology, called derivational morphology, makes for the creation of new words through the adding of affixes to a root. In French, suffixes like *-té*, *-esse*, and *-eur* added to adjectives can make nouns, e.g. *beau > beauté*, *triste > tristesse*, *noir > noirceur*; and nouns can make adjectives by the addition of suffixes like *-el* (*accident > accidentel*) or *-ien* (*Paris > parisien*). In English, suffixes do similar things, e.g. *-ness* added to adjectives can make nouns (*lonely > loneliness*), *-hood* added to nouns can make other nouns (*brother > brotherhood*), and *-less* added to nouns can make adjectives (*friend > friendless*). Derivation can also work by the adding of prefixes (*do > undo, tie > untie*) or even by adding infixes, though this is unusual (Matthews 1974: 131). These methods of affixation can be combined, as in a word like *redeployment*, which can be analysed as being structured from the root syllable *-ploy-* with the addition of two prefixes and a suffix. So here we have a mechanism that speakers can use for the creation of new words, though it might be more accurate to call it not a mechanism but a true competence. One need only be aware of the lexical inventions of children to realize that they spontaneously make full use of it, more so no doubt than adults. We notice it when children make up words which we know do not belong to the vocabulary of our language, but which we see as perfectly acceptable. Here are some examples of spontaneous morphological creation by children, in both French and English: *se dépyjamiser* (meaning 'to take off one's pyjamas'); *treindre* (instead of *tenir*, meaning 'to hold'); *explicages* (instead of *explications*, meaning 'explanations'); *senture* (instead of *odeur*, meaning 'smell'); *déprocher* (instead of *éloigner*, meaning 'to distance'); *abritement* (instead of *abri*, meaning 'shelter'); *proposement* (instead of *proposition*, meaning 'suggestion'); *décorages* (instead of *décorations*); *my Mum's a good cooker* (instead of 'a good cook'); *hooving* (= 'using a Hoover vacuum cleaner'); *bander* (= 'musician playing in a band'); *windscreepers* (= 'windscreen wipers'); *boredness*.

It is interesting to note that we can immediately understand the meaning of most of the words invented by children, even though we may never have heard them before. Our general ability to form words by analogy must play a part in this derivational innovation, though it is not the only thing to consider. For instance, 1.7 per cent of French words start with *con-*, which is a considerable proportion. In that initial position, the syllable usually derives from the Latin morphological marker *cum-*, meaning 'with', an example being *consonne* ('consonant'), and, as Molière's philosophy master says (see p. 139), consonants are called consonants because they sound 'with' the vowels. Latin's ease of morphological creation has been largely lost in French and children seem to know it: none of them would invent a verb *conjouer* to mean *jouer ensemble* ('to play together'), which might be possible if morphological invention was only a general competence based on nothing but analogy.

The ability to create, via derivation, words which have a fair chance of being understood is a very interesting property for an open code of communication. It is a lexical competence, separate from the protolinguistic competence that makes it possible to create unprecedented meanings from the juxtaposition of words. Whereas the sentences of protolanguage, like those of language, are created freely by speakers then forgotten by hearers who focus on the meaning, words created by affixation have difficulty in being incorporated into the vocabulary, though if accepted they can become fixtures in it. The invented word *décorage*, for instance, would be perfectly acceptable in French, but the prior existence of *décoration* would make it difficult for it to become a recognized part of the lexicon as currently used. So derivation, as a competence, seems to be an indispensable tool for speakers using an open lexicon. Does it follow that our ancestors who first started using a referential code of communication were able to create words after the manner of present-day children who make them up? Derivational processes as they can be observed in our modern languages have two effects: they generally alter the grammatical category of the original word; and they induce semantic change. For example, the adjective *full*, which can have a suffix added to make the noun *fulness*, serves to affirm a property of an entity, whereas the noun indicates the property. Semantic change is the only one of these two effects to concern protolanguage, since we have said that protolanguage cannot have the property of distinguishing between grammatical categories.

In modern languages, the morphological structure of words can at times reveal the semantic category they belong to. This is the case not only with derivational morphology, which makes words from pre-existing words, but also with inflectional morphology, which marks words in accordance with the semantic category of the entity they denote. In French, for example, sex is marked by the gender of nouns and adjectives. Many languages use class morphemes (see Chapter 2 for a mention of Chinese in this respect). Steven Pinker cites Kivunjo, a Bantu language, which marks sixteen different semantic classes (Pinker 1994). If semantic distinctions were as integral to protolanguage as they are to language, we may wonder whether our predecessors used inflectional morphology. There are arguments against that hypothesis. Class morphemes have an important grammatical function, that of making agreements. In French, subject–verb and adjective–noun agreements are obligatory. If we leave aside any idea of grammatical function, the function of inflectional morphology seems to be to distinguish semantic classes, whether they are concrete, like the man–woman distinction, or abstract, like property–entity. Such distinctions are category distinctions and nothing suggests they might have any protosemantic function. Although most animals, including sexed unicellular ones, can tell males and females apart, it is not true to say they manipulate categories of male and female. Protosemantics presupposes a capacity for representation via mental images, but not a capacity for making category distinctions. We shall come back to this fundamental difference between protosemantics and semantics. In addition, in Chapter 10 we shall see that the reason for the existence of inflectional morphology is syntactic and that the semantic distinctions which it introduces among words are a means and not an end. The lack of category distinctions in protosemantics, like the lack of syntax in protolanguage, makes us doubt the presence of morphology in protolanguage.

8.6 Protoconversations

The preceding analyses make it possible to sketch an identikit picture of *Homo erectus*'s mode of communication. As with any identikit picture, there is no guarantee that it will be a close likeness, as all we have to go on is a few clues, like the structure of pidgins, the different functional components of the linguistic competence of present-day human beings, and especially the locally optimal fit between any form of language and the system of meanings that it can express. As with an identikit picture identifying someone wanted by the police, the purpose of this attempt is to identify our ancestors' form of communication. Unless we are to suppose that *Homo erectus* and all the ancestors who preceded them were totally mute, we must try to define functional subsets of our own capacity for language, in an attempt to ascribe them to one species or another of our ancestors. To the objection that this is a futile endeavour, since language activity leaves no fossils, we may reply by citing the work of Bickerton, not for its conclusions but for the new questions that it makes us ask. Once defined, the concept of protolanguage is something of an encumbrance; and the reason why humans should possess this unused second code of communication is something of a mystery. This code, characterized by its lack of grammatical words and syntactic structure, groups words as semantic components into short sentences. Bickerton takes the view that it is a fossil. As such, it is of course a very different thing from bits of bone that one can hold in one's hand. As a behavioural fossil, its functional character obliges us to wonder about its usefulness, present or past. Just as palaeontologists try to reconstruct the stature or the diet of our remote ancestors from a single tooth or a fragment of femur, so we can attempt to postulate, in a way that is just as provisional, an identikit picture of the mode of communication used by the same species, drawing upon the vestiges of protolinguistic competence that survive in our behavioural inheritance. What follows should therefore be read as no more than a tentative reconstruction, whose main value may be that it tries to assemble a number of observations into a coherent model.

The communication used by *Homo erectus* was referential. Unlike animals which generally communicate their emotional or hormonal state, *H. erectus* could make reference to concrete states of the perceived world. In this lay the main originality of their protolanguage. They put words together, relying on their hearers' ability to combine the mental images created by the words. In this way they contrived to produce in hearers' minds a copy, albeit imperfect, of the scene they had in their own minds. Protolanguage, as it can be reconstructed from observations of pidgin languages, appears to be perfectly adapted to this function of concrete reference: by using only signifying words grouped into semantic constituents, speakers of protolanguage facilitate the interpretive work of their hearers.

The structure of protolanguage can only be understood if it serves referential communication. In order to communicate the few emotional states that our ancestors might have wished to manifest, sentences were not needed. On the other hand, to refer to objects and events in the perceived world, *Homo erectus* needed a vocabulary that was extensive enough to enable them to indicate a fair number of different situations. This would have been an open vocabulary, using the generative potentialites of phonology. Limited as it was to indicating concrete entities that could be represented mentally, it presumably entailed no abstract distinctions such as action, entity, quality, and manner, which are the semantic counterparts of verbs, nouns, adjectives, and adverbs. For the same reasons, the words making up this vocabulary probably had no morphological structure, since morphology as we know it serves mainly to mark or modify the semantic class of words; and the concrete protosemantics that we ascribe to *H. erectus* has no scope for such abstract distinctions between semantic classes. Our ancestors had the ability to picture concrete images and scenes from words spoken; but the processing they could give to these images and scenes was limited. They may have been able to go from one to the other via associations, as is possible with all mental representations, but they had no way of categorizing them abstractly.

Like us, *Homo erectus* did not go in for communicating about no particular situation. They tried to impress on their interlocutors the salience of situations worth commenting on. Assessing the salience of a situation, for instance its unexpectedness, was very likely one of the main processes that they were capable of. In our own case, we do that instantaneously and effortlessly, as can be seen from this exchange, observed between two children aged eight and ten, talking about hot-air balloons:

M: Did you see there's more balloons up there this morning?
Q: Yes, I know.

M: You, be quiet! I'm not talking to you, I'm talking to the others. [To his father] Did you see there's balloons up there this morning?

M's mention of balloons, in the minds of the others, clearly constitutes a salient situation. Like the other participants in the scene, M instantly recognizes that the spectacle of dozens of hot-air balloons drifting overhead is a most unusual occurrence. As mentioned in Chapters 1 and 3, drawing others' attention to such a thing is more or less a reflex action on the part of anyone witnessing it. Q's attitude and M's response suggest too that drawing people's attention to a salient situation is not a matter of no consequence: being the one to point out the presence of balloons has a degree of importance for M; and it is an importance that could be nullified by Q's reaction. This sort of importance presumably also existed for speakers of protolanguage and possibly even earlier for speakers of pre-language.

Thus far, we have considered only single utterances. But language, in its most current and spontaneous usage, is first and foremost conversational. This naturally raises the question of how protoconversation took place among our ancestors. Consistency with the identikit picture requires us to rule out any possibility of argumentation, with its implications for abstract links such as causal relations, negation, and logical compatibility, none of which fits with protosemantics. For all that, our ancestors' language may not have been made up of disjointed utterances. Q's reply, 'Yes, I know', or an equivalent of it in protolanguage, was no doubt conceivable as one in a range of possible replies; and the same probably goes for more positive responses such as exclamations expressing recognition of the salience of any situation indicated. The effect of these two modes of response was to make for a public assessment of the quality of the information supplied by the speaker.

For reasons which we shall analyse in Part III, speakers belonging to the species from which we descend probably did as we do when we try to impress people by being the first to bring genuine news of salient situations when they arise. So M's initial statement in the preceding example resembles the sort of thing that might have occasioned speech among our ancestors. This is a type of behaviour that each of us indulges in several times a day, and is no doubt one of the things which we share with our *Homo erectus* ancestors and perhaps also with their predecessors. The argument put forward in this chapter has been that protolanguage evolved in the service of this behaviour of reporting salient situations. The implication of this is that protolanguage was locally optimal in this role, an idea that is compatible with what we can surmise about its form. This scenario, plus the picture of protolanguage just presented, gives us an internally consistent idea of what could have been our ancestors' communication behaviour. Advantageous though this clarification may be, it seems to leave us with a deeper mystery. For if protolanguage was perfectly adapted to its function, what events might have brought about the appearance of real language?

9 The mechanics of syntax

The most evident and perhaps the most impressive quality of human languages is their syntax. The accurate placing and assembling of words and markers of agreement appear to result from complicated computations effected in real time by speakers and used by hearers to grasp the exact meaning of what is being said. Every language in the world has a grammar. There can be nothing fortuitous in such universality. In the twentieth century, Noam Chomsky was the linguist who argued most strongly for the existence of a faculty of language, rooted in our biology and seen as the source of that universality. If we accept that idea, it makes sense to wonder about the biological reason why our ancestors were selected to master the invention and use of a grammar as part of their code of communication. Syntax is not an obvious and expected extension of protolanguage, but rather an unexpected and peculiar development of prehuman communication, activated by the appearance of new abilities in representation.

9.1 The phenomenon of syntax

Here again is Molière's M. Jourdain, this time having a lesson in syntax:

M. JOURDAIN: Well, upon my soul! I have been speaking prose unawares for more than forty years! Ah, I am greatly obliged to you for having taught me that. So I would like to write a note to her, saying 'Beautiful Countess, your lovely eyes make me die of love.' Only I would want it to be said in a gallant manner, with a fine turn of phrase.

PHILOSOPHY MASTER: Tell her that the fires of her eyes reduce your heart to ashes, that day and night you suffer for her the agonies of—

M. JOURDAIN: No, no, no, I don't want any of that. I just want what I said: 'Beautiful Countess, your lovely eyes make me die of love.'

PHILOSOPHY MASTER: But you must spin it out a little.

M. JOURDAIN: No, I tell you, all I want put in the letter are those very words, but with a fashionable twist to them, a posh sort of arrangement. Please tell me, for the sake of argument, the various ways they could be put.

PHILOSOPHY MASTER: They can be put firstly as you have spoken them: 'Beautiful Countess, your lovely eyes make me die of love.' Or else: 'Your lovely eyes make me, beautiful Countess, die of love.' Or else: 'Of love, beautiful Countess, your lovely eyes make me die.' Or else: 'Die of love, Countess beautiful, your lovely eyes make me.' Or else: 'Me your lovely eyes, Countess beautiful, of love make die.'

M. JOURDAIN: And of all those ways of saying it, which is the best?

PHILOSOPHY MASTER: The one you said: 'Beautiful Countess, your lovely eyes make me die of love.'

M. JOURDAIN: Why, I did it right at my first attempt! And yet I have never studied! I thank you with all my heart and trust you will come back tomorrow morning.

Speaking is natural to all of us. Without effort, every sentence we speak is an original work. Like M. Jourdain, we should be amazed at this. We spontaneously fit words into the proper arrangement to express our thought, although many other arrangements are possible, most of which would be incorrect in a language like French. Of the 3,628,800 ways of ordering the ten words of M. Jourdain's sentence in English ('Beautiful Countess, your lovely eyes make me die of love'), very few would be grammatically acceptable. So, with all his complaints about never having been taught anything, how does this unlettered man know the best way to put his sentence together? We must of course suppose that, like every other human being, M. Jourdain was immersed since early childhood in a linguistic environment which exposed him to several million properly structured sentences. Yet he has never heard the one he now wants to make for the Countess. Similarly, it is highly unlikely that the following sentence would ever have been written before: *He says to him that the car at the corner of John's street was damaged through his negligence.* We can recognize this as a common-or-garden sentence, perfectly correct and couched in standard English. But an examination of its structure affords us a certain amount of evidence about our linguistic abilities. First, it contains embedded structures known as phrases, some of which are set within other phrases of the same kind. For example, the prepositional phrase *of John's street* is included inside the prepositional phrase *at the corner of John's street,* just as the clause introduced by *that* is embedded in a larger clause which is the whole sentence. Embedded structures of this kind are universal and can be made in any of the world's languages. This was not the case with protolanguage (cf. Chapter 8). A second noticeable feature of the sentence is that it contains some inflections, obligatory changes to words in accordance with agreement and case: the verb *says* has the marks of the present tense and the third person singular; *John's* is marked as a genitive case; and *to him* and *his* are dative and possessive forms of the masculine pronoun *he*.

Further analysis of the sentence reveals other facts. Intuition tells us two things: that it cannot be John who is making the statement and that it is not addressed to him either. What is the basis of this intuitive certainty? It can only be the structure of the sentence and the relative positions in it of *He* and *John*. We also surmise that it was *He* who damaged the car. It is also conceivable that it was actually John's brother who was responsible for the damage and that *He* had concealed this. It is important to note that our surmise about the lack of identity of *He* and *John* is in fact a deduction which we may call purely syntactic, for it depends solely on the structure of the sentence and not on the meaning of this or that word. The last thing we may observe is that the verb *say* is being used with all its complements, but it could easily not have been. If the prepositional phrase *to him* had been omitted, as it could have been without harm to clarity, it would still have been understood that the statement was being made to somebody unspecified.

The characteristics revealed by this simple sentence—structuring in embedded phrases, inflections, constraints on the reference of pronouns, the obligatory presence of certain complements—are universal and integral to all language. None of them, however, is to be found in protolanguage (Bickerton 1990). It can be added that the sentence also contains grammatical words like pronouns (*he*), prepositions (*at, through*), and determinants (*the*), all of which little words, though essential to the understanding of the structure of the sentence, play a very restricted semantic role. These too are absent from protolanguage. What must also be noted is that the topic of the sentence is an abstraction, a confession of fault, or a denunciation. And in accordance with the hypotheses canvassed in Chapter 8, the protosemantics underlying protolanguage cannot cope with the representation of any such idea. It can therefore be observed, on the one hand, that a whole set of properties which are syntactic in nature appear along with language; and on the other that a considerably increased power of expression comes into being, affording notably access to abstraction and a great reduction in ambiguity. It may seem plausible to assume that, in a world where protolanguage with its associated protosemantics had been functioning for hundreds of thousands of years, the syntax and semantics observable in human languages should have arisen together. But do these two innovations really go hand in hand? Is it possible that the invention of syntax, with the greater complexity of expression that it offered, opened the way to abstract ideas? Or was it the opposite that happened? Did the construction of a new dimension of meanings, separate from the perceptual world, bring with it the need for a more complex code that could cope with the communication of abstract conceptual relationships? According to the first hypothesis, it would have been the possibility of saying *John's book*, thanks to the genitive case marker and the obligatory disymmetry it makes between *book* and *John*, which opened access to the marking of an abstract relation between two entities, in this case the concept of possession. According to the second hypothesis, it would have been the ability to conceive of such abstract relations that brought about the grammatical means for their clear expression and for disambiguating between *the sister's father* and *the father's sister*. Before choosing between these two possibilities, we must first assess how independent the mechanics of syntax is from the meanings it enables us to express.

9.2 The importance of relations between words

The most fundamental difference between sentences in protolanguage and in language lies in the relations between the words. In protolanguage, the only links between the words are semantic. In a protosentence, the link *dog cat* will only be acceptable if the hearer is able to see a scene in the utterance combining the image conveyed by *dog* with the image conveyed by *cat*. But in language, associations of words are governed by different laws. Words are distributed according to grammatical functions such as subject, verb, or complement, and the association of these functions is not free: it is not usually acceptable to say *cat cushion kind*, though it might conceivably have a meaning in some contexts. What are the reasons for the existence of these grammatical functions and the rules governing their combination? If, as must be supposed, protolanguage is locally optimal for its protosemantic reference function, then we must also suppose that any refinements introduced by language serve a new function. What for example is the point of the distinction, present in all languages, between subject and verb? Typically, in a language like English, verbs express actions and subjects are the entities that do the actions: in the scene described as *The cat is eating*, the word *cat* denotes the actor. What makes semantics different from protosemantics is that it introduces roles, such as actor (the person or thing doing the action), patient (the person or thing undergoing the action), theme (that which undergoes motion during the action), or destination (the arrival point of motion) (cf. Chapter 11). In *Peter upsets Paul*, the patient is *Paul*, whereas in *Paul spills water on Peter*, the destination is *Peter* and *water* represents the theme. In Chapter 12 we shall analyse the purpose of these different semantic roles.

Comparison of language with protolanguage brings to light a remarkable fact: there is a typical but not systematic link between grammatical functions and semantic roles. For example, in English the subject is typically the actor, the complement is the theme or the patient, and the verb represents the action. What is remarkable about this connection is that, in language, not only the words themselves carry meaning but the grammatical relations they have within the sentence do so too. However, it is easy to see that the connection is not systematic: in *Peter is assaulted by Paul* the grammatical subject is also the patient and not the actor. This shows that there is a modicum of arbitrariness in the relation between grammar and semantics. Just as the arbitrariness of the link between lexicon and meanings enables phonology and the lexicon to exist as autonomous systems, so the degree of arbitrariness in the relation between grammar and meaning helps give autonomy to syntax. Some authors argue that the arrangement of the words in a sentence is a more or less direct consequence of the constraints of semantics. This would mean that the necessary distribution of semantic roles in the sentence would suffice to explain the order of appearance of the words, as well as their inflections, as long as certain general properties of each language are borne in mind, such as the Japanese one of placing complements before the verb (Van Valin and LaPolla 1997). If this hypothesis is right, syntax has no autonomy and it is pointless to wonder what brought about its appearance during evolution. The only thing of any importance would be the meaning of language acts; and that could be arrived at by combining the meanings of the words. The sentence resulting from the linear sequence of the words would be nothing more than the sound image of a mental operation bearing essentially on meaning. Against this, there is the idea that syntax

TABLE 9.1 *Examples of different uses of preposition* de *with associated semantic roles*

X de Y	semantic role of Y
voiture de Paul ('Paul's car')	possessor
poupée de chiffons ('rag doll')	matter, composition
chute de Jean ('Jean's fall')	theme
crime de Jacques ('Jacques's crime')	actor
accident de Jean ('Jean's accident')	patient
rêve de Jean ('Jean's dream')	experiencing subject
vacances de rêve ('a dream holiday')	qualifier
route de Paris ('the Paris road')	destination
lac de Genève ('Lake Geneva')	location
trait de scie ('saw cut')	instrument
etc.	

is indeed autonomous, with its own constraints determining the order of the words. This would mean that to process meaning into a sequence of words and to reprocess it from them at the other end are acts of coding and decoding. A good number of syntacticians do take this view, arguing that the meanings of the words often have little bearing on the arrangement of them, as in German for instance, where the verb systematically occupies second place in the main clause, regardless of which verb is used. Conversely, particular arrangements of words may correspond to very different meanings, as can be seen in Table 9.1 illustrating the fact that a French construction like *X de Y* can express a range of semantic relations.[1]

Thus the link between semantics and syntax cannot be a straightforward word-for-word one. The strongest argument for the autonomy of syntax is provided by the fact that judgements of grammaticality can be made. If a non-English speaker says *He claims to his friends of being a painter*, native speakers will understand the meaning well enough, though they will notice there is something wrong with the form of the sentence. Conversely, native speakers will have great difficulty in making sense of *The door's garden undoes the lamp*, despite which they will have no hesitation in

---

[1] The semantic diversity illustrated in the table is only partly to be explained by the fact that the preposition *de* is polysemic.

recognizing it as being grammatically correct. They may also turn it into a passive structure: *The lamp is undone by the door's garden,* despite the fact that they may have not the slightest notion of a context in which it might make sense. The grammaticality of that example comes more from the syntactic categories of the words than from their meaning. We are going to inspect some mechanisms peculiar to syntax which will enable us to see it not as a reflexion of semantic phenomena but as a device whose workings, though they serve the expression of meaning, follow their own logic.[2]

9.3 Some facts about syntax

Phrases

One of the most remarkable properties of syntax is without doubt the structural likeness between phrases built out of syntactic categories such as noun, verb, adjective, etc. It is quite simple to see the structural resemblance between a verb phrase and a noun phrase, e.g. *John succeeds in the competition* and *John's success in the competition* or *John hates his uncle* and *John's hatred for his uncle.* As these examples show, nouns can have complements just as verbs can, in these cases *in the competition* being a complement of the noun *success* and *for his uncle* of the noun *hatred.* It can also be seen that in all four examples *John* is a subject. The sub-assembly formed by the noun and its dependents constitutes a noun phrase. Noun phrases behave like nouns, which means that, from a syntactic point of view, the 'subject' of the noun and its complements are optional. Thus the syntactic behaviours of *success* and of *John's success in the competition* are identical. The word *success* is said to be the 'head' of the phrase. Noun phrases, with their head, their subject, and their complements, are similar to verb phrases, which are made from a verb, its subject, and its complements. The same analogy can be drawn with prepositional phrases: in *the worm is in the apple,* the words *the apple* play the role of complement to the preposition *in* and *the worm* may be seen as the subject of *in* via the intermediary of the verb *to be.* Similarly, in *He is proud of his daughter* the words *his daughter* are the complement of the adjectival phrase whose

---

[2] The syntactic phenomena discussed in the next few pages are set forth in greater detail in many works, e.g. Cowper (1992), Haegeman (1991), and Radford (1997). Pollock (1997) shows how they apply to French.

head is *proud* and *he* plays the role of the subject. In the latter pair of examples, the verb *be* is what is known as a copula, that is it does not have the existential semantic sense it has in structures meaning what does or does not exist, e.g. *There are black swans in Australia* or *I think, therefore I am.* A similar copular use is seen in the French verb *être* functioning as an auxiliary in structures like *Il est parti,* where *Il* is the subject of the verb *partir.*

The temptation is to see such analogies of structure as reflections of analogies of sense. Each of the preceding examples can be argued to show a property applied to two terms: being proud, applied to a father about his daughter, being in, applied to a worm in relation to an apple, or success, applied to John with regard to a competition. The fact is, however, that though the structure of the phrases makes it possible to express such properties, it is not linked to that function. In the statement *Put your brother's jotter into the bookcase* there is a verb phrase, three noun phrases, and one prepositional phrase, some of which have complements, and yet no property is explicitly expressed in the sentence.

Syntax is rather like a building set in which the basic bricks are phrases. When the bricks are assembled so as to fit properly with each other, it is possible to build constructions that make sense. But just as it is possible to join little plastic building blocks together and end up either with a house or with a shapeless something or other, with phrases it is possible to build either meaningful sentences or collocations of words which, though syntactically acceptable, remain semantically obscure.

Assembling phrases

All human beings are able to carry out complex syntactical operations in their native language, using mechanisms of which they remain unaware. Some of these mechanisms they have acquired in the process of learning to speak their language; but if we follow Chomsky's arguments, they have in addition other innate abilities, which are possessed by any healthy human being and are thereby universal. According to this theory, learning the grammar of a language consists of memorizing certain configurations among all the possible combinations allowed by the innate mechanisms. Among the latter there figure the movements of phrases, which are very good at revealing the mechanics of syntax. Take the sentence *Vous imaginez qu'il a parlé à Pierre* (1) [= 'You imagine that he spoke to Pierre'], from which an interrogative form can be straightforwardly derived: *Vous imaginez qu'il a parlé à qui ?* [= 'You imagine that he spoke to whom?']. When spoken, the interrogation is marked by intonation, though most languages have syntactic methods for marking interrogation. This can be done in French, by shifting the phrase *à qui* to the head of the clause, thus: *Imaginez-vous à qui il a parlé ?* [= 'Can you imagine who he spoke to?'] or even *À qui imaginez-vous qu'il a parlé ?* (1') [= 'Who do you imagine he spoke to?']. Or take this sentence: *Vous imaginez ce qu'il a dit à Pierre* (2) [= 'You can imagine what he said to Pierre'], to which someone hard of hearing might say: *Vous imaginez ce qu'il a dit à qui ?* [= 'You can imagine what he said to whom?']. If this question is to be reformulated, the French native speaker may introduce a hesitation after: *À qui...*, then might go on with a slight alteration of the question: *À qui a-t-il dit ce que vous imaginez ?* [= 'To whom did he say what you imagine?']. However, no one will give to this question the following form: *À qui imaginez-vous ce qu'il a dit ?* (2') [= 'To whom do you imagine what he said?']. Syntactically, that form of the question is improper. And yet the same shift has taken place as at (1), moving the phrase *à qui* to the head of the sentence. Three questions arise here. Why is this mechanism all right for (1) but not all right for (2)? How do we know? And why would no native French speaker ever dream of making that shift at (2)? The presence of *ce* in (2) affords us a clue. Traditional grammar defines the *que* in (1) as a conjunction of subordination, the equivalent of *that* in English and *dass* in German, whereas the *que* in (2) is a relative pronoun which when combined with the *ce* is the equivalent of English *what* and German *was*. This, however, does not explain why the shift of *à qui* to the head is possible in (1) but not in (2). The structures of (1) and (2) can be represented as follows:[3]

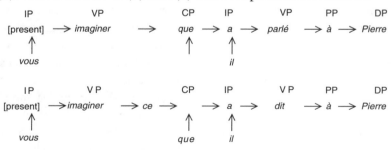

[3] This mode of representation is close to the system adopted in Chomskyan x-bar theory. Here the phrases are represented by their heads, the specifiers point towards the heads and the heads point towards the complements.

In this representation, VP = verb phrase, PP = prepositional phrase, DP = determiner phrase (i.e. a phrase involving a determiner or, as here, a proper name), CP = complementizer phrase, typically containing a subordinator. The only phrase that is slightly strange in the diagram is IP, inflectional phrase, a marker of tense, here the present; in some cases it can be occupied by an auxiliary. As will be seen, positing the existence of such a phrase helps explain certain things. Each phrase has at most one vertical arrow, from its subject, and can point an arrow at its complements.

By means of this sort of representation, movements like those which happen in the shaping of questions can be simply and neatly described. Questioning is indicated by the insertion of a complementizer phrase on top of the structure:

CP   IP   VP   CP   IP   VP   PP   DP
→ [present] → *imaginer* → *que* → *a* → *parlé* → *à* → *qui*
↑   ↑   ↑   ↑
vous   *il*

In Chomsky's view (Chomsky 1995: 290), the presence of the complementizer phrase in a language like French will attract the verb and the questioned element. If the questioned element stops halfway, the result is as follows:

CP   IP   VP   CP   IP   VP   PP
imaginez → → → *(que)* → *a* → *parlé* →
↑   ↑   ↑   ↑
      vous   *à qui* *il*

The subordinating *que* is replaced by the pronoun *qui* (though in certain registers it is maintained: *Vous savez à qui qu'il a parlé?*). The prepositional phrase *à qui* can continue its drift towards the subject of the first complementizer phrase:

CP   IP   VP   CP   IP   VP   PP
imaginez → → → *que* → *a* → *parlé* →
↑   ↑   ↑   ↑
à qui   *vous*   *il*

In the case of (2) the movement of *à qui* in two stages is blocked from the outset by the presence of the pronoun *que* in the position of the subject of the second complementizer phrase, which makes formation of the question impossible. The speaker gets round the difficulty by a sort of sleight-of-hand questioning of the sentence *Il a dit à Pierre ce que vous imaginez* (= 'He told Pierre what you can imagine') which is semantically very close to (2).

The idea of phrase movement may be no more than a convenient image for a cognitive reality that is very different; and the division into phrases used to analyse the examples may be faulty in some details. Nevertheless, the fact remains that an explanation in structural terms of the ungrammaticality of (2') seems more convincing than any attempted explanation on the basis of the meaning of sentence (2). The blocking of the headward shift of *à qui* would be difficult to explain on purely semantic grounds. The ungrammaticality of (2') is a manifestation of how the mechanics of syntax require proper linking of phrases with each other. The way interrogatives are formed in French is revealing in that respect. In examples (1) and (2) there are inversions of verb and subject. Are such inversions just a sort of gratuitous ploy for the marking of interrogation or are they too a consequence of phrase movement? In the question *Isabelle a-t-elle mangé ?* (3) [= 'Has Isabelle eaten?'], it would appear that the interrogativeness comes not from inversion but from the interpolation of the pronoun *elle* with its repetition of *Isabelle*. Representation of the syntactic structure as phrases helps to give a unified account of these different forms of questioning. Question (3) can be represented as follows:

$$CP \quad\quad\quad IP \quad\quad\quad VP$$
$$a \quad\longrightarrow\quad\quad\quad \longrightarrow \quad mangé$$
$$\uparrow \quad\quad\quad\quad\quad \uparrow$$
$$Isabelle \quad\quad\quad elle$$

This form can be derived from the basic form by movement of both the auxiliary and the grammatical subject:

$$CP \quad\quad\quad IP \quad\quad\quad VP$$
$$\longrightarrow \quad a \quad\longrightarrow\quad mangé$$
$$\uparrow \quad\quad\quad\quad \uparrow$$
$$\quad\quad\quad Isabelle$$

In many languages akin to French, interrogation is achieved solely by movement of the verb (the auxiliary in the example), which would give the non-French form *A Isabelle mangé ?* [= 'Has Isabelle eaten?']:

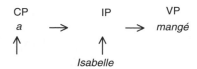

Such a form, unacceptable in French, is quite correct for example in English 'Has Isabelle eaten?' and in German: *Hat Isabelle gegessen?* A second movement, of the grammatical subject *Isabelle*, towards the subject position of the complementizer phrase CP, gives *Isabelle a mangé*, which, leaving aside intonation, is indistinguishable from the affirmative form of the sentence. In order to mark the movement and hence the interrogation, the grammar of French requires that the trace left by *Isabelle* at the starting point of its movement be marked explicitly by a pronoun agreeing with its antecedent, which is the form taken by the question in (3). From this point of view, it must be said that French, with its double movement for the formation of interrogatives, has not gone for the simplest solution. The subject-verb inversion in (1') can also be explained by a description in structural terms like the one just discussed. In this case, the position of subject of the complementizer phrase CP is occupied by *à qui*, blocking the upward movement of *vous* which stays behind the verb. But French can get round this type of blocking. Take the sentence *Qui Isabelle a-t-elle aidé ?* (4) [= 'Who did Isabelle help?'], where it looks as though the blocking has not eventuated and as though *Qui* and *Isabelle* occupy the same position, in apparent violation of the structural principles governing the assembling of phrases. In order to abide by these principles, it would be necessary to postulate a double interrogation, forming (4) from *Isabelle a-t-elle aidé qui ?* [= 'Isabelle did she help whom?'], which would give the following structure for (4):

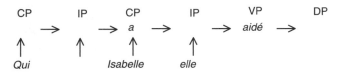

This may appear too complicated. The same structure, however, does enable us to give a neat explanation of the rather weird *Qui est-ce que* of French, as in *Qui est-ce qu'Isabelle a aidé ?*: [= 'Who did Isabelle help?'; 'Who was it that Isabelle helped?']:

CP	IP	CP	IP	VP	DP
est →	→	→	a →	aidé →	
↑	↑	↑	↑		
Qui	ce	que	Isabelle		

This representation also shows why a question like *Qui est-ce qu'Isabelle a-t-elle aidé ?* is improperly formed, as the position that would allow movement of the verb is taken by *que*. Even though such representations structured as assemblies of phrases may be revised and improved (there have been several such rethinkings in the history of linguistics), it is undeniable that they offer a mechanism that explains phenomena like movement of phrases.

The role played by the structure of phrases and their modes of assembly can also be seen in a remarkable way through analysis of the link between pronouns and their antecedents, as will be seen in the next section.

The mechanics of coreference

In connection with some examples, we have already noted that the coreference of a pronoun and a noun to the same entity can be impossible in certain syntactic arrangements (see p. 67). In the following example *Il pense que le frère de Jean est sourd* (5) [= 'He thinks that John's brother is deaf'], *Il* and *Jean* cannot be construed as being coreferential (short of supposing a split personality). However, no such impediment exists in *Jean pense que son frère est sourd* [= 'John thinks his brother is deaf'], where there is no difficulty about *Jean* and *son* referring to the same person. The causes of this type of blocking of coreference are structural rather than semantic. A representation structured in phrases gives a clear interpretation of it:

IP	VP	CP	IP	AP			
[present] →	penser →	que →	est →	sour d			
↑			↑				
Il			DP	NP	PP	DP	
			le →	frère →	de →	Jean	

The structural reason why *Il* cannot refer to *Jean* is that the pronoun 'c-commands' *Jean*: the phrase which is just 'above' *Il* in the structure of the sentence is 'above' *Jean* (in this context, 'above' means to the left of a horizontal arrow or above a vertical arrow). The expression 'c-command' indicates a relation of dominance among phrases as sentence constituents. This is not affected by the distance separating *Il* from *Jean* in (5), as is shown by the example in Chapter 3 (p. 67). On the other hand, in *Jean pense que son frère est sourd* [= 'John thinks his brother is deaf'] the possessive *son* does not c-command *Jean*, and so coreference is possible. Nor should it be thought that the blocking is effected by the mere fact that a pronoun comes before its antecedent in the sentence: in *Le fait qu'il soit malade ennuie Jean* [= 'The fact that he is ill bothers John'], the pronoun *il* precedes but does not c-command *Jean*, so coreference is possible:

```
     IP          VP            DP
[present]—> ennuyer  —> Jean
     ↑
 DP          NP         CP        IP          AP
   le   —>   fait   —>  que  —>  soit   —>  malade
                                   ↑
                                   il
```

Although *Il* precedes *Jean* in the word order of the sentence, the IP just 'above' *Il* is not 'above' *Jean* in the structure and so coreference is possible, though not obligatory, of course. The role of the syntactic structure is basic to an explanation of the phenomenon. Coreference may well be a purely semantic phenomenon (whether a pronoun and a noun can indicate the same entity), but it is largely under the control of syntactic structures. A referential expression such as *Jean*, with its fixed reference to an entity in the perceived world, must not be c-commanded by a pronoun referring to the same entity. This is a rule that seems to apply not just to the syntax of French but to all languages. It is this universality and the difficulty of imagining that something so universal might result from learning which made Chomsky deduce that it derives from a faculty for language. And it is a rule of syntax, not of semantics.

Another phenomenon which is a good illustration of a strictly syntactic aspect of our faculty for language is the traces left by the movement of phrases.

The hidden presence of traces

In the example *Isabelle a-t-elle mangé ?*, the presence of the pronoun *elle* is interpreted as a visible trace left by the phrase *Isabelle* when it migrated to the position of subject of the complementizer phrase marking interrogation. Similarly, in the question *Qui Isabelle a-t-elle aidé ?*, it can be assumed that *Qui* has left a trace where it was before its assumed migration, that is, in the position of the complement of the verb *aider*. The invisible presence of the trace is at times indirectly revealed. In *L'homme qu'il a surpris* (6) [= 'The man [whom] he surprised'], there are of necessity two individuals (or again a mode of split personality). A representation of the structure of the sentence, showing the trace, explains the phenomenon:

DP		NP		CP		IP		VP		DP
le	→	homme	→		→	a	→	surpris	→	[trace]
				↑		↑				
				que		il				

It is apparent that the pronoun *il* c-commands the trace. If we assume that the latter behaves like a referential expression, it cannot be c-commanded by a pronoun like *il* if the pronoun indicates the same entity. The situation is exactly the same as in sentence (5), as long as the existence of the trace left by *que* at the starting point of its movement is taken into account.

If postulating the existence of invisible words seems injudicious, it should be remembered that such things are common in science. In physics, for instance, the existence of elementary particles has often been taken for granted, though there is no direct proof of their presence. In this case, however, the presence of traces can be shown by the phenomenon of agreement in French. A slight alteration to sentence (6) forces, as it were, the trace to appear: *La femme qu'il a surprise* (6') [= 'The woman [whom] he surprised']. The feminine form of *surpris* is naturally explained by the presence to the right of the word of a trace whose antecedent is *La femme*. The agreement of the past participle, in the case of a phrase movement, can be analysed via the presence of the trace left by the movement. The grammar of French requires us to make a distinction between the past participles (*entendu* and *vues*) in the two sentences *Les idées que j'ai entendu exprimer* [= 'The ideas I have heard expressed'] and *Les feuilles que j'ai vues s'envoler* [= 'The leaves I have seen flying away'], the reasons for which lie in the position of the trace left by *que* in its movement. An amusing sidelight on this is provided by the two different meanings to be seen in a single sentence, depending on whether the agreement is invariable or made with the plural antecedent: *Les enfants que j'ai vu changer* [= 'The children I've seen being changed'] and *Les enfants que j'ai vus changer* [= 'The children I've seen changing']. However, this semantic influence is not direct; it works through an alteration of the sentence structure which, though it concerns only the invisible element of the traces, is nevertheless real.

The syntactic phenomena just considered, the existence of phrases, their mode of assembly, the constraints on reference, and the hidden presence of traces reveal the existence of mechanisms peculiar to syntax which any healthy human being is capable of mastering. The relative complexity of these mechanisms suggests that our ability to exploit them is not a matter of chance. If, as seems likely, they reveal the existence of a syntactic component in our faculty for language, then that component must be locally optimal for a certain function (cf. Chapter 6). If we are to understand the reasons for the emergence of language in human descent, we must first understand the function of syntactic mechanisms, so as to assess their evolutionary local necessity.

10 Syntax and meaning

The only function there can be for our ability to put words together in a particular way must be a communicative one. Poetry, for example, may play with syntax in making its effects, but the function of syntax cannot be versification. If evolution has endowed us with a capacity to learn the grammar of human languages, it must be in order to facilitate the communication of meanings. In Chapter 9 we inspected some aspects of the workings of syntax and noted the extent to which they have their own logic. If their purpose is the communication of meanings, we must understand their role in the construction of semantic representations.

10.1 From protolanguage to language

In order to assess the role of phrases, their mode of assembly, and their ability to move within the syntactic structure of any given sentence, we must come closer to defining what the meaning is that these mechanisms help create. As presented in Chapter 8, protolanguage is purely referential. A word is used in protolanguage to refer to a concrete entity and the collocation of words refers to a composite scene thanks to a mechanism of composition of images. Any addressee hearing *bread table* will visualize, given the context, a new loaf lying on the table. As protolanguage expresses no relation between *bread* and *table*, such as their positions with respect to each other, that relation remains implicit in the image constructed via protosemantic interpretation. One manifest feature of language is that it does express relations and properties: *the bread on the table* expresses a spatial relation between two entities; *The runner wins* expresses that the property 'winning' applies to the 'runner'. Relations and properties are generally represented by 'predicates' and the entities concerned by the 'arguments' of these predicates. Thus, in accordance with the mode of representation adopted for the purposes of this chapter, *On(Bread, Table)* and *Win(Runner)* represent the meanings of the two examples.[1]

Protolanguage is not completely unhelpful when it comes to expressing predicates: to express *Win(Runner)* it is perfectly possible to say *Runner win*. It suffices to state the relations and properties and to express their arguments contiguously. In this way we have the form of protolanguage spoken by human beings, pidgin, some examples of which were given in Chapter 8. This expressive power of protolanguage may suggest that predicative semantics appeared in the absence of syntax, as opposed to Bickerton who argues that what brought about access to a new way of representing meanings was the appearance of a new way of putting words together, that is to say the more or less fortuitous appearance of syntax.[2] In this chapter it will be argued that it was probably the opposite that occurred. The syntax of language presents many peculiarities which can only be explained if they serve to express predicates by means of words. Though able to express the predicates of semantics, protolanguage was not perfectly adapted to this new function. In what follows, we are going to assess language as used by our species to see whether it is better adapted than protolanguage to the expression of predicates. This will entail determining in what way the devices of syntax are more effective than those offered by protolanguage for dealing with predication. The answer to that query is not straightforward.

The type of phrase which is the natural vehicle of predication is the verb phrase. Verbs, with their grammatical subjects and possible complements, are the prototypical forms via which predicates are expressed. It might appear plausible that, by introducing the verb–noun distinction into protolanguage, one could achieve an acceptable mode of conveying predicative relations, the noun expressing the entity and the verb expressing the predicate that bears on the entity. Pidgins as described by Bickerton function with nouns and a verb phrase; and Genie said things like, *Father take piece wood*. So prima facie the value of what is added by phrases other than noun and verb phrases is not self-evident. If we examine the semantic

---

[1] The word 'predicate' in this use is borrowed from the language of logic. It entails a written form of the type $P(x, y, \dots)$, which expresses merely that the property P applies to the entities indicated by the 'arguments' $x, y, \dots$ A predicate should not be seen as a static or universal known, memorized as such by individuals. In Chapters 11 and 12, predicates will be shown to be the result of a dynamic process, 'thematic segmentation'.

[2] Bickerton has more recently revised this point of view (Bickerton 1998).

function of adjectival and prepositional phrases, for example, we find that they too express predication. In *The bread is on the table*, the predicate is represented by the preposition *on*. In *Peter is unhappy*, the predicate takes the form of an adjective. Yet both phrases are superfluous if their role is solely that of predication, given that predicating can be done by verbs. Even so, we are quite conscious of the fact that in a typical sentence the predication conveyed by prepositions and adjectives is not playing the same role as that played by the verb. In *Paul buys the little book on the shelf*, the main predication, bearing on buying, takes the form of an assertion. However, the purpose of such a sentence is not generally to state that the book is a small one or that it is lying on the shelf. So both of the secondary predications contribute to the reference: by specifying that the book possesses the property of smallness, the speaker facilitates the determination of the book bought; and the same goes for its lying on the shelf. In this case, it is the preposition *on* which expresses a predicate of position and thereby contributes to the determination of the argument. Verb phrases can also play this role, on condition that they are introduced in a complementizer phrase, as in *the woman who is singing*. Under these circumstances, it can be seen that the range of different types of phrase can be of use in facilitating the determination of the objects to which statements refer.

Predication is what makes the difference between protosemantics and semantics. Protosemantics is solely referential, whereas semantics is predicative. The words of language, except proper nouns attached to definite entities, express predicates. Thus the word *book* does not represent a definite entity in the perceived environment, but a property that entities in our environment may or may not possess. In contrast to the words of language, which express predicates, it can be said that the words of protolanguage behave more like proper nouns. Not that this prevents them from being ambiguous in some cases, just as in some contexts the name John can mean more than one person. Conversely, a word like *book* may come to have the value of a proper noun, for instance if a sacred text is referred to as *the Book*. However, most of the words used in everyday language do not have this proper noun connotation and are interpreted as predicates.

Because of this use of predication, reference is replaced by an operation of determination. In a particular context, a proper noun like John can refer directly to a definite entity, in this instance a person. But adjectives, prepositions, complementizer phrases, or even common nouns make no direct reference. Through their expression of predication, they afford hearers a way to determine for themselves which entity is meant. As they do this, hearers are resolving a kind of equation. The phrase 'the green book' will make them seek in the perceived context for an entity x which is a book and is green, in other words the solution to *Book(x) & Green(x)* = *True*. In this way, predication is used indirectly to make reference.

A mechanism of this sort leads inevitably to a recursive system. A typical sentence expresses a predication, for instance the assertion of the purchase of the book by Paul; but this predication bears on arguments, the book and Paul, which have to be determined for the interlocutor. Such a determination, when it is indirect, also uses predication. In its turn, this latter predication may require determination of *its* arguments, and so on. For example, in the sentence (1) *Paul's brother buys the book that John got from Jack's sister,* at least three levels of predication may be observed: *Buy(x, y)*; *Brother(x, Paul), Book(y), Get(John, y, z)*; and *Sister(z, Jack).* It is only the first level that constitutes an assertion. The later levels are used recursively for the determination of the arguments at the preceding levels. Semantic recursion is rather like a set of Matryoshka dolls: as long as there are more dolls inside a doll, it must be opened, since they all contain elements facilitating the determination of arguments. But dolls are also like dolls: every predication contains arguments; every argument can go into a new predicate which helps determine it, and so on. This is a perspective that gives a rather fractal image of semantics, like a snow crystal which stays identical at all degrees of enlargement.

How does this recursiveness express itself in words? A predicate may be expressed by a word, for instance the adjective *proud* which expresses the predicate of *pride*. It is a predicate which requires arguments, and proto-language can supply these: *Peter proud Mary* may mean that Peter is proud of Mary. But if a speaker feels the need to use predicates to determine the arguments of *proud,* as in *Peter proud of his daughter,* then protolanguage cannot manage it. The solution adopted by language as we know it is to assemble phrases onto other phrases, as we saw in Chapter 9, which is itself a recursive system. We must try to understand in what way syntactic recursion, with its bearing on phrases, is useful or even locally optimal in enabling the determination of arguments of predicates.

10.2 Semantic recursion and syntactic recursion

The key to the role of syntax lies in a rather unremarkable observation, which is that the words of spoken language make a linear sequence. What is not unremarkable, though, is the fact that we are obliged to speak words one after another. We must not only express a certain number of predicates but also indicate that they have arguments in common. A possible solution would be to use a number of variables to designate the shared arguments: *x bought y; x is Paul's brother; y is a book; John got y from x; z is the sister of Jack* (1'). This procedure consists of using unambiguous variables to identify the arguments of the predicates, while being sure to use the same name whenever the variable designates the same entity.[3] The systematic use of variables solves the problem of how to convey meaning via a linear sequence of words. The recursive aspect of predication is coded into the name of the variables so that the resulting representation is 'flat', that is without apparent ramification. The predicates can then be expressed one after the other in random order. For example, the five predications of (1') may be stated in any order,[4] since their dependences can always be identified from the names of the variables: *z is Jack's sister; x bought y; John got y from z; x is Paul's brother; y is a book* (1').

Language involves a system of variables, including notably its pronouns (*him, who, the latter*), its possessives (*its*), and its indefinites (*something*), which play something of the semantic role of x, y, and z in the preceding paraphrase. A different paraphrase of (1) contains for example three explicit variables (*something, somebody, who*): *Paul's brother buys something that John got from somebody who is Jack's sister and that something is a book* (1'''). However, this system of pronouns cannot possibly cope with expressing all the variables in a sentence, such as those found in (1'). In contexts where there are several different possible antecedents for the pronouns, their reference becomes ambiguous, which shows the limitations of the system.

Furthermore, the accumulation of pronouns as in (1''') makes the expression feel clumsy, which can soon become irksome, confirming that the role of variables in language is merely ancillary.

---

[3] This form of expression resembles the way meanings are given to computers, for example with the Prolog programming language.

[4] Experts will recognize in this the property known as declarativity, the main advantage of Prolog.

Evolution might have endowed us with the ability to cope with an efficient system of variables, such as at (1'), capable of expressing the links between predicates. The fact is, though, that human beings do not spontaneously express themselves in that way. They use syntax based on the assembling of phrases. If we compare sentences (1') or (1''') with (1), the solution devised by evolution for the expressing of semantic relations does not seem the worst possible. The real problem with a system of variables is that it is bothersome and repetitious. And it is a problem that can be avoided by expressing semantic relations through the assembling of phrases.

The first technique used in syntax to express dependence among predicates consists of bringing together those which have arguments in common. The predicates expressed in (1) can be structured in an order that is close to the order in which they are spoken:

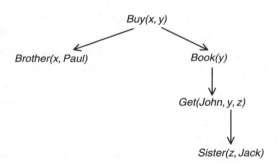

This representation shows four levels of predication, but as the variable *y* affects *Book* as well as *Buy*, the predicate *Get* could also have linked to *Buy*, which would reduce the representation to three levels. In some cases the argument is itself a predicate, as in *Peter thinks that John is ill* (2), which makes the representation even more directly recursive:

$$Think(Peter, x)$$
$$\downarrow$$
$$Ill(John)$$

This type of diagram in the form of a tree or a graph shows the recursive aspect of the semantic representation that remained implicit in (1') or

(1"). But a tree does not lend itself straightforwardly to linear sequences. A tree must be read in a particular order. In a way that seems natural to us, the syntax of (1) shows a possible reading of the tree, though many different readings would be possible, for instance: *Jack has a sister from whom John got a book which Paul's brother is buying.* The transition from semantic representation to syntactic representation, even when the former is in the form of a tree or a graph, is not immediate. Syntax must do two things: it has to express each predicate with its arguments; then it has to express the dependences between predicates. There is nothing surprising in the fact that, to express the recursiveness of the dependences, we are endowed with a syntactic system which is also recursive. It may, however, be surprising to realize that syntactic recursion is markedly richer than semantic recursion. This richness is not very obvious in a sequence of phrases such as *Peter's cousin's neighbour's brother's father,* though it is more apparent in *Peter's brother is proud of his adopted daughter,* a statement in which precise syntax makes for a concatenation of phrases. The art of putting phrases together is a particularly elaborate response to the semantic need for recursive determination of the arguments of the predicates. One may well wonder why it is so elaborate, with its range of different phrases and the numerous constraints it puts on the concatenation of them. Can semantics really require all that? From a semantic point of view, recursion generally follows an unvarying pattern: it links two predicates by making them share an argument. If we are to understand why syntax and its features are as they are, we must grasp the means by which it contrives to express dependences between predicates.

10.3 The principle of semantic linking

To express predicates, syntax makes use of phrases. A typical phrase consists of a head, a subject, and a complement.[5] The specimens of syntactic structures inspected in Chapter 9 were all built on this pattern. One of the functions of this mode of structuring is to express the relation between a predicate and its arguments, the predicate being expressed by the head while the arguments are represented by the subject and complement of the phrase. Thus, the predicate *Love(Peter, Mary)* translates

---

[5] According to Chomskyan x-bar theory, this is the structure of all phrases. In some versions of the theory it is possible to have multiple complements.

naturally into the phrase *Peter loves Mary*, in which Peter occupies a subject position allowing it to enter the predicate *Love* as an argument, while *Mary* in the complement position is interpreted as a supplementary argument of *Love*. So if predicates can be expressed by phrases, how do dependences between predicates translate? Phrases, with their two positions of subject and complement, have not only an internal structure that enables them to translate the structure of predicates but also the possibility of being hitched together. It is this property that is exploited for the recursive expression of links between predicates.

From the point of view of semantics, predicates are generally linked by their arguments. For instance, *Brother(x, Paul)* and *Buy(x, y)* are linked by the fact that they share a variable in the argument position, that is to say there is an entity, designated here by *x*, which has the twin properties of being both the brother of Paul and the actor of a purchase. The nature of the connection between the phrases is different, in that one phrase is joined to the subject or complement position of another phrase. For example, in *The brother buys*, the determiner phrase with *The* as its head occupies a subject position.[6] This means that phrases connect through structural links, either the link to the subject or the link to the complement. This system is radically different from the sharing of arguments. How can such structural links express semantic links?

We have an implicit awareness of what it is about phrases that links their form to their meaning: predications conveyed by a phrase share an argument with the predicate associated with the head of the phrase. In *Give me the little book off the pile*, the noun phrase translates the expression *Book(x) & Little(x) & Off(x, y) & Pile(y)*. The adjective occupying the subject position of the noun phrase expresses the predicate *Little(x)*, which shares its argument with the predicate associated with the head of the phrase *Book(x)*. Similarly, the predicate *Off(x, y)*, expressed in the complement position of the noun phrase, also shares an argument with the head predicate. We can call this rule on argument sharing among predicates the *principle of semantic linking* and define its functioning as

---

[6] In the mode of analysis adopted here, the noun phrase *brother* occupies the complement position of the determiner phrase (DP) of which *The* is the head; and it is this DP which occupies the subject position of the inflectional phrase IP. The same procedure was followed with the examples used in Chapter 9.

follows: the predicate expressed by the head of a phrase is semantically linked to the predicate expressed in the subject position and to the predicate in the complement position. This linking translates generally as argument sharing. In a sentence like (2) *Peter thinks that John is ill*, the linking does not consist of an exchange of arguments. Rather, the predicate expressed in the complement serves as argument for the head predicate. It should be noted that the principle of semantic linking does not specify which argument is the one to be shared, which can lead to curious ambiguities. In *the overtaking of the car*, it is not immediately clear whether the translation should be *Overtake(x, y) & Car(x)* or *Overtake(x, y) & Car(y)*, since that would depend on whether the car is overtaking or being overtaken. Each of these translations abides by the principle of semantic linking, which is why there is an ambiguity. In other cases, the ambiguity arises not from the choice of variable to be shared but from the choice of the predicates which effect the sharing. In the French sentence *Jean reçoit la médaille de Jacques*, which could mean either 'Jean receives the medal from Jacques' or 'Jean receives Jacques's medal', interpretation will vary depending on whether the prepositional phrase *de Jacques* links to *reçoit* or to *médaille*:

IP   VP   PP   DP

[present] $\longrightarrow$ *recevoir* $\longrightarrow$ *de* $\longrightarrow$ Jacques

$\uparrow$ $\downarrow$

Jean   la $\longrightarrow$ *médaille*

=Receive(Jean, x, Jacques) & Medal(x)

The interpretation induced by this syntactic representation is that it is Jacques who gives the medal (i.e. *de* = 'from'). If the phrase *de Jacques* links not to the verb[7] but to *médaille*, the principle of semantic linking requires the associated predicate to share an argument with *Médaille(x)*

---

[7] Recently, some authors including Chomsky have argued that in some cases the verb may stand 'above' the group formed by its complements (Larson 1988, Radford 1997: 201, Chomsky 1995: 62). In our example, one could say *Jean reçoit la médaille des mains de Jacques et les fleurs des mains de sa fille* ('Jean receives the medal from Jacques's hands and the flowers from his daughter's hands'), which suggests that the two complements *la médaille* and *des mains de Jacques* belong together in a single phrase which the verb commands though not belonging to it. This distinction would not alter the analysis of the example.

(i.e. *de* = 'of'). The preposition *de* is then interpreted as the predicate of belonging (*appartenance*):

IP   VP   DP   NP   PP   DP
[present]→ *recevoir* → *la* → *médaille* → *de* → *Jacques*
↑
Jean

=*Receive(Jean, x, y) & Medal(x) & Belong(x, Jacques)*

In accordance with the principle of semantic linking, syntax can establish dependences among predicates without any need of a system of variables. It does this by bringing together in a single phrase the two predicates to be linked. This affords us a further opportunity of noting that syntax is an autonomous mechanism serving semantics. It uses phrases like tools which bring together inside the same structure the predicates that have to be linked, after the biological manner of an enzyme attracting two molecules to the same site and bringing about their joining. Semantic structure, even in tree form (illustrated in 10.2), cannot be straightforwardly conveyed by a linear sequence of words. One possible solution would be to represent meaning by a system of variables whose names make it possible to link predicates by their arguments (cf. p. 214). The result would be a 'flat' semantic structure in which the links between predicates are marked implicitly in the names of the variables. Such a mode of representation could without difficulty be communicated via the serial flow of words. And yet the solution that evolution has provided is radically different. The semantic structure translates into another structure, also in tree form, which expresses the relations between predicates by bringing them together inside the same phrase. The principle of semantic linking, along with a number of other principles, enables hearers to reconstruct meanings through an understanding of which variables are shared among the predicates. Syntactic structure lends itself to sequential utterance. Phrases are spoken in a relatively constrained order which varies from one language to another. French prefers the subject of the phrase to precede the head, which in turn precedes the complement, whereas in Japanese the head follows the complement. However, in all languages, phrases are read 'depth first': if the subject of the phrase, for example, consists of another phrase, then the latter is uttered before the rest of the phrase containing it. In this way, phrases are embedded within each other like Matryoshka dolls and they never partially overlap.

So the system of phrases fulfils its function, which is to express predicates and their relations of dependence. To do so, it uses the principle of semantic linking. It also uses other mechanisms, whose functioning, though serving the expression of meaning, illustrates the autonomy of syntax from semantic structure.

10.4 The autonomy of syntactic mechanisms

Syntax is a tool working on behalf of the expression of meaning. As such, it has a structure and rules of functioning which are peculiar to it, though the purpose of this structure and these rules can be explained by the function they fulfil. If we consider for example the movement of phrases, it is not possible to say *Paul buys John has got the book*, since the principle of linking prohibits *Buy* and *Book* from sharing their arguments. In *Paul buys the book that John has got*, the insertion of a complementizer phrase allows the second argument of the predicate *Get* to move to a position where it can be shared with the predicate *Book* (cf. 9.3):

The book that John has got

syntactic structure   semantic structure

DP	NP	CP	IP	VP	DP	*Book(y)*
The $\rightarrow$	*book* $\rightarrow$	*that* $\rightarrow$	*has* $\rightarrow$	*got* $\rightarrow$	[trace]	

$$\text{Get(John, y, z)}$$

with *John* below *that / has / got*.

At its starting point in the verb phrase, the variable *y* is an argument of the predicate *Get*. As a result of movement, it comes to a position where the principle of semantic linking can apply inside the noun phrase whose head is *Book*. The variable *y* can thus be shared between the predicate *Book* and the predicate at the head of CP, represented by *that*, for the CP phrase occupies the complement position in the noun phrase. Syntax here offers an original means, without counterpart in semantic representation, for indicating that an argument is shared by two predicates. In *Paul buys the book John has got* the whole CP phrase, though present, remains covert. The hypothesis of an unexplicit or empty predicate at the head of CP reinforces the formal character of the principle of semantic linking and its independence from semantics.

In semantic representation the arguments are on an equal footing in the predicate, whereas this symmetry does not obtain inside the phrase. In the preceding example, movement is necessitated by the enclosing of an argument in the complement position. When the sharable argument is in the subject position, the bringing together can sometimes be simpler. The reason is that the subject occupies an external position within the phrase, whereas the complement occupies an internal position. In *Paul buys a book and steals an umbrella, Paul* is the grammatical subject of both verbs, though stated only once. In the semantic representation that we have adopted, *Paul* occupies the position of first argument: *Buy(Paul, x) & Steal(Paul, y)*. In speech, the 'factorizing' of *Paul* is possible because the grammatical subject is 'above' the verb. In the examples of syntactic structures that we have inspected, the grammatical subject turns up in the subject position of IP, that is outside VP, a consequence of which is that the grammatical subject is 'farther' from the verb than the complement is. This clarifies why the same factorizing is more difficult to accept for the complement: *Paul buys and Jacques steals a book*. Ellipsis can also result in a sort of factorizing: *Paul buys a book and Jack too*. There, the excentric position of the grammatical subject allows sharing of the verb-complement set marked by the simple echo *too* in the second clause. This device is a neat way of expressing *Buy(Paul, x) & Book(x) & Buy(Jack, y) & Book(y)*.

The functioning of phrases makes for a radical divergence between semantic representation and syntactic representation. The most obvious manifestation of this can be seen in the form taken by recursion. Semantic recursion is implicit. Every predicate, with its arguments, forms a whole. We think *Buy(x, y)*, in which x and y indicate definite entities, for instance a person we know or an object we have seen. Then we think to define x for our interlocutor by means of the predicate *Brother(x, Paul)*. Next, y must be defined by means of another predicate, and so on. Recursiveness lies in the fact that predicates may require to be defined by other predicates. This is an 'algorithmic' mode of recursion, for it can only be seen during the course of a procedure. Recursiveness in syntax, as it appears in a sequence of words, is different in nature; it is 'structural'. The stating of a phrase ends only when all the phrases that it contains are themselves stated. Consequently, the syntactic expression of a predicate is not done all at once. In sentence (1), the stating of *Buy(x, y)* is interrupted by the stating of the other predicates *Brother(x, Paul)* or *Get(John, y, z)*. The intricate embedding of these predicates during utterance may be more obvious in *He gives the book that John got from Jack's sister to his brother*, where the third argument of *Give* remains undetermined until after the full stating of *Get(John, y, z)*. This structural embedding is the price syntax must pay for making it possible to bring together predicates that share a variable. Representation on the basis of named variables (p. 214), by being structurally 'flat', avoids this drawback, but it requires a detailed interplay of variables and multiple repetitions.

Evolution set us on the path to structurally recursive expression of semantics. Fundamental aspects of syntax owe their existence to the need to express meaning with the least possible ambiguity, examples being the way phrases are interlinked or can move, as we have seen. If we bear in mind the principles stated in Chapter 6, we must assume that syntax is locally optimal for its function. If that is the case, we are bound to wonder why such a system of interlinking of phrases should coexist with a second system which, as we are about to see, seems to fulfil the same function.

10.5 Another form of syntax

Languages like French or English rely largely on the position of their words for the expression of meaning. Any change in the word order within a sentence usually results in an incorrect sentence or in a change of meaning. This strict order is the result of fitting together the components of the sentence in a way which, starting with the basic words, produces bit by bit an edifice in which everything hangs together. But there are other languages with syntax that is radically different from this; and an encounter with them can be extremely disconcerting. Sentences spoken in Dyirbal, one of the Aboriginal languages of Australia, give no appearance of requiring a set word order:

ba-la-n	*ɖugumbil-ø*	*ba-ŋgu-l*	*yaɽa-ŋgu*	*buɽa-n*
the-ABSII	woman-ABS	the-ERG-I	man-ERG	see-PAST

'the man saw the woman'

It seems that the five words of this sentence can be uttered in any order without the meaning being changed or the sentence sounding ungrammatical (Dixon 1972, quoted in Van Valin and LaPolla 1997: 1). To some extent a similar flexibility can be seen in a language like Latin: *Petrus Paulum ferit*, *Paulum Petrus ferit*, and *Paulum ferit Petrus* are three different ways of saying 'Peter hits Paul'. We might wonder whether this flexibility of word order does not invalidate everything we have observed on the rules of phrase linking and their effect on the expression of meaning. What is syntax for if the positions of the words are of no importance? The alleged total freedom of word order in Dyirbal probably cannot be taken at face value. We are dealing here with a language spoken by about forty people, which makes it difficult to elicit reliable pronouncements on grammaticalness. In spoken French, not only is a statement like *La voiture, la femme, hier, elle l'a vue* (literally 'The car the woman yesterday she saw it') grammatically acceptable, but its four components could be ordered in very different ways, such as *Elle l'a vue, hier, la femme, la voiture* (literally 'She saw it, yesterday, the woman, the car'). For a more complicated sentence the choice is more restricted; and if we add *devant le magasin* ('in front of the shop'), then a sentence like *Elle l'a vue, la femme, devant le magasin, la voiture, hier* (literally 'She saw it the woman in front of the shop the car yesterday'), begins to sound a bit too much like Monsieur Jourdain's countess beautiful. It seems likely that the same goes for Dyirbal. Nevertheless, it is a fact that constraints on the position of words in some languages are laxer than in others and this may appear to invalidate any analysis in terms of phrases.

In the preceding example from French, it is semantic constraints that enable us to tell that *elle* refers to *la femme* and *l'* to *la voiture*. In languages like Dyirbal or Latin, this role is played by case markers. In the example from Dyirbal, the absolutive (ABS) and the ergative (ERG) mark respectively the patient and the agent of the action. Also, agreement makes plain which noun each of the determinants applies to. Speaking more generally, the system of case marking seems to solve without further ado the problem of argument sharing among predicates. The word *yaṛaŋgu* in the example translates as the predicate *Man(x)*. It shares its argument with the predicate *See(x, y)*, expressed by the verb *buṛan*, for the simple reason that *yaṛaŋgu* is case-marked as ergative and this case identifies the actor of 'See'. So it would appear that, for expressing argument sharing among predicates, the case-marking system offers a solution that is different from phrase linking. Ray Jackendoff stresses the independence and concurrence of the two systems:

> ... the two systems of grammar are built independently on top of the system of protolanguage, each refining communication through its own expressive techniques. I see no immediate argument for the temporal priority of one over the other in the course of evolution. (Jackendoff 1999)

The system of case marking can lend itself to a fair degree of complexity, to be seen in its wealth of inflections. Steven Pinker cites *Näïkìmlyìià*, a word from Kivunjo, a Chagga dialect spoken in Tanzania near Mount Kilimanjaro, which means 'he is eating it for her' and is composed of eight parts: *N-*: a marker of focus; *-ä-*: a subject agreement marker, there being sixteen gender classes, including human singular (as here), human plurals, thin objects, extended objects, objects in pairs or clusters, clusters themselves, instruments, animals, parts of the body, diminutives for small or 'cute' things, abstract qualities, precise locations, and general locations; *-ì-*: present tense (other tenses can refer to today, earlier today, yesterday, no earlier than yesterday, yesterday or earlier, the remote past, habitually, ongoing, consecutively, hypothetically, in the future, at an indeterminate time, not yet, and sometimes); *-kì-*: an object agreement marker, here indicating that the thing eaten belongs to gender Class 7; *-m-*: a benefactive marker, indicating that the beneficiary belongs to gender Class 1; *-lyì-*: the verb 'to eat'; *-ì-*: an applicative marker, indicating the presence of an additional role, that of the beneficiary; *-à-*: a final vowel, which can indicate indicative versus subjunctive mood (Pinker 1994: 127–8).

In French, for example, such richness of morphology, here bearing upon the verb, is almost unheard of. A verb part like *je partirais*, say, is produced by adding to the root of the verb a marker of the conditional mood and another marker indicating the first person singular. Kivunjo, however, is a language which marks the verb according to the semantic features of its argument, thus allowing them to be identified in the sentence. This is a system of marking which, combined with its agreement rules, enables straightforward linking between the predicates of the sentence. Does this mean that systems of marking and phrase linking are two quite independent syntactic systems?

The fact is that in most languages the two systems coexist and are interdependent. In a language like German, the nominative case is given to the grammatical subject, regardless of whatever semantic role it plays: in

Der Sohn isst den Apfel ('The son eats the apple') the subject *Der Sohn* is marked as nominative; and the same happens in the passive version, where it is *Der Apfel* which is nominative: *Der Apfel wird von dem Sohn gegessen* ('The apple is eaten by the son'). And yet, from a semantic point of view, in one example the subject fulfils the role of the actor (the eater) and in the other it is the patient (what is eaten). So case depends on syntactic function. The close connection between case marking and phrase linking is seen also in agreements: in German, the complement of the preposition *zu* ('to', 'towards') always takes the dative; and in a similar way, adjectives have the case of the nouns they qualify. In the light of this interdependence, it seems quite legitimate to wonder whether the existence of two syntactic systems is not something of a redundancy.

Prima facie there is an obvious difference between phrase linking and morphological marking. The latter makes for identification of the arguments of the predicates, though it plays no role in predication. Morphological markers for gender, case, or, as in some languages, class, are not predicative.[8] The dative in German indicates at most a role, typically the role of beneficiary. The fact that *den Kindern* ('the children') takes the dative in *Ich gebe den Kindern einen Apfel* ('I give the children an apple') adds no predication but serves to link the predicate expressed by this phrase to the predicate 'Give'. This, however, does not indicate any exclusiveness in the markers. French makes notable use of non-predicative prepositions to clarify simple links between two predicates: *donner à Pierre* ('to give to Pierre') translates as *Give (x, y, Pierre)*, in which the preposition *à*, like the German dative, expresses no predicate but presents an argument to the predicate of the enclosing phrase. On the other hand, in *la médaille de Jacques* the preposition *de* is predicative and expresses belonging, whereas in *Il la reçoit de Jacques* ('He receives it from Jacques'), its only function is to introduce the argument of 'Receiving'. Such non-predicative prepositions are transparent when the principle of linking applies, though they constrain the choice of shared argument. So the presence of *à* in *donner à Pierre* forces recognition of *Pierre* as the recipient of the gift, in other words as the third argument in the representation of 'Giving', and not the object of the giving. In many languages, this function is served by morphological marking.

---

[8] It should be noted that there are a small number of predicates, including Seeming, Causing, and Willing, which can be expressed by an affix.

Nevertheless, though marking is not predicative, it is closely linked to semantics. This can be seen in the class markers of Kivunjo or even in the typical roles associated with cases in German, such as the role of theme for the accusative, actor for the nominative, possessor for the genitive, or beneficiary for the dative. The link between marking and semantics can also be seen in connection with gender. In French as in German, the gender of nouns can serve to mark the sex of individuals. But this also shows how marking can diverge from semantic connotations, gender being allotted to common nouns mostly in accordance with fortuitous convention: *la table* is feminine in French, though its German counterpart *der Tisch* is masculine. This can lead to amusing confusions between the gender of nouns and their associated semantic connotations, as in a sentence like the following, containing *le mannequin* (a masculine noun for 'model', i.e. indicating a person who is more usually feminine) and *la sentinelle* (a feminine noun for 'sentry', i.e. indicating a person who is more usually masculine): *Le mannequin a épousé la sentinelle; il* (or should the agreement be *elle?*) *a accouché d'un beau bébé* (literally: 'The model married the sentry; she has just had a fine baby').[9] There, though agreement between *le mannequin* and the masculine pronoun *il* is grammatically logical, agreement with feminine *elle* would be intuitively logical, but that would then wrongfoot the reader or hearer who expects *elle* to refer to *la sentinelle*. Such discrepancies must strike us as disconcerting, if we take the view that the function of the marking system is to facilitate the semantic categorization of entities mentioned in statements. Actually, marking does not directly serve semantic interpretation. What it does do is utilize semantic categorization for syntactic purposes, as can be seen clearly in the example from Kivunjo: the existence of sixteen semantic classes of possible agreement between a verb and a word contained in the sentence makes it almost impossible to misassociate the relevant word and the argument marked in the verb. It might almost be said that whether conventions governing classes depart from semantic reality or not, as happens with the gender of nouns in French, is unimportant. It does not prevent the marking system from making effective differentiations between words in ways that facilitate the linking of predicates, despite the fact that in some instances the system may function pointlessly, marking

[9] I am grateful to my colleague François Yvon for drawing my attention to this example.

distinctions which are superfluous (Carstairs-McCarthy 1998), the genders of nouns in French being perhaps a case in point.

Are there any languages which function without morphological marking or other languages which do without phrases? English is an example of a language that has very little in the way of inflectional morphology, even less than French. Both languages are practically devoid of case markings, except for those effected by pronouns such as *she* and *elle* which can become *her* and *la* (or *lui*) depending on the case assigned by the verb. There are, however, linguistic theories which posit the presence of an unmarked case to explain sentences like *Peter seems to be getting better*. This would mean that the phrase *Peter* had migrated from its position as subject of *getting better* that it would normally occupy in *It seems [Peter] to be getting better*, to take up the 'empty' position occupied by the impersonal *It*. The reason alleged is that, as no verbal phrase in the infinitive such as *to be getting* in that example can assign a case to its subject, *Peter* must move so as to receive its case from the subject position of *seem* which happens to be available. If we accept this type of interpretation, the case system may turn out to be universal, even where it has no morphological reality. On the other hand, can we imagine a language without phrases? Here again Dyirbal might be thought to be relevant. However, in a sentence like *Balan yabuɵ baŋgul ŋumaŋgu gigan banagaygu* (word for word 'the mother the father say return' = 'the father told the mother to return'), the subset *Balan yabuɵ* ('the mother') is considered to be the grammatical subject of both *gigan* ('tell') and *banagaygu* ('return'), while *baŋgul ŋumaŋgu* ('the father'), in its capacity as actor for the predicate 'Say', is the complement of *gigan*[10] (Dixon 1972, in Van Valin and LaPolla 1997: 542). These subject and complement functions suggest that what we are dealing with here is the phrases to be found in any language. The sentence under discussion also contains an embedded phrase: the clause made of *banagaygu* and its understood subject is embedded in the main clause built round the verb *gigan*. The structuring of sentences in Dyirbal is consequently, at least in part, based on the linking together of phrases, in particular verbal and prepositional phrases. The flexibility of the word order, underpinned by this basic structuring, derives from the richness of

---

[10] As Dyirbal is an 'ergative' language, the grammatical subject typically plays the role of patient while the complement of the verb plays the role of actor.

the morphological marking and can be exploited in ways that stress some elements for rhetorical purposes.

The interdependence between phrase linking and morphological marking in languages may be explained by the fact that present-day humans possess the ability to use both systems. What is unknown is whether a mode of syntax could exist that would function through just one of them. Seen from this point of view, the two systems are not equivalent, for morphological marking, unlike phrase linking, is not a recursive system. Take for example two German sentences: *Der Vater des Schülers schämt sich* ('The schoolboy's father is ashamed') and *Der Vater schämt sich des Schülers* ('The father is ashamed of the schoolboy'). There, the only thing that makes it clear that *des Schülers* is a complement of *Vater* in the first one and a complement of the verb *sich schämen* in the second is the positioning of the phrases. The genitive marking has the effect of linking the predicate *Schoolboy(y)* to one of the two other predicates that could be linked in this way, *Father(x, y)* and *Shame(x, y)*, and the potential ambiguity is resolved in this case by the positioning of the phrases. In a simple sentence involving only two levels of predication, this type of ambiguity is not possible. As the number of levels increases, the risk of ambiguity increases rapidly. Marking can reduce the likelihood of ambiguity by broadening the range of possible markers: genders, cases, class markers. A more foolproof system would entail a mode of recursive marking combining markers on the same word. This would mean that the word *Schüler* in the first sentence would bear two cases simultaneously, the nominative and the genitive. In some contexts, such as *I am ashamed of the teacher's friend's son*, a single word might bear three genitive marks. However, it does not appear that any such system exists in any human language.

The lack of recursiveness in morphological marking should not be seen as a total drawback. Each of the two syntactic systems used by human beings has its advantages and disadvantages. The functions they have in common are to express predicates and to indicate which predicates share an argument. The system of phrase linking is recursive, which makes it possible to express without difficulty several levels of predication. However, if there is no marking, it also requires strict word order. This must count as a disadvantage, since word order cannot then be exploited in the service of other parameters such as emphasis or rhetorical effect. In addition, the principle of semantic linking does not clarify ambiguities, since it does not identify which argument is shared (cf. *the overtaking of the car*). This entails the use of non-predicative phrases such as certain prepositions used to clarify the semantic role of their complement, e.g. *by* to indicate the actor (*It was bought by John*) or *to* to indicate the receiver (*given to John*), etc. Non-predicative phrases of this sort have the effect of overloading the structure. Marking systems, on the other hand, can avoid these disadvantages, but they too have their own built-in limitation, in that, by not being recursive, they are incapable of expressing unaided several levels of predication.

Human beings possess two syntactic systems which, though they coexist in present-day languages, are functionally independent from each other. Given that they both appear to fulfil the same function of expressing links between predicates, it is worth wondering whether they arose independently.

10.6 The origin of syntax

If it is a fact that each of these two syntactic systems has its own justification, then it is understandable that they should coexist in languages spoken today. If we are to discover whether one or other of them existed without the other at some time in the past of our species, we must answer two questions. Is each of them functional in isolation from the other? Is each of them locally optimal? As we have just seen, the answer to the first question is 'Yes'. On the second question, the syntactic mechanisms outlined in Chapter 9 and in this present chapter suggest that each of the two syntactic systems is locally optimal for linking predicates to their arguments. This would give us three competing hypotheses: (1) that morphological marking existed first on its own, and was followed by the appearance of phrases; (2) that phrases existed first, followed by the appearance of marking; and (3) that the appearance of predicative semantics induced the simultaneous emergence of both systems. In the present state of knowledge, as Jackendoff says, it is difficult to choose one of these possibilities rather than another. Intuitively, one may feel attracted to the view that a system of marking, rudimentary to begin with, might have become a complex innovation once predicative semantics had emerged, which would seem to rule out the second of the three possibilities. The interdependence we can see between phrases and marking in today's languages could be evidence supporting the third hypothesis, simultaneous emergence. But the complexity of phrase linking, with particular features such as recursion and movement, makes the first of the three scenarios very plausible.

The aim of this chapter has been to show that the machinery of syntax, which represents the originality of language in relation to protolanguage, though relatively complex, is also well regulated and, unlike what was previously imagined (Chomsky 1975; Piattelli-Palmarini 1989), does not owe its existence to chance. Syntax is based on a specific biological faculty, two essential elements of which are a capacity for morphological marking of words and a capacity to link phrases together. This syntactic faculty has a basic function which justifies its existence from an evolutionary point of view: it enables the expression of relations between predicates in the serial flow of words. To be compatible with the mechanisms of evolution set out in Chapter 6, the syntactic faculty must conform to the principle of local optimality. From the point of view of functional organization, the procedures that our syntactic faculty allows us to perform appear to be locally optimal, in the sense that it is not possible to improve them without thoroughly altering them. This last point is still the subject of debate, some linguists arguing that the system of phrases is not optimal (Lightfoot 2000). However, the fact that some aspects of syntax seem imperfect (for instance, the difficulty of extracting the complement of a subordinate clause by a movement) does not necessarily invalidate its local optimality which presupposes the making of a number of compromises among competing demands, such as the concision of the message, flexibility of expression especially with regard to word order, reduction of ambiguities in the linking of predicates, a reasonable cognitive load for encoding and decoding of the message, and the ease of children's learning of the particular syntax of their language from the examples to which they are exposed. It is possible to imagine a radically different system as a reasonable alternative that would satisfy all these constraints, for instance a system modelled along the lines of Prolog, with named variables (cf. p. 214). However, no one has yet suggested any changes to morphological marking or to the system of phrases likely to make for better performances over the whole set of criteria set out above.

This finding refers, of course, to the human ability to operate a syntactic system and not to the syntax of any particular language. The variability of syntax from one language to another can be explained, in part, by the relation established in each one between marking and the system of phrases. This variability is also affected by phenomena internal to each of the two systems, such as the order within phrases of the subject, the head, and the complement, lexical insertion within phrases, the choice of markers and entities marked, morphology, the rules of agreement, etc. Some authors argue that when the general principles of language become implemented in any particular language, they can give rise to sub-optimal deviations (Carstairs-McCarthy 1998). However, this does not invalidate the adapted character of the syntactic faculty itself.

The fact that syntax constitutes a functional whole derives entirely from the pre-existence of a predicate-based semantics. Details of syntactic organization may be described in isolation from a structural point of view; but their functional role, as we have seen, can only be understood via a demonstration of their ability to express links between semantic predicates. In our quest for the reasons why language emerged, we must now try to understand why predicative semantics appeared in a world which hominids could only perceive through their protosemantics. The key to the problem lies perhaps in the birth of the semantic faculty. Whatever the case may be, the syntax of language certainly owes its existence to this.

11   The structure of meanings

There would be no communication among human beings, no languages, no phonological systems, no words, no syntax, if languages with their sounds, their words and syntax did not enable speakers to create in the minds of their interlocutors thoughts related to their own. What do the meanings brought about by language consist of? Do they resemble what animals may experience? Why did our ancestors' brains evolve to manipulate these novel meanings? These are crucial questions if we are to understand the emergence of the human system of communication. Were it not for the operation of understanding, language would be nothing but pointless noise or at best a restricted signalling code. The crux of the mystery surrounding the appearance of language lies in this question of meaning. We can all have an intuition about what a sentence 'means', but to describe from the outside what that meaning consists of is not easy. It is even less easy to have a clear idea of the cognitive difference between a human being capable of understanding any given sentence and another primate incapable of such understanding. In this chapter, it is not our aim to bring these issues to definitive resolution, but rather to arrive at a description of the essential aspects of semantics from a functional point of view. If we can give a convincing account of the functional anatomy of meaning, however sketchy, we shall then be able to canvass the reasons why it emerged.

We have already encountered two modes of interpretation of speech. The concept of protolanguage, examined in Chapter 8, presupposes protosemantic competence in dealing with images and concrete scenes. Predicate-based semantics, on the other hand, which we drew on in Chapter 10 for our account of the role of syntax, is a world away from protosemantics. The aims of this present chapter[1] are first to clarify the

---

[1] The ideas presented in this chapter and the following one were developed in collaboration with Laleh Ghadakpour.

nature of these two semantics and the relation between them and then to canvass their respective roles in the evolution of the capacity for language.

11.1 Concepts, images, and definitions

Here once more is Molière's M. Jourdain, this time learning about predicates:

M. JOURDAIN: What? The son of the Grand Turk said that about me?
COVIELLE: Yes. As I had told him that I knew you very well and that I had seen your daughter, 'Ah!' he said, '*marababa sahem,*' which means 'Ah! I am so much in love with her!'
M. JOURDAIN: What? *Marababa sahem* means 'Ah! I am so much in love with her!'?
COVIELLE: Yes.
M. JOURDAIN: Well, upon my soul! It is as well you told me that, since for the life of me I would never have thought that *Marababa sahem* might mean 'Ah! I am so much in love with her!' What a fine language Turkish is! . . . His Turkish Highness does me too much honour and I wish him all prosperity.
COVIELLE: *Ossa binamen sadoc babally oracaf ouram.*
CLÉONTE: *Bel-men.*
COVIELLE: He says you should go quickly with him to prepare yourself for the ceremony so as to see your daughter right soon and draw up the marriage settlement.
M. JOURDAIN: So many things in two words?
COVIELLE: Yes, the Turkish language is like that, it says a great deal in few words. Do go along with him.

In everyday use, the average adult commands several thousand words and understands several tens of thousands. This would appear to mean, following the logic of Chapter 10, that any adult has access to tens of thousands of different predicates. An individual who hears and understands a word is able to recognize the predicate that it expresses. Recognition associates meaning with the words heard and, thanks to syntax, also with the sentences. Monsieur Jourdain knows intuitively that, as an equivalent of the translation given by Covielle, *Bel-men* must be rather approximate. Lexical words refer to meanings which we represented in Chapter 10 by predicates; and when he hears Cléonte say *Bel-men*, he expects the meaning of this utterance to amount to one or two predicates. But 'quickly', 'with him', 'to prepare oneself for the ceremony', 'to see one's daughter', and 'draw up the marriage settlement' express at least five separate ideas. To represent the meaning of a sentence, the evidence of Chapter 10 would lead one to expect roughly as many predicates in it as there are words. Where would these predicates come from in such numbers? A partial answer may be provided by the ways in which predicates relate to each other.

Predicates are not mental representations unconnected to one another. Most lend themselves to analysis via other predicates. *Kill(x, y)*, for example, is more or less equivalent to *Cause(x, z) & z=Die(y)*; and *Stallion(x)* gives a meaning close to *Horse(x) & Male(x) & Unsterilized(x)*. The philosopher Jerry Fodor, however, resolutely opposes the idea that any such breaking down plays a part in our understanding of statements. According to him, when we hear sentences like 'The stableman killed the stallion', we do not set about breaking down each of the predicates in the sentence so as to reconstitute its meaning. Our understanding of such a sentence does not depend on whether the predicates can or cannot be analysed via other predicates. If it did, understanding *The stableman killed the horse* would systematically require less effort, which is not the case (Fodor et al. 1980). However, if we accept Fodor's argument on this, it leads to rather untoward consequences. In particular, if predicates cannot be analysed into definitions, if they are actually atoms of meaning, then what is not clear is where we get the knowledge that seems to define them. Yet this knowledge is known to the people who use the words associated with the predicates. Ask any adult what a stallion is and the right answer will very likely be given. There are of course many words which are polysemic and can therefore represent different predicates. However, most people are aware of the meaning *Horse(x) & Male(x) & Unsterilized(x)* and are able to make sense of it if required to.

The problem with definitions, in Fodor's sense, is complicated by the fact that not all predicates are as easy to define as *Stallion*. Can one explain what a horse is to a child without showing one or at least a representation of one in a photograph or a drawing? No child would understand a definition such as 'mammal of the genus *Equus*'. It would appear that perceptual representation is indispensable: so *that's* what a horse looks like! Even so, a concrete predicate like *Horse* is not resistant to all definition. If you are asked how many lungs a horse has, or even a kangaroo, it is not your image of the animals that will help you answer 'two'.

Predicates relate to words, to perception, and to other predicates. Which of these three relations defines them? A commonly made distinction is that between the 'signifier', that is the word or the linguistic form, and the 'signified'. We have been using the term 'predicate', which belongs to logic, to mean the signified. It is a term which fits well with a formal use in which predicates combine to form definitions. However, it does blur the close link that exists between the meaning of a word and an image, as in the case of *Horse*. When we think of the difference between a horse and a donkey, the thing that helps us most is no doubt our images of them. The term 'concept' may seem more apt than 'predicate' for indicating the meanings of words; and it is certainly more commonly used. One advantage of it is that it does not require a choice to be made between the perceptual and the logical aspects of meaning. However, for that very reason it is ambiguous. It can be applied both to the associated image, for example in the case of the concept *Horse* to the image of the prototypical horse at a canter, and to the logical definition which sees the horse as having two lungs. Choice is in fact a necessity here, for it can serve no useful function to conflate in a single imprecise notion two representations as distinct as an image and a logical definition. Actually, whichever term we choose, we appear to be confronted by insurmountable difficulties. If concepts were nothing but definitions, no child could ever learn what a horse is; if concepts were nothing but images, we could never be sure whether a kangaroo has two lungs. To opt for saying that a concept is both an image and a logically defined entity comes too close to playing with words, for the problem of knowing how the connection gets made between the image and the definition remains unsolved.

In the empirical tradition, concepts are linked to perception, a concept being identified with a class of objects that we have some experience of. Recent empirical thinking focuses on the idea of typicality. A class of objects is organized about an ideal exemplar, a prototype, so that an object's belonging to the concept is gradual. Sparrows and nightingales belong 'more' to the concept of 'bird' than do geese or ostriches. Empirical theory is consistent in that it declines to consider the existence of logical relations between concepts. When the source of all knowledge is experience, any relations between concepts are purely a matter of statistics. So kangaroos have two lungs because animals resembling kangaroos generally have two lungs; and kangaroos have a heart because animals resembling kangaroos generally have a heart. However, human knowledge is not purely a matter of statistics. We can say that the heart and lungs are indispensable to breathing and to the circulation of the blood and that no kangaroo lacking these organs could live. In that case, their presence in the kangaroo's body is perceived as necessary. A strictly empirical theory is unable to explain this relation of necessity between concepts, since statistical relations are always contingent and cannot rule out exceptions.

The rationalist tradition, by contrast, stresses the idea of definition. A concept is defined in terms of other concepts. The rationalist system applies to concepts the principles which codify the organization of mathematical knowledge. Any new mathematical idea is defined in terms of ideas already known. If such a system is to avoid turning into a vicious circle, the existence of primitive notions which do not require definition must be presupposed. In mathematics the notion of number was considered for a long time to be primitive; then the introduction of sets as a new primitive notion at the beginning of the twentieth century led to a definition of numbers. Similarly, we must imagine that certain concepts used by human beings require no definition and are primitive concepts which serve to define all other concepts. To the rationalist, such concepts can only be innate. Several objections can be raised against this way of conceiving of the system of concepts, the most obvious of which is that there appears to be no reason why concepts thus defined might be of any use. A concept such as *Horse* is useful insofar as the entities we categorize as horses present consistent aspects and behaviours; but a concept bringing together all objects that are two-and-a-half feet high would almost certainly be useless. If concepts owe nothing to experience and everything to their definition, then there is no prima facie reason why the concepts we form should have the slightest usefulness, unless we agree with Descartes that the hand of God guarantees harmony between our mind and the universe. A second objection against a system of concepts organized like mathematics is raised by Fodor, who shows that understanding of concepts requires no analysis of their definition: if we want to be clear about the difference between a *Horse* and a *Donkey* or between *laying* and *throwing* a book on a table, it comes to us as an image rather than as a logical definition.

The choice here is an impossible one. If the meaning of a word cannot be broken down into predicates, then it is equally impossible to see it as an image or a prototype. The main objection against the empirical theory is its inability to exclude. If all concepts are kinds of average perceptions, prototypes, then nothing is impossible and all we have is at best atypical things. Empirical astonishment and rationalist astonishment are therefore different in nature. If somebody claims to have seen a sheep without a mouth, empiricists will be surprised by the novelty of the thing; but if they then come across a few hundred more mouthless sheep, they will stop being surprised. Rationalists, on the other hand, will not react in that way: they will want to know how such a sheep could eat. Rationalist astonishment is not susceptible to things statistical; and even after seeing their ten thousandth mutant sheep, rationalists will go on seeking an explanation. A fundamental characteristic of human beings is not just their ability to be astonished over lengthy periods but also the ability to clarify the reasons for their astonishment and to make others share it. Although this is, as will be seen, an essential aspect of language use, a strictly empiricist conception of human understanding can offer no explanation of it.

Coming now to a consideration of the biological role of conceptualization, we can see that here too there is a clear dichotomy between the empiricist and the rationalist conceptions. Depending on whether concepts are perceptual representations or logical representations, accounts of their origins will not coincide. On the one hand, roughly speaking, empiricist discourse will hold that concepts derive from the capacity for categorization and that the use of them in language comes later. The rationalist view, on the other hand, says that the reason why we have concepts is a logical one: they arose along with language. Their categorizing power is thereby seen as a consequence of their being used predicatively. So did language create meaning? Or was it the improvement of our ability to see the world as segmented that profoundly changed our ancestors' way of communicating?

The solution to this dilemma proposed in the following pages consists not of a loose compromise between the rationalist and the empiricist views of concepts, but rather of a suggestion that we abandon the idea of a concept as a single representation in favour of a dual representation. This choice of duality is pregnant with consequences; of necessity, it will entail first justifying the existence of two cognitive apparatuses operating in tandem, then considering two separate biological functions. And it will lead to the reconstruction of two separate evolutionary histories. That is what we are about to embark on.

11.2 Thematic segmentation

In Chapter 10, the meaning of utterances was expressed through predicates. A sentence like *John goes to London* would be represented by a
predicate of the type *Go(John, London)*. Once we have analysed the process
of thematic segmentation, this notion of predicate will come to seem
merely a convenience of expression. Entities analysed as theme, frame of
reference (or reference point), or agent will replace the arguments of the
predicate; and the predicate itself will take on the appearance of a simple
relation linking them.

Theme, trajectory, and reference point

There is a limit to our ability to vary the meanings that we express.
Semanticists have observed systematic parallels in our ways of expressing
relations between objects, locations, or properties. Here are five sentences:
(1) *John goes to London*; (2) *The light turns red*; (3) *John gives his support to
the chairman*; (4) *John leaves the house to his sister*; (5) *We are approaching
Christmas*. Each of these five situations can be analysed as dealing with
movement in a physical object, except in (3) which speaks of a more abstract
entity. The examples show great variation in the spatial dimensions in
which the movement takes place. In (1), the space is physical; in (2) it is a
space of colours, limited here to three, green, amber, and red; in (3) the
place of movement is a set of individuals; in (4) the house does not move
physically, but a change of possession is translated, as in (3), by an entity
passing from one person to another; and in (5) there is movement in time.
Ray Jackendoff, following the lead of Jeffrey Gruber (Gruber 1965), sees the
analogy common to these examples as the mark of our way of conceptualizing thematic relations (Jackendoff 1983: 188). In any movement, the
theme is the entity that moves. The other elements are linked to the
trajectory of the movement. In examples (3) and (4), the trajectory is
explicitly limited by two entities, John and the chairman and John and his
sister. In (1), the starting point is John's present position; in (2), the light
'moves' from its initial colour, which in certain contexts may be inferred to
be amber, to red; in (5) Christmas day or the Christmas period is the end of
the trajectory. Jackendoff, Gruber, and others argue that the meaning of
many linguistic expressions is informed by ideas of movement or location:

Language translates all non-visual relationships into spatial relationships. All languages do this without exception, not just one or a group. This is one of the invariable characteristics of human language. (Porzig 1950: 156, in Lorenz 1973: 129)

In any expression referring to a situation, whether concrete or abstract, there are to be found a theme (the entity moved or located) and a reference point or frame. If there is movement, then the trajectory fulfils the function of the frame of reference. In the following examples the frame of reference is an entity or a region of concrete space or an abstract space: (6) *John lives in Bath*; (7) *John lives between Leeds and York*; (8) *John lives near Glasgow*; (9) *The ice is threatening to crack*; (10) *John prevents Joe from succeeding*. In (6) the frame of reference is the geographical surface corresponding to the town of Bath and the theme is typically John's house. In (7) the frame of reference may be seen as a line or strip linking the two towns. In (8) the frame of reference is an area centred on the town; and we shall see how the size of the area is determined. The last two examples aim to show that even in a space that is more abstract than geographical space, the ideas of theme and frame of reference remain relevant. Imagine that the context in which (9) is spoken is one where two people are standing on a frozen lake. What is to be understood? One interpretation could be that the weight of the two people comes close to that at which the ice will start to break. There are of course other interpretations, for instance a temporal one that would mean the time is coming close when the ice will start to crack because it is thawing. If we take the first interpretation, we can consider that the theme is the combined weight of the two people and that this theme is located below a reference point, the threshold weight which will break the ice. Another interpretation of the 'is threatening' metaphor would give the opposite result: the theme, subject to changing location, is the breaking point of the ice and the reference point is the weight of the two people. In either case, (9) is analogous to (8), since the theme is to be found close to the reference point. One may wonder whether an interpretation in terms of theme and reference point might be inappropriate in (10), yet a faithful paraphrase of (10) is: *John prevents Joe from achieving success*. There, *Joe* appears as the theme and *success* as the reference point. Though this distribution of roles may seem quite natural, the fact is that the space in which the thematic relations in (10) can take place seems less obvious. From the example it may be deduced that some people have success and some do not.

There is naturally an inside-outside relation, Joe being outside the set of people who have success. Also, we understand from the word *prevent* that Joe as theme should move from outside the set to inside but that an action by John thwarts this eventuality.

It is clear that thematic segmentation, that is to say the making of a distinction between the theme and the reference point in a particular space offers an explanation of part of the interpretation brought about by reading examples (6)–(10). If we generalize, we could say that any interpretation requires a topographical type of thematic segmentation: the theme is positioned or moves in relation to a reference point within either a metric space (that is, the space of geography or weights and measures) or a topological space (as in the inside-outside duality of example (10)); the movement or the maintenance in position can be caused by an action exercised by an agent, of the sort that Talmy describes as a simplified force (Talmy 1988). Before testing the validity of this generalization and its consequences for the origin of language, we would do well to inspect in greater detail how thematic relations work. This we can do by examining an area different from concrete space, namely time.

Thematic segmentation of time

Most linguistic statements are time-related. In order to understand them, hearers must often engage in a process of temporal reasoning. This makes for an interesting situation, since unlike spatial thinking, it entails a clear distinction between mental representations and perception. It is not easy to separate our conceptualizations of spatial relations, such as nearness or innerness, from what perception shows us. But in the case of time, there is a greater separation between perception and conceptualization. One could be forgiven for thinking that both of them are based on linear time as used in science. Time as we conceive of it as a natural phenomenon, linear time comprising an infinity of instants, is an idealization somewhat removed from the way we express and think of temporal relations in language and reasoning. The idea of objective time as used in the physical sciences, logic, and artificial intelligence is a recent cultural construct requiring a command of the mathematical concepts of infinity and continuity (Lakoff and Núñez 2000). According to this concept, an interval of time is made up of an infinity of juxtaposed instants infinitely close to each other. Such a conceptualization, which does not exist in most cultures, plays no part in our cognitive processing of temporal relations. Here are some examples: (11) *The plant died during the drought*; (12) *Paul was the president long before the Fifth Republic*; (13) *She showered for ten days (and then she began to save water)*; (14) *In 1918, after John came back from the war, he had lunch with an old friend who formally handed over a letter to him.* In example (11) we see a standard thematic relation: the death of the plant, standing for the theme, is located inside a frame of reference, the drought. In (12) the presidency of Paul, seen in its entirety, is the theme; and as such it is located outside the frame of reference of the Fifth Republic. The thematic segmentation of (11) and (12) is thus analogous to what we saw in examples (7) and (8). Much can also be learned from the other examples. To interpret (13) we must create a repeated event: the shower in question is generally not understood as a single event lasting for ten days. How do we know? The use of the preposition 'for' obliges the hearer to mentally extend the event recounted so that it coincides with the duration stated. In *She showered for ten minutes* the extension is compatible with the normal duration of a shower. In (13) that would be impossible, as the typical duration of a shower cannot be extended to ten days. In this case, the mind interprets the situation by making the event repeat itself. The frame of reference is no longer a single shower, but a recurring one; and the theme 'Ten days' can now fit inside the frame of reference, enabling the expression of a temporal constraint. The repetition operation shown in (13) is a basic cognitive practice also applicable to space: in 'The table is covered in flies' the table is situated inside an area defined by the repeated presence of flies. If we accept Jackendoff's arguments, this repetition operation as it applies to time and space is the same one we apply to our conceiving of plurals; and to go from 'a tree' to 'trees' activates the same mental process as going from the single to the repeated (Jackendoff 1990: 30).

Example (14) reveals another mental operation. As we interpret the handing over of the letter, we are on a timescale of a few seconds, the time it takes to give a letter to somebody. This is far from the timescale on which we can place the year 1918. Interpretation of (14) requires first that 1918 be placed in relation to the present, then that the return from the war be set within the year 1918, and finally that the lunch with the friend be also located. This gives four successive themes (1918, the return, the lunch, and the handing over of the letter) and four successive reference points (the present, 1918, the return, and the lunch). These successive locations in time function on different timescales. The salient fact is that when we are on one of the timescales, the events on the other scales cannot be conceptualized, so that when conceptualizing the handing over of the letter, we have no direct access to the other three themes or reference points, the present, 1918, and the return.

The way we interpret temporal statements reveals several aspects of our semantic faculty. Before going further, it should be established that there is nothing linear in our mental processing of time. We do not follow a line of objective time made of infinitesimal instants. Nor do we even make use of some such line in order to position ourselves. Convenient though it is in the physical sciences, it is an abstraction that is unusable in any attempt to model mental operations. It would require a virtually infinite memory to store events on a line that was dense enough to enable interpretation of a statement like *Fifteen billion years ago during the first four nanoseconds of the universe*. The method employed by our mind to interpret this sort of statement relies on a recursive mechanism of positioning via changes of timescale. We take as a starting point a scale on which the theme and the reference point can appear together, for example the present moment and the birth of the universe. Then when finer distinctions are called for, distinctions that are inaccessible on the first scale, we change scales and the process starts over again until positioning has been achieved. It is exactly the same recursive technique that we use for orienting ourselves in space. For instance, in interpreting *In London, not far from Euston, in the pedestrian zone, right next door to the Oddbins* we also apply a recursive change of scale.

The reason why we have this mechanism of mental positioning lies in the poverty of any representations we can construct on a given scale. When speaking of going from Glasgow to London, we have no representation of any Oddbins or pedestrian zone, or even of Euston. Nor is it remotely likely that Carlisle, Leighton Buzzard, or Harrow and Wealdstone will figure on the mental map that we draw up. When we mentally locate the birth of the universe in relation to the present time, not only do we not see a film of all the events that have taken place since then, we probably form no representation of any of them. Why then, it may be asked, speak of scale, since this is a word that presupposes the existence of a mental map? Might not the recursive change that we have considered be a mere repeated change of focus induced by the fact that we are constantly attending to different objects situated in time or space? The answer to that is no: a mental map, for all its poverty, does deserve to be called a map, for it possesses topological and metric properties. The processes via which we interpret an event as being included in or prior to some other event are topological. And if we mentally position the pedestrian zone close to Euston we are also conducting a metric operation. Such operations and processes are carried out on a mental map of minimal structure, sufficient to feature the reference point and the theme and to make clear their relative positions: separateness, inclusion, proximity. If there is a change of theme, a new map is required to position it, which entails the discarding of the earlier one. Our mind seems to be unable to function on two different scales at the same time. Nevertheless, the system of mental positioning is fully functional and makes for an arbitrarily great degree of accuracy in temporal or spatial location, which would not be the case in a positioning system with a fixed scale.

Positioning and thematic roles

The significance of the system of recursive positioning whose functioning we have just seen in the interpretation of temporal statements goes well beyond the question of location of events in time or space. The mere fact of mapping a reference point or frame and a theme onto a scene, whether concrete or abstract, helps us identify semantic roles; and by positioning the theme with respect to the reference point or frame we can create a relation that did not previously exist. We might, for instance, be looking at various objects on a desk: a telephone, a computer, a few books and papers, a rubber, a desk calendar. Between perceiving this whole scene and realizing that the rubber is on the desk there is a qualitative difference. The mechanism through which we realize the rubber is on the desk entails mental mapping of the scene. The map ignores the other objects and locates the rubber and the desk as respectively theme and frame of reference. So it makes for accurate definition of the topological relation that can translate as the predicate *On(Desk, Rubber)*. The mental operation of conceptualizing a spatial relation is qualitatively different from perception. Perception of the whole scene, with the desk and the objects scattered over it, is a rapid process in which we take in the objects more or less simultaneously. Mostly we go no further, though at times we conceptualize some thematic relations: the rubber is on the desk top, the telephone under the papers. Such conceptualizations are slow and successive. The ones figuring in the example are based on perception, though their nature is not perceptual. In the examples illustrating temporal relations we noted that, for conceptualization to occur, perception was not necessary. In understanding *Paul was the president long before the Fifth Republic* we perceive nothing; but thanks to a very sketchy mental map we are able to place Paul's presidential term in the past outside the period covered by the Fifth Republic.

What I am suggesting here is that this principle can be generalized. Conceptualization of situations requires systematic use of a small number of means, which include mental maps, whether spatial, temporal, or abstract. Behind this system of maps there is no doubt a single positioning mechanism. This means that conceptualizing the idea that *Bill is nicer than Josephine but not as nice as Dorothy* is no different from understanding a statement like *Bonfire Night is after Hallowe'en but before Christmas*. In each case we position a theme and two reference points on two successive very simplified maps.

The means we have at our disposal for conceptualizing statements are not limited to mapping and the segmenting of theme and reference point. For instance, attribution of the semantic role of actor can be arrived at through location of the source of a force acting on the theme (Talmy 1988). An example of this is sentence (10) above, in which the theme is kept outside the frame of reference by the action of John. Furthermore, conceptualization of a statement generally involves several operations of thematic segmentation. In *Last year he was smaller than his father* the situation has to be thematically segmented both in terms of time and the scale of heights. However, even allowing for these points, the fact remains that conceptual segmentation, which produces predicates, is a result of the systematic application of a small number of mechanisms.

Thematic segmentation and metaphors

If the preceding generalization is correct, we may well wonder why mechanisms of conceptual segmentation are so closely patterned on functions as concrete as spatial location, movement, or application of forces. What comes to mind is that this way of analysing the phenomenon is a mere analogy, a spatial and dynamic metaphor similar to any other metaphor that can be thought of to relate areas of meaning to each other. This is a conclusion that would certainly be approved of by George Lakoff, who has always argued that language is largely based on the use of metaphor (Lakoff and Johnson 1980). In the preceding sentence, for example, the word 'based' is metaphorical (language, not being an object, cannot have a base) as is the adverb 'largely'. Metaphor is a powerful tool for transferring meaning from one field to another; but if analysis of thematic segmentation in terms of local maps or forces is nothing but a metaphor, it can teach us nothing about the biological origin of our semantic faculty. A metaphor must adhere to the parallelism of the analogy but apart from that constraint the choice of image is relatively free. For example, instead of saying that language is 'largely based on the use of metaphor', I could have said 'language draws heavily on metaphor', or even 'language is studded with metaphors'. That being so, equating thematic segmentation with mapping or the application of forces would appear to show nothing more than our ability to bring together different areas of meaning. If a spatial metaphor brought us to consider local maps, what would some other analogy have produced? Lovers may use metaphors drawn from botany, astronomy, cooking, meteorology, or warfare to express their feelings for one another. Can the roles of theme, reference point, and actor be systematically expressed via such metaphors? Jackendoff's view on this is resolutely negative:

[T]he most remarkable aspect of metaphor is its variety, the possibility of using practically any semantic field as a metaphor for any other. By contrast, thematic relations disclose the same analogy over and over again: time is location, being possessed is a location, properties are locations, events are locations. That is, the theory of thematic relations claims not just that some fields are structured in terms of other fields, but that all fields have essentially the *same* structure. (Jackendoff 1983: 209)

The example of time, discussed in detail above, is informative in that respect. It is not through mere metaphor that we locate events in relation to each other according to insideness, outsideness, or overlapping, in other words according to topological relations (Desclés 1990). No author has ever suggested a non-topological mechanism for representing the difference of meaning between (16) *The telephone rang while he was speaking* and (17) *The telephone was ringing while he was speaking*. In (16) one can imagine typically that the duration of the ringing is completely enclosed inside the duration of the speaking: for instance, the telephone rings and somebody answers it while the speaking continues uninterrupted. In (17) one can see more readily that the duration of the speaking, perhaps a single sentence, is completely enclosed inside the duration of the ringing. If the speaking lasts for a long time, the meaning taken will no doubt be that the telephone rang repeatedly, as in *The telephone kept ringing while he was speaking*. One would be hard put to it to find a metaphor capable of explaining the difference between these examples without having recourse to topological relations of inclusion. A metaphor is always optional, in the sense that one can choose not to use it or to use another one, whereas the interpretation of (16) or (17) requires that the topological relations between the events be correctly determined with regard to the context. This is very different from the stylistic and optional effects of metaphor, in that what is being determined is meaning.

It is striking that our way of grasping conceptual relations, of understanding 'Who does what to whom', as Steven Pinker says, should be so stereotyped. The means employed by the main mechanism enabling this conceptual segmentation of any situation resembles a system of spatial positioning: a map, a reference point, a theme, and a simple relation of a topological or a metric kind (insideness, separateness, closeness) between the theme and the reference point. This mechanism along with several others creates a part of meaning, the part that deals with thematic relations. Meaning, however, as we shall see, is not reducible to thematic relations.

11.3 Double meanings

The thematic segmentation examined in the preceding section is a basic element of the human semantic faculty, but only an element. It enables us to construct a predicate from a situation, by isolating what it is that makes the different arguments of the predicate and then putting them back into a certain relation. For example, a thematic analysis of *John goes to London* yields *John* as the theme and *London* as the reference point, and establishes a topological relation putting *John* on a trajectory limited by *London*. The predicate *Go(John, London)*, like all the predicates used in Chapter 10, is merely a convenient shorthand for expressing this topological relation between two entities.[2] Thematic segmentation plays an essential part in

---

[2] Strictly speaking, predicative shorthand is impure, since it retains a power of evocation. The word *go*, used to characterize the predicate *Go(John, London)*, conveys more than a location on a trajectory. This is why predicative shorthand, despite its usefulness in Chapter 10 for describing the interface between syntax and semantics, cannot be used in this chapter, since the purpose here is to make a clear distinction between the two components of our semantic faculty.

the predicative analysis of situations and in guiding the syntactic expression of meaning (cf. Chapter 10).

However, it must not be forgotten that thematic segmentation expresses only part of meaning. As a way of dealing with what words are capable of bringing to our minds, it is actually extremely limited. Take a spoken sentence as simple as *Peter hit Paul*. The only reason it would be spoken to us is that we know the two people in question; and we may even be familiar with where the act took place, at a village celebration, say. When we hear the sentence, the scene we can imagine is quite richly detailed, with the village people eating at trestle tables, glasses of *sangría*, paper plates, the squabble erupting, people intervening, Peter lashing out, Paul bleeding a little, the squaring off, the insults, etc. Or we may be ignorant of the exact circumstances of the event; and it is even possible that we do not know where it occurred or who Peter and Paul are. Whatever the case, it will inevitably be more than a mere thematic segmentation, which does no more than locate the event before the present on a local temporal map. Going a little further, thematic segmentation may analyse the situation by showing the theme, Paul, as subject to a force whose actor is Peter. If the situation is analysed more closely, as in *Peter gave Paul a thump*, segmentation produces a theme (the blow struck), a trajectory from Peter to Paul, and a force exercised by the actor (still Peter) on the theme. It is clear that this type of description is too meagre to fully represent what is brought to mind by the sentence *Peter hit Paul*.

Thematic segmentation is shown to be an extreme simplification of a scene. Although we may conceptualize the fact that an action was done by Peter to Paul or that something was transferred from Peter to Paul, we are still very wide of the semantic mark. The verb *hit* conveys much more than some indeterminate relation between two people. Everyone hearing it, by virtue of their experience and the situations in which they have heard the verb being used, will be bound to construct a more or less richly detailed representation of what actually took place between Peter and Paul. And their representations will vary depending on whether the verb used is *hit* or one of its more or less close synonyms, like *struck, punched, slapped, bashed, assaulted, knocked him about, roughed him up, gave him a bunch of fives*, etc. Despite which, the thematic analysis would be basically the same for all those variants, though some of them, such as 'knocked him about', suggest a repetitive theme. As this example shows, thematic analysis is too poor to catch the shades of meaning separating words.

What precedes suggests that the meaning produced by interpretation of linguistic utterances is not reducible to a single type of representation. Meaning is not limited either to thematic relations or to a mental scene stimulated by words. The interpretation of language results in two representations which are different in kind, one of them being a thematic representation and the other a representation which, in concrete contexts, consists of a scene. In Chapter 8, as part of a definition of the semantics associated with protolanguage, we discussed the evocative power of words. Protosemantics consisted of associating a concrete scene with a juxtaposition of words. It is tempting to see the protosemantics of our ancestors as a functional component of our own semantic capacity. This would produce a sort of equation: protosemantics + thematic segmentation = semantics. Such an analysis takes on its full significance when seen in an evolutionary context, with the appearance first of protosemantics as a functional whole, then the emergence of thematic segmentation with *Homo sapiens*, a development which would have resulted in the emergence of syntax. However, this way of conceiving of the semantics of language does raise problems, the first of which is related to the concreteness of the scenes constructed by protosemantics. Another one is the problem of defining what relations and even what conflicts there are between representation based on scenes and thematic representation. There is also the difficulty of understanding how such a composite could be functional and locally optimal.

Any limitation of protosemantics to concrete scenes would appear to rule it out as a functional component of semantics. This is the argument that Bickerton uses against those who claim that we think in images (Bickerton 1995: 22). Here once again is the example he uses against the idea that representation requires images: *My trust in you has been shattered for ever by your unfaithfulness* (see p. 177). This point appears to be a very strong one, given that the abstract content of the assertion gives little scope for any concrete visualization, and that, though some readers may well claim to 'see' the meaning of the sentence, it is highly unlikely that any two of them would be seeing the same thing. There are of course thematic aspects associated with the sentence, since the theme *my trust in you* passes from one state to another under the influence of an actor, *unfaithfulness*. There is also a temporal relation which locates the change of state in the past and leaves the new state unlimited. Thematic relations can also be seen in *in you*, in which *you* plays the part of frame of reference to locate the theme *my trust*, as in 'the trust I place in you'. Similarly, the prefix *un-* can be analysed in a thematic way, as the degree of faithfulness shown by the interlocutor is outside the area required for trust. But if we were to go no further than these thematic relations, we would end up understanding merely that 'something that was somewhere changed its state in the past because another thing was not in the right area', which is slightly reductive. The Bickerton argument, which says there is something absurd in the idea that concrete images contribute anything to the meaning of the sentence, seems to rule out any other possibility. If, however, we stretch the idea of an image a little, to cover whatever is perceived or felt, including emotions and sensations, then there is a marked reduction in the absurdity.

The different words used in Bickerton's example have evocative power. Admittedly, this power does not run to the creation of concrete scenes; but its evocativeness is no less real. The word *trust* for instance can summon up a feeling that is quite unambiguous in the context in which it is used, as can *unfaithfulness*. In this sense, we do not think with words, unlike what Bickerton appears to mean: we think with what words bring to mind. This is the very principle that we saw at work in protosemantics, except that our words refer to something more than images and concrete scenes. The words of human languages are able to convey in a more or less simplified way whatever we are able to perceive or feel. By being part of what we may call a 'scenic representation', these simplified perceptions and feelings are also part of the meaning we attribute to spoken statements.

This aspect of meaning seems to bring us close to the empiricist view that concepts are simplified perceptions. What comes to mind with a word like *hit* is in fact a prototypical scene, for instance a person landing a blow on another person's face. However, the empiricist view of the prototype falls far short of what would be required to explain the scenic part of semantics. As I said before, the mechanisms on which the empiricist tradition focuses are statistical and the prototype is constructed out of repetition of experiences. This makes the prototype merely an average perception, simplistically shorn of all the contingent details which vary from one experience to another. The interpretation of language requires a more powerful mechanism for the constructing of prototypes. As we saw in Chapter 8, human beings have the capacity to combine concrete scenes. The mechanism that enables combinations of this sort cannot rely solely on experience, since scenes made in this way can be completely novel and non-experiential, even physically impossible, after the manner of what we see in dreams. Prototypes on the empirical model cannot function in such combinations; they are not even sensitive to contexts. Also, human beings are able to form prototypes from a single perception. You only have to see one compressed-air corkscrew to form a prototype of it, a simplified representation that will leave out many details of the real object but in which the functional properties will be retained. With that difference, the simplified perception that a word or sentence may bring to mind does have some relation to the empirical idea of a prototype.

The foregoing discussion leaves us with a two-part view of semantics. One part of meaning comes from thematic segmentation; the other part consists of the stimulation of images or simplified sensations, making a scenic representation. Such an assembly does not give the immediate impression of being a working system. We must have a clearer idea of how it functions if we are to understand why and how it arose in the past of our species.

12 The emergence of meaning

If we adopt the parameters set in Chapter 8 and see protolanguage as a forerunner of language, and protosemantics as a forerunner of semantics, then the coming of a new ability like thematic segmentation must be explained in functional terms. In this chapter, I intend to make a distinction between the respective roles of the two components of our semantics with the aim of defining the place they had in the evolutionary history of the faculty of language.

12.1 The dissociation of the two forms of meaning

The apparent redundancy of thematic segmentation

On hearing a sentence spoken, human beings activate two simplified representations, one of which is a scene made from sensations sometimes barely sensed and the other a thematic analysis that locates a theme and a reference point in relation to each other on an extremely schematic mental map. What is contributed by the second of these representations? Nothing at all, prima facie, it would appear. Thematic analysis is so sketchy that it seems to overlap entirely with scenic representation. If, on hearing the statement *The apple falls off the tree*, we can visualize the scene, even in the most perfunctory way, we have no need to analyse it into a theme and a trajectory. Thematic analysis is rather like a stupid paraphrase which omits or ignores the fine detail and subtleties of a phenomenon that we can grasp much more aptly in the sensations awoken in us by the words—we can see the apple dropping, the ground covered in windfalls, or other apples still on the tree, etc. Obviously this perception is relatively poor: the other apples are not always there; the movement of the apple is not as uniform in its acceleration as it is in reality; we are unaware of how many apple trees there are in the immediate vicinity. Nevertheless, for most people visualization has taken place; they can say, for instance, that it was daylight when the apple fell and that they perceived the scene from a point of view outside the tree. It is difficult to see what might be added by thematic segmentation.

To have a clear grasp of the respective functions of the two modes of semantic representation, it is probably necessary to avoid seeing them as being in competition with one another. Though it is clear that thematic representation cannot be substituted for even an impoverished scenic representation, we must attempt to see clearly what it is that thematic representation contributes that scenic representation cannot. With that in mind, one way of proceeding would be to envisage situations in which one or the other of the two semantic components produces a result that is wrong. We shall examine two phenomena: mirror inversion and Zeno's paradox.

Mirror inversion

A friend who enjoys perplexing you asks you to explain why it is that mirrors invert right and left but not top and bottom. This inversion of right and left is an everyday experience for all of us. In the reflection, our right hand turns into a left hand, hanging to the left of the body seen in the image and with its fingers ordered like those of a left hand, that is, the opposite of a right hand. If you read a text in a mirror, the image is inverted, for instance any letter *d* looks like a *b*. Yet the text is not inverted vertically and no *d* ever looks like a *p*. How can you explain this perplexing phenomenon to the poser of conundrums? One's astonishment comes from the fact that the mind draws an inference which contradicts what is perceived. When the problem is posed, you visualize the situation, drawing on your capacity for scenic representation, and realize that right and left are in fact inverted, but that top and bottom are where they should be. The posing of the conundrum also makes you do an exercise in thematic segmentation. On hearing that right and left are inverted, you create a theme, the shape of a hand, say, which moves in an abstract space from one value to another different value. The fact that these values are called 'right' and 'left' is immaterial to the analysis, which is exactly the same as when it concerns an inversion of top and bottom: that is, a theme moving through a trajectory between two values. The thematic analysis tells you that the mirror is the cause of the right-left transposition. In Talmy's terms, the mirror exercises an abstract force that propels the theme on its trajectory, turning the shape of a right hand into the shape of a left hand. The mirror ought to exercise its influence in the other dimension too, by inverting the vertical alignment, since the ingredients are the same as in the horizontal. Thematic analysis says roughly that the same causes produce the same effects and so, in the absence of any other force, the mirror should invert a shape such as *d* from an upwards-facing position to a downwards-facing one.

When somebody faces you with this problem of mirrors, you understand it. You make a thematic segmentation of the situation that can only confirm what seems obvious: if things are turned from right to left, then they should also be turned from top to bottom. Yet your visualization of the scene treats the two dimensions differently. Which of the two apparatuses is mistaken? If you look at your own image in a spoon, the vertical axis seems to be just as inverted as the horizontal. Why should the behaviour of a flat mirror be any different?

It so happens that in this case it is our capacity for scenic understanding that produces a faulty representation. The spoon inverts both right-left and top-bottom (which equates to rotation), whereas in fact the flat mirror does neither. I compare my reflection with myself, except that the other self raises its left hand rather than its right. In order to be the other self looking at me, I would have to turn through 180 degrees horizontally. Nothing turns in the mirror, where every point stays opposite its own image. But if I hold up a text to the mirror, I see a reflected text in front of me. I compare the reflection with my own text and the letters and words seem to have been horizontally inverted. If I want to see my sheet of paper the right way round, I will have to turn it through 180 degrees. If I present my right thumb to the mirror, it points to my left both in reality and in the reflection, meaning nothing has turned. I still cannot help seeing the right hand as a left hand, though my expectation is to see a right hand; and I deduce wrongly that the mirror has made a right-left inversion. How does such a faulty perception of the situation arise?

The hand I see in the reflection is not a real one. It is what is known in optics as a virtual image, produced by an inversion. The virtual hand looks unmistakably like a left hand, which is why we are mistaken. What it is in fact is a hand inverted from front to back, a right 'anti-hand'. Nature has given us a left hand that looks like a right 'anti-hand', which is why we make the mistake. This is the source of our deduction that a right-left inversion has taken place and of the resulting paradox. The thematic interpretation was not mistaken when it noticed no difference. In all these mirror experiments, the only right-left inversions are produced in our own mental imaging and not in the mirror. I turn round mentally to compare myself with the anti-self facing me; I mentally turn my text or my hand to compare them with what I can see in the mirror. These attempts fail, as my shape once turned round does not coincide with my back-to-front inverted shape. The text becomes legible once it is turned, though the reflection is as illegible as the text was before rotation, for example if I had read it from behind on transparent paper. My right hand once turned does not fit with the anti-hand shown by the mirror. Right-left inversion never comes from the mirror, but from the rotation that our capacity for mental imaging feels obliged to effect in its interpretation of the anti-objects shown in the mirror. It should not be concluded that our mental imaging is in any way inferior because it is capable of making such gross errors. In the next section, the boot is on the other foot and the mistake is made by our thematic segmentation capacity.

Zeno's paradox

The feeling inspired in us by Zeno's paradox is the perfect illustration of the difference in functioning of the two components of our semantic faculty. In 460 BC, Zeno of Elea came to the rescue of his master Parmenides, one of whose theses had been subjected to ironic criticisms. Parmenides taught that Being is unbounded, indivisible, and unmoving. Plurality and movement are mere illusions. It was Zeno's achievement to argue that the idea of movement is an absurdity; and his arguments, which bothered his contemporaries, remain bothersome to this day. We can reuse the example of the falling apple to illustrate one of his paradoxes.

Zeno's idea was to decompose movement. Before reaching the ground, the apple must fall half of the distance. Having done so, it must then fall half of the distance remaining. When it has done that, it has still not reached the ground; and before it can reach it, it must still fall half of the distance to the ground, and so on. The result is that the apple can never reach the ground. This reasoning is powerful. Children presented with this paradox say that there comes a moment when the distance to the ground is so small that the apple covers it at one go (Núñez 1994). This is the atomist position: beyond a certain limit, further subdivision is impossible. Zeno's position makes this untenable and the atom must be subdivided: just before touching the ground, the apple is still airborne and must still cover half the remaining distance to the ground. It is an argument which seems unanswerable.

Numerous attempts were made to resolve the paradox. Aristotle had already understood that time, like space, could be infinitely subdivided so that the bits of time put together would form a finite duration. In mathematical terms, Zeno's series of time intervals is a convergent series. Nevertheless there is still something mind-boggling about the reasoning. Our intuition does not manage to let the apple touch the ground. What happens just before it touches? To explain why we still find the paradox mind-boggling, even though we know the mathematical solution, we must be aware that it sets at odds the two components of our semantic faculty. Our scenic representation shows the apple falling, making contact with the ground, bouncing, and rolling along; and spontaneously we would go no further. However, Zeno's reasoning makes us undertake an operation of thematic segmentation, by asking us first to separate the apple as theme from the ground as reference point. This segmentation can reach the conclusion that the theme eventually reaches the limit of its trajectory, though it is unable to show how. If, like Zeno, we oblige a subject to conceptualize the reaching of the limit, thematic segmentation goes into a loop and fails. We are then beset by a paradoxical feeling, for though we can imagine perfectly well the apple falling, we just cannot conceive of it.

Thematic segmentation produces a static representation, the mental map, which relies in large measure on the inside-outside distinction, the theme being located either inside or outside the frame of reference. We can conceptualize the apple inside its trajectory, but in such a conceptualization, the apple is motionless. Zeno demonstrated this with another of his famous paradoxes, the one in which he asks us to imagine an arrow in flight towards its target. At any given moment, the arrow occupies a volume; and in that volume, it does not move. Equally, it would be absurd to say that, where the arrow is not, it is moving. Ergo, the arrow is motionless. This is the perfect demonstration of the fact that our thematic representation is static. With a little concentration of mind, anybody can imagine the apple detaching itself from the branch, dropping, and rolling along the ground. In thematic representation, however, the apple, just like Zeno's arrow, is conceptualized in a static way. And that is how Zeno springs his trap. He asks us to conceptualize the apple just before it reaches the ground. Thematic representation draws a first map, on which the apple as theme is separate from the ground. The separation produces a space which becomes the frame of reference of a new map. The following position of the apple is placed inside the new map. This is not the end of the matter either, for Zeno once more forces us to separate the apple's new position from the ground. This makes us once again draw two new maps one after the other, the first to make the separation and the other to include the new position inside the space of the separation. The problem lies in the fact that this pair of new maps is indistinguishable from the previous pair. This is when we realize we are caught in an endless loop. To get out of it, there are only three possibilities: we can give up and accept Zeno's conclusion that movement does not exist (or at least that it cannot be conceptualized); or like children and some mathematicians,[1] we can cheat and say that, once a particular degree of enlargement has been reached, it is no longer possible to zoom in and separate the apple from the ground and that the apple takes advantage of this to reach the end of its trajectory in a single burst, so to speak; or else, as in standard mathematics, we can stick with constant scale and assume that the series of an infinity of time intervals set end to end converges. When Zeno's reasoning contrives to make us change scale, the mathematical solution is no longer satisfying to intuition. The mind is torn between a scenic representation which shows the apple touching the ground and a thematic representation which sets the endless loop in motion and never allows the apple to finish falling. So Zeno's paradoxes afford a fine illustration of the separation of our understanding into two components.

12.2 A functional role for thematic segmentation

Why go beyond the stage of protolanguage?

The double dissociation just discussed suggests that the two aspects of meaning we associate with statements derive from two components of our

---

[1] There are still some mathematical authors who feel the need to seek solutions to this paradox which they hope consist better with intuition. For instance, non-standard analysis of atomistic inspiration has been applied with the aim of giving reality to the notion of the infinitesimal and thus explaining that the movement happens without our being able to see it! (McLaughlin 1994)

understanding and that they correspond to two different cognitive apparatuses. As we have seen, the question at issue is to define a function for the second of these. In Chapter 8, protolanguage was presented as a locally optimal system serving a protosemantics which was also locally optimal. That any added value from thematic segmentation should not be evident is not surprising. The first idea that comes to mind is that syntax must be the evolutionary justification of thematic segmentation. Through thematic analysis of a situation we can establish the relations represented as predicates in Chapter 10. Once the segmentation process has been completed, syntax becomes a natural way of economically expressing the relations between predicates via the serial flow of words. Thanks to thematic analysis of situations, we can express for instance *John goes behind the church* with some chance of being understood by an interlocutor, who will analyse the syntax of the sentence back into two thematic segmentations: *John* as theme, moving towards a place. The place, specified as *behind the church*, is the theme of a new segmentation in which the church's role is to be the reference point. The place where John is going is the element common to both thematic analyses, which is why it enables the verb phrase and its complement to join up, in accordance with the principle of semantic linking (cf. Chapter 10.3). Thematic segmentation thus makes syntax possible and necessary. This enables us to see the faculty of segmentation of situations, with its distinction between theme, reference point, and possibly agent, as a way discovered by evolution to allow syntax to develop the power of expression with which we are familiar. However the phrases of sentences may be linked or embedded, the principle of semantic linking enables the hearer to reconstruct the thematic placings as conceived by the speaker, which is a first step towards the reconstruction of the scene itself.

Do we need to enquire further into a biological reason why we have a faculty for thematic segmentation? It is a faculty that opens the way to the use of syntax. As a means for the description of scenes, syntax as used by humans is vastly more efficient than protolanguage. Because of its accuracy, it even makes for easy access to abstraction. Is this not enough to justify both its own emergence and the emergence of a faculty for segmentation of scenes which makes it possible? This way of reasoning raises several problems, the most manifest of which is that it puts the cart before the horse. The evolutionary justification of the existence of syntax relies on the pre-existence of a system of thematic segmentation.

This makes it difficult to argue that it was the virtues of syntax that explain the emergence of a faculty which must have preceded it. A second difficulty, perhaps less obvious, lies in the alleged advantage offered by the accuracy and abstraction that come with syntax. Given our knowledge of protolanguage, this advantage cannot be taken for granted. Just as we are tempted to believe, wrongly, that chimpanzees would reproduce better if only they were able to speak (cf. Chapter 4), so we think that our prehuman ancestors would have been much better off if they had enjoyed a more accurate system of description of things and access to abstract communication. But if we try to see this issue from the point of view of prehuman communication, none of that necessarily follows at all. Our own semantic system is less than ideal, if judged against criteria of accuracy and abstraction, as can be seen whenever one has to explain an itinerary to somebody or follow mathematical reasoning of any degree of complexity. Would our ancestors have had the use of semantics as rich as ours if, as was suggested in Chapter 8, the aim of their communication had been simple drawing attention to salient situations? If someone asks what time it is, we do not give it to the nearest hundredth of a second. Similarly, it is likely that an over-accurate system of semantics, because it makes for cumbersomeness in communication, would not have been of benefit for the communicative needs of prehumans. If that is the case, the appearance of a semantic faculty in *Homo sapiens* remains a mystery.

Inferential ability

In Chapter 4, we questioned the plausibility of the idea that before our ancestors could speak they had become more intelligent. Various arguments now support the opposite view, that it was in fact human beings' reasoning abilities that developed out of their communicative abilities, or more precisely that developed out of their use of these in communication. This means that reasoning is of less use in solving the problems of daily life than in conceiving of meaningful contributions to make to linguistic exchanges. Seen like that, the two components of the semantic faculty (the ability to represent scenes and thematic segmentation) are apparently in competition with each other. Both of them provide simplified representations of a state of affairs that our senses have perceived or could have perceived; and both of them enable us to draw inferences from these representations. Think again of the example of the falling apple. Our system of mental imaging assures us that the apple finishes its fall by hitting the ground. Thematic segmentation arrives at the same conclusion: at the end of a movement, the theme is supposed to be inseparable from the limit of the trajectory, in this case the ground. As before, one or other of our two semantic systems seem to be redundant. The following example, however, may show something different. Without drawing any of the figures, try to imagine first a cube with a sphere just behind it; then to the right of the sphere, have a mental image of a pyramid. If you now imagine that you move a little to one side so as to have a line of sight from the cube to the pyramid, the question is: On which side is the sphere? Of the two systems that enabled you to interpret the instructions for this experiment, which is the one that enables you to find the answer? Most subjects say that they can 'see' the sphere is to the left. This is a conclusion that is arrived at through the system of scenic representation. It is an inference, a conclusion arrived at without the assistance of any concrete enactment of the experiment. The sphere is on the left because that is how we see mentally that it must be. The system of thematic segmentation cannot cope nearly so well with that example. Each of the three objects functions in turn as theme then as reference point. By the time the pyramid is mentioned, the cube is no longer part of the thematic relations. As for the rotation, the system of local maps is too poor to calculate the consequences of it. This example is another illustration of the apparent superfluity of thematic segmentation. Even so, it is in dealing with inferences that its added value will become manifest.

What if one of the subjects doing the preceding experiment claimed to see the sphere on the right? How could we convince such a person that this answer is wrong? By doing a drawing, of course. But if we were talking by telephone, we would have immense difficulty in demonstrating that the sphere is actually to the left of the observer. The mental imaging which led to that conclusion is unable to justify it. Let us suppose, in the example of the apple falling off a tree, that somebody refuses to believe that it really is on the ground. Our capacity for scenic representation can only register the fact that this person must be mistaken, that typically the apple should fall to the ground and stay there. Not that this constitutes a demonstration. Thematic segmentation, on the other hand, can deal with it better. If the theme, that is the apple, has not reached the ground, then of necessity it is separated from it. An interlocutor is then constrained to explain how this separation can continue, given that an abstract force, in Talmy's sense, is pushing the theme on its trajectory. The essential difference is that, unlike mental imaging, this type of reasoning does not derive from a typical situation. Mental imaging makes choices: the fall of the apple happens in daylight, the observer is outside the tree, there is grass on the ground, etc. How can we be sure that these parameters have no effect on the outcome of the fall? How can we demonstrate to an interlocutor that it will turn out the same in the present instance? Our system of imaging makes the outcome so obvious that to ask such a question may seem strange. The trouble is that, faced with doubt, imaging can draw on nothing but its subjective conviction which is rooted in a self-evident habit.

Thematic representation, on the other hand, can provide a demonstration of the apple making contact with the ground. If it never reaches the ground, it stays separate from it, within the confines of its trajectory. But the apple cannot remain motionless, since the force (in Talmy's sense) causing the movement of the theme on its trajectory has not ceased to operate. There would have to be a second force preventing the theme from continuing, as in example (10) on page 239. This demonstration is not conclusive, though one would have to be called Zeno to notice it in this case. That, however, is not the point. What is important is that thematic segmentation can produce an explicit reasoning. And anyone who can produce an explicit reasoning will convince people who can follow it. The only thing that can overcome the effect of such reasoning is a second reasoning that demonstrates it to be false. Therein lies the essential difference between the two components of our semantic faculty. Either of them can draw inferences; but thematic segmentation is the only one that can produce explicit reasoning to support the inferences. As we shall see, this explicitness underlies logical reasoning.

The birth of logical reasoning

Human beings, with their faculty of thematic segmentation, can produce a new form of reasoning. This type of reasoning relies on the topological structure of local maps (cf. p. 261). Since the topological properties of interiority and exteriority are mutually exclusive, stating such exclusions verbally is likely to produce inferences which appear as though logically necessary. By way of illustration, let us look again at the example of the mouthless sheep (cf. p. 237), which will give us the opportunity to reconcile the empiricist and the rationalist whose disagreement over this ovine question we examined earlier. Anyone who claims to have seen a mouthless sheep creates astonishment in people. This astonishment is initially the astonishment of the empiricist, because the image of such a sheep is a significant departure from the likely prototype of the animal. The prototype may entail an image of a sheep; but since there has been a mention of a mouth, the image or the one following it will be for example a sheep grazing. This will only make the atypical aspect of the mouthless sheep all the more obvious, thus reinforcing the salience of the first speaker's account. With this example, however, thematic segmentation will play a very different role.

The two preceding scenes can be mentally processed or thematized in various ways. On hearing about a mouthless sheep, a subject can analyse the statement as a theme (the mouth) coming out of a reference point (the sheep). Scenic representation then provides an atypical image of a sheep without a mouth that a hearer can analyse thematically by placing the observed sheep outside the abstract space representing the property of being a sheep. At this point, subjects may verbalize their astonishment. They have transformed the typical image into a definition: a normal sheep must have a mouth. If, however, a subject thematizes a typical grazing scene, it is the grass that will be the theme and the sheep the reference point. If the mouth is omitted, the theme stays outside the frame of reference and feeding does not take place. Verbalizing their new reasoning, subjects can elaborate a process of argumentation to show that such an animal without a mouth could not feed. It is scenic representation that brings the subject to the conclusion that the animal in question is atypical or that the absence of a mouth interferes with the typical process of feeding. However, it is thematic analysis of the scenes that makes for the construction of reasoning that can be verbalized. Thematization makes argumentation possible.

The topological relations represented in local maps of thematic analysis enable the production of compelling inferences. We are constrained to accept for example the fact that the theme cannot stand outside the frame of reference when it ought to be inside it, that the theme cannot move without being subject to an action (a force, in Talmy's terms), or the opposite fact that the theme must move if it is subject to an action. This type of extremely simple inference has the property of being easily communicable. Unlike the elaborate inferences made possible by scenic representation (remember the position of the sphere in the experiment with the three figures), inferences from thematic representation (after the manner of 'the theme is inside, therefore it cannot be outside') are easy to put into words and have a much greater power of conviction. The communicability of thematic reasoning is explained by the extreme simplicity of the distinctions made in a mental map. Basically, they are binary, of the all-or-nothing variety. The cognitive operation which consists of going from a scenic representation, with its numerous gradual and continuous aspects, to an all-or-nothing type of segmentation can be modelled, for example by the use of dynamic mechanisms producing topological 'catastrophes', like those used by Bernard Victorri (Victorri and Fuchs 1996).

Thematic representation makes for extreme simplification of scenes. This it does in the interests of power of conviction. Though we are all rationalists, we are also empiricists able to analyse our experience and scenic representations so as to abstract from them the simple relations of thematic segmentation. This means that, instead of just prototypes, we now have capacities of definition and deduction. This takes us far away from the idea (criticized rightly by Fodor and the empiricists, albeit for very different reasons) that concepts are stored in the mind as definitions (cf. p. 234). The preceding development offers an alternative to that idea of definitions, as well as to the purely empiricist conception. Definitions, and the logical deductions that they support, can have a transitory existence, but they are the result of a thematic analysis done on a scenic representation.

12.3 The emergence of human meaning

In the description of the semantic faculty just offered, thematic segmentation of scenes is the strictly human element, as against scenic representation which, as argued by Chapter 8, was an attribute of protohumans. In line with what precedes, we can say that the function of thematic segmentation is to enable explicit logical reasoning. This way of presenting semantics reinforces the idea announced in Chapter 4, that human cognitive faculties, in particular the faculties of reasoning and problem-solving, did not appear before the language faculty but were produced by it. What is primarily of value in an explicit and logical process of reasoning is not that it solves a problem; it is that it is communicable and that it may convince. Thanks to their capacity for scenic representation, protohumans were able to draw inferences. In most situations, it is that same capacity which enables us to reason. Try to work out, from the look of a figure-of-eight knot, how to tie one. In so doing, you are using your capacity for mental manipulation of the scene you can see. However, this mental work is not only difficult to communicate, it is also unlikely to convince anyone who might question its validity, for example by criticizing the conformation of the resulting knot. Reasoning deriving from the use of thematic segmentation avoids these two drawbacks. The extreme simplicity of thematic representation makes it easy to communicate and to show its inferences as self-evident. And therein lies the essence of logical reasoning.

This description makes us adopt a 'species relativism'. Logical reasoning as made possible by thematic segmentation is a very particular faculty. Confined as we are in our human condition, we find it difficult to see how fortuitous this faculty is from the point of view of evolution. Thematic analysis is a way of simplifying the world as we perceive it. We may well suppose, though it would be a difficult thing to assess, that this simplification is locally optimal for the production of the type of logical inference that we as humans are capable of. However, we have no way of assessing any of the alternatives that evolution may have confronted. There is only one form of logical reasoning that we can observe and it is the form we are endowed with.[2]

Unable though we are to say why we happen to have this form of logic rather than some other, we can at least try to analyse the function it fulfils. What hangs on this is as follows: a biological scenario that explains the faculty of communicating logical reasoning will justify the existence of thematic segmentation; indirectly, the appearance of syntax, which is of such great service to thematic segmentation, will also be justified. The evidence of the examples we have considered in this chapter is that logical

---

[2] I use the word 'logical' to describe the mode of reasoning underlying argumentation. So called 'classical' logical formalism was developed first by philosophy, then by mathematics. During the twentieth century, logicians conceived of many variants of classical logic, such as multivalued logics, possibilistic logic, fuzzy logic, modal logics, locology, temporal logics, etc. These developments derive from a desire to increase inferential power (with each of them it is possible to make types of inferences that classical logic cannot make) rather than from any desire to model argumentation. At present, for detecting inconsistencies, non-classical logics provide no plausible mechanism as powerful as the human system of argumentation (see Chapter 15).

reasoning is a tool for convincing. What we must understand is the reason why, at a particular stage of evolution, a need to convince should have become so important. This is a question which is central to any knowledge of language and its biological function. It can only be properly discussed via a study of language in the context of its conditions of use. Part III of this book proposes to do just that.

PART III

The ethology of language

Introduction to Part III

No attempt to study the characteristic behaviours of an animal species, to analyse their adaptive functions, or to understand their evolutionary origin can be limited to the stereotyped and controlled reactions that a specimen produces in the laboratory. In his preface to a book by Konrad Lorenz (1990), Rémy Chauvin tells the story of the Bombyx caterpillar. In rigorously controlled and frequently conducted experiments a caterpillar is inserted into a glass tube which is then closed. One end of the tube is turned towards the sunlight. The animal crawls down to that end; when it reaches it, it stops and eventually dies from heat. This is a fine example of an automatic and unadapted behaviour. To define accurately the mechanical and purposeless character of the caterpillar, graphs and tables of figures are drawn up documenting the speed of the animal relative to its age, the intensity of the lighting or the heat. In such a context, Chauvin says, one can only imagine how rash anyone would have to be to remind the scientific orthodoxists busy translating the crawling of their caterpillar into equations that the Bombyx caterpillar does not live inside glass tubes. In its natural habitat, when the sun shines on the leaves where these caterpillars are found, they actually turn round and crawl into the shade. Their bizarre behaviour inside the tube is a simple consequence of their inability to reverse or turn round.

In the twentieth century there were two radically opposite ways of studying animal behaviour. On the one hand, behaviourism, which originated in the USA in 1915, relied exclusively on experiments designed to confirm the validity of conditional reflexes, as illustrated by Pavlov's experiment, and of conditioning by reward or punishment, as used in animal training. According to this narrow conception of experimental psychology, the animal has little choice other than behaving as it is expected to behave. On the other hand, ethology is marked by the study of spontaneous behaviour. Konrad Lorenz, the founder of ethology, took the view that animals should be observed before any theorizing takes place. In trying to decipher the nuptial displays of ducks, measure the learning abilities of jackdaws, or understand the phenomenon of imprinting which makes goslings mistake a human being for their mother, Lorenz began by observing and attempting to understand what he could see without trying to control everything from the outset. What distinguishes ethology as a science of animal behaviour is its method, which consists of observing behaviours in their unprompted expressions. This approach by Lorenz and his fellow workers brought about a significant shift in thinking about animal behaviour in the first half of the twentieth century, because it was an attempt to see it from a Darwinian perspective and to rehabilitate the idea that there are some behavioural components or releasing stimuli which are inborn. Spectacular results were obtained from the study of various species, ranging from social insects (for instance, von Frisch's honeybees; see Chapter 1) to the chimpanzees studied in their natural habitat by Jane Goodall. In this respect, our own species is no different, as is shown for example by the studies done by Irenäus Eibl-Eibesfeldt (1967, 1975) on universals in the behaviour of humans.

The third part of this book is of ethological inspiration. Any ethologist who wants to make sense of the behaviour of a new species looks first and foremost to understand its most characteristic way of behaving. A study of nightingales that completely ignored their singing would be a very strange study. It would be equally strange to do a study of the behavioural biology of human beings and leave out the species' most characteristic type of behaviour, namely language. In keeping with the spirit of ethology, language will be considered here in its most apparent and spontaneous use, namely casual conversation.

13 Conversation behaviour

Essentially, human beings use language for conversing. Talking to one another is one of their main waking activities. As a way of behaving, it is quite characteristic; no other species devotes so much time to exchanges of messages which are always new and different from one another. The purpose of earlier chapters was to describe the structure of our capacity to convey these messages and the function corresponding to that structure. However, nothing or almost nothing has been said so far on the biological role of these acts of communication. The pieces of the puzzle are being fitted together: we can understand how our phonological faculty is locally optimal for the making of a lexicon of a particular size (cf. Chapter 7); we can also understand that syntax is useful for the expression of predicative relations (cf. Chapter 10); we have distinguished between two semantic competences, one of which functions to elaborate scenes and the other to produce a segmentation of the thematic elements of those scenes (cf. Chapter 12). And yet the emergence of all these faculties depends totally on the biological importance for human beings of speaking, or rather conversing.

13.1 An apparently unimportant behaviour

It may come as a surprise to explain the whole system of language as an outcome of a behaviour as seemingly unimportant as casual conversation. One might expect that the phonological, syntactic, and semantic mechanisms activated for the slightest sentence might be there for a nobler purpose. Some authors have put forward the idea that language is an evolutionary by-product of humans' overdeveloped cognitive faculties. In Chapter 4 we considered the arguments against that way of seeing language as essentially an outgrowth of intelligence and incidentally as a tool of communication. If evolution endowed us with language and the cognitive means associated with it, it was not for the purpose of speculating about the world into which we have been brought, of collaborating on the building of bridges or rockets or even devising systems of mathematics. It was so that we could chat.

That may be a difficult conclusion to accept; but the facts are there. No other behaviour involving language fulfils the conditions required to serve as its basic function: universality, spontaneous use, systematic and frequent use, exploitation of the whole range of linguistic possibilities. Of course, language can be used for giving orders, for singing, reciting poetry, punning, coordinating group activities; it can be used as an aid to rational thought; with language, one can tell lies, manipulate other people, or appeal to them for help, and so on. Some of these uses of language, poetry for instance, are not universally practised; others, such as singing, are practised infrequently by most people. And there are others again, such as thinking, which do not require the use of certain aspects of language, such as phonology, syntax, prosody, or bodily movement. Casual conversation, though, does require the full range of language competence. It is also a universal and spontaneous activity. Ethnologists have described spectacular differences among cultural customs; but no one has ever described any fundamental disparities of spontaneous conversational behaviour. In all countries and at all periods, whether in industrialized societies or among hunter-gatherers, people have spent and continue to spend a large part of their day conversing. This they do in various ways, quarrelling, storytelling, discussing, but every one of these ways is universal. And there is an obligatory aspect to conversation: when individuals are together, sooner or later they feel the need to converse. This phenomenon is very noticeable in what has been called the 'cocktail party effect', which happens when everyone is obliged to raise their voices so as to be heard over the noise of other conversations. In such cases, satisfying the need to converse requires a considerable physical effort; and the din it creates, when one becomes aware of it, represents an astonishing manifestation of the specificity of the human race. Any ethologist who can view his or her own humanity with enough objectivity cannot help being struck by such original behaviour, especially when the form of expression it takes is so disproportionate in comparison with animal communication (cf. Chapter 1).

An ethologist studying any animal behaviour observes its spontaneous expression and tries to understand how the action of the individuals promotes their survival or reproduction. Accordingly, the starting point for an ethological approach to language is observation of spontaneous conversation. We should, however, beware the dangers of adopting an approach that is too narrow. Though study of conversations is essential, it should not function as a framework limiting the events to be considered to those that happen during the time of an exchange. Theories which restrict themselves to measuring how important the information exchanged or the actions effected through speech are to the participants are hampered by their self-imposed limitations. If language really had such a utilitarian function, then we would certainly not speak when there is nothing to say. The insignificant nature of some of our conversations is inexplicable within such a framework. The function of language, as will be seen, is not to be explained by the achievement of an immediate benefit. Behind our daily verbal interactions, even when their apparent insignificance and superficiality might seem to belie it, there is a force of biological import. To discover what it is, however, we must consider elements from outside observable conversational exchanges.

We should also beware the fact that spontaneous verbal exchanges are phenomena of great richness which can be analysed in many ways depending on what one may be looking for. It is not my purpose here, any more than it has been in discussing other aspects of language, to give a restrictive and reductive description of conversational interaction. My aim is to identify structural elements which may help to determine the biological function of language. As with the other components of language, it is through an understanding of the structure of conversations that we may be able to define the biological function of these elements. That structure does not depend on the importance or the unimportance of the subject being talked about.

Here as an example is a conversation between two women, called A and B, in which A is surprised that B's Christmas tree has not dropped its needles. At the end of the extract, A jokingly suggests that it must be an artificial tree:

Context: three weeks after Christmas the tree is still green
A1 What? Is this still the tree? That's amazing!
B1 Yes! It hasn't dried out!
A2 And no roots?
B2 No roots. It's not even losing its... We've already cut off all the lower branches.
A3 It's odd that it's not losing its...

B3 Yes, I can't think why.
A4 It's a plastic one! [laughter]

This extract is representative of what we might call 'true' language, language as used spontaneously in daily life, as against the somewhat idealized language found in examples used in linguistics or the more highly wrought language of written texts. It does not contain all the different subtleties of spoken language, in particular markers of intonation and certain minor hesitations. Nevertheless, the extracts featured in Part III are sufficiently realistic for us to notice unfinished sentences, questions, exclamations, and especially the alternation of utterances. This alternation is the most basic thing in conversational behaviour, with a biological function that must be defined.

Many studies of conversation look at strictly linguistic things, such as the conditions governing the use of markers like 'well' or 'actually', the syntactic distortions peculiar to spoken language, or elocutionary hesitations. I shall have nothing to say on such matters. Some models designed to explain conversation look at aspects of social interaction. They derive from the view that conversation is a mode of interaction among others, akin to the ways we act on each other or on our environment. If one is trying to identify the biological impact of conversational behaviour, this type of model has a certain attraction. For example, the theory of 'speech acts' offers a view of language as a means through which human beings can act on each other in society. If language really is nothing but a way of affecting the behaviour of others, then there is no need to seek any further biological justification. However, that is a view of the function of language that we cannot accept without some refinement, mainly because it offers no explanation of conversational behaviour. Paradoxically, though conversation is a spontaneous and relaxed activity that we readily engage in, it is in fact a form of interplay governed by strict rules. By studying some of these rules, we shall arrive at a partial definition of the biological importance of language.

13.2 Some attempts to explain speech events

Why do we engage in a speech event? Why do we express at a particular juncture one particular message rather than another? These questions, which would be seen as natural if asked as part of a study of communication in an animal species, were bypassed for a long time in studies of human language. Although much research effort was expended on understanding the phonology of language, its syntax or its semantics, comparatively few attempts have been made to discover the laws governing its use in real situations. At any given moment of a conversation, it is not possible to say everything. Yet there are few models providing a definition of the range of acceptable conversational moves. There are two possible reasons for this. It has been assumed either that such laws did not exist or that our freedom in communication is governed by laws of extreme complexity. We are going to inspect some of the theories which have been hazarded as explanations for the content of our conversational utterances.

Doing things with words

In the 1960s, the philosopher J. L. Austin pointed out that language could enable us to act upon the surrounding world through the intermediary of other individuals, and conversely that there are acts which can be effected only through language. A typical example is promises. Promising consists not only of speaking a sentence; it is a genuine act which generally has tangible consequences, both for the promiser and for the person to whom the promise is made. It would be difficult to imagine such an act being effected without the use of language (Austin 1962). The same goes for most orders or official declarations, as in a court room when it is declared that the court is now in session. It may be objected that this use of language is highly particular and unrepresentative of everyday usage. Austin, like Searle after him, extends the definition to include all uses of language: we speak to act; language, like other forms of behaviour, is a way of carrying out social acts. In order to make this generalization, Austin and Searle have had to broaden also the definition of an act. By coining the idea of illocutionary acts, they wish to range numerous speech acts into a single category which covers the doing of a defined social act. Speech acts include stating, describing, asserting, warning, remarking, commenting, commanding, ordering, requesting, criticizing, apologizing, censuring, approving, welcoming, promising, objecting, demanding, or arguing (Searle 1969: 23). These acts may be 'successful' or not, a distinction that depends on certain conditions. If you declare that the court is now in session though you are only a barrister or a witness, then it is an 'unsuccessful' speech act. A promise that you will win the lottery cannot be a successful speech act. One of the conditions is that the speaker should have, at least in theory, the ability to accomplish the act spoken of. In this, the actual future accomplishment of the act spoken of in the promise is irrelevant; the success or lack of success of the promise is decided in the present. You can make a successful act of promising if you promise to stop smoking, whether or not someone else doubts that you really will.

The theory of speech acts brought with it the hope that the problem of the use of language could be reduced to a theory of action. From an ethological point of view, this would amount to a complete denial of the extraordinariness of language. All animals can affect their fellows by acts, many of which can be quite elaborate. The speech-act theory makes language merely a less material way of bringing these acts about. According to it, language behaviour is no different from other behaviours, in that its usefulness for individuals must be assessed by its immediate impact. What is more, the impact is assessed against criteria that are independent of language. Thus, the success of a promise, at the moment when it is made, depends on the sincerity of the promiser and on his or her ability to do the thing promised. In general, neither the sincerity nor the ability has anything to do with the functioning of language. Austin's and Searle's system roots the detail of the functioning of verbal interactions in the system of social interactions. And that raises some problems.

Interesting though it is, the theory of speech acts is also faulty, at least in its all-encompassing version that seeks to account for the totality of language phenomena. A first objection can be raised against the taxonomies proposed for the classification of speech acts. Although the theory is useful in analysing situations in which promises are made and orders given, it must be said that human beings do not pass their time making promises and giving orders. The great bulk of daily conversation, that is the bulk of language as it is used, hardly lends itself to analysis in terms of acts. Either the range of possible acts is too great to support a parsimonious theory, or it is necessary to include ill defined categories such as 'information' or 'assertion', which unfortunately cover the greater part of contributions to talk. In both cases, the predictive ability of speech-act theory, when applied to conversation, is extremely poor. It is assumed, for instance, that a question entails an answer. The theory is incapable of predicting the content of the two speeches or even the need for them to alternate. A second objection concerns the very object of the theory of speech acts. Dan Sperber and Deirdre Wilson take the view that it is a theory not of language but of human institutions. If one applies it to the game of Bridge, for example, one can try to define the conditions in which the bid 'Three no trumps' is an appropriate act. However, in so doing, one is developing not a theory of language but a theory of Bridge (Sperber and Wilson 1986: 245).

It is tempting to try to see communication as similar to other human activities with a view to defining the rules of its use and indirectly the reasons for its existence. But language resists such treatment. The earlier exchange on the Christmas tree cannot be reduced to a description viewing it as a mere set of questions and assertions. It would be pointless to hazard any more detailed description aimed at deducing from each of the speeches what type of act either of the two women is trying to bring to bear upon the other in speaking it. Take for example speech A2: 'And no roots?' How can it be explained? Intuitively, for A it is a way of justifying her astonishment: if the tree has no roots, it is understandable that somebody would be astonished that it has retained its needles. What is the act that is being done here? It would be too reductive to say that a question is being asked. It would be too vague to say that the woman's speech is an act of justification or argumentation. By that reasoning, A1 could be defined as an act of astonishment and B3 as an act of misunderstanding. But if everything is an act, if every speech event is a different act, the theory of speech acts becomes no more than a paraphrase without predictive power.

Attempts to explain language as just a particular instance of social interaction have so far been unsuccessful, since the reality of conversational interactions cannot be reduced to a mere list of social acts labelled in accordance with a set of unvarying specifications. Something new is at work in language interactions. The words exchanged are more than acts; they are the elements of a system which contains its own organization: conversation. It is to be expected that the justification of language, an original thing that emerged only with our species, should itself be original. Most of the time, when we speak it is not with the aim of acting directly on one another. A mode of speech that may hold good for an army on active service does not hold good for daily interactive talk. The biological motivation for such speech lies elsewhere; and the purpose of this chapter and the one following is to come closer to an understanding of it.

Conversation as an outcome of a desire to cooperate

The example offered by the theory of speech acts is an encouraging one. But ultimately, because it removes the essential motivation of speech acts from the field of language and locates it in the field of social action, it closes off any possibility of predicting the specificity of conversational behaviour. The essential distinction is that the sequence of social acts in daily life does not resemble the sequence of utterances in conversation.

In this context, the originality of the approach argued by H. P. Grice in his seminal article of 1975 becomes clear. He sees communication as an exercise in cooperation. Conversation would be impossible unless talkers took a whole set of precautions to make themselves understood by one another. By referring to the following map we can see an example of this.

Suppose that, after a bicycle trip, I have returned to the town of Lars and that I explain to friends where I have been. As they know the region well, all I say is that I went to Saint-Sauveur and then Vesonne, without mentioning either that I went through Rhodes or that I did not go via Crozes or Villeneuve. However, I might say that I did not go through Fronsac, for Grice's reason, which is that, because I am trying to be cooperative, I impose a number of rules upon myself: I say only things

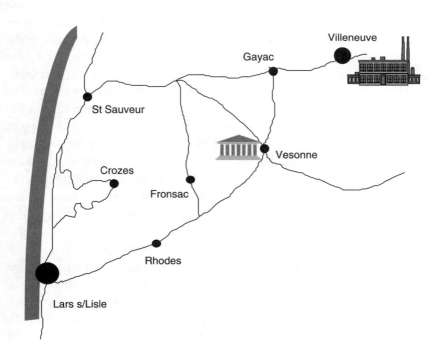

that I hold to be true; I give no pointless details; the only information I give is related to the subject; and I try to be relevant. To say, *I came back via Rhodes*, for instance, is pointless, since that information is automatically reconstructed by the hearers. It is, however, useful to state that I went through Vesonne and it may be useful to specify that I did not go through Fronsac, if going through Fronsac is our usual itinerary. Because they know I am cooperating, my hearers infer that I went neither to Crozes nor to Gayac, because if I had gone that way I would have said so.

Grice's hypothesis on cooperation seems likely to offer an explanation of the content of utterances. Unfortunately, it presupposes mechanisms that Grice does not spell out. Of the mechanisms that he does touch on, the most essential to an understanding of what makes people speak and give a particular content to their message is undoubtedly his maxim of relevance. Yet he gives us nothing but the statement 'Be relevant'. He does not even invoke the intuitive idea of usefulness which led us to omit mention of Villeneuve as irrelevant in the previous example. Another problem raised by Grice's theory is that it is of no help in accounting for the influence of context. If I am talking to my friends in Lars, with whom I had discussed several different possible rides before setting off on the trip, I can explain my actual itinerary; but I cannot accost some random passer-by in Lars and give the same information. If I did, the passer-by would stare at me in bewilderment and wonder what I was on about. The reason for this is that there are some things which it is acceptable to say in a certain context but which will be unacceptable in a different context. Grice's maxim 'Be relevant' has little light to shed on this phenomenon.

Grice's principle of cooperation is linked to the idea of a social convention. Like the theory of speech acts, though in a lesser degree, it views the structure of language exchanges as being a result of rules of a social nature, in this case a rule of proper behaviour that makes people cooperate. This cooperation continues, as Grice would have it, even in the case of a dispute: when two people shout and abuse one another in a verbal squabble, they are continuing to abide by the maxims which he argues underlie the principle of cooperation. This mode of cooperation is more like a reflex behaviour than it is like a moral principle. Structural properties of language such as phonology or syntax are for the most part, as we have seen, independent of the idea of convention. It would not be surprising if the use of language was likewise controlled in part by something completely different from a sort of contract freely and explicitly agreed to. It is hard to imagine that evolution would have endowed us with a faculty whose use was entirely subject to arbitrary convention. It is probable that the cooperation argued by Grice does not come from a deliberate choice of action on the part of speakers. If it derives from a biological predisposition to language exchange, as is suggested by the universality of conversation behaviour, then we must understand its mechanisms in detail and not restrict ourselves to mere intuitive statements such as the maxim of relevance.

The idea of relevance

Sperber and Wilson, in an attempt to identify principles that explain the content of utterances, have taken the ideas of Grice farther, simplifying and systematizing them (Sperber and Wilson 1986). Their first hypothesis is that Grice's various maxims all derive from the same requirement for relevance. Anyone who tries to be relevant will avoid making statements that are obviously false, will not weary an interlocutor with futile detail, and will endeavour to say things that have a bearing on the topic of conversation. That being the case, it is superfluous to stipulate that speakers must abide by maxims relating to the quantity and quality of information given to interlocutors; anyone adhering to the criterion of relevance will ipso facto abide by them. Sperber and Wilson then try to solve two problems left unanswered by Grice: why do we strive for relevance and how do we achieve it?

In their solution to the first problem, Sperber and Wilson rule out any possibility related to convention. Let us take the point of view of hearers: when they perceive an intention to communicate in a speaker, they presume that he or she also has a second intention, namely to be relevant. This principle of the presumption of relevance as stated by Sperber and Wilson can be illustrated by a rather extreme example. In 490 BC, Phidippides, after running the thirty-six kilometres from the battlefield of Marathon, arrived in Athens where he delivered his message then died from exhaustion. What were his interlocutors thinking about before he spoke? Certainly not that this man who had just run himself almost to death to bring them news was about to deliver himself of some totally trivial comment on the weather. Their presumption of relevance could not have been greater: he was clearly about to deliver a message of the most crucial importance. To a lesser extent we all have the same presumption about any person who appears to be on the point of communicating with us. The presumption of relevance is universal and is linked to the very principle of intentional communication.

The most original contribution of the Sperber and Wilson argument is its attempt to define relevance. The principle of relevance that they propose is designed to describe the content of our verbal interactions. This leads us to the very heart of the problem of language. If we can understand what it is that makes people say what they say, we may be able to understand the biological processes which endowed us with this behaviour. According to Sperber and Wilson, messages conveyed by speakers are calculated to produce a certain effect on hearers. The greater the effect, the greater the relevance. What does this effect consist of? It can be measured by the amount of new knowledge that a hearer can infer from the message. Referring again to the example of the bicycle ride, we can say that the mention of Vesonne allows a hearer to infer more knowledge than a mention of Rhodes. If the speaker added that he did not go through Villeneuve, this would add no knowledge and to mention it would not be relevant. This theory defines a relevant message as one which is able to produce knowledge in the minds of hearers.

Unlike previous models of language use, such as the theory of speech acts or Grice's theory, the explanation offered by Sperber and Wilson is explicitly cognitive. It views the message produced by a communicative act as a result of an intent in the speaker, an intent calculated to produce the maximum of cognitive effect in the mind of the hearer. If we are ever to explain the richness and variety of conversational exchanges, the need for a cognitive approach seems self-evident. On this very point, however, Sperber's and Wilson's theory does not go as far as one would like. As we have presented it so far, their model is incomplete. Their explanation of relevance is convincing for anybody who knows intuitively which inferences will be drawn or not drawn. With every example on which the theory is tested, we draw inferences and we assess the amount of new knowledge. The model's only role is to translate the assessment into relevance. In the example of the cycling trip, we know intuitively that a mention of Villeneuve would not enable the hearers to draw additional inferences and we deduce that any such mention is not relevant. The danger is that the model may lose all its point. If all it can say is 'A relevant message is one which produces a cognitive effect', and if the idea of cognitive effect remains intuitive, then it has no very significant contribution to make.

Sperber and Wilson cope with this difficulty by trying to describe the mechanism that makes us draw inferences. Their conception of inference consists of an extension of the idea of deduction. The cognitive effect can then be assessed against the set of deductions that can be made from the message. However, this way of conceiving of cognitive effect brings us up against a familiar problem in logic. Logic describes valid deductions, those that can be made without risk of error; it does not specify those that may or may not be of interest. The problem is as follows: the number of deductions that can be made from any particular knowledge is infinite. As Sperber and Wilson remind us, from the statement *The Prime Minister has resigned* it can be logical to deduce both *The Prime Minister has resigned or it's a little warmer today* and *If the Prime Minister hasn't resigned, the tiger will become extinct* (Sperber and Wilson 1986: 97).[1] If we can always produce an infinite amount of 'knowledge' of this type, most of which is clearly of no interest, by what criterion can we decide which knowledge will actually be produced? No such criterion is provided by logic. The solution adopted by Sperber and Wilson is to make use of an idea of 'cognitive effort'. The deductions produced are those that can be easily drawn. The idea of cognitive effort has been roundly criticized. Apart from the fact that it resembles the ill-defined notions of mental energy used by nineteenth-century authors, its absence of formal definition leaves us with an incomplete account of cognitive effect. The purpose of Sperber and Wilson was to give a very general definition of relevance, applicable to any situation of intentional communication, whether through text, gesture, speech, signalling, facial expression, or whatever. When what we are looking for, however, is a way to predict the content of language exchanges through talk, we are acutely aware of the requirement for a formal definition of relevance, even if it is more circumscribed.

The ideas of inference and cognitive effort still do not offer an explanation, for example, of why my account of my cycling tour can appear relevant to my friends in Lars but not to a randomly chosen inhabitant of the same town. The latter may draw quite a few of the same inferences as they do, for a comparable cognitive effort, since his knowledge of the region is as good as theirs. Despite which, not only will the relevance of my

---

[1] The validity of these deductions comes from the fact that, formally, p implies (p or q) and p implies (not p implies q) are tautological.

statements very likely not be apparent to him but he may even think I am suffering from a mental disorder. We do not go up to unknown people in the street and tell them we have just been to Saint-Sauveur and Vesonne. On this point of relevance, what explains the disparity between the expectations of my friends and those of the passer-by? It is not just a matter of inferences.

The conversational situations which show most clearly the limits of the Sperber and Wilson model are cases of non-relevance. Whatever sentence interlocutors may be hearing, it will always be easy for them to make some deductions. In the middle of a conversation, if someone suddenly says *Three times thirty-nine makes 117*, the bald statement will be seen in most contexts as irrelevant. The least to be expected is that the speaker will go on to explain either what the statement has to do with the subject of the conversation or why this message had to be conveyed. Sperber's and Wilson's theory cannot explain this. On hearing the statement, we could easily have deduced that 117 is not a prime number, that 117 divided by three makes thirty-nine, etc. According to the theory, such inferences ought to lend a measure of relevance to the message, yet that is not the case. The fact is that we do not make that sort of inference but Sperber's and Wilson's theory cannot say why. To rely on the argument of cognitive effort would be very artificial in this instance. What the theory lacks, if one wishes to apply it to an analysis of the everyday use of language, is a mechanism that genuinely limits the inferences actually drawn by hearers from verbal interactions.

Nevertheless, the idea of relevance does appear to be the key to an understanding of the use humans make of the faculty of language given to them by evolution. It makes perfect Darwinian sense to see the use of language as having a bearing upon the survival and the reproduction of individuals. To discover how language bears upon the lives of human beings, we must understand why some messages are produced and others are not. The messages produced are the relevant messages. What we need is a way of defining accurately what relevance is, not in the absolute as Sperber and Wilson try to do it, but in the particular instance of conversational exchange. And that is what we are now going to attempt.

14   Language as information

Chapter 13 led us to a phenomenon that has to be explained. Interlocutors do not have complete freedom in conversation; they must be relevant. We now need to understand how this is done and why it must be done, which will be the subject of this chapter and the following ones.[1] Analysis of how speakers contrive to make messages that are acceptable to their interlocutors will lead us to the observation that they use language in two fundamentally different modes of communication, the origin of which we shall endeavour to grasp. This chapter deals with the first of these two modes, the one which makes for the production of messages perceived as informative. The second one, the argumentative mode, will be discussed in Chapter 15.

14.1 The constraint of relevance in conversation

In relaxed social situations, such as a conversation among friends, we do not have the feeling that our behaviour is strictly constrained. Our impression is that we can say whatever enters our heads and that we speak without giving much thought to what we say. This contrasts markedly with how we try to weigh every word during a tense discussion in a professional setting, for example if the point at issue is the signing of a contract which will have some bearing on our future. In everyday talk we are in a very different situation. For most people, conversing is a pleasure. We speak almost without thinking and the content of what we say comes to us naturally. It appears to be the case, however, that we are actually subject to severe constraints, though most of the time we are unaware of this. One such constraint which is well known is that we cannot skip about from one subject to another. But there is another constraint which restricts

---

[1] The comments of Laleh Ghadakpour have been of assistance to me in clarifying the ideas set forth in Chapters 14 and 15.

much more our freedom in conversation and that is the constraint of relevance. At every juncture, there are things that can be said and other things that cannot be said. Even though there is a great range of relevant utterances that would be possible at any particular moment, they are negligible when compared with the huge number of imaginable utterances. How do speakers contrive almost instantaneously to find relevant words and to assess the relevance of words spoken to them?

As a parameter of conversation, relevance is an omnipresent and necessary condition. If we take an extreme case, anyone whose utterances are consistently non-relevant is soon dismissed as mentally ill. When we take our turn to speak, we very likely have several different objectives, of which we are more or less aware: making a social contact, passing the time of day, enjoying speaking, answering a question, trying to be seen at our best, etc. But one of the foremost of these aims is the wish to say something relevant: we would like to think that the interest of our hearers will be aroused; and at the very least, we hope to be seen as somebody who is sensible and a good conversationalist. In most situations we would not say something like *I have a female cousin whose girl friend owns a bike*, even if it is true. I sometimes make students do a simple experiment that consists of saying something irrelevant when among friends or in their family circle, so as to observe the way hearers react. Here are two examples:

Context: experiment, with a green rubbish bin close by:
C1 The bin's green.
D1 What are you on about?
Context: experiment, with the family:
E1 The table's made of wood.
F1 Hey, being a student isn't your strong point.

The reactions of hearers are remarkable by their consistency, as anyone who tries the experiment will find out. D1 is not justified semantically. The speaker was perfectly aware that C had spoken about the nearby rubbish bin and had referred to a property relating to the colour of it. What D did not understand was the reason why C made the comment. In the second experiment, F decides that E1 is not relevant and replies with sarcasm.

These experiments, which are very easy to reproduce, show that the first speaker, the one who introduces a new subject into the conversation, is subject to certain constraints. The intuitive requirement is that what is said must be of interest. Our problem is to find a way to define this requirement.

14.2 Relevance in the informative mode

We are all capable of playing our part in everyday conversations. For the most part, however, this expertise is every bit as unconscious as the ability that enables us to assemble words into grammatically acceptable sentences. With a modicum of objectivity, we can actually have an idea of how we choose the content of our utterances. For instance, there are stories we can tell and stories we cannot tell. I cannot just recount that I got up this morning, had my breakfast, listened to the wireless, got washed and dressed and then left the house. Anyone listening to such a story knows something essential is missing. And the something essential that is missing, something that is common to all narratives of this type, is a mention of a salient feature. Any speaker who manages to convey to his or her hearers the feeling that the facts recounted are of interest, perhaps because they are out of the ordinary, is being relevant. Relevance, in this case, can be gauged by the salience of what is recounted. It should be noted that similar facts can also be told of in the present, as in the example about the hot-air balloons (see pp. 191–2), where the child drew attention to the presence of many balloons in the sky as he spoke of them.

Relevance in this mode depends very much on whether the hearer makes a proper assessment of the fact recounted. If you tell people who have no idea of fast times in swimming that the girl next door can do the 100 metres freestyle in under fifty-eight seconds, they will be unable to see relevance in your statement. They may well ask whether fifty-eight seconds is a good time, in the hope of gauging the salience of what you are talking about; and if you explain that it is a time close to the national record, your statement will be more likely to be properly assessed.

In Part II of this book, we observed that language is structured in a precise way. Pronunciation obeys rules that bear particularly on the structure of syllables; analysis of the syntax of a sentence presupposes identification of the relations between phrases and their morphological marking; meaning, in the form of scenic and thematic representations, is constructed from these relations between phrases and from what the phrases call to mind. The selection of a relevant message by a speaker and the understanding of its relevance by its hearers also depends on a precise procedure. The main argument of this chapter is that part of the procedure is well modelled by probability theory. We may see something of how probability and relevance are linked by varying the parameters of the last example.

Let us assume that the girl next door can swim 100 metres not in fifty-eight seconds but in one minute eighteen seconds. Any hearer who knows something about competitive swimming may well wonder why you bother to mention it. The number of girls who can match her performance being quite high, there is no huge improbability in your actually knowing one of them. If you then state that she is a child of eleven, you restore the improbability and by the same token the relevance. A further parameter that has a gradual bearing on the relevance is the 'distance', whether concrete or abstract, between you and whatever girl you speak of. If she is your sister, there is greater relevance than if she is some girl who happens to live in the same town as you but whom you have never met. There too probability theory can predict the phenomenon. The greater the 'distance' in question, the greater the probability of finding someone within it who will be capable of equalling the performance and the less relevance there will be. The same phenomenon of distance can function in a temporal aspect. You can draw attention to a lady wearing an outlandish hat; you can exaggerate a little and say that, just an hour ago, you saw a lady wearing an absolutely outlandish hat; it would be much harder to say that ten years ago you saw a lady wearing an outlandish hat, unless you rescued your statement from non-relevance by stressing the hat's unlikely character (for instance, that it featured a bird's nest with a real bird in it). The more time has elapsed since the event recounted, the greater the probability of some such situation having happened; and the relevance of the story diminishes accordingly. In journalism, this influence of concrete or abstract distance on the relevance of events reported is well enough known for it to have a particular name: the death-to-distance ratio. All other things being equal, for deaths to be featured on the front page, the number of them must compensate for the distance: no Paris daily will give space on page 1 to a pile-up on a motorway which kills ten people if the event took place in Australia. This phenomenon is well predicted in probability theory.[2]

---

[2] It can be shown that the number of deaths proportionate to the distance can compensate for the latter. For rare events, modelled by Poisson's law, it is enough that the number of deaths increases in accordance with the square root of the distance. The distance used must not be simply geographical, some countries being 'nearer' than others at a given period (Dessalles 1992; Bousquet 1999).

People have an intuitive perception of what an unlikely event might be. The art of the raconteur consists of knowing how to toy with that perception, making much of the improbable features, adding details to increase credibility and lessen the perception of distance, and stressing his or her own astonishment. Here is an extract illustrating this strategy:

> Context: a discussion on the specificity of Alzheimer's disease
> G1: Who do you mean?
> H1: People with Alzheimer's. They just walk about aimlessly, you know.
> G2: Not just people with Alzheimer's.
> H2: Sure, but people with Alzheimer's cover miles and miles every day... You wouldn't believe! They're clapped out.
> G3: Is that so?
> H3: I'm telling you! Some of them... They put, like, they did this test and everything. There was this woman that did at least sixty miles a day! I'm telling you, she was clapped out!
> I1: Well, that's really something.

The improbable nature of the thing being reported is reinforced by 'You wouldn't believe!' in H2, the later mention of the test, the more or less conscious exaggeration of the sixty miles. However, the narrator is not the only person deploying narrative skills. The other two interlocutors are also active in the same register of probability: at the end, I1 shows one of them sharing the narrator's astonishment, while G's attitude has been quite different—in specifying that people with Alzheimer's are not the only ones who walk about aimlessly, G trivializes the fact reported at H1 and thereby makes it appear more probable. This strategy of trivialization is particularly frequent, almost systematic. In its simplest form, it consists of saying that one is already in possession of the knowledge being conveyed. In the previous example of the hot-air balloons (p. 191), it can be seen in the remark of the second child, 'Yes, I know'. It can, however, often take a form that is more constructive. The best way to apply this strategy of trivialization is to quote an instance that is analogous to the fact reported. In the following extract there are two examples of this:

> Context: on New Year's Day 1987, the temperature seemed exceptionally mild
> J1: At any rate, the temperature today is the highest you could expect until, until about the middle of February!
> K1: Yes, that's a fact.
> L1: Well, I know for a fact that in the winter of 1977 there was a Föhn type of weather... On the 1st January 1977, the temperature was 20 in Biarritz.

K2: I can remember a year when we were children, I can remember it very clearly. Round about the 20 December... My sister and I were in frocks, our summer frocks. Summer frocks! And it had been a very exceptional year.

The temperature of 16° is seen as exceptionally mild. L can contribute the information about a former New Year's Day, ten years earlier, when he says it was 20° in Biarritz. Likewise, K can report another instance of a very mild day for that time of year. Probability theory confirms that the effect of L1 and K2 is to trivialize the circumstance mentioned at J1: for observers who have no accurate or reliable weather figures, the probability of there being a very mild New Year's Day increases if they know that it has happened before. Let us assume for example that New Year's Day 1987 seems at first to be the mildest in the speaker's memory. After L1, the probability increases to be about one chance in ten, which is not all that exceptional. The more recent the analogous instance, the more effective the trivialization. From this point of view, K2 is not as effective as L1, since it extends the frame of reference several decades into the past. Similarly, the higher the temperature is in the analogous instance, the less remarkable it will seem in the present situation. On this point, K tries to go one better with her reminiscence about the summer frocks and the exaggerated way she stresses it. As these examples show, probability theory supplies a neat model for this trivialization behaviour. This strategy of quoting an analogous instance makes for what has been called 'story rounds' (Tannen 1984: 100), in which each speaker contributes an anecdote. The conversation then consists not of simple utterances as in the previous example, but of sequences of stories lasting for ten minutes or more. The initial motivation for each of the stories is trivialization of the one before. But as the effectiveness of the trivialization increases proportionately to the greater unlikeliness of the most recent story, the device is self-sustaining. In the previous example, it is possible that K2 is as much an attempt at trivialization as J1.[3]

I define as 'informative' this conversational style in which the first speaker wishes to draw attention to a salient situation.[4] Conversations in

[3] The trivialization phenomenon consisting of adding on analogous examples suggests a possible explanation for the prohibition put on non sequiturs and disjointed subject matters. In transitional moments, interlocutors expect, as in story rounds, that there will be evident analogies or associations between consecutive subjects of conversation.

[4] Claude Shannon (1948) defines the quantity of information of an event as the logarithm of the inverse of its probability: $\log_2 (1/p)$. The more the presumed probability p of an event is small, the greater the information its coming to pass will provide. If an

this mode do not always deal with unlikely events. Speakers may also inform hearers about pleasant or unpleasant happenings, as in the following two examples:

> Context: two people talking about a mutual friend
> M1: Did I tell you they've accepted Peter's application to do that course in Japan?
> N1: No, you didn't. That's marvellous!

> Context: O has bought some postcards to send to particular friends
> O1: Oh, damn! I've done it wrong. I've written this one to C.
> P1: Well, what difference does it make?

In the first extract, the salience of the situation reported in M1 is how pleasant it is, whereas in O1 the salience lies in how unpleasant the situation is. There is a close analogy between these conversations about pleasant or unpleasant things and the stories dealing with unlikely events. In both situations, the intensity of the salience is gradual; it depends on distance (something dramatic that happens close by affects us more than a similar thing happening farther away); and it is subject to trivialization by an interlocutor. Both types of information can be found on the front pages of newspapers where one finds cheek by jowl with one another the most untoward facts and dramatic events.[5]

Figure 14.1 plots the constraints on the freedom of a speaker using the informative mode (the dimension of pleasantness, symmetrical with that of unpleasantness, is omitted). Events that can be mentioned as new subjects of conversation in the informative mode must be outside a 'triviality area' marked by high values of probability and low values of unpleasantness. Figure 14.1 shows the triviality areas at three and five bits. In probabilistic terms, these areas correspond respectively to events with more than one chance in eight and more than one chance in thirty-two of

event is salient because it is improbable, a statement about it must provide significant information. If an interlocutor trivializes the event, thereby increasing the estimate of the value of p, the amount of information associated with it will be accordingly reduced.

[5] In technical parlance, one can measure the amount of information contained in an event of probability p and presenting the disadvantage d (going from 0, for neutral situations, to 1, for the most unpleasant ones) with a formula which is a straightforward generalization of Shannon's (see previous footnote):

$$I = \log_2 \left[\frac{1}{p(1-d)} \right]$$

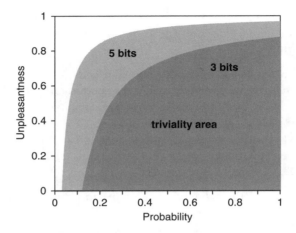

FIG. 14.1 Representation of the constraints of the informative mode, in terms of two parameters: the *a priori* probability and the unpleasant character of the event recounted. The latter must be located outside the two grey areas, if it is to convey three bits of information or five bits respectively.

happening. The two parameters of the figure, the *a priori* probability of the event and its pleasant or unpleasant character, are the two factors that most clearly affect conversations in the informative mode.[6] Other parameters with a bearing on salience include the aesthetic value of the event and more generally the intensity of the emotions it inspires. However, it is not always easy to disentangle these factors from the influence of probability, intense emotions being by definition unusual, as speakers do not fail to point out. In particular, if the salient situation is not being experienced in the present, the improbable aspect becomes necessary. This explains why speech motivated by emotion is infrequent in corpuses of recorded talk, which consist essentially of conversations on reported situations. A complete analysis of the different factors that combine to make a situation into a relevant event worthy of being spoken of in the informative mode has not yet been done.

The use of language in the informative mode obeys rules which speakers cannot avoid. It is difficult to interest hearers in stories that are trivial. In this mode, relevance requires the opportune production of a salient event,

---

[6] This conclusion is based on the corpus of conversations that I have compiled, which contains several hundred extracts.

that is to say typically one with a character that is both improbable and either pleasant or unpleasant. The constraint of relevance, as we have seen, affects also the reactions of interlocutors, whose only choice is either to acknowledge the salient nature of the event (as in I1 or K1) or else to employ the strategy of trivialization. A typical trivializing method consists of citing an analogous event, which makes for the sequences of speeches known as a story round. We must now move on to two things: a consideration of the abilities that interlocutors must possess if they are to converse in informative mode; and an enquiry into why our ancestors came to have those abilities.

14.3 Creatures responsive to information

Human beings are responsive to salient events that they observe or learn about. This ability is one that should not be underestimated. It depends on various mechanisms via which we can assess the salience of events. Let us focus specially on events we see as unusual. One mechanism works by making a judgement on frequency: any scenes which are simply out of the ordinary from a statistical point of view[7] draw our attention, awaken our interest, and may well activate a communication reflex in the informative mode. For example, if you live outside London but happen one day to bump into one of your cousins in the Haymarket, once you are back at home you will probably think this encounter salient enough to be recounted. However, our competence in recognizing salience is not restricted to the noting of statistical exceptions. We know, for instance, that a conjuncture of improbable events is even more improbable. Bumping into into one cousin in the Haymarket is unusual enough, but to bump into two of them quite separately on the same day is even more unusual[8] (in the interests of simplicity, let us assume that the encounters

---

[7] The complexity of such a measure of frequency should not be underestimated, since it deals with objects that are richly structured, namely the scenes produced by our mechanism of semantic representation. Most importantly, we cannot rely solely on statistical methods, for they presuppose a way of measuring the similarity of events.

[8] Mention must be made of the well known experiments by Amos Tversky and Daniel Kahneman, which would appear to refute this phenomenon of probabilistic conjunction (Tversky and Kahneman 1974, 1983). However, these authors restrict themselves to the scope of the conclusions they draw from their experiments. Although the subjects seem to be mistakenly judging that $(A \& B)$ is more probable than A, it is likely that they see A and B as prototypes rather than as sets of possibilities.

are emotionally neutral). We are also alert to the separateness of events. In the example of the two cousins, the event is genuinely highly improbable only if the presence of each of them in town on the same day is independent of the presence of the other (which would not be the case if this happened to be the day of a family reunion). In addition, effects of proximity impinge on our consciousness; and in the case of the two cousins, proximity in time is important, since there is a lesser *a priori* probability of meeting them within ten minutes of each other than within ten days.[9] Similarly, from a spatial point of view, to have a chance meeting with a cousin 200 miles or 2,000 miles away from home is more improbable than meeting him just two miles away. A consideration of proximity enters into more abstract areas too, for instance cousinhood itself: for most people the *a priori* probability of meeting a first cousin is lesser than that of meeting a distant cousin, given that the former are generally fewer in number. Our awareness and assessment of improbability also draw upon knowledge we may have of a situation. If we know, for example, that our cousin often comes up to town, then a chance meeting with him is less improbable. In short, our assessment of the improbability of an event and hence of its information value, depends on a precise mechanism which takes account of the frequency of events, their conjunction, their proximity, and any knowledge we may have that affects them. The way this mechanism functions, as revealed by detailed analysis of it, seems every bit as precise as the functioning of other aspects of language such as phonology or syntax (Muhlenbach 1999).

Informative behaviour is deeply rooted in all of us. In the presence of their mother, infants between nine and twelve months start to point at salient events or things, such as the arrival of their father or a dancing doll used by an experimenter (Carpenter, Nagell, and Tomasello 1998). What is remarkable at that age is that pointing does not indicate a desire to have the object but is an attempt to draw the mother's attention to it. Tomasello and his collaborators observe that this behaviour is unknown among the other primates. Even if their attention is drawn to salient events, they never attempt to share that attention with any of their fellows. Furthermore, it

---

[9] Probability theory can quantify this phenomenon. If we represent the probability of a chance meeting with one cousin by Poisson's law, the *a priori* probability of meeting both of them within a space of time Δt is inversely proportional to Δt.

seems they are also unable to decipher gestures designed to draw their attention to something. While chimpanzees, with their inquisitive nature, are perfectly capable of following the gaze of other chimpanzees and will even bestir themselves to go and look at what others are looking at, they do not understand gestures or looks aimed at informing them intentionally of where they might find a hidden sweet (Call, Hare, and Tomasello 1998). In our own species, attention-sharing behaviour directed at salient events is universal and automatic. The automatic quality was first mentioned in Chapter 3, with the example of the naked man. Human beings are creatures who are responsive to information; and language can be seen to be a way of sharing information.

14.4 The biological grounding of the informative mode

There is a common belief that as children develop they learn to converse, much as they learn good manners. This would mean that during childhood we learned the various ways of being relevant in our verbal interactions by imitating the example set us by adults. It is a fact that children are not always relevant, as can be seen in this example:

> Context: a little girl of three and a half speaks to her uncle about Leo, the family cat:
> Leo's got claws.

To an adult, such a statement lacks relevance (something which in a young child is not only accepted but is seen as touching), for there is no *a priori* salience in cats having claws. The child herself may see the fact as salient; but she is not trying to make sure that her impression is shared by the adult. Though very young children often say irrelevant things like that, as they grow older the relevance of their utterances is apparent to their interlocutors; and by the age of six, they are fully competent as speakers, capable of engaging in coherent conversation.

It might be thought that it is solely through their social interactions that children learn how to play their part in conversation. But there are problems with this instructional view of how conversational competence is acquired. For one thing, it affords no understanding of any mechanism whereby children might develop a responsiveness to salient events based only upon interactions with the people among whom they live. This responsiveness, as discussed in the previous section, presupposes perception of frequencies of events and taking account of factors such as their independence from one another, or the distance, whether real or abstract, between them, to say nothing of the capacity for trivialization. Proponents of the environmentalist view of conversational competence ought to explain how children can pick up the ability to recognize salient events just from the instances offered by their family circle. For another thing, the environmentalist hypothesis cannot explain why conversation behaviour is both universal and systematic. We have no knowledge of any peoples, any cultures, any human groups in whom this behaviour is lacking. No culture has ever been described in which spontaneous talk is conducted in ways different from what has just been analysed. If conversation were a cultural behaviour like jazz for instance, it would not be systematic and a significant number of people might opt out of learning how to do it. But that does not happen. Whereas a great many people neither play nor listen to jazz, it would be impossible to find, in any culture under the sun, more than a minute proportion of the healthy population who systematically abstain from all conversation.

Against the exclusively environmentalist view, there is the hypothesis that sees the capacity for conversation as deriving from specific biological predispositions. It can be argued that, just as children do not have to make up from scratch their ways of putting together the sounds and words of their language, so they can avail themselves of mechanisms that help them to become speakers with relevance. That would explain not only the early development of this ability in children but also the universality of conversation in its informative mode. The biological predisposition is a natural extension of the other biological predispositions underlying phonology, syntax, and the making of meaning. If we possess some such faculty and if we spend so much time using it to share information, it must be because it fulfills an important biological function.

14.5 Instinctive sharing of information

Many, indeed sometimes most, of our spontaneous language interactions function in informative mode. This is a fact that Sperber's and Wilson's general theory takes no account of. The criterion of relevance which applies here is unrelated to deductive inferences. Speakers' perception of the salience of any of the events they speak about comes essentially from two of its properties, its *a priori* probability and its pleasantness or unpleasantness. The behaviour of interlocutors, whether they recognize the salient aspect of the first utterance, as at I1 and K1, or whether they employ a strategy of trivialization, as at G2, L1, K2, and P1, is motivated by the same mechanism of assessment of amounts of information (cf. note 5, p. 287).

In Chapter 8, analysing the functioning of protolanguage in the minds of our ancestors, we tried to conceive of a language without syntax in which words are put together on the basis of their meanings. We tried to reconstruct the protosemantics of concrete scenes expressed by such a protolanguage. And we canvassed the question of what type of use our ancestors might have had for their protolanguage. Next I advanced the idea that protohumans communicated about salient scenes, a term which has now acquired a more exact meaning: salient scenes are those situations which, when spoken of, convey information. The hypothesis expounded in Chapter 8 was that protohumans conversed in the informative mode. No doubt their descriptions and narratives were poorer than ours. Human beings can draw on their other conversational capacities to stress the salience of their utterances. Nevertheless, according to the scenario set forth, our protohuman ancestors had the capacity to note salient events and the reflex to make them into acts of communication. The considerable advantage of this hypothesis is that it gives a consistent function to protolanguage. The fact that this mode of communication has survived to become an integral part of our own ways of communicating adds weight to this argument. The hypothesis suggests that the informative reflex which makes human beings draw others' attention to situations they see as salient was inherited from *Homo erectus*. From a structural point of view, conversation in this mode depends on the ability to detect informative value from *a priori* probability and the pleasantness or unpleasantness of the event perceived. So we must assume that our predecessors possessed this faculty of perception which functions both in our noting the salience of situations and in our strategy of trivialization.

Not all conversation among human beings takes place in informative mode. The second of our ways of communicating may be what makes us most fundamentally different from our immediate predecessor.

15 The birth of argumentation

The aim of this chapter is to show that the use of language has passed through two separate stages. The first of these, marked by the informative mode described in the preceding chapter, was very likely associated with the protolanguage spoken by the species of hominids which preceded us. The second, peculiar to our own species, is marked by the capacity for argumentation.

15.1 Relevance in the argumentative mode

The logical mode

Sharing of information is not the only remarkable behaviour in conversation. This can be seen if we look again at the example about the Christmas tree not losing its needles (p. 270). Up to B2, it might appear that the exchange between the two speakers is restricted to the informative mode: here is an uncommon fir, fully three weeks after being cut down, yet still keeping its needles. It can be said, however, that from A3 onwards the speakers are no longer in informative mode. Together they have begun canvassing an explanation for the phenomenon. This means that the plane on which they are now functioning is a logical one. Between the two conversation behaviours there is a clear difference and it is important to what follows. Neither of the speakers tries to trivialize this instance of B's Christmas tree. For example, A could have mentioned a niece of hers whose tree still had its needles after a month or something of that kind. Instead, she expresses her astonishment in a different way, using the term *odd* at A3. At B3 the speaker, noting the register in which A is functioning, expresses shared astonishment with *Yes, I can't think why*. The closing remark (A4: *It's a plastic one!*) is not meant to be taken seriously, though we can note that it actually functions as an explanation: if it really is a plastic tree, there is nothing astonishing about it.

Astonishment that seeks an explanation is not the same thing as responsiveness to untoward events. Situations that are out of the ordinary draw our attention because we perceive them as salient. When this interest in unusual situations gives rise to an act of communication, it is often one which stimulates the trivialization reflex. However, the other mode of astonishment, the one that activates the search for an explanation, is stimulated by the perception or the mention of an event seen as prima facie impossible. If narrative astonishment is probabilistic, explanatory astonishment is logical. The example of the Christmas tree shows that one and the same fact can stimulate both sorts of reactions one after the other. However, these two modes correspond to behaviours that are qualitatively different. An illustration of the difference can be seen in the following extract from Deborah Tannen (Tannen 1984: 62):

Q1: But anyway... How do you happen to know his stuff?
R1: 'Cause I read it.
S1: What do you do?
Q2: [? ?] Are you in... sociology or anything?
R2: Yeah I read a little bit of it. [pronounced *reed*]
Q3: Hm?
R3: I read a little bit of it. [pronounced *red*]
Q4: I mean were you... uh studying sociology?
R4: No.
Q5: You just heard about it, huh?
R5: Yeah. No. I heard about it from a friend who was a sociologist, and he said read this book, it's a good book and I read that book 'n
Q6: I had never heard about him before I started studying linguistics.
R6: Really?
Q7: Yeah.[1]

This extract is quite remarkable, in that the explanation requested by Q and S is not given till R5 and it looks as though it has been dragged out by Q. The effect of reply R5 is to allay Q's and S's astonishment by an explanation of what was inexplicable up to that point, namely how R had acquired any knowledge of the work of the sociologist in question, Goffman. The fact is that, although the reply R1 sounds like an explanation and seems to be offered as such, since it states that R has

---

[1] I have omitted some minor transcription details.

read Goffman, it is not acceptable as it stands. Why is this? What Q and S really want is that their astonishment should be allayed and R1 does not do that. Tannen asked R the following day why he had reacted as he did and it turned out that he had been perfectly aware of the non-relevance of R1-R4 but that he had felt intimidated by the abruptness of the questions starting at Q1. So his momentary infringement of the rules governing relevance in conversation had resulted from a conscious choice.

The logical mode, which I have called elsewhere the mode of paradox (Dessalles 1985, 1996b), derives from a behaviour which follows a particularly straightforward pattern: first, one finds something astonishing, then one tries to find an explanation that allays the astonishment. The preceding extract shows how relevance in this mode constrains the behaviour of interlocutors: R has only one way to be relevant and that is to offer an explanation. It is rather striking to note that situations of spontaneous conversation, which might be thought to give plenty of freedom of expression to interlocutors, actually impose strict constraints upon them at certain moments. What they must grasp, then solve, is a sort of logical enigma. Anyone who fails to do so runs the risk of being non-relevant and of incurring the social cost that this entails.

The preceding extract is an example of argumentation. The participants have to deal with a problem, an apparent paradox in this case, by putting forward arguments designed to reinforce or alternatively to resolve the problematic situation. This conversational mode is possible because speakers possess a capacity for argumentation. Situations of logical astonishment are not, however, the only ones in which people deploy their argumentative ability, as we are about to see.

The issue-settling mode

Many argumentative utterances in conversation deal with situations in which something is at issue. Interlocutors generally try to find a way of settling the issue. Here is an example:

Context: a conversation between students preparing to show slides
T1: But can't you put the projector here?
U1: Well, I put it there because I didn't dare put it on your desk. But if I put it here, it'll be projecting on the door handle. That'll be lovely!
T2: Well then, put a few books under it. Can't you lean it over a bit?
U2: That would skew the picture.

What is at issue here is finding a suitable place for showing the slides. U has brought the equipment, minus a screen, expecting to be able to use a white door instead. How can we define the behaviour of the interlocutors in this mode? As we have seen before, their behaviour is not a matter of total chance; and though we may at times have the impression that we can say anything at all in a conversation, it is an illusion. In this mode of issue-settling, interlocutors actually have little room for manoeuvre: either they point out an unwanted problem or they show how such a problem could be avoided. The extract above begins when the problem has already arisen: the unwanted problem is that the door does not lend itself to projecting a good image. T1 suggests a way of coping with this difficulty. U1 is in several parts. First, U gives the impression, no doubt in jest, of believing that T's desk is a space not to be invaded, contriving in this way to explain that there was something problematical in the solution proposed at T1. The second part of U1 functions in exactly the same way, since shining the pictures onto the door handle is equally undesirable. At T2, T again manages to solve the difficulty but U once more finds something wrong with the solution proposed. Such alternation between identifying an unwanted problem and avoiding it is characteristic of this mode of conversation.

The previous extract illustrates the fact that the typical outcome of conversations in this mode is a decision arrived at by the interlocutors or a plan of action that they agree upon. However, this mode of conversation need not entail an explicit mention of actions, as the following example shows:

Context: a windy day at a ski resort
V1: I think we're in for a bit of a blow.
W1: Yer, well, at least it'll get rid of the clouds.

There, the role of W1, unlike that of V1, is not informative. W's intention is not to draw attention to a salient situation. Nor is it to propose any action to change the situation. If W had suggested putting on more clothes, not going up to the higher slopes, or not going skiing that day, the situation of the skiers would have been changed so as to avoid the unwanted difficulty. But although W does nothing in that line, W1 has an effect on the problem pointed out at V1. After W1, though the situation remains unchanged, W shows that it is not unmixed: it is negative in some respects but they are balanced by more positive ones. This strategy, which consists of weighing up the pros and the cons, is peculiar to the issue-settling mode.

In this mode, relevance imposes strict constraints. When the problematical nature of an unwanted situation becomes apparent, one's expectation is that interlocutors try either to solve the problem or to show that the drawbacks are matched by advantages.

The interplay of conversational modes

It may well be asked whether there is at bottom a genuine difference between the two conversational uses of language, the informative and the argumentative. Is there not something arbitrary in saying that one of them deals with salient situations and the other with problematical situations? It is tempting to see a parallel between, on the one hand, improbable situations and paradoxical situations, and on the other between unpleasant situations and situations in which an issue requires settling. What matters is not distinguishing situations according to their 'objective' features. In absolute terms, no situation ever presents any of the features mentioned, improbable, paradoxical, unpleasant, or requiring settlement. These aspects exist only in the way interlocutors perceive the situations. It is not the same thing at all to consider a situation as being prima facie unlikely and prima facie impossible. There are situations which, though they are perfectly habitual, may be perceived as paradoxical: personally, I have never been able to understand why downhill skiers use poles with baskets when they are travelling at more than sixty miles an hour. Similarly, one can hear of something unpleasant, for instance an accident in which several people lost their lives, without necessarily looking on it as an issue requiring settlement. An issue, like a paradox, is an open-ended problem. What is required is that one should either reflect or decide, opt for an explanation or a solution. However, the attitude one adopts towards information is not the same; one is content to assess it for salience. It is of course possible, in any given situation, to have several different attitudes one after the other. On hearing of the suicide of a prime minister, for example, one may see it at first as unusual and unpleasant, then try to think of some explanation for it, and finally face the problem that his death raises for the country's future political development.

The most persuasive reason for making the distinction between the informative and the argumentative uses of language is that the mechanisms they activate in interlocutors are different. As we saw in the previous chapter, conversations in the informative mode depend on assessments of parameters such as the probability and the pleasantness or unpleasantness of situations. These assessments enable interlocutors to identify salience and also to trivialize situations. The argumentative mode, however, functions through a mechanism which is radically different, namely the detection of a cognitive conflict.

15.2 The idea of cognitive conflict

On the face of it, there appears to be a great disparity between the logical mode and the issue-settling mode. In the former, there is a state of affairs seen as strange for which an explanation is sought. In the latter, there is an unwanted state of affairs and a desire for it to end. The two behaviours are those of the investigative detective and the politician; and the favourite cognitive activity of a Sherlock Holmes is very different from that of a Winston Churchill. The sole concern of the first is to understand; the other's aim is to act. From a formal point of view, however, both activities share a basic cognitive mechanism which consists of the resolution of conflicts between representations.

Finding an explanation for a strange occurrence and finding a solution to an unwanted state of affairs are not unrelated activities. What constitutes a strange occurrence? It is an occurrence that we think ought not to have occurred: we perceive that a fact F has occurred and we have reason to believe that *not F* should have prevailed. In the example about reading Goffman (p. 295), Q and S perceive that R has some knowledge of the sociologist's books (F), but they were under the impression that a non-sociologist would have no reason to read them (*not F*). This constitutes what we may define as a cognitive conflict: Q and S believe two things which are mutually exclusive, F because they perceive it and *not F* because it follows from their knowledge that R is not a sociologist. And in a conversation in issue-settling mode, the situation is similar, in that the participants are in a state of wanting two things which are mutually exclusive. In the example about the projector, they want to lean the machine over a bit (F) so that the door handle will not show in the pictures, but at the same time they do not to lean it over (*not F*) because that would skew the image. What we have is once more a conflict between a representation and its negation.

To define such a conflict as cognitive is proper, for there is a conflict not between individuals but between mental representations. If conversation is to function, each of the participants must understand the conflict and experience it. It may well be that one of them espouses *F* and the other one *not F*, which may lead to disagreement between individuals or even to conflict within a relationship, but that is not what concerns us here. So as to defend their point of view in such circumstances, interlocutors must understand where the problem lies, that is to say the conflict of beliefs or desires between *F* and *not F*. The cognitive conflict lies inside each of the participants.

Identification of a cognitive conflict by a subject, just like the identification of the salience of an event in the world of information, is a phenomenon peculiar to the pragmatic level of language. Decisions about what it is apt to say in any given context are made at this level. The semantic level of language, discussed in Chapters 11 and 12, functions only in determining *F* and *not F*. The pragmatic level begins where subjects either identify a salient feature (notably, improbable and pleasant or unpleasant) or else realize that there is a conflict between their beliefs and their wishes. In the experiments with the green bin and the wooden table (p. 282), C and E make statements that are semantically unexceptionable. Their interlocutors, D and F respectively, have no difficulty in knowing which bin and which table are being spoken about or in understanding how the objects are described. What they cannot grasp is whatever salience there might be in the situations drawn to their attention by C and E or how they might give rise to a cognitive conflict.

A cognitive conflict exists only when the beliefs and wishes which constitute it have some degree of intensity. If one does not really believe that *F* is true or false, if one has no great desire or aversion for *F*, there can be no conflict between *F* and *not F*. An example might be the sight of a beggar waiting in a queue at an ATM, which makes you think both that he must have money (*F*) and that he has none (*not F*). At first these beliefs have some degree of intensity, in part because of what you can see: the man is unkempt and in rags, which is an image closely associated with people who are completely without money (*not F*). On the other hand, the belief in *F* is linked to the association between queueing at an ATM and withdrawing funds. This conflict is immediate and obvious to any person who makes the two associations. However, the cognitive mechanism that makes for the identification of the conflict should not be underestimated. The initial reflex consists merely of seeing the scene as salient; the image of the dosser queueing at the ATM is first and foremost incongruous, atypical, and improbable. The conflict can appear only after a thematic analysis (cf. Chapter 11). Such an analysis can take the beggar as theme and locate him either outside the property of having money (*not F*) or inside it (*F*). There is a manifest logical incompatibility between the two terms.

However, doing a thematic analysis of the situation is not enough to create a cognitive conflict. What is also required is that the terms of the conflict should have a degree of necessity. The necessity of a term *F* is the propensity of the subject to believe or desire *F* at a particular moment.[2] In the case of the beggar, the perception and the associations it brings to mind are strong enough to confer significant necessity both to *F* and to *not F*, thus setting up a cognitive conflict. In a model which I recently proposed (Dessalles 1998a), a cognitive conflict is represented thus: $(F, n_1) \uparrow (not\ F, n_2)$. The arrow represents the incompatibility and n_1 and n_2 represent the respective necessities of *F* and *not F*. The incompatibility is a consequence of thematic segmentation; but the conflict is experienced because n_1 and n_2 have significant values. We may define the intensity of a cognitive conflict as the product $n_1 \times n_2$. Thus, if n_1 or n_2 should happen to have a negligible value, the conflict disappears even though the incompatibility persists. This is how the search for solutions to cognitive conflicts is conducted.

15.3 The recursive nature of argumentation

Resolution of cognitive conflicts

The argumentative mode would not be a conversational form in its own right if it depended solely on the identification of cognitive conflicts. Argumentation, so widely practised by conversing human beings, grows out of the participants' collective efforts to find a solution to the cognitive conflict that they share once a subject is raised. To understand what it is in the biology of human beings that impels them to share cognitive conflicts

---

[2] The 'necessity' is related to the idea of propositional attitude, which is used particularly in philosophy of language. However, the philosophical idea of necessity is richer than that, since it includes the idea of truth, which many philosophers of language see as ontological rather than epistemological and which they therefore exclude from any cognitive approach such as the one concerning propositional attitudes.

which they then try to solve together, we must analyse the procedures whereby such conflicts are identified then resolved.

Faced with a conflict between F and *not F*, each participant will aim to invalidate the weaker of the two terms, that is, the term which seems at any given moment to have a lesser degree of necessity. If this is achieved, the conflict is resolved. In the case of the beggar, let us suppose that initially his impecunious appearance is so marked that the necessity n_2 of his having no money is strengthened. An observer's attention will therefore be directed towards the other term, to try to invalidate the idea that he has some money. He does appear to have some, since he is apparently about to make a withdrawal. However, there is also the possibility that he is standing in the queue for some completely different reason, for instance because he is hoping to be given some money by the person in front of him or so as to amuse his friends by pretending to have a bank account. But if we suppose that neither of these is the case—the person in front of him is having nothing to do with him and there are no friends of his to be seen—, then the beggar does appear to be waiting his turn to withdraw money. This has the effect of strengthening n_1 and of turning *not F* into the weaker term of the conflict. Why do we believe the man has no money? Because he is a beggar. To the mind of the observer, a beggar is bound to have no money. So if the necessity of his having money is n_1, the necessity of his not being a beggar also becomes n_1. By this stage, the conflict has shifted: is he or is he not a beggar? The process of resolution starts again with the weaker term, for example the idea that the man is a beggar. We take him to be a beggar because of the way he looks. But what if that is just a disguise? And so on.

The procedure for resolving cognitive conflicts, which is the driving force of argumentation, follows a simple pattern. It can be described as follows: (S1) assessment: assessing the terms of the conflict and focusing on the weaker one; (S2) abduction: seeking the cause of this term and imagining a situation in which the cause would not make for its effect; (S3) negation: if this fails, denying the cause. In the preceding example, the idea that the man is expecting to be given money or pretending to wait his turn is a result of the abductive strategy (S2).[3] The same goes for the idea that he might be disguised. In either case, the weaker term of

---

[3] The word 'abduction' is generally taken to mean the ability to discover the causes of a state of affairs.

the conflict disappears from the new situation imagined: whether he is begging or pretending, it is no longer possible to say he has money; if he is disguised, it is no longer possible to say we are dealing with a beggar. As for the negation strategy (S3), it gets us out of an intractable situation: when lack of imagination means we cannot apply strategy (S2), we deny the cause of the weaker term. When having no money becomes the term of lesser necessity and we deny its cause, the fact of being a beggar, we shift the conflict onto being a beggar versus not being a beggar.

Assessment of necessities (S1) and negation (S3), being purely pragmatic, make sense only as part of the process of ending the conflict. Strategy (S2), however, depends largely on our semantic abilities. It is called abductive because it consists generally of seeking the cause of the phenomenon to be eliminated and then of imagining some disruption to the causal link. Let us suppose that you throw a glass over your shoulder: you expect to hear the usual noise made by a glass breaking; if there is no noise, a conflict arises. You apply (S2) to the weaker term, in this case the existence of a noise. How can the situation be changed in a way that makes the noise stop being necessary? Here, the imagination may be quite productive: perhaps the glass landed on a thick carpet; someone may have caught it; it could have flown out of a window that happened to be open. Each of these possible solutions would constitute a disruption to the causal link between a glass falling and making a noise as it breaks. It is natural to see abduction in the search for a cause then an 'anti-cause', that is to say some event that prevents the effect from following its usual cause. Such an abductive search is semantic in nature, for it involves mainly our capacity for scenic representation. In the instance of the thrown glass, it is via a process of reasoning about the scene that we can alter the situation in such a way that the noise does not happen.

There is a mechanical aspect to the process of ending a cognitive conflict, particularly with respect to the sequence (S1)-(S2)-(S3) and the (S3) strategy itself. It should be noted, however, that for the most part it is in the (S1) and (S2) strategies that whatever common sense and intelligence we may attribute to one another in any given situation are to be found. The effectiveness of these two strategies depends on the experience and the creativity of the person who can assess the necessity of the elements of the situation and can find solutions by abduction.

A recursive procedure

We are insufficiently surprised at the fact that human beings communicate by constructing conversations. Taken as a whole, the sequence of speeches making up a conversation can run to an impressive length. In my own archive of recordings, there is a conversation of 355 speeches lasting more than half an hour on the detailed planning of a lunch in honour of a foreign guest, with its main course, the entrées, the dessert, etc. We have no evidence that any other form of life goes in for anything remotely resembling such a system of communication with its lengthy, elaborate, and highly structured exchanges. Nor do any of the existing models of human communication, either the theory of speech acts or theories of cooperation (see Chapter 13.2), help to explain the dimensions and evident complexity of conversational exchanges. Why are our language interactions not limited to exchanges on the binary pattern of question and answer, statement and reply? One mechanism that initiates complex exchanges is peculiar to the informative mode and comes from the possibility of story rounds, in which each new fact contributed entails a trivialization of the one before it. In the argumentative mode, which is our concern here, the lengthy sequences can be explained differently, being linked to the recursiveness of the procedure through which cognitive conflicts are resolved.

As stated previously more than once, recursiveness is at work in language, for instance in the organization of phrases (cf. Chapter 9) or in discarding and changing local maps (cf. Chapter 11). It is also present at the pragmatic level. Strategy (2), by creating a new situation, resolves the present conflict, but may thereby bring about another. The process starts again with the new conflict. The hypothesis that the dosser is expecting to be given money resolves the initial conflict; but it then comes into conflict with the perception of the behaviour of the beggar and of the person queueing in front of him. This type of second-guessing is one cause of recursion in conversation. Strategy (3) also triggers a recursive call to the procedure of resolution by shifting the conflict onto one of its causes: any observer who decides that the person cannot be a genuine beggar is instantly put into a new conflict between that conclusion and what can be plainly seen, the man's poverty-stricken appearance. So strategies (S2) and (S3) both lead to a recursive call to the resolution procedure. In the example about the slide projector, moving the machine onto the desk resolves the current conflict caused by the fact that in its present unsuitable position the picture is too small. Then another conflict is revealed when the picture is projected onto the door handle, which is not what is wanted. The expedient of leaning the projector a little to one side, though it resolves this conflict, creates another one by the unwanted deforming of the picture. This sequence of conflicts and attempts at resolution of them can be explained by the recursiveness of the procedure that the two participants engage in to settle the original cognitive conflict.

Logic and language

The argumentative procedure adopted by the participants in a conversation enables them to solve problems collectively, as can be seen in the extract dealing with the slide projector. Their interaction on the problem will lead them to a shared solution of the difficulty of projecting the image in a satisfactory way. What can be deduced from the strange resemblance between argumentation and problem solving? For some, it will no doubt be an argument in favour of seeing language as a product of the human capacity for reasoning. However, we should perhaps not jump to that conclusion.

A comparison of human performance with that of animals in the area of problem solving shows a striking contrast. Take the chimpanzees, some groups of which, as Darwin observed,[4] know how to break open very hard nuts, such as palm nuts. To do this, they use two stones, one as a hammer, the other as an anvil. To acquire the knack of it, the young animals have to go through a learning process involving the choice of the proper tools, the correct positioning of the nut, and the use of appropriate force. To master the technique, young chimpanzees living in the wild practise for years and need to make hundreds of attempts (Matsuzawa 1994). It is obvious, from videos showing young animals observing the adult experts then ineffectually struggling with a nut of their own, that they are unable to work out what they are doing wrong. When they first manage to do it properly, it is purely by chance. For instance, if the nut starts to roll along the anvil stone before it is struck, the young chimpanzee is incapable of dealing with this problem in any methodical way, such as altering the slope

---

[4] 'It has often been said that no animal uses any tool; but the chimpanzee in a state of nature cracks a native nut, somewhat like a walnut, with a stone' (Darwin 1871: 51).

of the stone. Whereas human beings perceive a conflict between what they want and what they achieve, then abductively try to discover a way of achieving what they want, all the chimpanzee can do is notice that what it achieves is not right. In this case, the mind of the chimpanzee is focused on actions. The procedure it adopts is one of trial and error. If it does not achieve the desired result, it repeats the action or else tries something else, whereas human beings can negate the unwanted result that they achieved and gradually try to solve the various incompatibilities that arise. In this, their reasoning is logical.

So it is not only in argumentation that assessment, abduction, and negation play a role; they also help to solve problems. The procedure for resolving cognitive conflicts that we have just outlined can actually be seen as identical with a procedure for solving problems (Auriol 1999). Does this mean that language as we use it is an outcome of our general reasoning ability? This is certainly the view of some authors, who see the use of language as in part the result of planning (Grosz and Sidner 1986; Grau, Sabah, and Vilnat 1994; Carberry 1988). We have more than once had occasion to canvass the hypothesis that language might be an expression of our general intelligence and of our reasoning power; and on each occasion we have rejected it as implausible (cf. Chapter 4). There is a further argument that can be raised against it. The human method of problem solving via assessment, abduction, and negation is highly peculiar. It bears little resemblance to the techniques of planning and problem solving developed by engineers, whose artificial methods rely systematically on probabilistic calculations for identifying the most promising course of action. In this, their methods are much more effective than anything that human beings are capable of. Such a statement may appear surprising, given the difficulties encountered by engineers in their attempts to design machines that can play chess at the highest level or that can even play a game like Go reasonably well. The superiority of human beings over machines does not lie, however, in any greater ability to plan but rather in the detection and matching of structures.[5] It is thanks to these abilities that chess champions beat the best computer programmes.

---

[5] The ability of good chess players to recognize structures enables them to be much better than beginners at replacing the pieces on the right squares if the board is upset during play. When there is an absence of play structures, for example if the pieces have been set out at random, good players are not much better at replacing them than beginners (Gobet and Simon 2000).

In planning ability, human beings are much less smart than machines, which are able to keep many potential solutions simultaneously in their memory and compare them.[6]

The fact that human reasoning as applied to planning is largely sub-optimal must be significant. It would be implausible to assume that evolution might have endowed us with the ability to resolve cognitive conflicts so as to enable us to solve our little practical problems. If that ability is locally optimal, it is not for the purpose of creating a species of primate engineers or primate strategists, but for a completely different one: that of producing a particular form of relevance in conversation. Human beings reason in the same way as they argue; and the assessment-abduction-negation process that they use for reasoning is marked by its conversational origin. A common view of language is that it is an outgrowth of the capacity for reasoning. On this view, human beings, who are intelligent because intelligence is 'useful' for their survival, take advantage of their intelligence to speak and argue. The preceding discussion makes it possible to turn this view on its head and see the capacity for reasoning as an outcome of our argumentative abilities. This would mean that the capacity for reasoning logically derives from the abilities necessary to conversation.

If the reasons why language exists do not lie in the reasons why intelligence exists, how can we explain the biological reason why argumentation exists? If the species that preceded us could do without argumentation, why did our *Homo sapiens* ancestors begin to become aware of cognitive conflicts and to wish to resolve them collectively through argumentation? The answer may lie in the effect that language can have on those who use it.

15.4 The proximal function of language

What use is language to interlocutors? The theories discussed in Chapter 13 afford different answers to that question: one of them sees language as a

---

[6] Technically, the assessment-abduction-negation method is a refutation method which works by what is called backward chaining, starting with the problem and trying to find a solution. It is a strictly sequential method, called 'depth-first', with no possibility of comparing more than two solutions at once. The goals, which are the negations of the weaker terms in conflicts, are produced in a deterministic way. All these features make it a largely sub-optimal technique of problem solving.

way of acting; according to another, language is all about intercomprehension and the cooperation of individuals to that end; the third view is that language is a way of bringing a partner to infer new knowledge. If we restrict the functions of language to such modest roles, it will be very difficult to understand the biological reason for its existence. On the other hand, definition of the two conversational modes makes it possible to see a more important function in language. We can go so far as to say that language enables human beings to share some of their thoughts.

In a largely unconscious way, people conversing abide by precise rules, some of which are social in nature and others linguistic. Socially, conversation is interplay between individuals. Linguistically, it is essentially a private exercise in which each of the participants creates messages that have a particular phonology, a syntactic structure, and a meaning. The process which most precisely affects the content of utterances functions at an intermediate level somewhere between the social and the linguistic, a level where conversation can be seen to be a collective game played with shared representations. Sperber and Wilson take strong exception to the idea that representations are shared; for them, representations exist only inside brains and each participant has only his or her own brain. If there is no shared brain, there can be no sharing of representations. This may be so, but it does not oblige us to draw the conclusion that Sperber and Wilson draw, namely that communication cannot enable a duplication of representations.

Something crucial hangs on this question of duplication. According to Sperber and Wilson, communication is merely a way of having interlocutors make deductions and there is no guarantee that they will draw the conclusions from any spoken message that the speaker may expect to be drawn. If that is so, if language is nothing more than a way of stimulating others to have thoughts that have no necessary relation to the thoughts of the speaker, then we may well wonder what biological usefulness it might have. It is hard to credit the notion that the accuracy of the phonological system of languages, which enables us to distinguish more than ten phonemes per second even in unfavourable acoustical conditions, that the complexity of our syntactic faculty, which allows us to express complex semantic relations through the linear flow of words, that the linking of our two systems of semantic representation, through which we can picture scenes and reason logically, that the only function of all this should be to stimulate chains of free deductions in the minds of our fellows. What conceivable selection pressure could there be for such a function? Why would natural selection have fashioned all these competences if the result of every utterance is so unforeseeable? Evolution may well be playing dice with the development of species, but its action is not totally arbitrary. An instrument as finely tuned as our faculty for language could not have been produced by natural selection unless it increased the chances of survival and reproduction of the beings thus endowed. It is difficult to see how the ability to stimulate chains of free deductions in the minds of their fellows could in any way improve speakers' chances of survival and reproduction. And even if it did improve them, there would still be a mystery in the fact that the great precision of expression afforded by language should have been selected for so meagre a purpose as to be a mere stimulus to the thinking of others.

This chapter and the previous one show that, if we wish to understand the biological origins of language, we must not base our arguments on general considerations about communication. The definition of relevance given by Sperber and Wilson, which they apply to every communicative act, is too broad to be of use in understanding what language enables people to do when they use it in real situations. Actual observation of conversational behaviour forces one to the conclusion that communication through language is much more precise and effective than Sperber's and Wilson's rejection of the duplication of representation would have us believe. It is clear that the speeches making up exchanges interrelate very closely with each other. Such a thing is possible only if interlocutors are working on identical representations. Some examples will illustrate this.

When one interlocutor trivializes a salient event, finds a logical explanation for something amazing, or thinks of a way to avoid some unwanted state of affairs, can one doubt that he or she has properly analysed what was said, whether it was the salience of the thing mentioned, its amazing or unwanted quality? In conversations, interlocutors expect precise things. If they are unable to analyse the mode in which a speaker is functioning, they know that some element is missing. For instance, when C says 'The bin's green' (p. 282), D responds not by a string of uncontrolled deductions but with an answer that makes it plain something is wrong with the statement, since there is no salience in it, no strangeness, and no issue requiring settlement. In this, D's behaviour is consistent with what was expected from the experiment. However, when A expresses astonishment at the state of the Christmas tree, B understands immediately, as can be seen from B1, that the astonishment is inspired by the fact that the needles have not fallen off, that being the untoward feature of this particular tree. Intercomprehension in conversations is generally excellent, even if the occasional misunderstanding may give the opposite impression. Misunderstandings are actually the exceptions that prove the rule, for they are quickly detected. Here is an example of such a misunderstanding:

> Context: the interlocutors have just been talking about very old people who are in good health
> X1: So, I mean, how old was Abraham when he had children?
> Y1: Well, yes, but that's not known for certain.
> X2: Registration of births wasn't very certain.
> Z1: I don't know if there's ever been a world record. It would have to be pretty old. Over eighty for sure.
> Y2: Sorry? What are you on about?
> Z2: To be....
> Y3: To be having kids?

The extract begins with X1, the function of which is to use the example of Abraham to trivialize the earlier mentions of people who are exceptionally old and exceptionally healthy. This leads to a logical exchange on how valid the example might be. However, Y is still thinking of the earlier conversation; so she takes Z1 to mean that the record of human longevity is more than eighty. Even though such a statement may be in no way illogical, it is conversationally out of place. Y recognizes this, as is shown by Y2. This very statement enables its speaker to catch up with the subject at Y3, even before Z has had time to spell out what was missing. Where there is a misunderstanding, normal conversation soon becomes impossible. Misunderstandings remain the exception; and the fact that they are detected by interlocutors shows that speakers mostly know that they are reasoning on the same evidence. In the informative mode, they expect the salient feature, which they may then try to trivialize; in the logical mode, they look for an incompatibility, for which they try to find an explanation; and in the issue-settling mode, they expect to find an unpleasant situation, which makes them look for a way of obviating it. Conversation abides by rules that are as clear-cut as those of a card game and the bids are utterly unambiguous. This does not mean there are no ambiguities on the social plane. Why does A feel the need to strike up a conversation about the Christmas tree (pp. 270–1)? Why does Q keep nagging S (p. 295)? The answer is not a simple one; and Deborah Tannen, who is Q in the extract, attributes her own behaviour to the conversational style peculiar to her own culture. The existence of these social ambiguities should not obscure the cognitive effectiveness of communication via conversation. People know full well what they are talking about. It may be that interlocutors do not share everything; but what they do share includes what makes it possible for speeches to follow one another in accordance with the rules of conversational modes.

What guarantee can we have that any thought content is duplicated in the brains of the different participants? The only guarantee is the one that they too rely on: if the reconstituted thought does not stimulate the perception of a particular conversational mode (salience, paradox, or issue to be settled), we can say that the process of duplication has broken down. This principle (we may call it the principle of conversational relevance) provides a criterion of validity which, though it may not be absolute, is still very effective, as can be seen from the relative infrequency of misunderstandings and the rapid detection of them. The principle of conversational relevance also offers an explanation of situations which are just not covered by standard theories of communication. If, for instance, one says, *Can you pass me the salt?*, the answer *Yes* is not conversationally relevant because it does not obviate the undesirable situation. Conversely, and for the same reason, it is understandable that if someone says it is cold, an interlocutor should offer to go and close the door. Because the rules of conversational relevance applying to the issue-settling mode make people seek to obviate the undesirable situation, the statements in these two examples are equivalent to the direct requests *Pass me the salt* and *Go and shut the door.*

The immediate effect of language when used in standard conditions, in other words its proximal function, is thus to share a conversational attitude (salience, astonishment, issue-settling) and the thoughts which the attitude pertains to. Obviously, this is not the only effect of language, given that its use may have, for example, immediate social consequences. Nevertheless, it would be difficult to find some other function better able to explain the structure of the language capacity at all levels. Sharing the thoughts that pertain to conversational situations requires a tool of the required precision of expression. No one who does not have an accurate enough means of expression could hope to share the salience of a past experience. Nor could one make someone else understand how an explanation designed to resolve an astonishing situation is well suited to that requirement. Such definite conversational needs require a particular level of accuracy. The faculty of language, as described in Part II, is adapted to conversational requirements and hence to the sharing of thought content and the attitudes it prompts.

15.5 The origin of conversational modes

It is natural to wonder when it was that our ancestors began to develop the conversation behaviour to which our species devotes so much time. It also seems plausible to assume that, since there are two basic conversational modes based on different cognitive faculties, these faculties did not appear together. If, as we have suggested in Chapter 14, it was the communication of salient situations that appeared first in one of our ancestral species, there are grounds for suspecting that the other conversational mode, the argumentative one, emerged with our own species. In other words, argumentation is peculiar to humankind.

The emergence of language as we use it is linked to the appearance of a new capacity, which was an awareness of cognitive conflicts. The detection of incompatibilities between facts and their opposites, the propensity to communicate these incompatibilities and to attempt to resolve them collectively by interacting with others, this could be what underlay the new way of using language as argumentation. This would mean that our use of language was a product of two components, information-sharing and argumentation, the first of them having appeared at the protohuman stage and the second being peculiar to ourselves. The consistency of this model, as will be seen, is strengthened by the symmetry it implies between the pragmatic and semantic innovations peculiar to *Homo sapiens*, for it would mean that argumentation appeared along with the capacity for thematic segmentation.

The emerging scenario is as follows. Protohumans, through their protolanguage and protosemantics bearing on concrete scenes, could draw attention to salient situations in their environment. Their human descendants, in addition to that ability, had syntax based on phrases and morphological marking, the semantic ability of thematic segmentation, and a capacity for logical reasoning. To explain the emergence of language, what must be shown is that each of these components fulfills a biological function and that this function is useful, either directly or indirectly, to the survival and reproduction of individuals.

The emergence of the syntactical faculty is understandable if we accept the need for some thematic segmentation. Concatenation of phrases and morphological marking are two different but locally optimal ways of helping to recursively detect thematic roles in a sentence (cf. Chapter 10). Having identified the importance of cognitive conflict to argumentation, we can now posit a role for thematic segmentation. The fact is that it enables us to detect cognitive conflicts. Segmenting situations thematically is a gross over-simplification, especially as a form of representation, since it duplicates scenic representation. Nevertheless, these simplistic thematic images enable human beings to detect topological impossibilities, which become apparent in the form of logical incompatibilities. An example of a topological impossibility is that an object cannot be simultaneously inside and outside a particular area. The dosser queuing at the ATM cannot be both 'inside' the property of having money and outside it. Translating this impossibility as an incompatibility, we sense it as a cognitive conflict.

A cognitive conflict, unlike the detection of a salient situation, is perceived as a choice between a state of affairs and its negation. Neurologically speaking, the ability to entertain such choices is located in the most anterior region of the brain (Deacon 1997: 263). This cortical zone is a recent acquisition, the part which has grown most when human brains are compared with the brains of chimpanzees. It is possible that the prefrontal zone of our cortex underwent significant development after the stage of *Homo erectus*, hand in hand with the emergence of the new capacity of detecting and resolving cognitive conflicts.

Because it offers the possibility of detecting incompatibilities, thematic segmentation can be seen to have a use that may justify its existence on biological grounds. This raises the question of how useful the ability to detect incompatibilities might be in a world of protohumans. The apparent self-evidentness of this question is misleading. It strikes us as self-evident only because we see it from our human point of view, which makes us believe that logic is manifestly useful. Yet the fact that all other animal species manage to go on living and reproducing perfectly well without the help of such an ability should give us pause. Among the very first representatives of *Homo sapiens*, who possessed exactly the same faculties as modern human beings, there was no spectacular demographic development before the invention of agriculture, which has only happened during the last 5 per cent of the period of their existence. In our colonization of several continents there is nothing more remarkable than the geographical expansion of our predecessor *Homo erectus,* who probably did not possess our faculty of logic. What needs to be explained is how biologically valuable this faculty of logic is.

At the risk of contradicting the accepted view that logic is a simple tool of reasoning, we must here reaffirm the Aristotelian principle that logic is the mainspring of argumentation. This puts the ability to tackle cognitive conflicts into a basic human dimension, in the seemingly trivial context of everyday intercourse with other people, where the ability to produce relevant arguments is required. It is in the ordinary exchanges of argumentation that we have each day with our friends, our enemies, or just with the janitor, that we can see a latterday reflection of the interactions which led to the faculty of logic taking its place among our essential biological capacities. The idea that will be developed in the remaining chapters is that the biological reason for the existence of our sensitivity to cognitive conflicts is resistance to lying. The only immediate difficulty encountered by liars is the need to make sure that their interlocutors do not detect logical incompatibilities in what they say. Therein, as we shall see, lie not just the biological justification of our ability to detect cognitive conflicts but also the justification of thematic segmentation and the syntactical faculties that it requires.

16   Language as an evolutionary paradox

If we accept the implications of what was said in the previous chapters, we reach a paradoxical conclusion. By rights, according to the laws of evolution by natural selection, communication of the human variety ought not to exist. The first effect of speech is that it enables hearers to benefit from the information and the knowledge possessed and conveyed by the speaker. If this behaviour represented mere gratuitous assistance, it should die out rapidly through the workings of natural selection. If it represented self-interested assistance, where is the quid pro quo? The aim of this chapter is to stress the apparent impossibility of human communication when one tries to apply Darwinian criteria to its individual and social consequences. If we are to understand why our lineage came to adopt a communicative behaviour which is so unusual among living things, we must find a proper solution to this paradox.

16.1   The theory of social bonding

Situations in which animals give food to unrelated fellows are infrequent. This observation is entirely consistent with Darwinian theory, which sees individuals as competitors for survival and reproduction. And yet, human beings spend a large amount of their time giving potentially profitable information to anyone who cares to lend an ear to them. How can the theory of evolution by natural selection, strictly interpreted, make sense of such apparently altruistic behaviour? The answer may lie in the role that language plays in establishing social bonds.

Most people who are asked about the function of language reply that human beings use it above all to create social bonds. It does appear that many of the relations that human beings establish among themselves are in large measure a function of language: friendships, hierarchical relations, esteem, and even love are about feelings which are often initiated or maintained via language. When it is obvious that language serves to hold human groups together and to improve their efficacy in the competition for survival, is there any need to seek some other function? Unfortunately, that way of seeing language, on the face of it, does not withstand critical examination.

The primatologist Robin Dunbar has suggested an unexpected comparison. He draws an analogy between language and another behaviour which is systematic among many primates. His baboons spend a fair amount of time in grooming each other. This behaviour serves no utilitarian purpose, contrary to what one might expect. Jane Goodall, for instance, states that chimpanzees, which spend hours scratching about in the fur of their fellows, only ever find twigs or dirt, since these animals in the wild, which is where she studies them, never have parasites (Goodall 1971). So why do they behave like that? It is obvious to anyone studying primates in their natural environment that grooming does not happen indiscriminately, at no particular moment or between random individuals. Typically, inferior animals in the hierarchy groom their superiors. Sometimes, after an outburst of aggression, when an individual adopts a posture of submission, the dominant animal will start to groom the submissive one (Goodall 1971: 246). Grooming may take place among several individuals who all groom each other at the same time. Dunbar's point is that, for us, language plays something of the role played by grooming among other primates (Dunbar 1996: 78). Individuals who spend time grooming one another establish a strong bond which manifests itself also in alliances and acts of protection. A network of 'friendships' is woven within the troop, which means that primates such as chimpanzees or gorillas live in groups with a complex social structure organized about differentiated individual bondings. Why do humans groom each other rarely or not at all and why would language have replaced this reciprocal cleaning system? The explanation does not lie in the loss of most of our fur. According to Dunbar, it lies in the increase in the size of groups. There is evidence, notably the correlation between the size of the neocortex and the size of groups among primates, suggesting that our hominid ancestors lived in groups that were much larger than those of chimpanzees (Dunbar 1993). In such conditions, grooming cannot continue to be the basis for social bonding as it is too time-consuming. The higher primates are not ants; their complex society is not based on close family bonds but on personal bonding which is the result of many different interactions. When the size of groups increases, there is a corresponding increase in the possibilities of interaction. Language, in Dunbar's view, by enabling individuals to interact with several other individuals simultaneously, is much more effective than lengthy physical contact as a way of establishing and maintaining social bonding.

Although it is undeniable that language does fulfil a social function, the one advanced by Dunbar appears questionable. The analogy he posits with grooming behaviour is surely reductive; it greatly underdetermines language. If language is merely about individuals' mutual assurances of their wish to stay together, then synchronized grunts would do the job just as well. Dunbar goes further, with the observation that a good part of the contents of conversation deals with third parties. In other words, conversation is not just about establishing and maintaining social relations; it is also a way of controlling these relations by publicizing the deviant doings of other members of the group (Dunbar 1996: 79). This would be a second reason for seeing language as a factor of social cohesion.

Dunbar rather exaggerates the importance of gossip. Tittle-tattle and other forms of gossip do of course account for a significant amount of our conversational interactions; but they often add up to a minority of those interactions. It is possible, perhaps even plausible, that the influence of this amount of gossiping on the use of language may be only fortuitous. What is undeniable is that the continuous monitoring of social bonds within the group is of paramount importance for its members. But that may be the very reason why gossip bulks so large in conversations, given that mentioning a shared issue is one of the ways of being relevant (cf. Chapter 15). In other words, if one considers, as we have done, the structure of conversational exchanges, one expects interlocutors to engage in gossip. This would mean that such an activity is a consequence and not a cause of our mode of communication. In the light of this, it is unlikely that the scope offered by language to praise or disparage the actions of others had any direct influence on the evolution of language behaviour. After all, language also serves for speaking of many other types of subject matter, factual, psychological, imaginary, etc. The diversity of topics of conversation is infinite; and the emergence of language during the course of evolution cannot be accounted for by any one of these various uses on its own (cf. section 4.5). Taken together, they make a congeries of things that are far too disparate to account for the evolutionary creation of a faculty that was as novel, as complex, and as integrated as language.

The idea that language is involved in the establishment of social bonding seems self-evident. However, when we look for support for that idea with a view to explaining the emergence of language as we know it, no explanation from the usefulness of social cohesion stands up to examination. The role played by language in social bonding or as a way of controlling the doings of members of the group is not up to explaining language behaviour as a whole. The inadequacy of the explanation from social bonding becomes even more blatant if we accept the fact that language, even when it serves to comment upon the behaviour of others, is an altruistic activity.

16.2 The altruistic character of language

Who benefits from language? If we judge by the pleasure people take in talking, language does as much good to those who speak as to those who listen. However, this is not the place to discuss psychological motivations. Biological motivations are what concern us, for these are what can create selection pressure. The only 'benefit' to be considered is therefore any consequence of conversational behaviour which is positively correlated with the survival and reproduction of individuals, without taking into account any other effect. The pleasure or displeasure associated with any particular behaviour is itself the product of evolution and not its source. In our genetic equipment, pleasure and displeasure are ways of broadly controlling behaviours. If conversational behaviour affords some pleasure to interlocutors, the reason is that the behaviour was once biologically of use to our ancestors and continues to be of use to us. If we are to understand what such use might consist of, we must ask again: Who benefits from language?

If we consider the mode of communication that we defined as protohuman, which consists essentially of drawing attention to salient situations, the answer seems immediate and obvious: acts of communication benefit hearers. Any speakers who take the trouble to point out a salient happening or phenomenon are providing their fellows with potentially valuable information. In this context, the adjective 'valuable' has a biological meaning, that is to say the speaker is passing on to others information which, in some cases, may improve their chances of survival or reproduction. Obviously, this does not happen every time somebody speaks. Mostly, the information is no sooner registered than it is forgotten. However, let us invert the perspective and ask what would count as biologically useful information.

Animals pick up many clues to what might be biologically useful to their survival and reproduction. There is a broad range of tastes and flavours, for instance, which attracts us towards whatever might provide proper nourishment for a hunting-and-gathering existence. Another example is attention: animals' faculty of paying attention enables them to focus their cognitive resources on the relevant part of their environment. How can we define such relevance? Ethology and earlier behaviourist studies have clearly shown that animals focus their attention on stimuli that might be a source of danger or pain and on stimuli that might lead to a reward or an opportunity to reproduce. Such stimuli have biological implications and it is understandable that animals' attention should be biased in their favour. So when speakers draw attention to an unpleasant aspect of their surroundings, they are passing on valuable knowledge. Can the same be said about drawing attention to an unlikely situation? Animals that are inquisitive, attracted that is by novelty, are not as numerous as those that are sensitive to the biological implications of situations; and the higher primates belong in that minority. One may well wonder why these animals are sensitive to the unexpected, unless it is because novelty is a good predictor of biological relevance. By definition, novelty is rare; and focusing attention on it makes no great demands on cognitive resources. Also, novelty is valuable for whichever individual is able to exploit it first. The potential implications of novelty, whether positive or negative, may be greatly increased by the fact that it is known only to a single individual or to a few. Implications and novelty are good indicators of biological relevance. It is understandable that many animal species have selective attention which can focus on these two aspects of the environment. What remains to be explained, however, is the astonishing combination of factors which led our species, and probably the species that preceded us, to turn these two focuses of attention into subjects of communication. In addition, we must understand why individuals whose attention is aroused by something should automatically assume that it must likewise arouse the attention of others, to the point that they set about telling everyone about it. Anyone who sees this behaviour as self-evident ought to explain why our species is apparently the only one to practise this type of communication.

The communication of salient situations becomes even less understandable when we take into account the fact that information known to a speaker will often lose some of its intrinsic value by being communicated. The attraction of novelty in particular is linked to the fact that the potential gain from the novel situation is not to be shared. If one makes a point of communicating every new thing to others, one loses the benefit of having been the first to know it.[1] The mystery of this human type of communication becomes even deeper when we realize that, in a species made up of individuals who all make a point of passing on to everyone else anything of biological value that happens, there should be no need to go and find out information. Inquisitiveness can often be a costly behaviour. It encourages foraging along the very edges of a territory, tasting unfamiliar foods, staying alert rather than sleeping, etc. If everything of biological value is supplied by others via language, what would be the point of spending time and taking even slight risks so as to get the information oneself? A species that practises systematic sharing of salient situations ought to be transformed in no time into something more like shoals of fish than structured groupings. Once a stage is reached where no one goes to get information, there is nothing left to communicate. Communication of salient situations would therefore appear to bring about its own negation.

The arguments just advanced are not the only factors that give evidence of the paradoxical nature of prehuman and human communication. If we try to understand how the predispositions underlying such a system of communication could have been selected, we soon reach absurdity. In an animal group, the contribution of individuals to the procreation of the following generation is what is called a constant-sum game: if for a variety of reasons some individuals have more viable offspring than the average, others have fewer. This lies at the heart of Darwinian theory. If we consider the members of a species at two different periods separated by ten generations, we find that some of the individuals from the first period are the ancestors of individuals in the second period, and that others are

---

[1] The mushroom seeker in south-west France is torn between the desire to tell his friends, who are also his competitors, about particular locations where he has come across extraordinary layers of cepes and the understandable need to keep them secret.

not. Not only have those who turn out to be ancestors reproduced, but it can be stated with a fair probability that they did more reproducing than their fellows who were living at the same time. This being the case, how can we explain a communication behaviour which consists of passing on to one's fellows information which is by definition useful for their survival? In such a scenario, everything points to the conclusion that the individuals who do not play by the rules, who keep useful information to themselves while benefiting from information given to them by others, will have a greater chance of having offspring, other things being equal. Such a conclusion would appear to mean that there is no possibility for language to exist! It also happens to be the best explanation of why the systematic sharing of information does not exist in other species.

Informing about salient situations, something that humans do every day of their lives, something that we may assume their predecessors also did, seems to contradict laws of nature, in particular the theory of natural selection. It seems clear that we have skipped a stage in our reasoning, for otherwise there would be no conversations, no language, no books, no readers, no human race and we would just be primates who are sensible enough to keep quiet when they have nothing to do. The human obsession with divulging anything of interest, instead of jealously keeping the information to themselves, requires an explanation. As we shall see, the explanations that come most readily to mind are not necessarily the best.

16.3 Language and cooperation

In attempting to solve the apparent paradox of language, some authors have speculated that it is best seen as symmetrical cooperation (Dunbar 1996; Ulbaek 1998). It must be admitted that on the face of it this view is not without merit. Conversation is an activity which is mostly symmetrical, in which interlocutors periodically exchange roles. In an economic type of cooperation such as bartering, individuals offer an object or provide a service which is voluntarily exchanged for an object or service supplied by somebody else. It is easy to see how this arrangement can be applied to conversation, where each participant provides information and takes advantage of the information supplied by others.

This analogy with economic cooperation derives in fact from a standard explanation of the problem of altruism among animals. A strict interpretation of the theory of natural selection would lead us to suppose that living beings ought to be motivated by utter selfishness, since helping or favouring other individuals of their own species could mean that it would be these individuals which would thereby have a better chance of surviving and reproducing. Since the making of the following generation is a constant-sum game, the members of a species at any given moment will more likely descend from individuals who were helped than from altruistic individuals. There are, however, two possible ways to avoid this line of reasoning. The first of them, advanced by William Hamilton in 1964, argues that altruism towards related individuals may be passed on by natural selection (Hamilton 1964, 1972). The most obvious example is altruism towards offspring: any individual which helps its offspring at its own expense can still have more descendants than some other individual which does not exercise the same parental care. And it is a fact that, in many animal species, parents markedly reduce their own chances of surviving by giving time, food, and protection to their young. More surprisingly, the same argument can be applied to collateral descendants. Individuals resemble not only their direct ancestors but also their uncles, aunts, brothers, or cousins. If these relatives behave altruistically towards them, this behaviour, via resemblance, may be passed on to later generations. The best known and most remarkable example of altruism towards collateral relatives is that of social insects. Moreover, this example resoundingly confirms the Darwinian explanation, as it is the only explanation that can predict correctly the altruistic behaviour of the sterile workers which, so as to help their reproducing brothers and sisters, make the total sacrifice of their own chances of reproducing. Unfortunately, however, this theory cannot apply to language. This is not because conversation behaviour cannot be focused on related individuals but because it is not restricted in any way to the family circle. Language is essentially a behaviour that is social and not kin-based, as protectiveness might be.

Altruism towards kin being irrelevant to language, only one other standard explanation might fit and that is the argument from reciprocal cooperation. This would make language acts symmetrical: participants give information to each other, bearing the cost of this behaviour, which is that they lose their exclusive possession of the knowledge they impart; but the final balance is positive since all participants benefit from the information they receive. Cooperation of this kind does exist in nature, the most clear-cut case being no doubt the process of reproduction in sexed species. In a couple, each of the two individuals needs the other in order to procreate; they each receive from the other something they lack, while at the same time affording the other the possibility of reproducing. The respective investments of the male and the female in this transaction are of course rarely symmetrical, but even though costs and benefits will differ, reproduction in couples is still a cooperative enterprise. In species of birds that stay by the nest until their young have become autonomous, cooperation is markedly more symmetrical and two non-kin individuals can be seen helping one another, since each task taken on by one of them is one task fewer for the other. Can we assume that human use of language works on this same principle? There are two major objections to any explanation of language through symmetrical cooperation; and it is those objections that we must now examine.

The most basic objection to a system of cooperation comes from the existence of cheats. Since the earliest studies of the role of cooperation in biology (Trivers 1971; Axelrod and Hamilton 1981), considerable attention has been paid, particularly in sociology and economics, to the problem of how well cooperation can withstand cheating. Computerized simulations have been done to test the efficiency of complex strategies calculated to thwart dishonest partners (Axelrod 1984). The problem of cooperation is that, if there is any possibility of cheating, we can never be sure that reciprocity will actually work. Anyone who takes the initiative must first be sure that their partner is trustworthy. The starting point of any attempt to apply the principle of symmetrical cooperation to language interaction must be to ensure that the problem of cheating is not so serious as to rule out cooperation. The object of the exercise is to find out whether speakers who communicate objectively useful information can become more numerous than individuals whose policy it is to remain silent.

I have studied a simplified version of this problem, in which the strategies of the individuals were fixed and systematic (Dessalles 1999). However, individuals were given some scope to choose the partners with whom they would interact. As in a biological species, individuals could cross-breed and have offspring who resembled them. Figure 16.1 illustrates the conditions in which cooperation can happen and continue to happen under the influence of natural selection. The results of the study are quite unambiguous. When detection of cheats is not good, cooperative

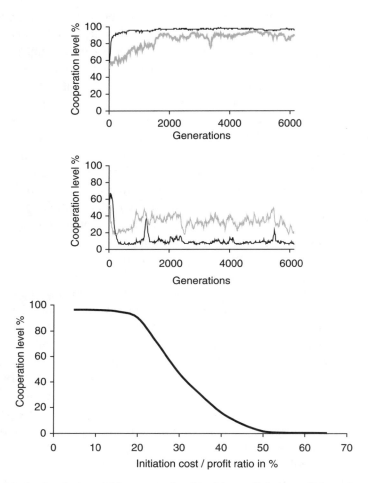

FIG. 16.1 A simulation with a genetic algorithm of the conditions in which cooperation can be maintained during evolution. The top graph shows the establishment of cooperation both for the individual who initiates it (in black) and for the individual who responds (in grey); the middle graph shows an instance where cooperation is not possible; the bottom graph shows that the level of cooperation depends on the relative cost of initiating it.

behaviour disappears. If cooperation is to be biologically stable, it requires the gains for both parties to be high to compensate for the risk of cheating and the costs entailed by cooperative behaviour. In the case of birds which cooperate in bringing up their young, the costs are heavy, but the benefits in terms of reproductive success are considerably higher than the birds would obtain with minimal investment. How does this apply to language? The average biological usefulness to a hearer of anything said in conversation should not be overstated. While it is true that we derive most of what we know about the world from our spoken interactions with other people, this benefit is spread over a large number of conversations. On the other hand, the cost of language seems to be quite small. Little energy is required for speaking. This might suggest that language thereby meets the requirements of stable cooperation. However, the cost of speaking is generally underestimated by authors who see language as symmetrical cooperation.

What is important is not so much speech as such, but relevant speech. To have something relevant to say, one must be in possession of relevant information that one can convey to others. But the getting of such information is not something that just happens by itself. If one is to give others relevant information about something one has been the first to observe, curiosity and time are required and risks may have to be run. This cost of acquiring information, often overlooked, raises doubts about the cooperative theory of the use of language.

16.4 Language and cheating

Through language, as we have said, it is possible to give useful information to others. Spontaneous conversation of course rarely amounts to an exchange of vital information. However, it is a fact that we know much more at second hand than through our own experience: we know about places where we have never been, people we have never met, happenings we have not witnessed, etc. Try for a moment to imagine what life must be like for any human being deprived of language. The lives of deaf people who have no access to sign language can give us an idea of it (Kegl, Senghas, and Coppola 1999: 199). Since the information we give each day to our fellows is valuable, we should only ever speak advisedly and with the intention of getting something equivalent in return; and conversely, we ought to be regularly consulted for what we know. Doctors are consulted by their patients, who repay them for the service they provide; and the aptness of this service is accepted without question. Why are language acts rarely the result of similar promptings? Why do they not always result in

the provision of some such compensatory service? Why are they systematically assessed? Some of the utterances in the examples used in Chapters
14 and 15 leave little doubt about the true nature of conversations:

> G2: Not just people with Alzheimer's. (p. 285)
> Q1: But anyway... How do you happen to know his stuff? (p. 295)
> U2: That would skew the picture. (p. 296)
> W1: Yer, well, at least it'll get rid of the clouds. p. 297)

The hearers' attitudes clearly do not amount to registering a valuable piece
of information and being invited to provide in return some piece of
information of similar interest. In each of the examples, the hearer's return
speech has the effect of questioning the interest or value of what the
speaker has said. The hearer's attitude is more like that of a customer
quibbling about the quality of the merchandise on offer, rather than that
of a friend to whom one has just done a favour and who is doing one
in return. Despite appearances, conversation is a fundamentally dissym-
metrical activity. Typically, a speaker draws attention to a salient situation
and the interlocutors assess the information on offer, either to acknowledge its value (for instance, *Yes, that's a fact* at K1, p. 285), to trivialize it,
or to question its interest or value, as in the other examples just quoted.

Assessment is a systematic behaviour which can be easily stimulated. If
the information you supply to your interlocutors is in their view not
salient enough, if for example you tell them something new to you but
which they already know, or if you say you have lost your wallet with very
little money in it, you systematically run the risk that somebody will say
either *Yes, I know*, as in the episode of the hot-air balloons (cf. Chapter 8),
or *So what?* Or you can see what happens when you make a statement
including a detail that is obviously false, by saying for instance, when the
subject is the economy of Brazil, that the population of the country is the
same as that of all European countries combined, or some such untruth.
If your interlocutors have the appropriate knowledge and the social
conditions are right,[2] they will make a point of correcting the mistake.
This sort of behaviour is so much a part of our nature that we do not pay
enough attention to its biological incongruity. Why should we point out
to people that they have made a mistake?

---

[2] It is assumed that the conditions in which such an experiment must take place are
those of ordinary conversation. There are social circumstances, such as wide divergences of
status between participants, which may inhibit spontaneous conversational behaviour.

The real meaning of this way that hearers have of assessing the quality of the information they receive can be seen if we invert the perspective. According to the logic of any cooperation, the person who runs the greatest risk is the one who makes the first step. If we apply this logic to language, speakers will only address individuals who can be expected to play by the rules of reciprocity and to give back information of comparable quality to the information they are given. But observation shows that speakers need no such encouragement to speak; and hearers do no more than assess the information they are given, either to acknowledge the value of it, to belittle it, or to express a doubt about it. Clearly, in the longer term, as soon as there is a change of topic there can also be a change in the dissymmetry of the attitudes of participants, who may exchange roles. It should, however, be noted that this inversion of roles is not systematic and of course if it does not happen, this is not seen as being out of place, as it would in a cooperative situation.

What we must envisage therefore is a mirror image of this situation, in which it is the speaker who has something to gain and the hearer who holds back. In other words, the real difference between the cooperative relationship and the way language is observably used in real life is to be found in where the risk lies. In cooperation, the greater risk is run by the person who makes the first step, whereas in language exchanges the risk clearly lies with the hearer. This inverse scenario still requires a biological explanation. But if we begin by accepting it, the reasons underlying many aspects of our conversation behaviour are made plain.

One of the most astonishing features of language behaviour, namely turn-taking, is neatly explained by this inverse scenario. Any explanation drawn from the cooperative model can apply to no more than two sorts of utterances, the opening one of an exchange and the reciprocal one: I tell you something of interest to you, you tell me something of interest to me, at which point conversation comes to an end until the next exchange, which has no reason to be a continuation of this one. Observation of real conversations shows that their structure is not as flat as a sequence of dyads. As soon as we abandon the conception of everyday language as a cooperative exchange, the depth of its embedded structure becomes perfectly comprehensible. The fact that hearers make efforts to assess or question the information being conveyed, thereby obliging speakers to add to it or to make their meaning clearer, explains the structure of conversation as it can be observed. Each of the two conversational mechanisms has its own type of structure. We saw in the previous chapter that an act of trivialization prompts another; and in the same way the detection of a cognitive conflict may be followed by the stating of a solution to it, though the solution may engender a new cognitive conflict. Conversation emerges from these two types of recursive sequences, which derive from the fact that in conformity with the inverse scenario the hearer assesses the quality of the information conveyed by the speaker.

16.5 The cost of communication

Observation of the structures of linguistic exchanges obliges us to adopt an inverse view of communication, in which the speaker is in the position of a supplicant. This conclusion seems to fly in the face of the evidence, since the speaker is the only person who has something tangible to convey at a particular moment, in the form of information about an interesting situation. This mystery becomes even stranger if we take account of the cost of acts of communication.

There is an argument, advanced by John Krebs and Richard Dawkins, which says that communication, when it is of benefit to the sender of a signal, evolves into signals that are exaggerated, repetitive, and costly (Krebs and Dawkins 1984). This principle is based on the simple idea that there is a balance between the manipulation of receivers by senders and the resistance that receivers can put up; and this balance inevitably evolves towards the use of exaggerated signals. All communication arises from the ability of an animal to interpret clues in the behaviour of some other animal, whether of the same species or a different one. These clues enable the animal to predict the future actions of the other. Any improvement in the predictive ability is advantageous, since a receiver can 'mind-read' the sender's intentions and so forestall them appropriately. For instance, you may suppose that a dog baring its teeth is making ready to bite; and this enables you to take early evasive action. According to Krebs and Dawkins, this situation cannot remain unchanged. The sender now has a powerful way of manipulating the other, by pretending to adopt the behaviour which the other will think it can forestall. In this, evolution contrives a way of increasing the life expectancy of senders. The dog baring its teeth may have no intention of biting; it may be adopting this hint of a coming behaviour because its ancestors learned that this was a way of getting out of a difficult situation by making it appear they were about to attack. However, receivers also evolve, even if they belong to the same species, and may become more and more difficult to manipulate. This makes for exaggeration of signals: if a dog is to be convincingly threatening, it will have to approach, growl, and crouch as though about to leap. Coevolution of these sending and receiving behaviours may lead to demonstrations that are as exaggerated and repetitive as the nuptial displays of some birds, the singing of crickets or territorial birds, peacocks' feathers, threatening behaviour in chimpanzees, etc. A similar logic can be seen at work in the eye-catching repetitiveness of advertising, a situation in which the aim is to manipulate a receiver who is able to read the message but who has learned to resist being manipulated. This type of 'arms race', when the outcome is important to the sender, evolves systematically into exaggeration of signals.

This finding confirms a theoretical prediction made by Amotz Zahavi based on another type of reasoning. Zahavi introduced what is known as 'the handicap principle'. His central idea is that any behaviour that is not costly is easy to counterfeit. Under the influence of natural selection, the possibility that cheats can imitate the signals of 'honest' senders opens the way to costly signals that only the honest senders can afford (Zahavi 1995; Zahavi and Zahavi 1997). An example is the spectacular stotting (vertical leaping on all four legs) of Thompson's gazelles when faced with a wolf. Zahavi interprets this apparently absurd behaviour as a signal to the predator meaning that the animal is in good health and so capable of fleeing if attacked. Zahavi's idea is that the signal evolved because it was 'reliable' and that it is reliable because it is costly. Other gazelles in the same herd, perhaps less healthy, will not stot, since the risk of making an unimpressive jump is that it will draw the attention of the predator to their poor physical condition. Once more the conclusion is that signalling evolves into costly and exaggerated forms.

These two theories help to explain a number of phenomena about communication in the animal world. Language, however, seems to gainsay them. If we accept what appears to be suggested by conversation behaviour, namely that it is speakers who have the possibility of cheating by conveying false information to hearers, then it is the former who can play the manipulative role. Evolution must endow hearers with an ability to resist, which would mean that language should either disappear or evolve into signalling that is exaggerated, repetitive, and costly. Yet clearly this has not happened. Language as used in conversation is none of those things. Zahavi accepts the paradox:

We don't know how symbolic word language evolved in humans.... The rub is that verbal language does not contain any component that ensures reliability. It is easy to lie with words. (Zahavi and Zahavi 1997: 222–3)

So the existence of language is an apparently insoluble problem. According to the cooperative model, it should be hearers who play the cheating role; yet it is they who take counter-measures. If it is speakers who play the cheating role, one would expect language to evolve into exaggerated and costly behaviours, which has not happened. However, this second term of the paradox, stressed by Zahavi, may be resolved by something suggested by the analysis of conversations.

The behaviour of interlocutors as described in Chapter 14 can be divided into two components, one which consists of pointing out or trivializing salient situations and one which consists of detecting cognitive conflicts and seeking solutions to them. The existence of these two components of our behaviour makes sense if we accept that it is hearers who run the risk of being cheated in verbal interaction. Trivializing behaviour helps them to keep a sense of proportion about the information they receive. By way of simplifying, we could say that trivialization is an antidote to exaggeration. Anyone who might be tempted to exaggerate the salience of an event recounted can be met with the hearer's ability to compare situations and thus to see them in relation to one another. The original role of the detection of cognitive conflicts can be made sense of as the attempts of hearers to guard against lying. This interpretation means we can see both components of our conversation behaviour as consequences of the fact that hearers run the risk of being misled by speakers.

Let us assume that whatever benefit speakers derive will increase with the salience of the situations they speak of. This makes for a strong temptation to exaggerate or even to tell lies. The risk run by a hearer is that of affording an undue benefit to the speaker. Against this risk, hearers have two strategies, trivialization through comparison with already known situations and detection of inconsistencies. Both of these rely on faculties with which natural selection has endowed human beings, among which are a sense of probabilities and the ability to detect cognitive conflicts (cf. Chapter 15). Each of these conversational mechanisms has thus much the same function as the other, that is the avoidance of cheating in communication. It must be admitted, however, that they each require very different cognitive mechanisms.

The effectiveness of the two types of counter-measures available to hearers makes it possible to resolve the paradox identified by Zahavi. He rightly observes that language signals are not in themselves costly. In conversation, the language used by speakers, unlike the language of advertising, is not full of repetitive and exaggerated signals. Shouting, repeating one's sentences, or attracting attention by any means possible are not ways to increase the effectiveness of what is said. However, he is right to stipulate that the only signals natural selection can favour are the reliable ones. With language, though, the difference is that the reliability of the message is not guaranteed by the cost of the signal carrying it but by its resistance to hearers' assessments. In conversation, a speaker tries to appear relevant in the opinion of others. The speaker's difficulty is to be able to tell of salient situations unfamiliar to interlocutors. Faced with their faculties of trivialization and argumentative criticism, there is no point in altering the signal so as to be heard. What is necessary is the possession of quality information; and it is in that necessity that the cost to the speaker lies. It lies not in the signal itself but in the difficulty of getting information from the environment in a way that enables it to be communicated appropriately in conversation. There is something intrinsically arduous in being relevant, given hearers' capacity for detecting poor quality information. It is not, *pace* Zahavi, easy to tell lies, even with words, as hearers test the logical consistency of what they are told. Nor is it easy to overdo the salience of a situation, since that exposes speakers to hearers' power of trivialization.

According to Zahavi's general idea, communication has to be a costly exercise for speakers, if the benefits of it accrue to them. This is indeed what we can observe, though the cost is not linked to the sending of the signal itself. Human beings spend a far from negligible amount of time and energy in gathering information. The spirit of inquisitiveness and exploration, which is so highly developed in our species, is in itself paradoxical. Life expectancy for the adventurous is shorter than for stay-at-homes. The cost of behaviours of inquisitiveness and exploration, of whatever intensity, can be understood in part if we see them as a way for individuals to cull information. If we accept that relevant speakers benefit from communication, we can see why they bother to seek out genuinely salient facts so as to convey them to fellows during conversation. This behaviour can be explained by the fact that their hearers have effective ways of assessing the quality of information supplied to them and that this makes it difficult to mislead them.

The fact remains that the use of language will continue to appear paradoxical until we try to understand the other element in the mystery, that is the reasons why hearers come to afford a benefit to speakers, despite the concomitant risk of being misled about the quality of the message. If we are to make progress on this fundamental point, we must determine the nature of this biological benefit which speakers derive from language interaction. The following chapter will be devoted to that question. For the moment, the points already made in this chapter and those before it make it possible to identify three qualitatively different phases in the evolution of language.

16.6 Three stages in the evolution of language

The following table, 16.1, has been drawn up with the aim of bringing together the large principles underlying the organization of language as they have been argued in Parts II and III, so as to give a coherent picture of the emergence of language.

In this model, the columns are cumulative, the contents of each box being added to whatever lies to their left. Each line describes respectively the name of the system of communication, its phonology, its syntax, its semantics, its communicative function, and its protective mechanisms against cheats. The matter of phonology remains in part a mystery, for there is a dearth of evidence about phonological systems which might have been used at the three stages of evolution shown in the table. Any clarification of it would depend on an analysis of the phonological competence of present-day speakers with a view to defining functional subsystems locally optimal for their function. It may be noted that the changes in the anti-cheating capacities (bottom line) go hand-in-hand with the communicative functions (second last line). When prelanguage limits speech to drawing attention to events in the perceptible environment, verification of whether they are salient enough can be done by mere observation of them. Protolanguage makes it possible to speak of non-immediate salient scenes, but the struggle against cheating requires

Table 16.1 *A model of the evolution of language in three stages*

Prehumans	Protohumans (erectus?)	Humans
Prelanguage ?	Protolanguage Combinatory phonology	Language
Separate vocal signals	Juxtaposition of words	Syntax (phrases & morphological marking)
Demonstrative gestures		
Communication of concrete scenes	Combining of images	Thematic segmentation
Immediate salient situations	Non-immediate salient situations	Unverifiable salient situations Conveying of cognitive conflicts
Immediate verification	Deferred verification	Detection & resolution of cognitive conflicts (argumentation)
	Comparison with known scenes (trivialization)	

that they must be verifiable via deferred testing. With the advent of detection of cognitive conflicts, communication about salient scenes that are both non-immediate and unverifiable becomes possible. Thanks to argumentation, interlocutors can just appraise the consistency of information supplied.

Though Table 16.1 contains a number of features which are of course conjectural, none the less it also presents a number of virtues. In drawing up such a table, the constraints are as follows: (1) the state described in each column must be functional; (2) the communicative functions (second last line) must be of advantage for the survival and reproduction of individuals; and (3) the contents of each box must be locally optimal for the communicative function of that particular column. In everything that has been said up to now there are arguments in favour of points (1) and (3). For instance, mere juxtaposition of words grouped according to semantic constituents, which is a mark of protolanguage, is locally optimal for a protosemantics consisting of the combination of images to make a concrete scene (cf. Chapter 8). Similarly, we have seen how the recursive linking of phrases and morphological marking make for the expression of thematic segmentation, which is itself a locally optimal way of detecting cognitive conflicts. Point (3), however, requires some further clarification. Each of the columns can be locally optimal only insofar as the following column to the right remains unavailable. As was argued in Chapter 6, species are systems in equilibrium. Any new species produced by evolution and endowed with different competences comes about by chance. This is why we must hazard some guesses to explain the existence of these three quite distinct stages in the evolution of language. One of these conjectures is to posit that the transition to protolanguage was a result of the invention of the mechanism for combining the images conveyed. Another one, which serves to explain the second transition, correlates the emergence of modern human beings with the invention of the mechanism of thematic segmentation. At the time they made their appearance, these two mechanisms were radically new developments. There are grounds for believing that they are examples of the type of sudden innovation that marks the process of speciation, unpredictably branching off in a different direction.

It may also be noted that, unlike most authors, I do not attribute the transitions between the systems of communication of our ancestors to the invention of new systems of syntax. In the model set out in Table 16.1, the two systems of syntax that we know of, phrase linking and morphological marking, are mechanisms which had the effect of facilitating the communication of thematic segmentations. This means that the latter preceded and that the syntactic faculties of modern human beings are subordinate to it. Both of the transitions in Table 16.1 are therefore explained at the semantic level, first by the invention of the ability to combine the images conveyed, then by the invention of the capacity for thematic segmentation of scenes so as to transform them into a simplified topological representation.

One of the fundamental conjectures of Table 16.1 concerns the function of language, which remains essentially the same throughout the three stages. In all three, individuals use language to draw attention to situations which interlocutors will see as salient. This is what explains the contents of the other boxes in the table. For instance, the explanation of why natural selection favoured an innovation such as thematic segmentation is that it was a mechanism which created cognitive conflicts, and this made it possible to detect liars who mislead their hearers by recounting falsely salient situations. The keystone of this construction is therefore the fact that speakers have something to gain by drawing their fellows' attention to salient situations. What is the biological justification of this behaviour? This brings us to constraint number (2) mentioned above and to the need to understand how drawing attention to salient situations can increase the viability of speakers or their reproductive expectancy. That hearers developed strategies for the detection of exaggeration or lying leads us to assume that they also grant the benefit to speakers. This situation, in which it is speakers who are the supplicants, is at variance with appearances, which tend to suggest that information is the only thing exchanged during linguistic interaction. What is the advantage that we are capable of granting to each other as a function of our conversational activity? That is the question which the following chapter will endeavour to clarify.

17 The political origins of language

When we try to explain why a faculty such as language could have emerged during human descent, we expect to find reasons peculiar to that faculty. If we are enquiring into the reasons why eyes were selected, the selective advantage they conferred is almost self-evident in the function they served. It seems clear that any creature endowed with the ability to detect shapes thereby has an advantage for its survival. In language, however, the link between the function and the selective advantage is not so direct. None of the many attempts to make direct correlations between language and an increased life expectancy or improved reproductive power has ever produced a proposition that consists with what can be observed in the actual use of language. The most striking instance of such attempts is the argument that language is a symmetrical exchange of information based on the principle of cooperation. The preceding chapter showed the contradictions inherent in this idea, the most blatant of which is that, though detection of uncooperative people ought to be the role of speakers, in fact it is hearers who develop strategies to counter the communication of poor quality information.

This means we must propose a theory of greater complexity, one allowing for the possibility that the link between the use of language and its benefits for survival and reproduction is not direct. The main purpose of this chapter is to offer a theory of the emergence of language which is not only internally consistent but also compatible with evolution through natural selection. As we shall see, the implications of the argument advanced here reach beyond the matter of the emergence of language.

17.1 How speakers benefit by being relevant

The previous chapter showed that, from the point of view of evolution, language is a paradox. Marc Hauser, who has made a compilation of animal communication systems, expresses quite appropriate surprise at the very existence of our mode of communication:

It remains unclear why selection would favor a more specific referential system than currently exists in nonhuman animals. What advantage would obtain from the ability to succinctly describe events in the world, both those currently experienced and those experienced in the past and stored in memory? (Hauser 1996: 67)

One answer to this question is, as we have said in earlier chapters, that language and the faculties that make it possible, phonology, syntax, and the capacities for representation, are used by human beings to tell each other of salient events. What is it that makes humans behave in this way? It means we are a very strange species. Even if salient situations are those which offer a potential biological value, why do human beings spend a large proportion of their time talking about them to their genetic competitors?

To resolve this paradox, we must abandon any idea that the only thing functioning in human interactions is the information that people give to each other about the surrounding world. The cooperation theory, with the contradictions which we have noticed, presupposes that what speakers receive is the same in kind as what they give. We must consider another possibility, an asymmetrical exchange in which the gratification afforded by the act of informing is not itself communicative in nature. It is not easy to posit such a hypothesis, for there is something by definition immaterial in conversational exchange. Nevertheless, what matters in conversation, intangible though it may be, is pregnant with consequences for interlocutors.

My research colleagues appreciate an analogy which I sometimes use. It makes a comparison between the situation in conversation, which is a privileged and representative mode of language use, and another situation which is highly particularized and governed by strict ritual, namely the publication of a scholarly article (Dessalles 1998b). Let us ask about academics the question asked about everyday conversation: what makes academics publish papers? This is an analogy with some point to it. Academics are eager for opportunities to speak or write. When they are given the chance to express themselves among their peers, they endeavour to set out their pet ideas in the best possible light. As colleagues, by working on similar subjects, they are well equipped to follow each other's papers; and they often know one another as friends. Professionally, though, they are in fact potential competitors who, like all scholars, try to publish their findings before anyone else does. One might therefore see something surprising in the apparent naivety of these academics rushing to be the first to pass on their brightest ideas to their competitors. This is a situation not unlike that of our first hominid ancestors who started pointing out to each other any situation worthy of interest, though they were also in competition with each other for access to reproduction. If we look at the world of the scholarly paper from a more realistic point of view, we can discover a plausible motivation, conscious or unconscious, for publicizing one's ideas. Those scholars who contrive to present papers seen as relevant by their peers enjoy an increase in their professional status within the academic community. And conversely those who do not publicize their ideas, either by writing books or presenting conference papers, forfeit their scholarly standing. No one has ever heard of academics leaving their published work unsigned or using some obscure pseudonym. Yet, if they had no other aim than the advancement of knowledge, that would surely be quite a frequent occurrence. Intellectual property, being the first to have new ideas, and making them known are omnipresent concerns in the academic world. This is reminiscent of how the child behaved in the extract about the hot-air balloons (Chapter 8, p. 191), trying to impress on his parents that he was the one who had been first to notice that the balloons were back.

This analogy with the academic world suggests that a speaker seen as relevant earns a measure of social kudos from language interaction. If we add this parameter to our ethological analysis of language, we have an explanation for the phenomena presented as paradoxical in the previous chapter. Among primates, high social status is a way of increasing individuals' chances of survival and their reproductive power, as it guarantees them privileged access to food and sexual partners. If being relevant in conversation is a way of bettering one's social status, it is understandable that speakers should be eager to speak and be at pains to stress the salience of the situations they speak of. In my own culture, there is actually competitiveness among speakers; and it is common to hear them interrupting each other, talking at the same time as someone else, and talking over one another. In other cultures, the competition is more covert, but it is still competition. The various conversational styles of different people (Tannen 1984) can be seen as strategies adopted in the hope of appearing relevant, in that some of them go in for quantity and frequency of speech, while others who favour quality will speak sparingly and more to the point. If relevance's reward is the granting of social favour, it is understandable that speakers should be strongly tempted to mislead hearers by exaggerating the salience of the events they tell of or even by recounting events that never took place.[1] It can be seen too why it is essential for hearers not to grant status on spurious grounds. So hearers have ways of resisting overstatement and falsehood. Their role in conversation can now be seen for what it is: comparing situations presented as salient with familiar situations and testing the logic of speakers' statements for inconsistencies. Hearers try to assess accurately the quality of the information presented to them so as to 'reward' it properly through granting status. This inversion of the roles played in cooperative relations now makes sense, for here it is the speaker who plays the supplicant's part, seeking a little social favour from interlocutors, and it is hearers who, by having to guard against the risk of cheating, play the judge's part.

This role of social favour can also explain other phenomena related to conversation, first and foremost being the fact that a person can without difficulty engage single-handedly in language activity with several interlocutors, something that the cooperative model would totally rule out. A person giving a lecture to an audience of several hundred is acting in complete conformity with his or her biological predispositions in taking the opportunity to be granted status by a large gathering (the butterflies in the stomach of the beginner underline the point that the risks are run by speakers). We can also say that the conversational behaviour of hearers fits into this same pattern. It makes sense that, hearers being umpires who can grant or withhold status, they should assess the salience and the logical consistency of what they hear. Why, though, should they talk of it, when they could keep the results of their judgements to themselves? Conversation would then consist of isolated speeches, disconnected from each other. The reason why conversation is a more structured system is that it is in hearers' interest to publicize their assessment.

It is in hearers' immediate interest that speakers be required to justify their statements. Just as bartering can produce a fair price, the real value of

---

[1] Fictional stories, in which a speaker narrates imaginary or exaggerated events, are in a separate category. Fiction exists only if a hearer is fully aware of the imaginary character of the events recounted. It entails a universal way of using language and relies on, among other things, hearers' ability to partly inhibit their critical reflex. The biological function of this ability to understand and appreciate fictions remains to be defined.

any information is determined by the interaction between the person who supplied it and those who are trying to put it into perspective. There is a second motivation that may make a hearer express an assessment, which lies in the fact that any hearers who do contrive to put a statement in perspective, or even to invalidate it, will be speaking with relevance. And this can mean that they too are granted status by other participants. After a lecture, for example, it is usual for questions to be taken from the floor, almost all of which will contain assessments of this or that aspect of the talk. This behaviour of publicly expressing an assessment is biologically motivated by the fact that whoever manages to make a relevant assessment is gratified by receiving marks of social esteem from the other participants.

It may be helpful to recall that our focus here is on the biological motivations of behaviours, which is not the same thing as their psychological motivations. We snatch our hand away from a flame because it is painful; but the biological reason for this behaviour is different. If our hand is burned by the flame, it would severely limit the uses we can put it to; and especially in a state of nature, that could eventually compromise our chances of surviving and leaving progeny. Conversation situations can be analysed in psychological terms: hearers' comments may be inspired by a desire to help speakers by pointing out their mistakes or by drawing their attention to a problem. Alternatively, hearers may wish to dissociate themselves from what has just been said or even to show their hostility to a speaker. People who participate in the interaction may experience it as a moment of relaxation or conversely as a sort of confrontation in which those who are proved wrong lose face. All this and more may take place; but the matter under discussion here is of a very different nature. Psychological motivations cannot replace biological determinants, being at best only intermediate products of these, which bias individuals' behaviour in certain directions. But by taking account of the status which individuals grant each other, we may appear to be infringing this principle of separation between psychological and biological causes. The status we give to a friend, a neighbour, or a colleague is first and foremost a psychological phenomenon. Trying to see it as a factor in the biological propensity to participate in conversation looks like a mixing of genres, which is why we cannot assume our explanation is entirely satisfactory as it stands. If speakers' conversational behaviour is related to the granting of status by interlocutors, what we have to do is find the biological motivation for granting status.

A first point to be noted is that there is no automatic link between the granting of status to speakers and the way interlocutors psychologically experience the interaction. Whether they are participating in a squabble or an agreeable chat is neither here nor there. The fact is that interlocutors, often unconsciously and independently of the feelings they may have for one another, can still grant each other a certain social importance. Though B may happen to show that A is mistaken, A can none the less give B a measure of status. In such interactions, the esteem that is apportioned, unlike a zero-sum game in which what is gained by one is lost by another, is generally mutual.

The idea that information is exchanged for status is an attractive one, for it resolves the paradox inherent in language by providing a biological motiv-ation for the act of speaking. Given this justification, we can see a reason for all the various features of language and it becomes conceivable that each and every component of it is locally optimized so that speakers can stress the relevance of what they have to say. That is, the rate of information delivery allowed by our phonological system, the wealth of relations that our faculty of syntax can easily express, and the ease with which we can combine images to make scenes are all capacities that can appear to have been designed to function as tools in the service of conversational relevance. This, however, may be jumping to conclusions. Admittedly, the idea that language entails an asymmetrical exchange seems to solve the problem of its emergence, but it is an idea that stands upon a sizeable assumption, namely that hearers are willing to grant status to relevant speakers. Yet if we examine the biological validity of that assumption, there is nothing self-evident about it. On the surface, it is reminiscent of the symmetrical exchanges of the cooperative situation. If we are to devise a consistent theory of the emergence of language, one in which the grant of status is a driving force, then we must begin by thinking of conditions in which hearers could be biologically advantaged by granting it to some of their fellows. In so doing, we shall have to inspect 'prestige theory' and what explains it on a genetic level.

17.2 Prestige theory

Amotz Zahavi is known for his idea of the handicap principle, which he uses to explain some of the more outlandish curiosities of the natural world, including many signals of communication. Zahavi is also the inventor of another theory, less often cited than the first one and sometimes confused with it, which serves to explain some altruistic behaviours without reference to cooperation. This is his prestige theory; and according to it, the altruistic behaviour of some animals is motivated by the fact that it affords them prestige among their fellows.

Zahavi has made a study of a species of desert-living bird, the Arabian babbler (*Turdoides squamiceps*, of the *Timaliidae* family). He notes that this social animal (it lives in groups of three to fifteen) has a number of different behaviours which it practises with extreme diligence. Babblers spend time feeding each other; they stand guard against birds of prey, 'barking' alarm calls when one appears and deterring it by mobbing. It may be thought that these are fine examples of disinterest and altruism. To explain how natural selection could have favoured such behaviours, one cannot help considering selection by kinship or cooperation. Altruistic animals take real risks, as proven by the ethologist's statistics; and presumably they do this to protect their young. But with the Arabian babbler, this is not the case. The bird's behaviour is the same whether or not it has had any opportunity to procreate within the group. Well, is it cooperative behaviour? In the wild, the altruistic behaviour of the little birds seems closer to fierce competition than to friendly cooperation:

If guarding were based on reciprocity, there would be no point in striving to do *more* guard duty than others. Even if one asserts that such competition is necessary to ensure that the group is never without a sentinel, one would still have to explain why each bird interrupts the watch of the one nearest to it in rank, rather than attempting to replace younger, more inexperienced babblers. (Zahavi and Zahavi 1997: 135)

Zahavi's idea is that the babblers behave in this way to earn prestige from their fellows:

A babbler who can stand guard longer than its comrades, give them part of its food, approach a raptor, take the risk of sleeping at the exposed end of the row— and can also prevent others from doing such deeds—proves daily to its comrades its superiority over them. By doing so, that individual increases its prestige and has an easier time exerting control. (Zahavi and Zahavi 1997: 144)

We might wonder why prestige is so hard to deserve that it requires those who aspire to it to accept privations and expose themselves to dangers. The ethological reality is that prestige pays off in increased chances of reproduction:

Greater prestige ensures an individual a bigger share of the partnership's 'gains'—
that is, a better chance to reproduce successfully. (Zahavi and Zahavi 1997: 149)

The costliness of the exploits to be carried out in the search for prestige is
consistent with the handicap principle. There is no possibility of cheating:
you cannot pretend to feed others; an alarm call will infallibly draw the
attention of a raptor; and a sentry who hides cannot claim to be standing
guard. Zahavi's conclusion is that the quest for prestige is analogous with
all those communication situations in which the possibility of dishonesty
leads to costly signals. If we leave aside the matter of cost, already
discussed, the parallel with human language looks to be inescapable.
However, Zahavi's demonstration is incomplete. What is missing is a
whole dimension of the story, the one which explains the forces impelling
these little birds to grant prestige to their fellows who accomplish the
exploits.

There is nothing neutral in granting status to others. As Zahavi points
out, birds singled out in this way earn an advantage which deprives other
members of the group:

Increased prestige for one partner means a loss in prestige for another. In other
words, it is a zero-sum game within the group. (Zahavi and Zahavi 1997: 149)

If this is the case, there is something not quite clear in the granting of
status to others, whether among Arabian babblers or in human society. A
tactic that would appear much more profitable from the point of view of
one's chances of breeding would be to let the others go to great expense
of energy in their displays of altruism, then refuse to give them priority in
feeding or in access to sexual partners in the full knowledge that their
previous actions have always been selfless. This ruthless reasoning would
appear to invalidate prestige theory. Direct computer modelling of the
phenomenon as it can be inferred from Zahavi's description fails to
reproduce the altruistic behaviour. As Figure 17.1 shows, when there is a
shortage of altruistic individuals, status granting is genetically neutral, as it
has too few opportunities to manifest itself. However, no sooner has the
proportion of altruistic individuals reached a significant level than the
proportion of status granters falls, since by virtue of their habit of giving
priority to the ones they honour, they end up leaving fewer descendants.

Nevertheless, the argument of this chapter is that the emergence
of language can be explained by a version of prestige theory. The
system of status-granting, if appropriately augmented, can be shown to

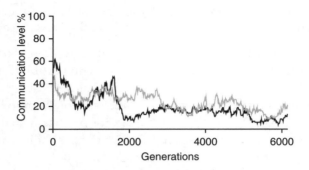

Fɪɢ. 17.1 A simulation of prestige theory, showing that in normal conditions there is neither the status-granting behaviour (in grey) nor the altruistic behaviour (in black)

be advantageous both for the individuals who grant the status and for those who benefit from it, which could explain why it appeared during evolution. The solution I propose consists of a 'political' mechanism whereby language is helpful in the forming of coalitions.

17.3 The political role of language in hominids

The emergent character of social status

Among animals, status is often taken by force. A wolf or a baboon that can establish its physical supremacy over other individuals imposes its control upon the group, makes decisions on its behalf, and has privileged access to sexual partners. Among humans, social status has considerable significance, though it is rarely based on the exercise of bodily strength, except among children. In most cases, status emerges from the respect that each individual grants to others. Human societies have of course reified status by marking it with badges, emblems, and various symbols. But that mode of status, even if it becomes hereditary, is merely an extension of the status gained from others. So the word 'status' as used here covers the whole range of positive or negative assessments that individuals make about each other. It ranges from the esteem that two close friends have for one another to the charisma of a political leader in the eyes of the crowd or the respect afforded us by the people we frequent. Going on what Zahavi says about prestige among babblers, human ways of granting status have their counterparts in the world of animals:

> Prestige reflects the *degree* of a superior individual's dominance, as recognized by subordinate members of the group. In other words, prestige is gauged by others. The dominant may claim prestige, but for the prestige to be real it has to be accepted by subordinates, and it is this acceptance that actually determines an individual's prestige. (Zahavi and Zahavi 1997: 144)

For babblers as for human beings, social status as granted in such a system has no material reality. Its repercussions, however, on the survival and reproduction of individuals are significant in the natural world. Among babblers, status is granted in accordance with the real testimony the birds can give about their ability to accomplish tasks that are of use to the group. As far as human beings are concerned, what we have to understand is why among the individuals to whom status is granted there are those who give testimony about their ability to be relevant. In our species, there are of course other ways of acquiring status, such as accomplishing feats of heroism. Between the extreme situations in which heroes demonstrate courage and the ordinary conversations of everyday life in which speakers show their ability to be relevant, can there be a connection which explains why both types of act should earn status for those who do them? The answer may lie in a socio-ecological characteristic shared by members of our species, their propensity to form coalitions.

The importance of coalitions in the lives of hominids

The social lives of animals are often governed by their genetic relations. In a colony of social insects, for instance, all its members are linked by relations of descent or sibship. However, in a number of species, unrelated individuals may at times choose to work together on certain tasks. Such more or less temporary groupings we can call 'coalitions'. In *Chimpanzee Politics*, Frans de Waal describes how chimpanzees make and unmake coalitions so as to take power within the wider group (de Waal 1982). Dolphins form alliances which enable them to resist attacks by other alliances (Connor, Heithaus, and Barre 1999). In Zahavi's description of Arabian babblers, the life or rather the survival of isolated individuals in the desert is very precarious. Forming coalitions so as to defend a territory containing bushes in which they can escape from birds of prey is vital for them. Robin Dunbar stresses the importance of coalitions among primates, in particular the baboons that he studies. The act of grooming can be seen to be a pledge of reliability among members of a coalition: if they keep each other engaged in lengthy sessions of mutual grooming, their coalition gains in stability, for admission to a coalition and keeping a place in it requires a large investment of time (Dunbar 1996).

When it comes to forming coalitions, human beings are masters of the art. We are bonded in families, in friendships, and in professional relationships; we belong to organizations, to trades unions, and to political parties. Legend has it that the survival of American pioneers, before the establishment of law and order in the person of a sheriff, depended on the fact that individuals belonged to groups which were determined to avenge any attack on a member. The coalition system can be seen too in the urban gangs of teenagers. Some people even see academic research environments as being structured by opposing coalitions. In any of these contexts, individuals would have little chance of making their way unaided. This behaviour of seeking alliances is so deeply rooted in us and so universal that it cannot be seen as a product of culture. Our need for friends is instinctive; and they are the people we rely on when we find ourselves in difficulties. The pleasure we find in spending time with them and the assistance they might afford us in case of need seem to us to be two very different things. They are, however, two inseparable aspects of belonging to a coalition.

For many species, including several species of primates, notably human beings, coalitions are essential to the survival of individuals. Among humans, there is an added dimension to this relationship, a political dimension, for it is a fact that coalitions can come into competition with each other. In a society of babblers, a coalition's enemy is not a raptor; it is other coalitions. For they can evict you from your precious bush and send you out into the unsafe environment where other bushes are rare. Among chimpanzees too a coalition's enemy is another coalition, either the one which holds power or the one which is trying to take power. Human beings are even more unlikely than chimpanzees to have the ability to impose themselves unaided on a group, if they do not have the support of other individuals. Nor can they ever hope to remain in power by themselves; faced with the coalitions of others who are out to depose them, they must be able to draw on the constant support of their own. Politics is a basic behavioural component of our species, arising from the confrontations of coalitions. In Dunbar's view, the necessity of coalitions to human societies is not a product of chance: the coalitions formed by our ancestors must have grown to a critical size, which was bound to produce qualitative changes, one of which would have been the appearance of language (Dunbar 1996: 78). We shall try to relate this hypothesis to the link we can see between language and social status.

Coalitions, status, and leadership

In general, the existence of coalitions can be explained by the benefit they can be seen to have for their members. Here, though, our focus is on a different question. Since belonging to a coalition is of such vital importance for individuals, what are the criteria on which they choose each other? The consequences of their choice being as important as they are, it would be surprising if people allowed mere chance to determine which partners are to share their destinies. In the case of de Waal's chimpanzees, it seems clear that physical strength is a determining criterion, for if one wants to be one of those who will take power in the group, it is best to belong to the coalition of the fittest. As their coalitions are typically formed of two or three individuals, the physical strength of a single chimpanzee can suffice to make the difference between losing power and holding on to it. If we accept Dunbar's arguments, human groups and coalitions were larger, for reasons as yet unclarified, than were those of other primates (Dunbar 1993). The consequence of this would have been that grooming could no longer serve as a token of reliability among members of a coalition, since the time that an individual can devote to it has to be shared out among all the members, which means that each one receives too little attention for it to be considered reliable. How could a behaviour like language, or rather prelanguage, have come to replace grooming as a criterion of selection among the partners in a coalition?[2]

One point that can be made here is that, as coalitions grew in size, of necessity physical strength would become less important, there being no great advantage in being strong if you are clearly outnumbered. And if bodily strength is no longer a determinant, then individuals must rely on other criteria for their choice of one another. The hypothesis I propose is

---

[2] Dunbar's solution, which sees language as a way of detecting cheating within the coalition, was discussed in the previous chapter.

that one of these criteria is the ability to be relevant (Dessalles 2000). Obviously, it could be asked: Why should language have this function, rather than, say, the colour of hair, the ability to collect bright objects, or some other characteristic of body or behaviour? Our ancestors' language behaviour, as I have tried to reconstruct it, consisted of drawing attention to salient situations. What relation can be seen between this behaviour focused upon information and the choosing of partners to make an effective coalition? We may find an answer to that by revisiting the idea of status.

We have observed that language is closely associated with the granting of status, in that relevant speakers are granted it by hearers, unlike those who have little of interest to say. As this mode of freely given status is not material, its tangible consequences must manifest themselves in the behaviour of individuals. My idea is that this granting of status is the very process whereby the choice of coalition partners is made. In other words, individuals try to ally themselves with others to whom they grant status. In particular, they try to ally themselves with the individuals who are most relevant. And conversely, the fact that some individuals attract others for that same reason makes their status visible within the coalition. This is why there is little chance that large coalitions, unlike friendships among a small number of individuals, will be egalitarian. Members of a coalition have come together because the esteem of all is focused on a small number of them, or possibly on just one. This is an inevitable development, a product of the dynamics of status-granting. If some individuals have a quality which earns them status from their fellows and if status serves as the basis for forming coalitions, then these individuals will function as centres of attraction and a coalition will form about them. Let us simplify things by calling these central individuals 'leaders', though the word is reductive of the reality that we want it to refer to. The behaviour that consists of granting status to individuals and trying to ally oneself with them on that basis is bound to give rise, once alliances grow beyond a certain size, to the forming of coalitions centred on leaders.

The choice of the word 'leader' is deliberate. In any coalition of a certain size, over five or six members, say, decisions affecting the collective membership are rarely emergent, unlike what happens in shoals of fish or flocks of starlings. Some members exert more influence than others on collective actions. The fact is that, in human groupings, the preponderant ones are those who have had status conferred upon them by the estimation of the others. In short, human beings grant status to each other in accordance with a gradual criterion, which we can call criterion *C*. They tend accordingly to join coalitions of individuals who show a high value for criterion *C*. The positions occupied by members of such coalitions are leadership positions, with influence over collective decision making. The larger the coalition, the greater the influence. This brings us to a consideration of what it was that made the ability to be relevant appropriate for playing the part of criterion *C*.

The function of language in the choice of coalition partners

Can a criterion which decides whether people will become allies and grant esteem to each other be indifferent? It might seem that any criterion, as long as it is a shared one, could lead to an integrated system of coalitions that are more or less manipulated by individuals who emerge as pre-eminent. This, however, overlooks the fact that a coalition has a purpose, the most typical of which, for primates, is to provide its members with protection against other coalitions and a measure of success in dealing with them. So the choice of one criterion rather than another is hardly a matter of no consequence. If members choose and grant status to each other according to criterion *C*, then the leaders of the coalition are among the best according to *C*. What becomes of the coalition is determined by the behaviour of these leading members. If members choose and grant status to each other according to the pigmentation of their hair, the future well-being of the coalition lies in the hands of the ones with the darkest hair. If members choose and grant status to each other according to their ability to speak relevantly, then it will be the ones who appear to be the most relevant who will have the greatest say in the coalition's destiny.

I have shown elsewhere (Dessalles 1999) that a 'good' criterion, that is a criterion that might be favoured by natural selection, must have the property of correlating with the success of the coalition in political competition. When the criterion is 'good', granting status in accordance with it is a profitable strategy, which means that prestige theory applies. Figure 17.2 illustrates this situation as applying to language. However, when there is insufficient correlation, the situation reverts to that illustrated in Figure 17.1. The existence of this phenomenon may explain why leaders' hair colour has little chance of becoming a criterion of alliance, for there is no reason for it to correlate with the success of their coalitions. In

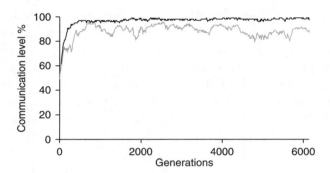

Fig. 17.2 Emergence of language behaviour (in black) when relevance is a good criterion, allowing the strategy of status granting (in grey) to reach a stable level

chimpanzees, the criterion of physical strength does correlate, whereas in coalitions of significant size, like those of human beings and no doubt also of our hominid ancestors, it is of no importance. The argument of this chapter is that the ability to be relevant in conversation is, for us and for them, a 'good' criterion of selection among members of coalitions.

What relevant speakers contrive to show is that they are able to get information, or to find out where it is, sooner than others. In the hypothesis expounded in previous chapters, this property was present as early as the prelanguage and protolanguage used by hominids. By drawing the attention of their fellows to salient situations, our ancestors were able to show that they were better than others at observing their environment, including their social environment, and getting from it what might be biologically relevant. It makes sense to assume that these individuals had more chance than others to influence the well-being of the coalitions they belonged to. If this was the case, a profitable strategy for all individuals was to join up with those who were able to show through language their ability to get relevant information from their physical and social environment.

In order for this explanation of the role of language to be consistent, the destiny of individuals must be closely linked with the destiny of the coalition they chose to belong to. This is confirmed by simulation and theoretical modelling (Dessalles 1999). Figure 17.3 shows that unless the impact of political competition reaches a certain level, the emergence of a behaviour like language is impossible. This means that it was the exist-ence of a social organization peculiar to our lineage which created the

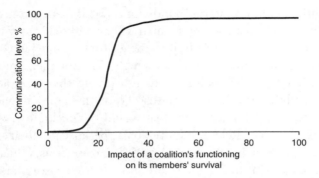

Fɪɢ. 17.3 Once the impact of a coalition's functioning on its members reaches a certain threshold, the emergence of a behaviour like language becomes possible.

conditions in which individuals could benefit from showing their ability to be relevant.

17.4 Language as showing off

The political scenario of the origin of language which has just been proposed presupposes a number of hypotheses which can be set out as follows:

(H1) Individuals who form coalitions use criteria to choose their allies; a 'good' criterion C, compatible with natural selection, is one whose effects are positively correlated with the success of the coalition.

(H2) In most coalitions, especially when they reach a significant size, some individuals have more influence than others on collective decisions, being those who are the best for C and who have the highest status inside the coalition.

(H3) Performance in conversation is a 'good' alliance criterion, for it demonstrates the ability of a speaker to get biologically relevant information from the environment; it is assumed that this ability is correlated with the ability to influence the coalition in the right ways.

The first of these three hypotheses is the easiest to validate theoretically (Dessalles 1999). (H2) seems less obvious, for it introduces a systematic link between performance of individuals with regard to C and their status in the coalition. Granting status to individuals is far from inconsequential: it implies giving them advantages which will be withheld from the rest of the coalition. Is it not possible to imagine a situation in which one might ally oneself with individuals who have a high *C*, letting them influence the collective destiny of the coalition but not giving them the advantages which normally accrue to high status? From the point of view of an individual member of a coalition, that would be ideal. However, such a situation is unstable. Relevant individuals, because of their ability to influence a coalition in the right direction, are seen as valuable by all potential members of it. It is therefore in their interest to make the best bargain, by offering themselves to the highest bidder, so to speak, that is to those who grant most status and, via status, most advantages. The emergence of a status system is thus an inevitable outcome of the existence of a membership market in which individuals who are seen to possess high value as measured by the alliance criterion become the most sought after.

We have already had occasion to examine (H3), in particular its correlation between conversational relevance and biological relevance (see Chapter 16.2). In trying to gauge the second correlation, that between individuals' capacity for relevance and their ability to influence a coalition in the right ways, let us suppose that the situation in other coalitions is the opposite and that it is individuals who are incapable of relevance who exercise the most influence. Who would bet on the long-term success of such coalitions, all other things being equal?

Obviously, (H3) does not state that language relevance is the only good alliance criterion in the human species. There are bound to be several others, which we could identify by thinking of behaviours which earn status for those who practise them. Courage is one that comes immediately to mind. Some authors, such as Edward Wilson (1978: 156) note that courage, though extremely costly, must be biologically advantageous, given the status it earned for heroes. What Wilson cannot explain, however, is the reasons why other people should grant status to heroes. Why, after all, should honour, whether touted at Agincourt by Shakespeare's Henry V ('The fewer men, the greater share of honour... If it be a sin to covet honour, I am the most offending soul alive') or by Corneille's Castilian count in *Le Cid* ('I may be reduced to a life without happiness, but not to accepting a life without honour'), be due to men of courage? That honour is a reality, and so coveted that some will endanger their very lives for it, can be seen in the attitudes of other people, who applaud, give pride of place, and grant prerogatives to heroes. Admiration behaviour, though deeply rooted in our nature, is most unusual in the world of animals. Of what advantage can it be to those who admire? It is not clear how our ancestors could have become our ancestors, by having more descendants than their more graceless contemporaries, if this was a result of their giving up substantial advantages to heroes. Even if the group as a whole can benefit from having heroes among its members, it should be in the interest of individuals to let others reward the courageous and not bother themselves about it. Admiration behaviour, so typical of our species and so inexplicable by standard theories, makes sense according to (H1) and (H2), which enable us to see it as a good alliance criterion, correlated to the success of a coalition. A similar explanation can be given of the fact that certain behaviours incur a loss of status for those who engage in them. This is the case with acts of cheating, treachery, or cowardice, which are understandably correlated negatively with the success of a coalition, especially when they are done by influential members.

If language relevance is one of the ways in which we expose ourselves to the judgements of our fellow human beings, it may appear surprising that so many conversations are so unremarkable. People should only ever speak when sure of being able to make the best possible impression, instead of holding forth about this, that, and the other, as most people do. But in fact both behaviours may be profitable. Compared with other alliance strategies, language relevance occupies a special place. The cost of language is relatively low, as Zahavi points out, unlike heroism. As a consequence, most people have no hesitation in being relevant at every opportunity, the result of which is everyday language activity and its subjects of conversation which can sometimes seem, from the outside, dreadfully ordinary. There are many situations in which it is possible to be more relevant than silence. When conversation flags, a comment on the disagreeable weather may enable somebody to evince a little relevance. It may earn speakers no status, but it costs almost nothing. While it lasts, at least they have a social existence. In conversation that is less ordinary, relevant individuals gain the esteem of their fellows. What they say plays a large part in the construction of their personality in the minds of their interlocutors. All that said, whether conversations turn on trivial or vital subjects, what participants say is always governed by the strict laws of conversational relevance and it is this that can earn status for speakers.

There seems to be nothing new in language as a way of showing off. Human beings like to be spoken about;[3] if need be, they will even do it themselves. Speaking offers thus the possibility not just of being noticed for our ability to be relevant but also, when possible, of showing by the content of what we say that we are a rather extraordinary person in some way or other. The fact that language is used like that by many people, perhaps even by everybody, cannot serve as a justification for its biological existence. If the esteem of others could be won merely by boasting, then the best strategy for hearers would be to turn deaf and the best for speakers would be to produce exaggerated and repetitive messages so as to overcome the deafness. That would be the type of communication to be expected from a system functioning along the lines defined by Krebs and Dawkins, of which advertising is a fine example. Human language does undoubtedly contain features akin to advertising, as seen in the efforts every person will make, when circumstances are favourable, to appear in the best light. None the less, it is not the speaker but the hearer who is in control of language exchanges, as they have developed out of our biological constitution. Hearers, to grant status, judge especially the relevance of what is said. Admittedly, clever speakers can take advantage of their own scope for manoeuvre to choose the content of what they say so as to show themselves off. But they must still function within the tight constraints of relevance. People whose talk about themselves too obviously trangresses accepted boundaries of pertinence in information-giving or argumentation run the risk of displaying their self-infatuation. Whatever status we may enjoy from our closest associates is not of our own professing; it must be earned. And it can only be earned if we play by the rules laid down by the biological organization of our species. The getting of status and existing within the different coalitions to which we may wish to belong can only be achieved, not by showing off, but by showing that we possess one very particular faculty: the ability to be relevant. Whenever the occasion arises, in other words dozens of times a day, we go through the ritual of displaying for other people's judgement our ability to give them a relevant message made of ordered thoughts.

The behaviours underlying conversation obey unconscious mechanisms. Speakers drawing attention to salient situations, hearers trying to

---

[3] Think of the writer who said to his critics, 'I don't mind if you say good things about me or bad things, as long as you spell my name right.'

trivialize them, others expressing doubts about the internal consistency of what they are hearing are all behaving instinctively. Reflex is what governs these actions. We exercise a degree of conscious control over the content of our utterances; but we find it difficult to resist the urge to speak. We cannot help trivializing what is presented as unlikely or questioning what appears strange. Human beings start to speak as soon as they meet someone. The cocktail-party effect, everybody trying to out-talk the noise of neighbouring conversations, and the din this creates, show how systematic language behaviour is and how deeply rooted it is in our biology. At stake in these conversations is something of vital importance to each of the speakers: who is going to have a close relationship with whom, who will rise in the estimation of others, who will gain the benefits and the influence that come with status. What we are unconsciously exercising in our conversations is a part of our biological programming. Behind the immediate stimulus of exchanging relevant information, what we are doing is assessing others' ability to decide what is good for the set of people who will choose to ally with them. Language can thus be seen more as a means than as an end. Just as phonology makes for the construction of an extended lexicon, so our use of language makes for the construction of coalitions.

17.5 *Homo loquens* or *Homo politicus*

The hypothesis argued in this chapter sees the function of language as lying outside language. When we spend our time exchanging information, it is not for the intrinsic value of the information. The information may of course be useful, even of vital importance to a hearer. But whatever usefulness there may be in the information exchanged, it is never systematic; nor can it be the biological reason for the emergence of language. Speakers are eager to bring gifts of information because they have something to gain from them. Human beings turn into interlocutors for a fifth of their waking lives because they are in a game which, when played under nature's conditions, is essential to their survival and procreation. The aim of the game is to discover whom to choose as allies and to determine who will influence collective decisions. It is a game which differs from the other one, the game of natural selection, because the winners are not the only ones who get to propagate their difference. In the coalition game, any players who try to keep all the status for themselves, rather than grant it to others, may end up paying dearly for it. It is better to stand second in a coalition that wins than first in one that loses.

What we know about political behaviour fits so neatly here that we may doubt whether it is a cultural phenomenon. Political behaviours are universal, whether they consist of seeking allies, agreeing not to dominate the coalition, or leaving a coalition that is badly led, etc. These are behaviours which do not have to be learned or invented. They appear as early as the play of children. We reproduce political competitiveness in sport, in the workplace, and in our friendships. Whenever we opt to support a team or join a party, when we make friends or cultivate a relationship, each of these choices belongs to the range of political behaviours. Man, said Aristotle, is by nature a political animal (*Politics* I, 2). The mechanisms that govern our social life are so closely linked to considerations of coalition and status that, ethologically speaking, our species could be called *Homo politicus*. If we analyse what we do, and what we do not do, in a day, we may become aware of how few of our choices are prompted by our immediate wishes. Our actions are influenced in large measure by potential profits and losses in social status. The much-mentioned importance of the 'gaze' of others reminds us that it is the eyes of people who judge us. We are sensitive to the way we are regarded by those with whom we wish to associate, that is to say members of the coalitions we belong to or would like to belong to. What I suggest is that it was this social organization of our species, structured through political competition among coalitions, which led to the emergence of language during the evolution of the line from which we come.

Jacques Monod saw language as 'one of the initial "choices" which determine the whole future of the species by creating a new selection pressure' (Monod 1970: 145). Here we depart from Monod and propose that this 'initial choice' was political functioning. Language of the human variety, consisting of drawing others' attention to salient situations and of testing the consistency of what is said, developed in a context peculiar to our lineage, namely a system of coalitions which constrains individuals to seek out the most promising coalition among those which are available. Through speech and relevance, individuals endeavour to become valued as coalition partners, in the same way as they endeavour, also through language, to assess accurately the quality of their own potential partners. Unlike what one might think, it was not our language faculties that helped us to bring about a complex social structure in which an individual can belong to various coalitions. It makes more sense to see the relationship of cause and effect as being the opposite of that: it was the social structuring peculiar to our species which created the conditions for the emergence of our type of human language. In other words, before our species became *Homo loquens*, speaking man, it was *Homo politicus*.

17.6 The other functions of language

Central to the functions of language is relevance in conversation. In the scenario just outlined, all aspects of the language faculty were selected for that single function. The language faculty, with all its phonological, morphosyntactic, and semantic components, was locally optimized by natural selection so that speakers could appear relevant. The size of the lexicon supported by our phonological system, the richness of phrase linking, or our capacities for combining mental images all evolved so that we could conceive of relevant contributions to conversation. None of this rules out, of course, the existence of a number of secondary uses of language which have no strict link to relevance. In singing, for instance, the relevance of the words is not always a criterion. It would be difficult to draw up an exhaustive list of these secondary uses. For example, among the functions of language in certain cultures, particularly cultures which use writing, are mathematics and poetry. Biologically, however, such uses, important though they may be culturally, are at best side effects of language competence, as well as being activities practised only by special-ists within the group. They are optional extras, an unexpected present given to our species by nature. The late development of culture, in the cumulative form of it that we know, is evidence that many of the secondary uses of language are epiphenomena of evolution.

Dunbar stresses the importance of language for analysing and com-menting on social relations within the group and for deploring any acts of cheating (Dunbar 1996). He strongly suggests that this is a biological function of language. It is not impossible that we should have a natural inclination to gossiping, though it would be necessary to define reasons for it. It should, however, be pointed out that commenting on social relations does not mean that the speaker is relieved of the need be relevant. A remarkable thing about the faculty of language is that nothing in its structure depends on the subject spoken about: whether the conversation deals with food, adventures, a particular technique of fishing, or what our next-door neighbour did to his wife, the same principles govern the way phonemes and phrases are put together and the combinations of mental images. If there is a natural inclination to gossiping, it is not directly linked to language but rather to the fact that we think there is something important in judging the actions of people with whom we have social links or who are our geographical neighbours. That importance inheres in the way human society is structured into coalitions and in our constant need for clear judgements about anybody with whom we might find ourselves in a coalition.

In some instances, the interest we take in what goes on round about us is influenced by our nature as political creatures, gossip being a case in point. Another example of this influence, not very different from gossip, affords a striking illustration of the importance of status in human social organization. It would be hard to see an event as minor as a tiff between a married couple as a salient situation, unless of course the couple in question were one's best friends or happened to be a king and queen. People are affected by anything related to individuals whom they see as in some way occupying high positions, which is why a girl living in the south of Africa may be intimately acquainted with the doings of a family living in Monaco, for the simple reason that the family is that of a prince. Humans living in modern societies may not all agree about which people are the ones who occupy high positions, but they do more talking about the ones they see as having status than about others. Though this favourite form of talk is not an intrinsic property of language, it may reflect a natural bias in our perception of what constitutes salience. This bias, like the one towards gossip mentioned by Dunbar, fits neatly into the political account of language given in this chapter.

During election campaigns, the candidates talk and debate, in an endeavour to show they are worthy of being entrusted by their fellow citizens with the running of the country. Ordinary human beings are involved in a similar process with the people among whom they live, albeit on a very different scale and usually without being aware of it as such. We all participate in a perpetual election campaign, the point of which is to elect our friends, our social contacts, and the people whose advice, orders, or suggestions we are going to heed. Every utterance we make in daily conversation contributes to this process. Mistakes are not allowed: if we say something incomprehensible or inconsistent,[4] this will cast doubt on what we are and distort the image that others have of us. The essence of everything that makes for the originality of our biological constitution, in particular our highly developed mental capacities and linguistic faculties, was selected so that we could stand a good chance in this elective process. There are two complementary ways of winning in this system of natural politics: either we ourselves have a chance of being seen as the best candidate or we will be smart enough to be in alliance with the best. My whole argument is that the faculty of language evolved to serve these two strategies.

---

[4] This does not apply to speaking in jest, a subject which would no doubt require lengthy discussion.

18 Epilogue

Research into the origin of language is in its infancy. Nevertheless, by drawing on findings from very different disciplines, which is what this book has done, it is possible to have an inkling of what separates non-language from language in human phylogeny. Before drawing some conclusions from this clearer understanding of our past, let us recapitulate the main elements of the outline we have given.

18.1 A genesis in three stages

If we extrapolate a little from Chapters 16 and 17, we can imagine a plausible sequence of the evolutionary events that led to language. Some of our ancestors who belonged to the first species of *Homo*, say, began to form sizeable coalitions. In such a 'political' context, finding good allies becomes essential. It can be assumed that individuals who were observant enough to notice salient things in their environment made valuable companions. This assumption is basic to the whole account. In a context of political competition, the gathering of information is of crucial advantage. Among other species, observation remained an essentially private matter; but among our ancestors it became something to be shared. Individuals began divulging to others the salient observations they made, not because of the intrinsic value of the information, but so as to demonstrate their ability to notice things sooner than their fellows. This was how a primordial mode of communication came about, for the purposes of which a perfect adaptation was what we call 'prelanguage', made of isolated words that drew attention to an actual situation, that is one which could be observed by the interlocutors. This initial stage of prehuman communication was stable. Cheating was not a possibility, as verification was almost instantaneous.

The second stage arose from a new semantic capacity, the faculty of combining the memories of perceptions brought to mind by words so as to make composite scenes, possibly scenes never before witnessed. Combinations of words could then express a meaning. This was the beginning of protolanguage as described by Bickerton, that is a language without syntax. What was its function, the function for which natural selection had favoured it? The increase in referential precision made it possible to speak of scenes in their absence or of scenes not experienced in the present. Speakers could prove their informative gifts by telling of salient facts that had happened elsewhere or beforehand; and hearers could visualize the scenes. However, this imperfect representation hindered perception of salience. Human beings, like other animals, are equipped to discern salient aspects in what they perceive, for example a suspicious noise, an unfamiliar animal, or an unexpected object. Such situations, when merely visualized, are hard to see as salient. In conversations among humans, salient situations, if they are not actually happening, are always presented as improbable (cf. pp. 191–2). We can imagine that the ability to estimate degrees of improbability arose with protolanguage and the conveying of absent situations. Recognition of salience ceased being a mere perceptual reflex and became in addition the consequence of a probabilistic estimation.

This mode of communication opened the way to possible exaggeration and lying. Protolanguage would not have existed if interlocutors of that period had been unable to protect themselves against these risks of cheating. Informers who exaggerate what they have witnessed or who report events that never happened are likely to derive undeserved benefits from this, by making hearers believe they are providers of reliable information. As a protection against this danger, individuals developed the strategy of trivialization, consisting of a comparison between the reported situation and previous situations, and offering a safeguard against fraudulent overstatements of salience. As for the problem of lying, it is likely that the only recourse open to protohumans was deferred verification. Liars were individuals whose statements were invalidated by further experience. This procedure limited communication to concrete and verifiable situations.

The third stage, human communication, began with the rise of a new semantic capacity, thematic segmentation. It enables us to make binary distinctions between the elements of a scene, for example by analysing that an object is inside, rather than outside, an area. This new capacity makes it possible for us to detect cognitive conflicts. When a speaker's words set up a cognitive conflict in a hearer's mind, the risk is that it arises from dishonesty. Invented facts are very likely to make for illogicalities, such as an object being in two different places or moving without cause. This is what makes it possible to controvert statements made by criminals under investigation or on trial. What this means is that here is a capacity which was selected as a way of guarding against lying, before itself becoming a component of communication. Reporting or drawing attention to a salient event was no longer the only way to be appreciated as a member of a coalition, for now one could also expose inconsistencies in other people's statements. This was the birth of argumentation. Since the ability to detect inconsistency was as valuable to a coalition as was the ability to detect salience, status was granted also to those who could argue cogently. By extension, humans began to notice inconsistencies in natural phenomena, with the result that detecting strange facts became a valued form of communication.

These new forms of communication constrained speakers to share their thematic segmentations. In this way, syntax arose, as a way to distinguish among the elements of a situation (typically theme, reference point, and agent) while marking a simple relation among them (typically a topological one). By extension, syntax became a way of referring to entities. For example, by stating that an object lies within a given frame of reference, one makes it easier to refer to it. In this, the recursive form of syntax shows its utility, for as each thematic segmentation is liable to entail a further segmentation to clarify its own elements, a way was required of expressing the segmentations through embedding. Human beings found this way in phrasal syntax.

There we have a brief version of the account given of the emergence of language by the various analyses making up the chapters of this book. If the broad lines of this account are accepted, language appears in a new light. Language behaviour has biological roots. It is a product of evolution by natural selection. As such, it is a product of no inescapable necessity, but only of a local necessity. It was only in the highly particularized context of a 'political' species that language could prove to be advantageous for those using it.

18.2 A new view of language

The genesis of language as described in this book obliges us to see it in a way that is radically new. Such a reappraisal may well prove to be agonizing. In most mythologies and in the conceptual frameworks provided by religions, language is of divine provenance. Authors who eschew such assumptions customarily examine the evolutionary history of species looking for a reason underlying another prejudice, namely that language was a culmination, a type of perfection towards which other species are still in the process of evolving. This is why the forms of communication used in the most 'advanced' species are seen by some as early versions of language, humans being the only species to have managed the quantitative leap which enabled its members to express 'everything'.

I hope I have laid this prejudice to rest. Members of other species do not speak because it is not in the interests of their survival and reproduction to do so. We humans do speak because a fortuitous change profoundly altered the social organization of our ancestors, who found themselves faced with the necessity, if they were to survive and breed, of forming sizeable coalitions. Language then arose as a way in which individuals might show off their value as members of these.

This new perspective on language within the animal world has other implications. Not only did language result from the fortuitous appearance of a highly particularized mode of social organization, but it was not a necessary result. That is to say, either language might not have existed or it could have existed in a radically different form. Take for instance argumentation, which structures many of our language exchanges. According to the idea developed in this book, argumentation arose as a consequence of a mechanism for the detection of lying. We tend to think that our capacities for logical reasoning are universal, that they must inevitably accompany any form of intelligence. But this is a total illusion. Evolution might well have endowed us with some completely different mechanism for checking the reliability of other people's statements.[1] This would have profoundly altered our intelligence and use of language, though they would not have been inferior to what they now are. The history of species has left no trace of this sort of alternative, but all the evidence suggests that even our ways of understanding and reasoning are a fortuitous product of evolution. If there ever comes a day when this planet is inhabited by

---

[1] Developments in information technology provide examples of validity testing which are not logical. For example, to check that accounts have not been falsified or data on human origin misconstrued, it is possible to test the frequency of appearance of significant digits. In the present state of the technology, however, it is difficult to imagine any way in which this might be transposed into a validity test applicable to a reported scene.

another life form capable of achievements on a par with ours, it is extremely unlikely that its way of thinking and its way of communicating (if it has any) would be qualitatively comparable to our cognitive functioning and language. If there is anything at all 'universal' in logical reasoning and language, it stops at the frontier of our species.

What other conclusions can be drawn from this discussion of the origin of the faculty of language? The question of origins has exercised the minds of many people. In addition to whatever benefit science can draw from a better understanding of our phylogeny, there is also the matter of how each of us makes sense of our lives. We must accept that our existence, whether as a species or as individuals, was unnecessary. Despite which, many aspects of our behaviour are not gratuitous, language being a case in point. An awareness of the biological reason for the existence of our language behaviour can give us a clearer understanding of our own behaviour and that of others. When people talk, they are not merchandising or selling information with a view to getting a quid pro quo. Talking is a way of existing socially. People who speak to others are giving them an opportunity to judge their use of a capacity which is essential to the proper functioning of coalitions—that is to say, their ability to be relevant. Those who can speak relevantly are sought after; and, other things being equal, those whose speech is full of platitudes, commonplaces, or wrong-headed judgements are less highly valued.

Language behaviour exists only because it is judged. We are constantly obliged either to provide reliable salient facts or to argue consistently. This means language is a game, in which the prize is to join a network of relationships, to be accepted, and to win a valued place in it. We are not generally aware of this. To say that we speak because we feel the need to or because we enjoy it is a psychological view of language. And it has been one of the aims of this book to see the origin of language from a very different perspective, one that helps us to analyse the real biological purpose of our everyday interactions.

18.3 Future perspectives

This work on language is part of a broader enterprise to re-examine human behaviour and cognitive abilities from an evolutionary perspective. Many other aspects of our behaviour can be rethought in this way.

Chris Knight has shown in a brilliant book how such an evolutionary perspective can lead to the discovery of a logic behind collective behaviours like rituals, celebrations, myths, body painting, or the rules governing eating and marriage (Knight 1991). Though ethnographers had been in the habit of seeing such things as products of cultural evolution, authors such as Knight interpret them as expressions of a biological programme the reasons for which lie in the phylogeny of our species. This 'naturalizing' work on human behaviours has barely begun. This book is intended as a contribution to this evolutionary rethinking.

I hope that readers who have followed the argument presented here will have altered their view of the origin of our species and its most characteristic behaviour, language. They should have encountered new ideas, some of which are quite original, particularly the idea of protosemantics and the division of semantics into two separate competences, the analysis of conversational behaviour as two components, one focused on salient facts, the other on argumentation, and my refutation of the cooperative theory of language, which I replace by an account based on politics.

Can this type of research into our origins be turned to any practical use? Any advance in our understanding of our own nature can lead to its being applied. One that can be mentioned here, by way of a small digression, is the explosion of new ways of using the internet that occurred in the early 1990s. For about a decade, scholars had been using the network to send messages to one another. Technically, the innovation which led to the existence of the Web was a minor one, a programme enabling the display of pages in a standard format and making it possible to go from one page to another, wherever they happened to be in one of the computers linked to the network. The original objective of the research which developed the project at CERN and the University of Illinois was to share documentation and sources of information. No one had foreseen the amazing way the new system would take off among private users. The French *Minitel* system offered a wide variety of services, but going directly from one page to another was not possible unless they belonged to the same provider. Why was there such a huge and immediate expansion in the number of pages put on the Web? Unlike *Minitel*, which was restricted to administrative and commercial services, millions of private individuals, quite spontaneously and without charge, started to put their pages onto the Web, most of them containing information of excellent quality. How can we explain this unexpected phenomenon?

There is nothing more facile than the hindsight which lets us see that an event was foreseeable. That said, there is a close analogy between what happened in the early days of the Web and the conditions in which language emerged at some time in the past of our species. What the Web offered was a way for people to draw attention to themselves. By offering useful information, they display themselves and their competence. We could say that the Web offers another way for individuals to exist socially. Yet, people who put a homepage on the Web are unaware of who might read it, there being no intention on anyone's part to attract the attention of particular individuals. In this way, those who put their pages on the Web are following their biological programming, exactly as they do when talking with friends. What both cases have in common is the display of a competence with the aim of being appreciated, which is what we do day in, day out in our ordinary relations with people we know. Through the Web we are able to do this non-stop and on a world scale. This book's analysis of the biological role of language turns a misleading appearance back to front: the Web is not a mere device for getting information; it is first and foremost a new way for people to attract the attention of others by supplying information they may find useful.

It can be seen that the discussion of the biological origin of our language behaviour may have a role to play in the analysis and forecasting of social developments. Our understanding of human interactions in the changing conditions of modern society is a significant field of study which will undoubtedly benefit from the longer perspective offered by biology. Nowadays human beings live in societies of hundreds of millions of their kind, in which their behaviours follow a biological programme that was selected for living in tribes of hunter-gatherers. According to a widely accepted view, human beings have replaced their biological programming with a set of rules based entirely on convention. This view, given what we can see at work in language, must be held to be dubious. There is no law or precept laying down how to use language in conversation. Our talk is no different from that of our ancestors as they did their wall paintings in the cave at Lascaux. In writing this book, I have attempted to 'naturalize' language by showing that speech is a component of our biological nature. It is to be hoped that this will lead to further work of broader scope.

References

Aiello, L. C. (1996). 'Terrestriality, bipedalism and the origin of language', *Proceedings of the British Academy* 88: 269–89.

Auriol, J.-B. (1999). *Modélisation du sujet humain en situation de résolution de problème, basée sur le couplage d'un formalisme logique et d'un formalisme d'opérateur.* Paris: doctoral thesis, ENST.

Austin, J. L. (1962). *How To Do Things With Words.* Oxford: Oxford University Press.

Axelrod, R. (1984). *The Evolution of Cooperation.* New York: Basic Books.

—— and Hamilton, W. D. (1981). 'The evolution of cooperation', *Science* 211: 1390–6.

Barone, R. (1976). *Anatomie comparée des mammifères domestiques.* Paris: Vigot.

Bergson, H. (1940). *Le rire, essai sur la signification du comique.* Paris: Presses universitaires de France.

Bickerton, D. (1990). *Language and Species.* Chicago: University of Chicago Press.

—— (1995). *Language and Human Behaviour.* London: UCL Press.

—— (1998). 'Catastrophic evolution: the case for a single step from protolanguage to full human language', in J. R. Hurford, M. Studdert-Kennedy, and C. Knight (eds.), *Approaches to the Evolution of Language: Social and Cognitive Bases.* Cambridge: Cambridge University Press.

Bonner, J. T. (1980). *The Evolution of Culture in Animals.* New Jersey: Princeton University Press.

Bousquet, O. (1999). *Pertinence et probabilité.* Paris: Mémoire de projet, ENST.

Brenot, P. (1984). 'Langage et hominisation', *Revue de phonétique appliquée* 71/72: 217–25.

Call, J., Hare, B., and Tomasello, M. (1998). 'Chimpanzee gaze following in an object choice task', *Animal Cognition* 1: 89–100.

Carberry, S. (1988). 'Modeling the user's plans and goals', *Computational Linguistics* 14 (3): 23–37.

Carpenter, M., Nagell, K., and Tomasello, M. (1998). 'Social cognition, joint attention, and communicative competence from 9 to 15 months of age', *Monographs of the Society for Research in Child Development* 255 (63): 1–143.

Carré, R. (1996). 'Prediction of vowel systems using a deductive approach', *Proceedings of the International Conference on Spoken Language Processing.* Philadelphia, PA, 434–7

Carstairs-McCarthy, A. (1998). 'Synonymy avoidance, phonology and the origin of syntax', in J. R. Hurford, M. Studdert-Kennedy, and C. Knight (eds.) *Approaches to the Evolution of Language: Social and Cognitive Bases.* Cambridge: Cambridge University Press.

Cavalli-Sforza, L. (1999). 'Des gènes, des peuples et des langues', in *Les langues du monde.* Paris: Belin, 52–9.

Charbonnier, G. (1961). *Entretiens avec Claude Lévis-Strauss.* Paris: Agora, Pocket (1969 edn.).

Cheney, D. L. and Seyfarth, R. M. (1988). 'Assessment of meaning and the detection of unreliable signals by vervet monkeys', *Animal Behaviour* 36: 477–86.

—— —— (1990). *How Monkeys See the World: Inside the Mind of Another Species.* Chicago: University of Chicago Press.

Chomsky, N. (1968). *Language and Mind.* New York: Harcourt, Brace and World.

—— (1975). *Reflections on Language.* New York: Random House.

—— (1981). 'A naturalistic approach to language and cognition', *Cognition and Brain Theory* 4 (1): 1–22.

—— (1995). *The Minimalist Program.* Cambridge, MA: MIT Press.

—— and Halle, M. (1968). *The Sound Pattern of English.* New York: Harper and Row.

Connor, R. C., Heithaus, M. R., and Barre, L. M. (1999). 'Superalliance of bottlenose dolphins', *Nature* 397: 571–2.

Coppens, Y. (1983). *Le singe, l'Afrique et l'homme.* Paris: Fayard.

Corballis, M. C. (1991). *The Lopsided Ape: Evolution of the Generative Mind.* Oxford: Oxford University Press.

Cowper, E. A. (1992). *A Concise Introduction to Syntactic Theory: The Government-Binding Approach.* Chicago: University of Chicago Press.

Crain, S. (1991). 'Language acquisition in the absence of experience', *Behavioral and Brain Sciences* 14: 597–650.

Crothers, J. (1978). 'Typology and universals of vowel systems', in J. H. Greenberg, C. A. Ferguson, and E. A. Moravcsik (eds.), *Universals of Human Language, Vol. 2, Phonology.* Stanford: Stanford University Press.

Darwin, C. (1859). *On the Origin of Species.* London: John Murray.

—— (1871). *The Descent of Man.* Princeton: Princeton University Press (1981 edn.).

—— (1872). *The Expression of the Emotions in Man and Animals.* London: John Murray.

Dawkins, R. (1976). *The Selfish Gene.* Oxford: Oxford University Press.

Deacon, T. W. (1992). 'Brain-language coevolution', in J. A. Hawkins and M. Gell-Mann (eds.), *The Evolution of Human Languages.* Santa Fe: Santa Fe Institute Proceedings vol. XI, Addison-Wesley, 49–83.

Deacon, T. W. (1997). *The Symbolic Species.* New York: W. W. Norton and Co.

Dehaene, S. (1997). *La bosse des maths*. Paris: Odile Jacob.

Desclés, J.-P. (1990). 'State, event, process and topology', *General Linguistics* 29 (3): 159–200.

Dessalles, J.-L. (1985). 'Stratégies naturelles d'acquisition des concepts', Actes du colloque COGNITIVA 85. Paris: CESTA, 713–19.

—— (1992). *Les contraintes logiques des conversations spontanées*. Paris: Rapport technique TELECOM-Paris 92-D-011.

—— (1996a). *L'ordinateur génétique*. Paris: Hermès.

—— (1996b). 'Pourquoi est-on, ou n'est-on pas, pertinent ?', *Communication et Langages* 107: 69–80.

—— (1998a). 'The interplay of desire and necessity in dialogue', in J. Hulstijn and A. Nijholt (eds.), *Formal Semantics and Pragmatics of Dialogue*. Enschede: University of Twente, TWLT-13, 89–97.

—— (1998b). 'Altruism, status and the origin of relevance', in J. R. Hurford, M. Studdert-Kennedy, and C. Knight (eds.), *Approaches to the Evolution of Language: Social and Cognitive Bases*. Cambridge: Cambridge University Press.

—— (1999). 'Coalition factor in the evolution of non-kin altruism', *Advances in Complex Systems* 2 (2): 143–72.

—— (2000). 'Language and hominid politics', in C. Knight, M. Studdert-Kennedy, and James Hurford (eds.), *The Evolutionary Emergence of Language: Social Function and the Origins of Linguistic Form*. Cambridge: Cambridge University Press.

Dixon, R. M. W. (1972). *The Dyirbal Language of North Queensland*. Cambridge: Cambridge University Press.

Donald, M. (1998). 'Mimesis and the executive suite: missing links in language evolution', in J. R. Hurford, M. Studdert-Kennedy, and C. Knight (eds.), *Approaches to the Evolution of Language: Social and Cognitive Bases*. Cambridge: Cambridge University Press.

Dunbar, R. I. M. (1993). 'Coevolution of neocortical size, group size and language in humans', *Behavioral and Brain Sciences* 16 (4): 681–735.

—— (1996). *Grooming, Gossip, and the Evolution of Language*. Cambridge, MA: Harvard University Press.

—— (1998). 'Theory of mind and the evolution of language', in J. R. Hurford, M. Studdert-Kennedy, and C. Knight (eds.), *Approaches to the Evolution of Language: Social and Cognitive Bases*. Cambridge: Cambridge University Press.

Durand, J. (1990). *Generative and Non-Linear Phonology*. London: Longman.

Duve, C. de. (1995). *Poussière de vie, une histoire du vivant*. Paris: Fayard (1996 edn.).

Eibl-Eibesfeldt, I. (1967). *Ethologie - Biologie du comportement*. Paris: Naturalia et Biologia ed. scientifiques (1977 edn.).

—— (1975). *The Biology of Peace and War: Men, Animals, and Aggression*. New York: Viking Penguin (1979 edn.).

Eldredge, N., and Gould, S. J. (1972). 'Punctuated equilibria: an alternative to phyletic gradualism', in T. J. M. Schopf (ed.), *Models in Paleobiology*. San Francisco: Freeman and Cooper.

Encrevé, P. (1988). *La liaison avec et sans enchaînement*. Paris: Seuil.

Epstein, R., Lanza, R. P., and Skinner, B. F. (1980). 'Symbolic communication between two pigeons', *Science* 207 (1): 543–5.

Fodor, J. A., Garrett, M. F., Walker, E. C. T., and Parkes, C. H. (1980). 'Against definitions', *Cognition* 8: 263–367.

Frisch, K. von (1967). *The Dance Language and Orientation of Bees*. Cambridge, MA: Harvard University Press.

Gardner, R. A., and Gardner, B. T. (1992). 'Early signs of language in cross-fostered chimpanzees', in J. Wind, B. Chiarelli, and B. Bichakjian (eds.), *Language Origin: A Multidisciplinary Approach*. Dordrecht: Kluwer Academic Publishers.

Genette, G. (1983). *Nouveau discours du récit*. Paris: Seuil.

Gobet, F. and Simon, H. A. (2000). 'Five seconds or sixty? Presentation time in expert memory', *Cognitive Science* 24 (4): 651–82.

Goldberg, D. E. (1989). *Genetic Algorithms in Search, Optimization and Machine Learning*. Reading, MA: Addison-Wesley.

Goodall, J. (1971). *In the Shadow of Man*. Boston: Houghton Mifflin (1988 edn.).

Gould, S. J. (1980). *The Panda's Thumb*. New York: Norton.

—— (1996). *Full House*. New York: Three Rivers Press.

—— and Lewontin, R. C. (1979). 'The spandrels of San Marco and the Panglossian program: a critique of the adaptationist program', in *Proceedings of the Royal Society of London* 205: 281–8.

Grau, B., Sabah, G., and Vilnat, A. (1994). 'Pragmatique et dialogue homme-machine', *Technique et science informatique* 13 (1): 9–30.

Grice, H. P. (1975). 'Logic and conversation', in P. Cole and J. L. Morgan (eds.), *Syntax and Semantics, vol. III, Speech Acts*. New York: Academic Press.

Grosz, B. J., and Sidner, C. L. (1986). 'Attention, intentions, and the structure of discourse', *Computational Linguistics* 12 (3): 175–204.

Gruber, J. S. (1965). *Lexical Structures in Syntax and Semantics*. Amsterdam: North Holland (1976 edn.).

Grumbach, A. (1994). *Cognition artificielle: du réflexe à la réflexion*. Paris: Addison-Wesley.

Haegeman, L. (1991). *Introduction to Government and Binding Theory*. Oxford: Blackwell (1994 edn.).

Hagège, C. (1985). *L'homme de paroles*. Paris: Fayard.

Hamilton, W. D. (1964). 'The genetical evolution of social behaviour', *Journal of Theoretical Biology* 7: 1–16.

—— (1972). 'Altruism and related phenomena, mainly in social insects', *Annual Review of Ecology and Systematics* 3: 192–232.

Hauser, M. D. (1996). *The Evolution of Communication*. Cambridge, MA: MIT Press.

Hewes, G. (1992). 'History of glottogonic theories', in J. Wind, B. Chiarelli, and B. Bichakjian (eds.), *Language Origin: A Multidisciplinary Approach.* Dordrecht: Kluwer Academic Publishers.

Hickok, G., Bellugi, U., and Klima, E. S. (1998). 'The neural organization of language: evidence from sign language aphasia', *Trends in Cognitive Sciences* 2 (4): 465–8.

Jackendoff, R. (1983). *Semantics and Cognition.* Cambridge, MA: MIT Press (1995 edn.).

—— (1990). *Semantic Structures.* Cambridge, MA: MIT Press.

—— (1999). 'Possible stages in the evolution of the language capacity', *Trends in Cognitive Sciences* 3 (7): 272–9.

Jacob, F. (1970). *La logique du vivant: une histoire de l'hérédité.* Paris: Gallimard.

Kaye, J. D. and Lowenstamm, J. (1984). 'De la syllabicité', in F. Dell, D. Hirst, and J.-R. Vergnaud (eds.), *Forme sonore du langage: structure des représentations en phonologie.* Paris: Hermann.

Kegl, J., Senghas, A., and Coppola, M. (1999). 'Creation through contact: sign language emergence and sign language change in Nicaragua', in M. DeGraff (ed.), *Language Creation and Language Change.* Cambridge, MA: MIT Press, 179–237.

Kirchner, W. H. and Towne, W. F. (1994). 'The sensory basis of the honeybee's dance language', *Scientific American* 207 (6): 52–9.

Knight, C. (1991). *Blood Relations: Menstruation and the Origins of Culture.* New Haven: Yale University Press.

—— Power, C., and Watts, I. (1995). 'The human symbolic revolution: a Darwinian account', *Cambridge Archeological Journal* 5 (1): 75–114.

Krebs, J. R. and Dawkins, R. (1984). 'Animal signals: mind-reading and manipulation', in J. R. Krebs and N. B. Davies (eds.), *Behavioural Ecology, an Evolutionary Approach* (2nd edn.). Oxford: Blackwell Scientific Publications, 380–405.

Lakoff, G. and Johnson, M. (1980). *Metaphors We Live By.* Chicago: University of Chicago Press.

—— and Núñez, R. (2000). *The Infinity Blues: How the Embodied Mind Brings Mathematics into Being.* New York: Basic Books.

Langaney, A. (1999). 'La génétique des populations à l'appui de la linguistique', in *Les langues du monde.* Paris: Belin, 60–3.

Larson, R. (1988). 'On the double object construction', *Linguistic Inquiry* 19: 335–91.

Leroy-Gourhan, A. (1965). *Le geste et la parole.* Paris: Albin Michel.

Lewin, R. (1999). *Human Evolution.* Malden, MA: Blackwell.

Lewontin, R. C. (1987). 'The shape of optimality', in J. Dupré (ed.), *The Latest on the Best: Essays on Evolution and Optimality.* Cambridge, MA: MIT Press.

Lieberman, P. (1984). *The Biology and Evolution of Language.* Cambridge, MA: Harvard University Press.

Lieberman, P. (1992). 'On the evolution of human language', in J. A. Hawkins and M. Gell-Mann (eds.), *The Evolution of Human Languages*. Santa Fe: Santa Fe Institute Proceedings, vol. XI, Addison-Wesley, 21–47.

Lightfoot, D. (2000). 'The spandrels of the linguistic genotype', in C. Knight, M. Studdert-Kennedy, and J. R. Hurford (eds.), *The Evolutionary Emergence of Language: Social Function and The Origins of Linguistic Form*. Cambridge: Cambridge University Press, 231–47.

Lindblom, B. (1998). 'Systemic constraints and adaptive change in the formation of sound structure', in J. R. Hurford, M. Studdert-Kennedy, and C. Knight (eds.), *Approaches to the Evolution of Language: Social and Cognitive Bases*. Cambridge: Cambridge University Press.

Lorenz, K. (1965). *Studies in Animal and Human Behaviour*. London: Methuen (1970 edn.).

—— (1973). *Behind the Mirror: A Search for a Natural History of Human Knowledge*. London: Methuen (1977 edn.).

—— (1978). *Vergleichende Verhaltensforschung: Grundlagen der Ethologie*. Wien: Springer Verlag.

—— (1990). *Sauver l'espoir*. Paris: Stock. First pub. 1988 as *Rettet die Hoffnung*. Wien: Jugend und Volk.

Lot, F. (1956). *Les jeux du hasard et du génie: le rôle de la chance dans la découverte*. Paris: Plon.

McLaughlin, W. (1994). 'Resolving Zeno's paradoxes', *Scientific American* (November): 66–71.

MacNeilage, P. F. (1998). 'Evolution of the mechanism of language output: comparative neurobiology of vocal and manual communication', in J. R. Hurford, M. Studdert-Kennedy, and C. Knight (eds.), *Approaches to the Evolution of Language: Social and Cognitive Bases*. Cambridge: Cambridge University Press.

McNeill, D. (1992). *Hand and Mind. What Gestures Reveal about Thought*. Chicago: University of Chicago Press.

Maddieson, I. (1984). *Patterns of Sounds*. Cambridge: Cambridge University Press.

Malherbe, M. (1983). *Les langages de l'humanité*. Paris: Seghers.

Martinet, A. (1967). *Éléments de linguistique générale*. Paris: Armand Colin (1969 edn.).

Matsuzawa, T. (1994). 'Field experiments on use of stone tools by chimpanzees in the wild', in R. W. Wrangham, W. C. McGrew, F. B. M. de Waal, and P. G. Heltne (eds.), *Chimpanzee Cultures*. Cambridge, MA: Harvard University Press.

Matthews, P. H. (1974). *Morphology*. Cambridge: Cambridge University Press.

Mehler, J. and Dupoux, E. (1990). *Naître humain*. Paris: Odile Jacob (1995 edn.).

Michelsen, A. (1998). 'Danse techno chez les abeilles', *La Recherche* 310: 52–6.

Monod, J. (1970). *Le hasard et la nécessité*. Paris: Seuil.

Muhlenbach, F. (1999). *Pertinence des énoncés portant sur des événements improbables*. Paris: Mémoire de DEA de Sciences cognitives, EHESS-Paris VI-CREA.

Noble, W. and Davidson, I. (1996). *Human Evolution, Language and Mind*. Cambridge: Cambridge University Press.

Núñez, R. (1994). 'Cognitive development and infinity in the small: paradoxes and consensus', in A. Ram and K. Eiselt (eds.), *Proceedings of the Sixteenth Annual Conference of the Cognitive Science Society*. Hillsdale, NJ: Lawrence Erlbaum Associates.

Pelegrin, J. (1990). 'Prehistoric lithic technology: some aspects of research', *Archeological Review from Cambridge* 9 (1): 116–25.

Piaget, J. (1932). *Le jugement moral chez l'enfant*. Paris: Presses universitaires de France (1969 edn.).

—— (1967). *Biologie et connaissance*. Paris: Gallimard.

—— (1976). *Le comportement, moteur de l'évolution*. Paris: Gallimard.

—— and Inhelder, B. (1947). *La représentation de l'espace chez l'enfant*. Paris: Presses universitaires de France (1972 edn.).

—— —— (1951). *La genèse de l'idée de hasard chez l'enfant*. Paris: Presses universitaires de France (1974 edn.).

Piattelli-Palmarini, M. (1979). *Théories du langage - Théories de l'apprentissage*. Paris: Seuil.

—— (1989). 'Evolution, selection and cognition: from "learning" to parameter setting in biology and in the study of language', *Cognition* 31: 1–44.

Pinker, S. (1994). *The Language Instinct*. New York: Harper Perennial (1995 edn.).

—— and Bloom, P. (1990). 'Natural language and natural selection', *Behavioral and Brain Sciences* 13 (4): 707–84.

Pirelli, V. and Yvon, F. (1999). 'The hidden dimension: a probe paradigmatic view of data-driven NLP', *Journal of Experimental and Theoretical Artificial Intelligence* 11: 391–408.

Pollock, J.-Y. (1997). *Langage et cognition: introduction au programme minimaliste de la grammaire générative*. Paris : Presses universitaires de France.

Porzig, W. (1950). *Das Wunder der Sprache: Probleme, Methoden und Ergebnisse der modernen Sprachwissenschaft*. München: Lehnen.

Premack, D. and Premack, A. J. (1983). *The Mind of an Ape*. New York: Norton.

Prince, A. and Smolensky, P. (1993). *Optimality Theory - Constraint Interaction in Generative Grammar*. Piscataway: Rutgers University.

Pylyshyn, Z. W. (1980). 'Computation and cognition: issues in the foundations of cognitive science', *Behavioral and Brain Sciences* 3: 111–69.

Radford, A. (1997). *Syntax: A Minimalist Introduction*. Cambridge: Cambridge University Press.

Ruhlen, M. (1994). *The Origin of Language: Tracing the Evolution of the Mother Tongue*. New York: John Wiley and Sons.

Savage-Rumbaugh, D. M., Savage-Rumbaugh, E. S., and Sevick, R. A. (1994). 'Biobehavioral roots of language: a comparative perspective of chimpanzee, child, and culture', in R. W. Wrangham, W. C. McGrew, and F. B. M. de Waal (eds.), *Chimpanzee Cultures*. Cambridge, MA: Harvard University Press.

Savage-Rumbaugh, E. and Lewin, R. (1994). *Kanzi, the Ape at the Brink of the Human Mind*. New York: John Wiley and Sons.

Searle, J. R. (1969). *Speech Acts: An Essay in the Philosophy of Language*. Cambridge: Cambridge University Press.

Shannon, C. E. (1948). 'Mathematical theory of communication', *Bell Systems Technical Journal* 27: 379–423, 623–56.

Sperber, D. and Wilson, D. (1986). *Relevance: Communication and Cognition*. Oxford: Blackwell (1995 edn.).

Studdert-Kennedy, M. (1998). 'The particulate origins of language generativity: from syllable to gesture', in J. R. Hurford, M. Studdert-Kennedy, and C. Knight (eds.), *Approaches to the Evolution of Language: Social and Cognitive Bases*. Cambridge: Cambridge University Press.

Talmy, L. (1988). 'Force dynamics in language and thought', *Cognitive Science* 12: 49–100.

Tannen, D. (1984). *Conversational Style – Analyzing Talk Among Friends*. Norwood: Ablex Publishing Corporation.

Trivers, R. L. (1971). 'The evolution of reciprocal altruism', *The Quarterly Review of Biology* 46: 35–57.

Tversky, A. and Kahneman, D. (1974). 'Judgement under uncertainty: heuristics and biases', *Science* 185: 1124–31.

—— —— (1983). 'Extensional versus intuitive reasoning: the conjunction fallacy in probability judgment', *Psychological Review* 90 (4): 293–315.

Ulbaek, I. (1998). 'The origin of language and cognition', in J. R. Hurford, M. Studdert-Kennedy, and C. Knight (eds.), *Approaches to the Evolution of Language: Social and Cognitive Bases*. Cambridge: Cambridge University Press.

Van Valin, R. D. and LaPolla, R. J. (1997). *Syntax. Structure, Meaning and Function*. Cambridge: Cambridge University Press.

Varela, F. (1988). *Invitation aux sciences cognitives*. Paris: Seuil.

Victorri, B. (1999). 'Débat sur la langue mère', in *Les langues du monde*. Paris: Belin, 37–42.

—— and Fuchs, C. (1996). *La polysémie - Construction dynamique du sens*. Paris: Hermès.

Waal, F. B. M. de (1982). *Chimpanzee Politics: Poner and Sex among Apes*. Baltimore: The Johns Hopkins University Press (1989 edn.).

Williams, G. C. (1966). *Adaptation and Natural Selection: A Critique of Some Current Evolutionary Thought*. Princeton: Princeton University Press.

Wilson, E. O. (1978). *On Human Nature*. Cambridge, MA: Harvard University Press.

Worden, R. (1998). 'The evolution of language from social intelligence', in J. R. Hurford, M. Studdert-Kennedy, and C. Knight (eds.), *Approaches to the Evolution of Language: Social and Cognitive Bases*. Cambridge: Cambridge University Press.

Wrangham, R. W., McGrew, W. C., de Waal F. B. M., and Heltne, P. G. (eds.) (1994). *Chimpanzee Cultures*. Cambridge, MA: Harvard University Press.

Yvon, F. (1996). *Prononcer par analogie : motivation, formalisation et évaluation*. Paris: doctoral thesis, ENST 96 E 015.

Zahavi, A. (1995). 'Altruism as a handicap: the limitation of kin selection and reciprocity', *Journal of Avian Biology* 26 (1): 1–3.

—— and Zahavi, A. (1997). *The Handicap Principle*. New York: Oxford University Press.

Index